Privatizing Monopolies

Privatizing Monopolies

LESSONS FROM THE
TELECOMMUNICATIONS
AND TRANSPORT SECTORS
IN LATIN AMERICA

EDITED BY

Ravi Ramamurti

The Johns Hopkins University Press

Baltimore and London

© 1996 The Johns Hopkins University Press
All rights reserved. Published 1996
Printed in the United States of America on acid-free paper
05 04 03 02 01 00 99 98 97 06   5 4 3 2 1

The Johns Hopkins University Press
2715 North Charles Street
Baltimore, Maryland 21219-4319
The Johns Hopkins Press Ltd., London

Library of Congress Cataloging-in-Publication Data will be found at the end of this book.
A catalog record for this book is available from the British Library.

ISBN 0-8018-5135-1

Contents

Acknowledgments

This project could not have been undertaken without the generous grant provided by the North-South Center, University of Miami, and the steadfast support of its director of grant programs, Mary Uebersax. The conference held in Boston in September 1993 was cosponsored by the College of Business Administration, Northeastern University, and for that thanks are owed to Deans David Boyd and Roger Atherton.

The various essays benefited enormously from the comments of the anonymous reviewer selected by the Johns Hopkins University Press as well as those of Yair Aharoni of Duke University, Jorge Dominguez and Raymond Vernon of Harvard University, Pedro-Pablo Kuczynski of Latin America Enterprise Fund, Michael Einhorn of the U.S. Federal Trade Commission, Leroy Jones of Boston University, Gerardo Sicat of the World Bank, and Jim Molloy of Northeastern University. Lori Anne Daley and Thomas Hennlich helped organize the conference, Richard Harris and Marianne Penney ably handled the word processor, and Diane Hammond and Holly Webber copyedited the manuscript. At Johns Hopkins University Press, Henry Tom, Barbara Lamb, and Carol Zimmerman shepherded the manuscript through the many stages of production with amazing patience and diligence. Finally, like all my other undertakings, this project could not have been started or finished without the unflinching support of my wife, Meena, or the delightful distractions provided by our lovely children, Bharat, Gita, and Arjun.

Privatizing Monopolies

1. The New Frontier of Privatization

Ravi Ramamurti

When the privatization trend began in the developing world in the early 1980s, the enterprises selected for divestiture were typically small and operated in competitive markets. Firms of this description had fallen into government hands for a variety of historical or accidental reasons, and there was no compelling reason for state ownership of movie theaters, bakeries, restaurants, or factories that produced simple manufactured goods. Even in developing countries, the local private sector was quite capable of buying and managing these firms, and the competitive nature of their markets meant there was no need for regulation after privatization.

Until about 1987, despite any rhetoric to the contrary, the privatization trend in developing countries was confined to small firms of this sort in the periphery of the public sector (Vernon 1988; Vuylsteke 1988). To be sure, some governments had more ambitious plans, including the outright sale of large state-owned enterprises that dominated their markets; but few governments actually transferred control of those firms to the private sector. Even in Chile, the initial rounds of privatization consisted of the return of small, recently nationalized firms to their former owners (Hachette and Lüders 1993). By 1987, only Britain had privatized large enterprises, such as telephone, gas, airline, and road transportation companies.

Latin America, which is the focus of this volume, was not much different from the rest of the developing world. There, until about 1988, the state enterprise sector seemed safely intact, as governments floundered in their attempts to privatize even small firms (Ramamurti 1992a). With the exception of Chile, most governments merely reorganized the public sector, sold government shares in mixed enterprises, or divested state enterprises on the fringe of the public sector. Between 1982 and 1988, the Brazilian government raised only US$220 million through

1

privatization, or less than 1 percent of the net worth of federal state enterprises (Werneck 1991, 64); in a similar period, Argentina raised US $32 million through privatization, or less than 0.5 percent of the country's gross national product (Gonzalez Fraga 1991); and in Venezuela, the state enterprise sector probably expanded marginally in the five years prior to 1988, despite the privatization of a few hotels and agricultural marketing boards (Kelly 1988).

If the barriers to privatization in general were substantial (see, for example, Austin et al. 1986), the barriers to privatizing large firms with high market power seemed even greater. Although countries differed in the size and composition of their state enterprise sectors, at the core in most countries were a dozen or so large firms that dominated their markets, such as telephone companies, electric utilities, the airlines, railroads, heavy industries, and natural resource firms. To whom could the government sell such firms? Local buyers lacked the funds to buy them and, in many cases, the expertise to manage them. Foreign buyers might have had both the expertise and the capital, but the sale of "strategic" firms with high rents to foreigners seemed unlikely. After all, in many instances, especially in Latin America, governments had taken over firms in these sectors precisely because foreign ownership had been considered unacceptable or undesirable. Besides, one would have expected the opposition to privatization from workers, union leaders, government officials, and other current beneficiaries to be stronger and better organized in the case of large, monopolistic state enterprises than in the case of small, competitive firms.

If the feasibility of privatizing large firms with market power was in question, so also was the desirability of doing so. The gains to be had from changing the ownership of firms in businesses where a heavy dose of regulation was likely to be necessary after privatization, seemed unlikely to be large—certainly not large enough to justify the political risks of privatizing their ownership. To be sure, privatization would alter the goals and managerial motivations of the firm, but the incentive for cost reduction, innovation, or profit maximization would continue to be blunted by regulation. Indeed, it was sometimes argued that any efficiency gains to be had by privatizing the ownership of such firms would be offset by the higher transaction costs of regulating them through arm's-length contracts. Empirical studies on the comparative efficiency of public and private firms in regulated businesses yielded mixed res-sults: depending on the performance measure chosen, some indicated that private enterprise was superior to public enterprise, but others indicated the opposite. After reviewing the many studies on this topic, Vickers and Yarrow (1988) conclude that private ownership seemed superior to public ownership in competitive markets, but in noncompetitive markets, governments gained more from injecting competition into the sector or improving the incentive effects of regulatory policies than by privatizing ownership.

The argument for state ownership of sectors requiring regulation appeared to be stronger in developing countries, where the private sector was commonly unable or unwilling to invest in capital-intensive projects with long payback periods and where the institutions necessary to support the smooth working of the private sector, such as property rights, capital markets, and reliable regulatory mechanisms, were underdeveloped or nonexistent. After all, even rich countries like Japan relied on the government to take the lead in the early stages of economic development (Gerschenkron 1962). The regulatory task was also complicated by the higher degree of economic and political uncertainty in developing countries, which demanded greater flexibility in the regulation of firms with market power (Levy and Spiller 1994). Yet, flexibility was hard to build into arm's-length contracts with private parties, given the relatively low credibility of both the government and the private sector and the mutual distrust between the two sides. In the absence of impartial institutions, such as an independent judicial system, to mediate between private owners and regulators, direct ownership of such firms seemed the only real option. Jones (1982), among others, argued that developing countries created state enterprises largely for pragmatic reasons of this sort:

> Public enterprise can be understood as the response of pragmatic governments to similar problems faced in the process of development. . . . The public operation of a particular industry will depend on a comparison of the costs and benefits of public enterprise as compared to alternative intervention mechanisms. Benefits are conceived as following from intervention where *market failures* lead a private producer to behavior incompatible with social-welfare maximization. Costs occur as a result of *organizational failures,* and these vary with the intervention mechanism and the characteristics of a particular industry. . . . The empirically revealed preferences of LDCs suggest that public enterprise is most appropriate in industries that are large in scale relative to product and factor markets; are capital intensive; have high forward linkages; involve high rent and natural-resource export; produce standardized products; and do not require large numbers of decentralized establishments. (3–4)

Even if public policymakers in developing countries were unaware of these theoretical arguments about the merits of public versus private ownership, until the late 1980s they acted as if they were skeptical about the gains to be had from privatizing large, monopolistic state enterprises.

An Abrupt Change

Some time in the late 1980s—probably around 1988—the behavior of governments in the developing world appeared to change dramatically.

Suddenly, privatization moved into high gear, sweeping in its tide not just large firms but firms in the core of the state enterprise sector. In developing countries—which in one survey includes all former centrally planned economies except East Germany—the revenues raised from privatization grew from US$2.6 billion in 1988 to US$23.1 billion in 1992 (Sader 1993, 11). As a result, in 1992, for the first time, the privatization proceeds of developing countries exceeded those of the industrialized countries— US$23.1 billion, versus US$17.3 billion. About 33 percent of the developing countries' proceeds was accounted for by infrastructure sectors, such as power, telecommunications, transport, and water; about 25 percent was accounted for by banks and other financial institutions; and another 15 percent was accounted for by firms in the primary sector, that is, mining and extraction, particularly in oil and gas.[1] Within infrastructure, telecommunications accounted for more than half the total, while power accounted for 23 percent and airlines for 12 percent (see table 13-1, this volume).

In terms of geographic distribution, the leading region for privatization was not Eastern Europe, where there was much talk about wholesale divestiture, but Latin America and the Caribbean, which accounted for fully two-thirds of the US$60 billion raised through privatization in the developing world between 1988 and 1992. Latin America became the developing world's laboratory for large-scale privatization, which explains the geographic focus of this volume.

After 1988, country after country in Latin America announced plans to privatize airlines, telephone companies, electric power companies, or gas and oil companies; more surprisingly, they implemented these plans at a mind-boggling pace. Within the five-year period 1988–93, six of these countries privatized their telephone companies, nine divested their flag carriers, and between two and four privatized firms in the electric power, railroad, and water sectors.

Argentina went the farthest in the shortest time. President Carlos Menem, who assumed office in 1989, surprised most observers by announcing his intention to sell practically every core state enterprise in the country by the end of 1992. Within a year of assuming office, he had disposed of 85 percent of the government's stock in the national airline and 60 percent of its shares in the telephone company. Within another year, the government privatized two television stations, four petrochemical plants, 10,000 kilometers of national highways, and 5,200 kilometers of railroads (Alexander and Corti 1993). By 1994, the list of privatized firms included two electric power companies, the national water and sewer system, the Buenos Aires subway system, other parts of the national railway network, ports and harbors, the national coal company, a giant steel company, 50 percent of the national oil company, and several industrial firms, including defense firms.

Mexico, Peru, and Venezuela implemented less sweeping but equally broad-based programs, while in 1994 ambitious programs were under way in other countries in the region, such as Bolivia, Brazil, Colombia, and Ecuador, not to mention countries outside the region, particularly in Eastern Europe and the former Soviet Union. Not only were these ambitious programs implemented in many countries by the same parties that had fervently nationalized private firms in previous decades, in Jamaica and Venezuela the very same politicians who had once championed nationalization became advocates of privatization.

Issues and Research Design

This sudden and stunning acceleration of privatization in the developing world provided the impetus for the studies in this volume. The new evidence accumulating in Latin America and elsewhere demanded a reexamination of the rationale for state-owned enterprises, of the presumed obstacles to the privatization of large, monopolistic firms, and of the economic gains to be had if those obstacles were somehow overcome. Thus, the central questions explored in this project were (1) Why did the countries involved suddenly target for privatization large firms with high market power that constituted the core of the state enterprise sector in their countries? (2) How did they overcome the barriers to privatizing such firms, including the challenge of attracting private investors? And (3) what difference was privatization making or likely to make in the performance of those firms in the short and long run?

These three questions were explored through case studies of privatization in the telecommunications, airlines, and road sectors in a number of countries in the Latin America and Caribbean region by a team of North American and Latin American scholars. (A profile of the cases is presented in table 1-1.) The sample includes a case from Jamaica, a country far smaller than the other countries covered in this volume—but Jamaica was one of the first countries in the region to privatize its telephone monopoly.[2] In many ways, Jamaica's experience illustrates the pitfalls to avoid in privatizing monopolistic enterprises.

The decision to focus on the telecommunications sector, which alone accounted for one-sixth of total proceeds from privatization in the developing world between 1988 and 1992, requires no explanation. The transport sector was included because, like telecommunications, firms in this sector, especially airlines, were among the first to be privatized, thereby offering a longer record of postprivatization results than most other cases of privatization (see table 13-1). In the roads sector, where privatization gained momentum in Latin America only recently, the only case studied was that of Mexico, which had one of the most ambi-

Table 1-1. Profile of Cases Studied

Sector and Company	Year Nationalized	Year Privatized	Percentage of Government Ownership	Annual Sales (US$ mill.)[1]	Market Power[1]	Number of Employees[1]
Telecommunications						
TOJ, Jamaica	1975	1987	90 in local service company, 51 in international service company	63	Monopoly	2,199
TELMEX, Mexico	1972	1990	55	2,115	Monopoly	49,000
ENTel, Argentina	1946–48	1990	100	1,453	Monopoly	46,040
CANTV, Venezuela	1953	1991	100	550	Monopoly	19,861
Airlines						
LAN-Chile	1929[2]	1989	100	183	Duopoly in domestic market; regulated competition in international routes	1,635
Aerolíneas Argentinas	1950	1990	100	632	Same as above	10,791
Aeromexico	1959	1988	100	492	Same as above	7,015
Mexicana	1982	1989	51	744	Same as above	13,906
VIASA, Venezuela	1975[3]	1991	100	243	Same as above but with three airlines in domestic market	3,568
Roads						
Mexican toll-road program[4]	n.a	1990 onward	n.a.	n.a.	Local monopoly; competition from free roads	n.a.

[1] Data pertain in most cases to year before privatization.

[2] Firm created by the state.

[3] Started in 1960 as joint venture between state and existing private airline (Avensa); in 1975, government's share rose to 75%.

[4] The function of building and maintaining roads, previously carried out by CAPUFE, was thrown open to private participation through competitive bidding.

n.a. = not applicable.

tious toll road programs in the developing world (see chapter 10). Ideally, the study should also include cases from the energy sector, which ranks second only to telecommunications in the sums raised through privatization between 1988 and 1992 (US$7 billion), but unfortunately, much of that activity occurred after this research project was finished. Within the chosen sectors, the largest cases of privatization are included in our sample, with the notable omission of the Chilean telephone companies and the Brazilian airline, Viacao Aerea São Paulo (VASP).

At any rate, the research design permitted intercountry comparisons within the same sector as well as comparisons between sectors. The final section of the volume includes a chapter on the multinational corporation's perspective on telecommunications privatization and a chapter on the challenge of financing private investment in infrastructure sectors. Although politics played a major role in shaping policy in every case, the studies focused for the most part on the effects of politics on economic variables of interest, such as the manner in which the privatization was packaged, competition policy in the short and long run, choices made with respect to pricing and other regulatory issues, and the kinds of buyers targeted.

Finally, a word of explanation about this volume's title. *Privatizing* covers mainly the divestment of state-owned enterprises, although, in the case of roads, it refers to private participation in a sector previously limited to state agencies. To be sure, in several instances, divestment and deregulation occurred simultaneously. However, in every case of divestment studied, the government transferred management control over the firm to private hands rather than merely selling a few shares to private parties, although in several cases, ironically, the winning consortium included state enterprises owned by the governments of rich countries. *Monopoly* loosely refers to firms with high market power, not necessarily those with 100 percent of the market. Also, it covers both natural and artificial monopolies. For instance, in our sample, state-owned telephone companies were sole providers of both local and long-distance telephone service, the first of which is still widely regarded as a natural monopoly, while the second is not. In the case of the airlines, all the countries studied artificially restricted competition on both domestic and international routes. And in the case of toll roads, market power at the local level was complete, except for the alternative of free roads, which were usually of lower quality. However, in every case the high market power of the firm in question, whether or not justifiable on economic grounds, presented a challenge with which the privatizers had to contend.

Why Were the Enterprises Privatized?

As might be expected, the acceleration of privatization in the countries studied had several causes, some of which were firm- or sector-specific while others were broader in scope. Although the unit of analysis is the firm or the sector rather than the country, given the size and salience of the firms studied, the authors invariably stumbled onto larger political forces impinging on their cases.

One cause of privatization in most of the cases studied was the government's dissatisfaction with the state enterprise's past performance. Ironically, the governments concerned had nationalized all four telecommunications firms and at least three of the five airlines studied in this volume, with a view to improving their performance. In telecommunications, that hope was fulfilled in some degree in the initial years following nationalization: in Argentina, nationalization led to the consolidation and integration of thirty-one privately owned telephone companies, in Jamaica it ended the stalemate on pricing between regulators and a multinational firm that had slowed the sector's expansion, while in Venezuela it led to a decade of rapid expansion and the modernization of the network (see chapters 2, 4, and 5). In the airline sector, state firms helped to expand domestic and international service: Aerolíneas Argentinas, for instance, was created in 1950 to combine the routes, aircraft, and other assets owned by a number of regional airlines that had been nationalized in the 1940s (see chapter 7). However, by the late 1980s, most of these firms were registering poor performance.

In telecommunications, the problems were long waiting times, outdated technology, poor service, artificially low prices, and the capture of the firms by workers and unions. The longer a firm had been under state control, the worse those problems seemed to be: the performance of these firms in Argentina and Venezuela, where the time between nationalization and privatization was forty-four years and thirty-eight years, respectively, was worse than for similar firms in Jamaica and Mexico, where the corresponding period was only twelve and eighteen years, respectively (see table 1-1). In the airline sector, the typical problems were poor service, militant unions, and obsolete aircraft. In the case of roadways, the chief problems were the poor maintenance of existing roads and the lack of funds for new investment. In almost every case, performance worsened in the 1980s, when much of Latin America was mired in recession, inflation, budget deficits, and balance of payments crises.

Besides disappointment with the performance of the firms in question, other factors were at work in particular sectors and countries. One such factor was technology, which was evolving in the telecommunications field in a manner that increased the prospects for privatization. On the one hand, the state enterprise was seen as being unable to keep up with the needs of sophisticated users, who demanded cheap, reliable, high-speed networks for transmitting data, voice, text, and images. In Argentina, Mexico, and Venezuela, banks and other private companies were attempting to bypass the public network by creating higher cost, private networks (Ambrose et al. 1990). On the other hand, technological change made competition possible in areas that were once regarded as natural monopolies. Thus, long-distance service was no longer a natural monopoly, given the advent of microwave and satellite technology, thereby making privatization a more attractive option: no longer would privatization mean converting a state monopoly into a private monopoly.

In the airline industry, no such technological forces were at work, but two important exogenous changes propelled the privatization trend. One was the growing market for leased aircraft, which dramatically lowered the barriers to new entry. The other was the deregulation of the domestic airline service market in the United States, which the U.S. government followed with attempts to liberalize and deregulate international bilateral air service agreements. Under pressure from U.S. negotiators—or, as in the case of Chile, a voluntary application of the same policy—many Latin American nations found themselves liberalizing competition on their U.S. routes, thus pitting their state-owned airlines against increasingly aggressive U.S. carriers, such as American Airlines and United Air Lines. This exogenous shift in the level of competition exposed the weaknesses of the state-owned airlines and increased the appeal of privatization as a solution.

But, forces at the firm and sector levels only partly explain the privatization of the firms in question. If poor performance were the primary government concern a convincing case for privatization might have been made many years earlier. Conversely, the performance of some firms that were privatized, such as the telephone company in Mexico, could hardly be described as hopeless, either by regional or national standards. In addition, in only one case (Mexicana airline) did the government route the money raised from privatization into the coffers of the enterprise rather than the national treasury, even though many of the companies had suffered in the 1980s from insufficient funds for investment. Similarly, the technology that permitted competition in long-distance telephone service had been around for a decade or more; besides, none of the governments that privatized their telephone companies took advantage of this technology to create competition in long-distance telephone service! The more important explanations, it seems, lay in forces that transcended the privatized firms or their sectors.

One such force, whose importance can easily be overestimated, were international agencies such as the International Monetary Fund (IMF) and the World Bank. While they may have been important in halting the expansion of the state enterprise sector, in reducing subsidies to such firms, or in putting privatization on the national agenda, in every case but Jamaica, the decision of governments to privatize their telephone companies went far beyond what the international agencies were urging. Much of the reform that the World Bank had been seeking in the 1980s in sectors such as power, telecommunications, and transport assumed the continuation of state ownership of the core assets. In telecommunications, for instance, the World Bank would have been content to see upward price adjustments, delegation of powers from the government to the state-owned telecommunications authority, and private participation in cellular service, equipment supply, or value added service (see, for instance, Wellenius et al. 1989). In fact, once the governments of Argentina and Mexico announced that they intended to sell their telephone companies, the World Bank tried to slow rather than acceler- ate the pace of privatization out of concern that serious mistakes might be made. This is not to say that the structural adjustment loans offered by the IMF and the World Bank did not figure in the political calculations of local leaders or that these agencies did not provide these countries a great deal of valuable technical advice on privatization; the more limited conclusion is that the impetus for sweeping privatization came from national leaders—which raises the question of why they had such sud- den and dramatic changes of heart.

The answer to that question, if indeed there is one, must vary from country to country. In Chile, where privatization accelerated as General Pinochet's term of office came to an end, there was in fact no change of heart: Pinochet had long believed in free markets and private ownership. In the other countries, privatization accelerated with the arrival of a new leader, who sometimes belonged to a conservative party that had opposed nationalization in the first place, as in Jamaica—although even in this case the final stages of privatizing the telephone company were carried out by Michael Manley, whose party had nationalized the sector fifteen years ear- lier. In Argentina, Mexico, and Venezuela, the leaders who accelerated privatization did so immediately upon assuming office, but in all three cases they hailed from parties that had once argued in favor of nation- alization. Carlos Salinas of Mexico, it could be argued, belonged to a new generation of the Mexican ruling party and genuinely believed in free markets and private ownership; but how is one to explain the about-face in Argentina by the Peronist Party, which not only led the nationalization movement of the 1940s and 1950s but vehemently opposed plans to privatize the national airline and the telephone company only a year before Presi- dent Carlos Menem took office? Even more perplexing is the about-face in Venezuela by President Carlos Andrés Pérez, who had personally led an ambitious program of nationalization in a previous term as president.

What these facts suggest is that the privatization of giant enterprises like airlines and telephone companies was not only ideologically driven in some cases but also had a pragmatic appeal that transcended differ- ences in national histories, party ideologies, and conditions within par- ticular sectors or firms. One such pragmatic appeal, a very powerful one in fact, was the contribution that large-scale privatization could make to solving the countries' macroeconomic problems, particularly in reduc- ing budget deficits and public debt, which were spiraling out of control in the 1980s (Ramamurti 1992b). If foreign investors were allowed to participate in large-scale privatizations, the foreign exchange crises fac- ing these countries could be alleviated as well. Privatization may have carried political risks, but for cash-starved governments it may have been a lesser evil than cutting spending or raising taxes.

Thus, in the 1990s, the argument of the 1950s and 1960s that the state would make capital-intensive investments that the private sector shied away from was turned on its head: capital-short governments were not only willing to let the private sector make future investments in such sectors, they were prepared to raise cash by liquidating past investments in those sectors. Although the sale of both money-making and money-losing firms could strengthen a government's short-run cash flow, the former were clearly more attractive, especially if they were also large. Once governments overcame the real or perceived obstacles to privatizing such firms, the floodgates of monopoly privatization were opened. Raising cash was not simply a by-product of monopoly privatization but was often its overriding aim, leading in many cases to a privatization package that was skewed toward increasing the sale price of the firm rather than maximizing the prospects for improved efficiency. A high selling price, which usually meant selling the firm for more than its book value, was also important for the political reason that it minimized charges of giving away the "national patrimony" to private investors.

For telecommunications privatizations that were highly visible transactions, another very important purpose served by privatization was to send a signal to private investors that the country was embarking on a new economic course, one in which the private sector, not state enterprises, would play the lead role. In Argentina, Mexico, and to a lesser extent Venezuela, this seems to have been an important motivation. As one senior Mexican policymaker put it, "When we were selling TELMEX [Teléfonos de México] to private investors, we were selling Mexico as well!" The signal had to be loud, so as to register above the din of international news; it had to be sent quickly, so that private sector investment would occur early in a new president's term; and it had to be resoundingly positive, to make heads turn in international investment circles. To achieve the latter, the privatizers had to make sure that the sale was a "success," which came to mean selling the firm in the first attempt to one of several qualified bidders. If the bidders included well-known multinational firms in the industry, so much the better.

For the signal to be loud, quick, and positive, the firm targeted for privatization had to be large, easily divested, and attractive to private investors. The last requirement meant that the firm selected had to be a "plum" rather than a "lemon." In many countries, the telephone company satisfied these criteria better than any other state enterprise (see chapter 3). There was commonly no legal or constitutional obstacle to transferring control over telecommunications companies to the private sector—including, in three of the four cases, foreign investors. Although the past performance of these companies was not always spectacular, their prospects for raising prices and for future expansion were excellent. All four telephone firms studied suffered from overstaffing, but layoffs could be avoided by absorbing excess staff through future growth. Thus, telephone companies were desirable candidates for sale not because their past performance had been awful—which was undoubtedly true in countries like Argentina—but because in every case studied their future growth and profit potential were excellent. Therefore, in all four countries they were among the first big firms to be sold.

Publicly, governments argued that they were privatizing their airlines and telephone companies to improve their performance. Rarely, however, did they spell out how privatization would produce that outcome. Given the poor performance of state firms, such explanations may have seemed unnecessary; presumably, privatization would result in better management, greater access to capital and technology, a tougher handling of labor issues, or less political interference. As we shall see, in regulated industries, the relation between type of ownership and performance was much more complex than that.

To sum up, the three goals that explain the privatization of telephone companies and airlines are the following:

—Maximizing the proceeds from the sale to help end the country's fiscal and balance of payments crises.

—Sending a positive signal to private investors through a "successful" sale.

—Improving the performance of the enterprise or sector by encouraging competition and improving regulation and management.

These goals were not wholly consistent with one another. Maximizing proceeds and sending a signal were both advanced by selling a plum rather than a lemon, but the division of spoils between the government and potential buyers presented a conflict. Similarly, the goal of improving the performance of the enterprise, by strengthening competition in the sector or by keeping a tight rein on prices, directly conflicted with the objective of turning the companies into plums before privatization, which was important for sending the desired signal.

The manner in which these goals were balanced varied from one telephone privatization to another. Of the four countries, the signaling objective was most important in Argentina, where the government's credibility was so low and the economic crisis so deep that a quick, successful sale of the telephone company at any price became an end unto itself. It was also very important in Mexico, where President Salinas was anxious to regain the credibility with domestic and foreign investors that his country had lost in the 1980s. In Jamaica, the fiscal goal was probably paramount; the government saw partial privatization of the profitable telephone company as a convenient way to raise money quickly, and the temptation to sell more of its stock led eventually to its full privatization. In Venezuela, which was the last of the four countries to privatize its telephone company, the growing credibility of its Latin American neighbors allowed it to achieve the signaling objective without sacrificing the other two goals to the same extent as in Argentina and Mexico. Even in Venezuela, however, policymakers were more concerned about satisfying potential investors, obtaining a good price for the government, and placating employees than maximizing the interests of consumers.

The signaling objective was less important than the other two objectives in the airline privatizations. Although the sale of a flag carrier had considerable symbolic value, the airlines were closer to being lemons than plums, especially with each passing year. In the 1990s, the financial health of the airlines studied worsened, their labor relations soured, and competition on international routes intensified. Thus, even as governments became more eager to sell their airlines, prospective investors became less interested in buying them. Therefore, in many cases, the airlines were privatized only after one or two failed attempts.

How Were the Firms Privatized?

Given the size, market power, and visibility of the firms studied, it is not surprising that in every case there was much legwork to be done before privatization. Governments had to restructure the firms, negotiate deals with workers and their union leaders, clean up the firms' finances, redefine the regulatory environment, market the firms to potential buyers, and finally, close the deals. In performing these activities, governments were helped by foreign management consultants, accounting firms, lawyers, and investment bankers, many of them working in parallel. Besides financing many of these consultants, the World Bank itself provided a lot of technical assistance in Argentina, Mexico, and Venezuela.[3] However, despite all the high-paid consultants and World Bank experts at their disposal, the privatizers were in uncharted waters: no reform as ambitious had been attempted before in the public sector in their country or in any other developing country.[4] On the one hand, privatization involved the politically sensitive task of freeing up the firms from the clutches of current beneficiaries, such as workers, unions, ministers, legislators, and customers. On the other hand, it involved the technically complex task of restructuring the firms, redefining their regulatory environment, and marketing them to prospective buyers. Table 1-2 summarizes how these aspects were dealt with in the telecommunications privatizations, which were typically more complex than the airline privatizations.

Table 1-2. The Principal Elements of the Telecommunications Privatization

Elements of the Package	Telecommunications of Jamaica	Teléfonos de México	ENTEL of Argentina	CANTV of Venezuela
1. Restructuring prior to privatization				
a. Organizational	a. Local service and international long-distance companies were merged in 1985 to form the TOJ.	a. The idea of dividing TELMEX into two regional companies was rejected; instead, domestic long-distance microwave transmission network owned by a government agency was consolidated with TELMEX prior to privatization.	a. ENTEL was divided into northern and southern parts, with the capital city divided between the two and the regional companies equally owning the long-distance service company.	a. CANTV was sold as is.
b. Labor relations	b. None was reported.	b. Labor contracts were consolidated into a single agreement, categories of workers were reduced, and flexibility in deploying workers was increased.	b. The workforce was reduced through attrition; labor relations were strained in the run-up to privatization. The workweek was extended by 7.5 hours, job guarantees were ended, and workers rights were curtailed.	b. There were no reductions in the workforce.
c. Financial	c. None was reported.	c. The balance sheet was improved through debt buyback, but only company resources were used for this purpose; no additional debt was assumed by the government.	c. The government purchased hundreds of millions of dollars of equipment prior to privatization, adding to the company's inventories, while agreeing to absorb US\$1,757m in debt and leaving the buyers responsible for only US\$380m.	c. Before privatization, the government assumed US\$500m in long-term debt and accumulated interest owed to foreign creditors.

Table 1-2. (continued)

Elements of the Package	Telecommunications of Jamaica	Teléfonos of México	ENTEL of Argentina	CANTV of Venezuela
2. Competition policy	The TOJ was granted an exclusive right to provide public and private customers domestic and international service (including cellular) in all parts of Jamaica for twenty-five years, renewable for twenty-five more years.	TELMEX was granted an exclusive right to provide domestic and international public long-distance service for six years; entry into other services, including local service and private circuits, was unrestricted. TELMEX was also granted the only license to offer cellular service in all regions of Mexico. It was permitted to compete in all services, equipment supply and service, Yellow Pages, value added services, etc. through separate subsidiaries.	Each company was granted an exclusive right to provide local and long-distance service in its assigned territory for seven years, extendable to ten years if performance targets were met. A joint venture between the two regional companies was granted the right to be one of two providers of cellular service nationwide, with the requirement that entry occur no sooner than two years after rivals had entered. Both companies were permitted to offer other services through separate subsidiaries.	CANTV was granted an exclusive right to provide local and long-distance service for nine years, from 1992 to 2000. It already had the rights to one of two bands reserved for cellular service. All other services, including private lines, value added services, and terminal equipment, were opened to competition.
3. Pricing a. Initial levels	a. Prices for international calling were raised prior to privatization; an "informal understanding" was reached that the buyer would not raise local rates, which were very low, for five years; revenue per line stood at US$700 in 1990.	a. Special telephone tax averaging 40% scrapped; local and domestic long-distance rates were increased sharply in the run-up to privatization, while international rates were reduced; overall, revenue per line increased from US$450 in 1989 to US$745 in 1991.	a. Price distortions were not corrected, with very high rates for new connections and long-distance service continuing; overall rate for a basket of regulated services increased revenue per line from US$328 in 1990 to US$635 in 1991 and US$794 in 1993.	a. Two large price increases were granted before privatization, raising the revenue per line from US$275 in 1990 to about US$500 in 1992; rate rebalancing between local and long-distance service was to begin in 1994 and end in 2000 with an end to all cross subsidization; telephone tax on CANTV reduced from 5% of revenues to only

Table 1-2. (continued)

Elements of the Package	Telecommunications of Jamaica	Teléfonos of México	ENTEL of Argentina	CANTV of Venezuela
b. Subsequent pricing rules	b. Prices would be adjusted to yield 17.5–20% real after-tax return on equity, which would be revalued annually to reflect inflation and devaluations of the Jamaican dollar.	b. Thereafter, prices for the basket of regulated services were to be set according to the price cap method, with no adjustment for anticipated productivity gains.	b. Thereafter, price increases allowed according to the price cap method, with 2% per year adjustment for anticipated productivity gains in years 3–7.	b. Thereafter, prices for regulated services were to be increased according to the price cap method with no adjustment for productivity gains until the end of 1996, followed by a 3% per year adjustment on long-distance services up to 2000.
4. Labor participation	2% of shares were reportedly sold to workers.	4.4% of the stock were sold to a trust controlled by the workers at the same price paid by the core investors, financed under concessional terms through a state-owned bank. There was no worker representation on the board.	10% of shares were sold to workers at a price equal to about 20% of that paid by the winning consortium, with subsidized financing thrown in as well. Workers were assigned one seat on the board.	11% of shares were sold to workers at the price offered by the winning consortium but financed by a non-interest-bearing loan. Workers were assigned two out of nine seats on the board.
5. Performance obligations	No explicit goals were imposed except the requirement that the "company shall maintain standards of service which shall be no less than those prevailing immediately before" privatization.	Explicit goals were set for the rate of network expansion, universal coverage, public telephones, and quality of service, with financial penalties for nonfulfillment of targets.	Explicit targets were set for network expansion, public service obligations, and quality of service.	Explicit targets were set for network expansion, public service obligations, and quality of service.
6. Regulatory institutions	The preexisting regulatory agency was continued.	The idea of creating an autonomous regulatory agency was rejected in favor of continuing existing agency (SCT). A new set of telecommunications regulations was approved by the government specifying procedures for entering various segments.	A new autonomous regulatory agency (CNT) was created by presidential decree in 1990 but failed to function until 1992 and then was hamstrung by political interference. The agency was financed by a levy on telephone companies, but the budget still had to be approved by the ministry.	A new regulatory agency, CONATEL, was established by presidential decrees in absence of congressional approval of a new telecommunications law that would have created such an agency.

Table 1-2. (continued)

Elements of the Package	Telecommunications of Jamaica	Teléfonos of México	Enrel of Argentina	CANTV of Venezuela
7. Targeted investors a. Core investors or dispersed? b. National or foreign?	a. Core investors were sought. b. Cable & Wireless of the U.K. (C&W), which already controlled the international service company and was a minority owner of the local service company, was targeted. Government's intention of retaining control over the TOJ was dropped as it felt pressure to improve its fiscal position.	a. Core investors were sought. b. Control by Mexicans was required, although this could be done through a trust in which foreigners owned up to 49% of the shares.	a. Core investors were sought. b. Foreign control was permitted. Three bids were received for the two companies, with one bidder withdrawing in the final stages, forcing the government to work out a deal with the two that remained.	a. Core investors were sought. b. Foreign control was permitted. Two bids were received, both involving control by foreign firms, with local investors as minority partners in the consortia.
c. Divestment in tranches?	c. C&W acquired 70% in four stages, and 13% were sold to the Jamaican public in one offering.	c. In the first step, controlling shares were sold to a consortium of Mexican and foreign firms, including Southwestern Bell and France Telecom; subsequently, additional shares were sold through three international offerings.	c. In the first step, 60% of the equity of each company was sold to the winning consortia (Telefónica de España, Citibank, and an Argentine investor; STET of Italy, France Telecom, J. P. Morgan, and another Argentine investor). Subsequently, the government's remaining holding of 30% was sold through international offerings.	c. In the first step, 40% were sold to the winning consortium, with the right to appoint five out of nine board members, 11% were sold to workers, and the government plan to sell its 49% in tranches in the local and foreign capital markets was put on hold due to political circumstances in Venezuela in 1993 and 1994.

Table 1-2. *(continued)*

Elements of the Package	Telecommunications of Jamaica	Teléfonos of México	ENTEL of Argentina	CANTV of Venezuela
8. Selling price and terms	The government realized US$156 million for its 83% ownership of the TOJ, representing approximately US$1,700 per main line. All sales were for cash.	The government realized more than US$6 billion for its 55% of TELMEX, representing a price of US$1,750 per line from the core investors and more than US$5,000 per line in subsequent rounds. All sales were for cash.	The government realized US$3.3 billion from selling ENTEL, representing a price of only US$630 per line from the winning consortia and US$2,200 per line from the international offering, for an overall average of US$1,050 per line. Debt-equity swaps were allowed in the sale to core investors; international offerings were for cash.	The government realized a price of US$1.885 billion from VenWorld, a consortium led by GTE, which owned 51% of the consortium and included Telefónica de España (16%), ATT (5%), and two Venezuelan private firms. The sale was for cash.

Source: For Jamaica, chap. 2 and Adam et al. (1992); for Mexico, chap. 3, Ramamurti (1993), and Tandon (1994); for Argentina, chap. 4, Abdala (1994), and World Bank (1994); and for Venezuela, chap. 5, CANTV Annual Reports for 1992 and 1993, and Taylor and Vidal (1994).

Dealing with Stakeholders

Of all the stakeholders, workers and unions were probably the most ardent defenders of the status quo, especially in the airline industry. Governments used both the carrot and the stick to elicit their cooperation. Among the sticks was the threat of closing down the state enterprise, which the Chilean and Mexican governments carried through in the airline industry. In the process, existing employees were let go, old labor contracts were terminated, and new companies were formed that rehired a small fraction of the former employees and under tougher employment contracts. Governments also used strong-arm tactics to discipline workers and labor leaders who threatened to derail privatization, including sending in the armed forces to run state enterprises when they went on strike against privatization (Argentina). In Argentina and Mexico, the presidents confronted powerful labor leaders within months of assuming office, thereby demonstrating their resolve to push ahead with privatization.

Among the carrots that governments offered workers were generous severance packages that reduced the workforce, significantly in some cases, and assurances about job security after privatization, especially if labor contracts had been renegotiated before privatization. In every airline privatization, except Mexicana, and every telecommunications privatization, employees were also offered shares in the company, usually at a discount, and almost always financed by a concessional loan. Employees' share of equity varied from as little as 2 percent in the Jamaican telecommunications company to 25 percent in the airline Aeromexico. In Argentina and Venezuela, they were also granted a seat or two on the board of directors.

Governments also overcame with surprising ease the potential opposition to privatization from ministers, civil servants, and other members of the bureaucracy. In every country, the most important reason for this was the president's very strong commitment to privatization and his willingness to infiltrate and centralize the decision-making process.[5] Infiltration was achieved by appointing to the positions of minister, senior civil servant, and state enterprise manager individuals who shared the president's commitment to privatization. Centralization was achieved by assigning responsibility for privatization to an inner circle of trusted and committed privatizers. Thus, for instance, in Jamaica, the privatization of the telephone company was handled in a relatively secret manner by a handful of trusted presidential appointees; in Argentina, the president appointed special "intervenors" with extraordinary powers to privatize the airline and telephone companies; and in Mexico, companies slated for privatization were immediately transferred from the sectoral ministry to the ministry of finance, where a small but dedicated band of privatizers was located. Committed privatizers were also appointed to head the state enterprises targeted for sale so that the expertise and information inside the firm could be mobilized toward privatization. Despite these tactics, every president encountered pockets of opposition from the bureaucracy and ministerial ranks that delayed or compromised the privatization strategy, but nothing so overwhelming as to derail privatization.

Typically, two types of individual found their way into the inner circle of presidential advisers on privatization: one hailed from the private sector, and the other was usually a young person trained in economics, business, or law in the United States, in many cases holding a doctoral degree, as well. Even though these individuals seldom agreed among themselves on every issue and frequently turned to the president to resolve policy logjams, they shared a faith in private ownership and markets. They relished the prospect of replacing what they viewed as inefficient state enterprises with vibrant private organizations.

In keeping with the tendency to centralize the privatization process, the leaders concerned also minimized the involvement of the national legislature, even though the ruling party had the majority in it, lest opponents of privatization send the program into a tailspin. In Argentina, president Carlos Menem privatized the telephone company and the airline with a stream of presidential decrees following two broad-based laws passed by congress to deal with the country's economic crisis. In Mexico, the strategy for privatizing the telephone company deliberately avoided any component that required the legislature's approval—for example, to amend foreign investment laws to permit foreign control of the firm.[6] However, in Venezuela, where the democratic tradition was stronger, the privatizers had to maneuver through the many obstacles set up by legislators (see chapters 5 and 9). Therefore, the process took a little longer there.

In all the countries, the public at large was surprisingly receptive to the idea of privatizing large state enterprises. For instance, one opinion poll in Jamaica indicated that 54 percent of the public supported the government's decision to privatize Telecommunications of Jamaica, while another in Venezuela reported that 80 percent of the people believed public services would improve with privatization. Similar sentiment was reported in Argentina, where the state telephone company was renowned for its poor service. Thus, the public's dissatisfaction with state enterprises made it easier to gather support for privatization. However, it also created hopes for performance improvement that the buyers of the firms found hard to satisfy later, especially in the telecommunications sector, where prices were increased sharply at the time of privatization.

Luring Investors

In every country, the privatizers took several measures to make the state enterprises more attractive to investors. Where the firm was a lemon to begin with, they struggled to turn it into a plum, and where the firm was already a plum, they made it juicier still, by raising its profitability and reducing its risks.

Telecommunications   In the telecommunications cases, profitability was increased by raising prices for regulated services in the range of 65 percent (Mexico) to 95 percent (Argentina) before privatization, streamlining the workforce at the government's expense, and writing off or transferring to another state organization part or all of the outstanding debt (US$1,757 million in Argentina, and US$500 million in Venezuela; see table 1-2). In addition, in Argentina, Mexico, and Venezuela, special taxes on telephone users were lowered sharply or scrapped altogether. By 1990, the annual revenue per telephone line in three of the four countries was US$700 or more, a level comparable to that in the United States. In every country, the privatized firm was also given one of two licenses to provide cellular telephone service, a rapidly growing and highly profitable business.

In terms of risk, in every case the government insulated the telephone company from competition in basic and long-distance service for periods ranging from six to twenty-five years. At the same time, to protect investors from the risks of inflation and price regulation in the future, all countries but Jamaica adopted the price-cap method of rate regulation pioneered in Britain, wherein the privatized firm is permitted to raise prices automatically for regulated services to offset the effects of inflation, less an adjustment for anticipated productivity improvement.[7] However, unlike Britain, the three countries in our study assumed little or no productivity improvement after privatization, at least not in the rules governing pricing.[8] Since the potential for productivity improvement in the Latin American telephone companies was probably greater than that in British Telecom, the pricing regime approved in our sample countries was generous—apparently, deliberately so. In Jamaica, where the rate-of-return method of regulation was employed, investors were guaranteed an after-tax return of 17.5 to 20.0 percent on (revalued) equity. Everywhere, the privatizers argued that a lucrative pricing scheme was necessary to offset the risks of doing business in their country and to finance rapid expansion of the network. Finally, in Mexico and Venezuela, governments restructured the firms' equity capital so that strategic investors could control the company by buying only 20.4 percent and 40 percent, respectively, of the total equity.[9]

In every case, governments sought to transfer control of the firm to a core investing group, sometimes referred to as a "strategic investor," who would be responsible for running the firm after privatization. The government required that this group include both local firms and reputable foreign firms belonging to the industry. Local participation would avoid charges that the government was giving away the national patrimony to foreigners.[10] Foreign participation would not only allow governments to raise foreign exchange and send a signal to the international investment community, it would provide access to technology and expertise that local firms lacked. In three of the four telecommunications privatizations (all but Mexico), foreign firms were allowed to control the privatized firm. To minimize the risk that investor response might be lukewarm, the privatizers made promotional visits to major financial centers, such as London, New York, and Paris, and met with the senior management of multinational companies in Europe and the United States. Investors were also invited to visit the country and the firms. In addition, they were invited to comment on the government's privatization strategy. As might be expected, potential investors asked governments to make the package more profitable and less risky; frequently, governments obliged.

Despite all the preparatory steps and marketing efforts undertaken by the privatizers, the overall response of private investors was rather modest, showing just how low the credibility of these countries had sunk by the late 1980s. In every country but Jamaica, a dozen or more foreign telecommunications companies were prequalified, but in the end only two bids were received for the two halves of the Argentine telephone company, and two bids each were received for the Mexican and Venezuelan telephone companies.[11] (These facts mask the fact that, typically, more than one foreign company participated in every consortium.) One reason for the limited number of bids was the fact that, even after decades of development, only the largest, local firms in these countries could afford to bid for giant state enterprises. National firms participating in the consortia that purchased the telephone companies in Venezuela and Mexico invested US$450 million and US$850 million, respectively, which even in the 1990s were large sums for a single venture, especially at a time when so many other state enterprises were also on the auction block. Another reason, of course, was the perception of foreign investors that Latin America was still a very risky place to do business.

All foreign telecommunications firms that did submit bids undoubtedly concluded that their risk-adjusted returns were likely to be high. They may also have expected to gain some advantage from being the among first foreign firms to invest in this sector in these countries. Each would also get paid for consulting services rendered. In some countries, foreign firms were appointed as operators of the enterprise and paid management fees. However, each foreign firm had special motivations as well. Southwestern Bell was reportedly bullish about TELMEX and would have bought the company singlehandedly, had it been allowed, because its territory in the United States bordered Mexico. Like other Baby Bells, it was also looking for overseas opportunities to invest cash generated by its domestic operations. Telefónica de España was pursuing an active strategy of expansion in Latin America, a region with which Spain had special ties. By 1994, it had invested in telephone companies not only in Argentina and Venezuela but also in Chile and Peru. France Telecom and Cable & Wireless of the United Kingdom had both invested in the past in former French and British colonies, respectively, and seemed more at ease than the Baby Bells in making investments abroad. Surprisingly, privatized British Telecom did not participate in any of the Latin American opportunities. (For more on the foreign investor's perspective in this industry, see chapter 12.)

Airlines Governments had more difficulty turning their airlines into plums, because every airline in our sample faced competition in the domestic market from one or two other firms and on most international routes from at least one foreign carrier. Governments could not increase the market power of an airline in the domestic market without putting another national firm into trouble, and bilateral air service agreements precluded granting the national airline a monopoly on international routes. Latin American airlines faced particularly stiff competition from megacarriers such as American Airlines and United Air Lines, which took over the routes of weaker carriers such as Pan Am and Eastern Airlines in the late 1980s. Given these constraints, governments did what they could to sweeten the privatization package: for example, the Argentine government promised that for ten years after privatization no other national airline would be permitted to fly on international routes where Aerolíneas Argentinas enjoyed "sole designation"; the Venezuelan government made a similar promise with respect to its airline, VIASA. Governments also assumed most of the liabilities of the airlines. However, these inducements did not lure many buyers.

A second important difference between the airline and telecommunications privatizations was the growth potential of the two industries. As discussed earlier, every telecommunications firm studied had a huge, pent-up demand in its market and a monopoly position for at least the medium term, which translated into fat profits after privatization. In contrast, in the 1990s, airlines were plagued by excess capacity and were expected to grow at half the rates of the telecommunications firms.

A third factor that constrained airline privatizations was the requirement imposed by bilateral air service agreements that an airline flying international routes had to be controlled by nationals of the country whose flag it bore. In every country, the local private sector had some experience in the airline business, unlike telecommunications, but its track record was hardly spectacular: in both Argentina and Chile, private airlines had been bailed out by the government and reprivatized only recently. Consequently, governments were keen to attract foreign airlines as investors, even though they could not be offered a controlling interest in the national airline. However, this was probably not a serious obstacle to privatization, since governments were able to give foreigners effective control over the operations of their airlines without selling them a majority of the stock (Argentina, Chile, and Venezuela).

In several airline privatizations, governments received only one bid, and in no case did an American airline submit a bid. The only foreign airlines that bid were Air New Zealand, Scandinavian Airline System, and Iberia of Spain. Had it not been for Iberia, which bought two of the five airlines studied and was the sole bidder in Argentina and Venezuela, there may have been no story to tell in some of our sample countries. Apparently, Iberia's goal was to dominate the market for intra–Latin American and European–Latin American travel. Iberia also invested in a private airline in Chile and made an abortive attempt to buy the Bolivian airline.

What Difference Did Privatization Make?

Despite setbacks and disappointments, the governments involved were generally satisfied with the outcomes of the privatization transactions, especially in the telecommunications cases. In all four countries, the telecommunications privatization was the largest transaction until then. It yielded the government US$156 million in Jamaica, US$1,885 million in Venezuela, US$3,300 million in Argentina, and US$6,000 million in Mexico.[12] These amounts represented 1–3 percent of the gross national product of the respective countries. TELMEX alone raised four times as much money for the Mexican government as the 723 firms privatized before it.

The airline privatizations raised smaller amounts for the government, varying from a low of US$46 million for LAN-Chile, to US$140 million for Mexicana, US$145 million for VIASA, US$285 million for Aeromexico, and more than US$500 million for Aerolíneas Argentinas.[13] The Argentine privatizations and the Mexican airline privatization allowed buyers to pay for the equity of these firms with sovereign debt, which explains the participation in them of financial institutions like Citibank, Chase Manhattan Bank, and J. P. Morgan. In all the other cases, sales were for cash, and in all cases but Mexicana, that cash went to the treasury rather than the company. Thus, the short-run impact of these privatizations on the treasury's cash flow was positive, not only compared to the scenario without privatization but, in the telecommunications cases, also after netting out the liabilities assumed by governments at the time of privatization. Since half or more of the sale proceeds typically came from foreign investors, the transactions bolstered the country's foreign exchange reserves. The Argentine debt turned in by the buyers of the airline and telephone companies as part of their offers reduced that country's outstanding foreign debt by fully 10 percent.

In large measure, the signaling effect was also achieved by the telecommunications transactions. In less than two years, a new administration had restructured and privatized the country's telecommunications firm in the very first attempt, attracting in the process several well-known multinational companies as investors. The transactions were carried out more or less according to schedule, in accordance with a set of preannounced rules, and under the supervision of credible international agencies like the World Bank. Above all, the countries demonstrated their willingness to permit private investors to earn high returns in their countries, the full extent of which became apparent when the share prices of the telecommunications companies in Argentina and Mexico rose by a factor of two to three within months of privatization. As these shares soared, so did the local stock markets, whose prices were influenced heavily by how well the telecommunications firms did. In all three countries in which sending a signal to private investors was a motivating factor, after the telephone companies were sold, foreign investment surged, flight capital began to return, and the price of sovereign debt in the secondary market rose (Ramamurti 1992a).

In short, governments used privatization quite successfully to bolster their short-run cash flows and to gain credibility for their new economic strategies. But what about the impact of privatization on the firms' performance, which after all was touted by governments as a major reason for privatization? Each chapter presents the short-run results known to the authors at the time of writing, as well as speculations about the lagged effects of privatization. Our purpose here is not to render a verdict on privatization, which other studies have done very well, but to understand more fully the changes triggered by privatization.[14] To do that, we begin with the premise that the performance of any firm depends on the incentives facing its managers, which in imperfectly competitive markets depends not only on who owns the firm (public versus private) but also on the nature of competition in the market and the quality of government regulation of the industry (Vickers and Yarrow 1988). A discussion of the interconnection between these variables and performance in the telecommunications and airline industries follows (see figure 1-1).

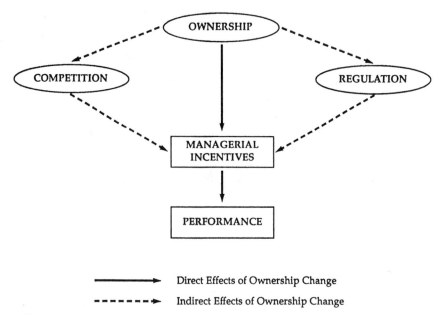

Figure 1-1. The Interplay between Ownership, Competition, and Regulation.

Ownership, Regulation, and Competition: Telecommunications

The most striking and consistent short-run result in the telecommunications sector was the rapid expansion of the network after privatization (see table 1-3). In the first three to four years after privatization, the network grew at 13 percent per annum in Mexico, 13 percent per annum in Argentina, more than 15 percent per annum in Venezuela, and 18 percent per annum in Jamaica. Not only were these rates double or triple the historic rates, they exceeded the targets set by governments. This growth resulted from a three- or fourfold increase in capital spending, compared to the period before privatization. The second dramatic result in every case but Jamaica was the explosive growth in labor productivity. Measured by the number of lines in service per employee, it grew by double digits in Venezuela, 13 percent per annum in Mexico, and 19 percent per annum in Argentina. As a result, the companies' sales and profits doubled or tripled after privatization. The companies also registered large increases in rural telephone service and the number of public telephones in operation. And while they improved the quality of service on average, they had difficulty meeting targets in one or two areas, especially in and around the capital city, where one-third or more of the telephone lines were concentrated. Customers complained about about billing errors, repair delays, unfriendly service, and of course high prices. As one Mexican observer put it,

"Consumers are complaining that they have to pay First World prices for Third World service!"

Ownership To what extent did the change in ownership account for these short-run results? Without doubt, it played an important part. For one thing, some agency problems that beset state enterprises were avoided under private ownership. Since governments turned over control to a strategic investor, there was a clear line of command in the firm that ended unambiguously with the owners who sat on the board, except in matters where the board's power was explicitly circumscribed by regulation. This differed markedly from the situation in the state-owned enterprise, which Aharoni (1982, 89) describes as "an agent without a principal." Besides a new chief executive officer (CEO), picked usually by the biggest investor within the consortium, the private management brought in dozens of new managers from the private sector.[15] Foreign firms contributed technical expertise in areas such as network expansion and operations management, while local partners contributed complementary expertise in labor management, local supplier management, and government relations.[16]

Privatization also resulted in a more focused and aggressive pursuit of profits, through both revenue growth and cost control. The participation of foreign state-owned firms, such as France Telecom and Telefónica de España, seemed not to dampen the consortia's profit motive one bit. Rapid expansion of the network after privatization was consistent with profit maximization and would probably have occurred in Argentina, Mexico, and Venezuela without government targets, as it did in Jamaica. The companies made money when they added lines, because connection charges were exorbitant;[17] they made more money every time new customers used their telephones, especially to make long-distance calls; and they made still more money when the volume of calls made by old customers grew because the network was bigger. Recognizing that profits could be earned by serving businesses better, the companies invested in fiber-optic overlay networks, data transmission facilities, digital exchanges, enhanced services, and cellular telephony. With guaranteed high returns, the companies reinvested most of their profits, even in Jamaica, where the government did not require it.

The new managements were similarly aggressive in controlling costs. The dramatic increases in labor productivity resulted from a deliberate effort to freeze the size of the workforce even as the network expanded by double digits. In Argentina, where workers were not promised job security after privatization, the new owners shed almost 50 percent of the original workforce, even as they hired younger persons with skills in areas such as information systems or marketing; companies recovered the US$15,000–20,000 spent on severance compensation per employee

Table 1-3. Results of Telecommunications Privatization

Performance Measures	Telecommunications of Jamaica	Teléfonos of México	ENTEL of Argentina	CANTV of Venezuela
1. System expansion and growth	The network grew at 18% per year in the first four years after privatization, versus 4.5% per year in the eleven years of state ownership. Telephone density doubled from 3.19 lines per 100 persons in 1987 to 6.58 in 1992. Capital spending averaged US$70m per year in the four years after privatization, versus US$16m in the four years prior to it.	The network grew at 12% or more per year after privatization, compared to 6–7% in the previous decade and an average of 9% in the three years leading up to privatization. Telephone density increased from 6.6 lines per 100 persons in 1985 to 8.7 in the first three years of privatization. Capital spending averaged US$2.2b per year after privatization, versus US$1.3b in the three years before privatization (and much less in the early 1980s).	The network grew at 12% per year in the first four years after privatization, versus 5% in the five years prior to privatization. Telephone density increased from 9.4 lines per 100 persons in 1985 to more than 14 in 1994. Average capital spending of US$1.2b per year after privatization was three to four times capital spending in the early 1980s.	The network expanded at more than 15% in the first two years after privatization. Telephone density increased from 8.2 lines per 100 persons in 1990 to 10 by 1993 and was projected to reach 20 in the year 2000. Capital spending in the first two years after privatization was US$1.1b and was projected to total US$6b between 1992 and 2000.
2. Labor productivity (measured by main lines per employee)	This worsened in the run-up to privatization and, at forty lines per employee in 1992, barely exceeded the 1985 level of thirty-seven lines per employee.	This improved by 13% per year in the first three years of privatization to reach 152 lines per employee in 1993, compared to a decline of 2% per year in the 1980s and a growth of 10% per year in the two years leading up to privatization.	This improved by 19% per year in the first three years after privatization, partly through workforce reduction, to reach 150 lines per employee in 1994, versus 6.5% in the years before privatization.	This improved by double digits in the first two years after privatization, when it stood at ninety-seven lines per employee, versus a small decline from 1987 to 1990.

Table 1-3. (continued)

Performance Measures	Telecommunications of Jamaica	Teléfonos of México	ENTEL of Argentina	CANTV of Venezuela
3. Quality of service	Quality standards were neither stipulated nor monitored by the government. However, by 1992, the network was reportedly 100% digitized, placing it ahead of most developing countries.	This improved in the aggregate by historical standards but with significant shortfalls in some areas compared to the (challenging) targets set in the concession agreement, particularly in the Mexico City region. Digitization rose from less than 40% to 72% in the first three years of privatization.	If company-reported data are accurate, significant quality improvements were registered in the first four years and the (easy) targets set in the concession agreement were greatly exceeded; however, as of 1994, regulators had not verified the accuracy of the self-reports. Digitization rose from 14% in the south and 11% in the north in 1990 to 53% and 72%, respectively, in 1994.	In the first year, the call completion rate improved from 48% to 53% for local calls, from 31% to 39% for domestic long-distance calls, and from 19% to 33% for international calls; in the aggregate, all quality of service targets in the concession agreement were exceeded. Digitization rose from 20% to 40%.
4. Financial performance	Between 1985 and 1991, after adjusting for inflation, sales and net profits grew by 47% and 54%, respectively.	In the first three years after privatization, sales and net profits rose to three times and five times, respectively, of their levels in the year before privatization.	Sales rose to 3.5 times in the year prior to privatization; losses exceeding US$500m in 1988 were turned into after-tax profits of US$660m in 1994.	Sales more than doubled in the first year of privatization (55% increase at constant prices), and a loss of US$161m in 1991 turned into a profit before tax of US$208m in 1992.

Source: see table 1-2.

in two years or less. The privatized companies were also able to redeploy workers more easily from one area to another and to curtail corruption by repair and other personnel. Unlike the government, private owners did not regard employment creation or its preservation as an objective of the enterprise.

The new owners were equally ruthless in shedding white-collar workers. Staff departments were closed or consolidated, but those workers who survived participated in stock purchase or bonus plans. They also reduced inventories through better control over purchasing and storage. Finally, equipment suppliers took a big hit. In Argentina and Mexico, local manufacturers had for years sold equipment at high prices to state enterprises, with the support of politicians. Under the threat of taking their business elsewhere, the new owners forced local suppliers to cut equipment prices by 25 percent in Mexico and more than 50 percent in Argentina.

Regulation Private ownership was necessary, but not sufficient, to produce the behavioral changes and outcomes described above. Changes in regulation that accompanied privatization were at least as important. When the firms were government owned, the government's role as regulator was never distinguished from its role as owner. It seemed that the enormous power vested in the government as owner, including the power to hire and fire the firm's CEO, made formal regulation unnecessary. Indeed, in Jamaica, when the telephone company was nationalized in the 1970s, the public utilities commission that once regulated the sector folded (Adam et al. 1992, 170). In Argentina, no formal license or concession agreement existed between the government and ENTel until the firm was privatized. Instead, the government made up rules as required and changed them as convenient. Privatization forced governments to formalize the regulatory relationship with the firm. In Mexico, for instance, a short, vaguely worded license agreement was replaced after privatization by a comprehensive one that was four times as long. The new agreement took advantage of international regulatory experience and stipulated targets for network expansion, universal service, and quality, with penalties for failing to meet the targets—including termination of the license. Although the agreements had flaws, especially in Argentina, in the short run, privatization produced a quantum improvement in the quality of regulation.[18]

In terms of content, perhaps the most important elements in the new regulations were (1) the sharp increase in prices before privatization, including the first steps toward rebalancing prices for local and long-distance service and ending the subsidization of the former by the latter, (2) the use of price-cap regulation after privatization for periods varying from six years in Mexico, to eight in Venezuela, and up to ten in

Argentina, and (3) the setting of explicit targets for quality and universal service. The increase in prices for telephone services was necessary not only to find buyers for the companies but also to motivate them to invest in the network after privatization. In Mexico, rates for local service were raised sharply at the time of privatization, but the connection charges for new lines and the rates for long-distance service, which were high to begin with, went up further or remained the same. In Argentina and Venezuela, local service rates were not increased as much, but long-distance continued to subsidize local service.[19] In Jamaica, the government and the privatized company had an understanding that local service rates would not be increased for five years.

Price-cap regulation, unlike rate-of-return regulation, gave the owners a strong incentive to reduce costs without fear that the resulting profits might be expropriated administratively by regulators. The importance of this factor is seen, for instance, in the very modest improvement in labor productivity after privatization in Jamaica (which used rate-of-return regulation) compared to the other three countries. Four years after privatization, the Jamaican company had 40 telephone lines per employee, compared to 97 lines per employee in CANTV, 121 lines per employee in Argentina, and 152 lines per employee in TELMEX. Similarly, the companies would probably not have bothered to extend telephone service to remote and low-income areas or worried about quality of service if targets had not been set in these areas in the concession agreement. In a few instances, regulators actually imposed penalties for failing to achieve targets.

Competition   If, in the short run, privatization and regulatory changes had a positive impact on the performance of the monopoly enterprise, competition had almost none. Governments paid lip service to promoting competition but, as mentioned previously, did so only on the fringes, such as cellular service, value added services, trunking, and paging, where competition would probably have been permitted even without privatization. In local and long-distance service, which made up 90 percent or more of the sector's revenues, the privatized firms enjoyed exclusivity, that is, monopoly power, for periods ranging from six years in Mexico, to eight in Venezuela, up to ten in Argentina, and twenty-five in Jamaica. The privatized firms were also granted one of two licenses for cellular service; in Mexico, the privatized firm was granted the only national license for cellular service. In no case was the privatized firm prohibited from diversifying into services open to competition, such as value added services, or into products for which the telephone company would be a captive market (for example, cables or switching equipment), as long as these activities were carried out through separate subsidiaries.[20] Most privatizations also protected the buyers against the risk of hostile takeovers for up to ten years, thus eliminating competition for corporate control in the medium term.

In Jamaica, the incumbent firm's power was strengthened by merging the local service and international service firms before privatization, presumably to make the package more attractive to Cable & Wireless, which owned 49 percent of the international service firm. In Mexico, the federal microwave network owned by a state agency was consolidated with the telephone company before privatization to satisfy the express request from potential buyers that the state should not be simultaneously regulator and provider of service. Only in Argentina was an existing state monopoly divided into two regional companies before privatization, for the explicit purpose of creating "competition by comparison." Yet, even here, the regional companies were made fifty-fifty owners of a third company, which provided long-distance service.[21]

In every country, the privatized firms seem to have adopted textbook tactics to make life difficult for companies wishing to offer new telecommunications services that were open to competition, such as cellular telephony and value added services. These providers had to connect their facilities with the monopolist's network, but the terms and conditions had to be mutually negotiated. The privatized firms haggled over the number of connection points, access charges, marginal investments required to facilitate interconnection, billing procedures, and so on. Eventually, regulators were available to settle the issues, but meanwhile delays were to the monopolist's advantage. Despite such stalling tactics, in every country but Jamaica, by early 1995, the telecommunications industry included a handful of firms with strong multinational partners and sales in the range of US$50 million to US$100 million. The nucleus of future competitors to the monopoly enterprise was created.

The Long-Run Outlook   The future results of privatization cannot simply be extrapolated from the results in the years immediately following privatization. However, one can gain some insights into the future by asking what is likely to happen over time to each of the variables in figure 1-1.

Considering ownership first, it is reassuring that governments locked in the consortia members for the long haul by barring the sale of their stock in the telecommunications firms for five to ten years. Also reassuring is the fact that neither the foreign firms in the consortia, which must worry about their image and reputation, nor their local partners, which had too many other investments in the local economy, have a strong incentive to behave opportunistically. Once the ban on selling shares ends, there are bound to be changes in the composition of the consortia, but this should not make a material difference in the performance of the firms as long as the principal investors do not leave or squabble endlessly (which in some cases they well might).

Turning to regulation, it is safe to predict that problems lie ahead, because most countries did not create strong new regulatory institutions to oversee the telecommunications sector. Despite pressure from the World Bank to do so, and despite a facade of independence and professionalism, the regulatory agencies were riddled with political meddling and bureaucratic constraints. Countries were relying on the concession agreement, drafted at the time of privatization, with an unusually large dose of foreign assistance, to see them through many years of regulation. But as the concession agreements become obsolete, they will have to be renegotiated by regulatory bodies whose expertise, information, and resources are vastly inferior to that of the privatized companies. There is a real danger of regulatory capture.

In every country, within the first few years agreements struck with the government at the time of privatization had to be modified, sometimes informally.[22] Both the number and the severity of such adjustments is likely to increase with time. First, as administrations change, the new officials will feel less obliged to honor every commitment made by their predecessors. In the absence of strong regulatory agencies and impartial courts, officials in the ministries are likely to wield effective power. Second, economic conditions, which were relatively good in the years after privatization, could become more turbulent, as they already had by 1993 in Venezuela and by January 1995 in Mexico. For instance, the price-cap method could become politically controversial if inflation is high rather than low, as it was in the years immediately following privatization. Finally, governments may want to renegotiate the agreements because the returns earned by the companies, which may have seemed reasonable ex ante, appear excessive ex post. (This is the problem of the "obsolescing bargain"; see Vernon 1971.) In at least a few cases, the resulting conflicts between governments and firms could turn ugly.

If the long-run outlook for regulation is worrisome, fortunately the long-run outlook for competition is encouraging, because it could flourish once the exclusivity periods end. In Jamaica, that period is so long that one can safely predict that a future government will go back on its promise before it expires. In the other countries, notwithstanding any attempts by the incumbent firms to extend their monopoly privileges, governments are unlikely to oblige. Instead, a few more players are likely to be permitted into each market segment or geographic region. Doing so will no longer exact a toll on a privileged state enterprise, as it would have in 1990; on the other hand, it will please consumers and the growing lobby of potential competitors waiting in the wings for exclusivity to end. To both the incumbent monopoly and potential entrants, the

Figure 1-2. The Three Stages of Telecommunications Reform.

government's threat to end exclusivity and introduce competition in all services by a specific date has been far more credible *with* privatization than it ever would have *without* privatization.[23] By the end of 1994, more than half a dozen firms were getting ready to enter the Mexican market in 1996, when TELMEX's exclusivity period would end. Similarly, local and foreign firms were jockeying for position in Argentina and Venezuela.

The final reason to expect competition in the future is technological change, which continues to chip away at the natural monopoly status of telecommunications, including local service. In all four countries, even with exclusivity in force, the privatized monopolies complained constantly about how those rights were being violated by illegal devices, such as callback services and the misuse of private data networks for voice communication. Thus, technology is on the side of the consumer and the regulator, serving in some degree as a counterbalance to the power of the monopoly firm.

In summary, as shown in figure 1-2, in the telecommunications sector, governments did not transform the state monopoly (stage 1) into a competitive, privately owned sector (stage 3) in one swift step, as in theory they might have done, but are likely to achieve the same final result via an intermediate stage of regulated private monopoly (stage 2). The incumbent firm is likely to become entrenched during stage 2, making it difficult even for industry giants, such as ATT or MCI, to dislodge it in stage 3. However, new entrants can be expected to contest the monopoly firm's stranglehold and keep it on its toes. In stage 3, regulators will have to ensure that new entrants can interconnect with the monopolist's network on reasonable terms and compete with it fairly. Competition will make the regulator's task easier in some ways, but more challenging in other ways.

It might appear that countries could have done better by moving directly from stage 1 to stage 3, without spending several years in stage 2. However, doing so would have robbed governments of the chance to solve their fiscal problems through privatization or to signal their commitment to market-oriented policies. And in the absence of those incentives, in some countries, the sector may not have been reformed at all. The adage, better late than never, may well apply here.

Reform without Privatization? One might reasonably ask whether governments could have implemented all the reforms they did, with the exception of privatization, and expected the same outcomes. For instance, could not governments have renegotiated labor contracts, raised and rebalanced prices, applied price-cap regulation, and prescribed targets for universal service, network expansion, and quality of service to the state firm as they did to the privatized firm? No such case was studied in this project, but our conclusion, based on this and other studies is, probably not (on state enterprise reform, see Shirley and Nellis 1991; Ramamurti and Vernon 1991).

First, governments seem to have difficulty being tough with labor except during economic crises, as seen in our cases. Even then, the threat to privatize was itself an important reason why unions made concessions to the government, apparently because they preferred negotiating with the known devil to the unknown (future private owners). It is unlikely that a state enterprise would have grown as rapidly as the privatized firms did without adding to its workforce, especially if it was making money hand over fist.

Second, officials in more than one country argued that the public would not have tolerated the sharp price increases that were made before privatization if the government had not also promised to privatize the firm. For instance, officials in Mexico claimed that the public would not have trusted the government and TELMEX to put the additional revenue to good use.[24] Thus, a sharp increase in prices was necessary to privatize the telecommunications firms, but equally important, privatization may have been necessary to increase prices. Whether or not one agrees with this argument, it illustrates the kinds of interdependency that exist between the variables in figure 1-1.

Third, it would have been difficult to apply price-cap regulation for any length of time to state enterprises. This method works because it allows the firm to retain, and do what it pleases, with the cost savings that exceed the productivity gains assumed in the *RPI - X* formula. Governments would have a hard time granting that kind of discretion to the managers of state enterprises, who after all are salaried employees, not owners of the firm. Perhaps, therefore, no country, to the best of our knowledge, has used price-cap regulation for state enterprises.

Finally, governments have tried unsuccessfully to formalize the regulation of state enterprises through performance contracts, wherein the mutual obligations of the government and the state enterprise are made explicit after lengthy negotiations. These contracts contain performance targets for the firm and promises about government conduct, similar to those in the concession agreements signed with privatized monopolies (for examples from Bolivia, see Mallon 1994). However, in developing

countries, performance contracts have had a disappointing record, because neither the firms nor the governments seem to take their commitments very seriously (Nellis 1991).[25] Promises made between one part of
the state (the government) and another (the state-owned enterprise)
seem to have less credibility than when those same promises and threats
are made by the state and a private firm to one another. To be sure,
privatized firms can also miss targets, as the firms in our sample did, but
this is more likely to cause dismay than when a state enterprise misses
targets. Odd as it may seem, the private monopolies in our sample
seemed more vulnerable to the pressure of public opinion than the
erstwhile state enterprises.

Ownership, Regulation, and Competition: Airlines

Data on postprivatization results are not uniform across the airline studies, rendering comparisons difficult. The available evidence is sufficient to
conclude that privatized airlines faced far more problems than privatized
telecommunications firms. Only Aeromexico, which was drastically restructured by the government before privatization, registered increases
in output, efficiency, and profits after privatization. Aerolíneas Argentinas and VIASA, which were losing money at the time of privatization,
continued to lose money for three years after privatization. Mexicana,
which was losing money before privatization, achieved record losses
after privatization, despite modest improvements in efficiency. And LAN-
Chile, which was quite profitable at the time of privatization, achieved a
big loss in the very first year after privatization, followed by declines in
market share and labor productivity.

The fortunes of the privatized airlines, like other airlines at the time,
were adversely affected by excess capacity in the industry and slower
than anticipated growth in demand. In addition, changes in ownership
and regulation did not make as much difference in the airline cases as
they did in telecommunications.

For one thing, the airlines were sold to weaker buyers than the
telecommunications firms. Aeromexico and Mexicana were sold to consortia that did not include any foreign airline, and the Mexican investors
had experience in only the reinsurance and hotel/resort industries,
respectively. In Chile, investors in Ladeco, the only national competitor
to LAN-Chile, were barred from bidding for LAN when it was privatized.
Its ultimate buyer included Scandinavian Airline System, but the firm
was run by a flamboyant local partner with no background in airlines. In
Argentina and Venezuela, management control was vested in Iberia, the
Spanish state-owned airline that was itself mired in problems and not
renowned for efficiency or good service. Indeed, in the early 1990s,

Iberia was charged by the European Commission with having covered its losses through huge subsidies from the Spanish government.

In addition, with the exception of Mexico, the governments involved continued to own substantial shares in the "privatized" airlines, because buyers could not be found for those shares. Two or more years after control of the airline had been turned over to the private sector, the government's share of equity stood at 43 percent in Argentina, 40 percent in Venezuela, and 26 percent in Chile. In Argentina and Venezuela, workers hesitated to buy the shares that had been set aside for them, because the airlines showed no signs of making a profit; eventually those shares were transferred at a price that amounted to a giveaway.

To be sure, the new owners of the airlines, like the buyers of the telecommunications firms, tried to expand revenues and contract costs. But neither came as easily in the airline business. For one thing, the airlines could neither raise prices with impunity nor expand volume as easily as the telecommunications firms in our sample. In the aftermath of the Gulf crisis, the ambitious fleet expansions by LAN-Chile and Mexicana saddled them with very high fixed costs, putting the first into technical bankruptcy within a year of privatization and forcing the second to sell out to its domestic rival, Aeromexico. On the cost side, the price of fuel, an important input, was entirely beyond the control of the owners. And the airlines, unlike the telecommunications firms, could not raise labor productivity without sharp reductions in the workforce, which cost Mexicana and Aerolíneas Argentinas US$35 million and US$75 million, respectively, in severance payments.

As in the case of telecommunications, in the short run, privatization cemented rather than loosened the artificial barriers to competition. To be sure, the airlines were not monopolies, but neither did they compete head-on with one another in the domestic market or engage in fare wars. Instead, they operated on routes allotted to them by government officials and charged approved fares. In Argentina and Venezuela, these practices continued after privatization, and were reinforced by the guarantee of "sole designation" on international routes to VIASA and Aerolíneas Argentinas for several years. In Argentina, privatization *weakened* domestic competition, because the consortium that purchased Aerolíneas Argentinas included the owner of its principal domestic competitor, Austral.

The opposite approaches to sequencing privatization and deregulation in Chile and Mexico offered some useful lessons. Chile deregulated the industry first, and privatized the state enterprise fully ten years later, while Mexico privatized first, and deregulated four years later. The advantage of the deregulate-then-privatize approach was that competition made the state enterprise's performance so bad that the political barriers to restructuring and privatizing it were greatly reduced; the disadvantage was that the state enterprise probably fetched less money after deregulation than it would have before. The advantage of the privatize-then-deregulate approach was that the state enterprise was restructured before competition set in; the main disadvantage was the risk that promises made to entice buyers at the time of privatization could make it harder for the government to deregulate the industry afterward, as may have happened in Argentina and Venezuela.

In countries like Argentina and Venezuela, the airline industry may go through a three-stage transformation process, similar to the one described for telecommunications (see figure 1-2). The first, or initial, stage involves imperfect competition with state ownership in the sector. The second stage involves imperfect competition among privately owned airlines. The third, and final, stage, which Chile and Mexico had already reached by 1995, involves relatively free competition among privately owned airlines.

One important difference between the telecommunications and airline industries is that incumbency seems to bestow far greater advantages in the former than the latter. Therefore, in stage 3, the privatized airline is under much greater risk of being put out of business by competition than is the privatized telecommunications firm. Will governments allow privatized firms to fail? Even in Chile, where the willingness to allow markets to work is stronger than in most developing countries, the government extended subsidies to the privatized LAN-Chile rather than allow it to go bankrupt. As long as governments feel compelled to put a safety net under their national airlines, or any other privatized firm, the argument that private firms, unlike state enterprises, operate under the threat of bankruptcy will not hold water.

Does Ownership Matter?

This research project began with the proposition that, in markets where competition is weak or absent, which we conveniently label monopolies, changing a firm's ownership from public to private while holding industry structure and regulation unchanged would make relatively little difference to its performance. Furthermore, we suggested that in developing countries privatization might conceivably worsen performance because the limited regulatory capacity of governments would make arm's-length regulation of private monopolies cumbersome and, possibly, unworkable.

But our conclusion is that ownership matters, even under conditions of highly imperfect competition, though not necessarily for the reasons one might expect. Although it is dangerous to generalize from a handful of case studies, we venture the following ten hypotheses:

1. Although economists assume that the main reason to privatize a firm is to improve its performance, that motivation may be less important in explaining why governments privatize large, monopolistic firms than (1) their desire to realize an immediate cash flow to shore up budgets and foreign exchange reserves, and (2) their desire to send a signal to private investors about a shift in economic strategy.

2. The real significance of privatizing monopolies lies not so much in its direct impact on managerial incentives but in its indirect impact through concomitant changes in competition and the quality of regulation, changes that might not have occurred without privatization. Although in theory, privatization, competition, and regulation are independent policy variables, in practice, they are highly interdependent.

3. In the short run, privatization of monopolies is likely to be accompanied by a strengthening of regulatory arrangements, because the government's roles as owner and regulator are no longer blurred, and some kinds of regulatory reform have more credibility and teeth when the government is not also the owner of the firm being regulated.

4. In the short run, the privatization of monopolies is unlikely to be accompanied by a strengthening of competition, even if such competition is technically feasible, because an important motivation for privatizing such firms has been to shore up government finances, an objective better served by selling the state firm with, rather than without, market power. This expectation will be less true as governments reduce their budget deficits and public debt through privatization and other means.

5. In the long run, regulatory agreements negotiated at the time of privatization will become increasingly obsolete and incomplete, because of unforeseen economic, technological, and competitive developments. Transaction costs associated with regulation will increase, relations between firms and governments will become strained, and the risk of regulatory capture will increase. Countries in which firms and regulators enjoy high mutual trust and in which regulators have both the expertise and the discretion necessary to reasonably adapt rules to uncertainty and change will continue to gain from privatization.[26] Unfortunately, few countries in Latin America, or elsewhere in the developing world, are likely to satisfy these conditions. Therefore, in the next decade, the record of privatized monopolies is likely to be choppier than it has been so far.

6. In the long run, however, privatization increases the likelihood that competition will be strengthened in monopolistic industries, to the extent this is technically feasible, because the state no longer has a vested interest in protecting the interests of the firm it used to own. Both the privatized monopoly and the potential entrants into the industry are more likely to believe the government's threat (promise) of introducing competition into the sector *with* privatization than *without* it. In industries such as telecommunications, the onset of competition could mitigate the regulatory shortcomings discussed in the previous paragraph.

7. In theory, many of the changes in regulatory policy that accompanied the telecommunications privatizations, such as the initial price increases, the use of the price-cap method of regulation, or the setting of targets for expansion and quality of service, could have been applied as well to state-owned enterprises. In practice, however, they are unlikely to be as effective, because (1) promises and threats made between two parts of the state, that is, the government and the state enterprise, seem to have less credibility than similar promises and threats between a government and a private firm, and (2) agency problems associated with state ownership make it difficult for governments to grant discretion to enterprise managers. Note that, if a country is able to overcome these two obstacles, because its governments are more disciplined and responsible in using power, the case for privatizing state-owned monopolies rather than reforming them will be weaker. (This may partly explain why privatization has not spread to monopoly sectors in many Asian countries.)

8. Thus, the real significance of privatizing monopolistic firms goes beyond its direct consequences, such as lower agency costs, better management, or clearer goals. It includes as well the greater opportunity that privatization provides, in the medium to long term if not in the immediate term, to use the disciplinary forces of competition and regulation to improve the firm's performance. That, in turn, is possible because privatization reduces the scope for opportunistic behavior by governments.[27] Most of the problems of the state-owned enterprise stem not from the enterprise but from the state; the discipline that privatization imposes on the state is probably more important than the discipline it imposes on the firm and its managers.

9. The assumption that private firms, unlike state enterprises, are disciplined by the threat of bankruptcy may not be true of private firms that are "too big" or "too important" to fail, for example, electric power, water, or telecommunications companies—and possibly airlines too. Under these circumstances, the moral hazard problem arises, with private firms taking higher risks than they otherwise would. If such risk taking proves unwise ex post, governments may be forced to bail out the privatized firms or, in the extreme case, to renationalize them.

10. Thus, in the case of monopolies, the functions and responsibilities of governments may change in kind after privatization, but for a long time to come, they are unlikely to disappear altogether.

NOTES

1. Data on privatization in this and the following paragraph are from Sader (1993).

2. The telecommunications cases appear in this volume in the order in which the firms were privatized. The Chilean telephone company was privatized a few months before Telecommunications of Jamaica.

3. Each of these countries obtained a structural adjustment loan from the

World Bank, whose conditions included privatizing the state-owned telecommunications firm. The World Bank's involvement was particularly deep in Argentina (see World Bank 1993).

4. In 1995, this may sound like an exaggeration, but it was certainly true in 1989 or 1990. Even Chile, the pioneer of privatization in Latin America, began to privatize monopolistic state enterprises only in the second half of the 1980s. To be sure, as the last of the privatizers in our sample, Venezuela benefited in some measure from the experiences of Argentina, Chile, and Mexico (see chapter 5).

5. For ease of presentation, the term *president* is used throughout, even though in Jamaica the head of government was the prime minister.

6. In both Argentina and Mexico, the economic crisis facing the country at the time made it easier for presidents to centralize decisionmaking.

7. This is the retail price index minus X, or $(RPI - X)$ formula, where X is the productivity adjustment factor. Initially, X was set at 3 percent for British Telecom, but by 1993 it had been raised to 7.5 percent.

8. In Argentina, the productivity adjustment factor was set at 2 percent after the first two years, rising to 4 percent after the seventh year, if the exclusive right to provide basic services was extended beyond the seventh year for three more years. In Mexico and Venezuela, a productivity adjustment factor of 3 percent kicked in after six and eight years, respectively.

9. This was done by concentrating the voting power in a special class of stock that was later sold to the winning consortium.

10. Indeed, in keeping with this sentiment, nationals headed the privatized telecommunications firms, even in those cases where foreign investors controlled the consortium.

11. In Jamaica, the government sold its shares to the foreign operator, Cable & Wireless, which already owned a piece of the company, without inviting competing offers. In Argentina, a third bid from a consortium led by Bell Atlantic fell through in the last minute.

12. The figures pertain to the government's entire holdings prior to privatization, which varied from 55 percent of the total equity in Mexico, to 83 percent in Jamaica, to 100 percent in Argentina and Venezuela. The figure for Venezuela does not include the 49 percent of CANTV's stock that the government had not divested by the end of 1994. The figure for Argentina includes an imputed value for Argentine debt turned in as part of the offer, valued at the prevailing price in the secondary market (19% of face value).

13. The amounts indicated are for 67 percent of LAN, 20 percent of Mexicana, 75 percent of Aeromexico, 60 percent of VIASA, and 85 percent of Aerolíneas Argentinas. In the last case, the amount shown includes an imputed market value of US$304 million for Argentine debt, with a face value of US$1.6 billion, that was turned in by the buyers as part of their offer.

14. For a rigorous cost-benefit analysis of twelve cases of privatization, see Galal et al. (1994).

15. In TELMEX, which was sold intact and reportedly had a good staff, in the first year only seven new executives were brought in at the highest levels; however, in Telefónica de Argentina, which resulted from splitting up a badly run

company, ENTel, the new owners hired 250 managers to form a new corporate organization. The company later shrank its original workforce by 9,000 persons while adding 4,000 others from the outside.

16. For instance, in TELMEX, the local partner assumed control of finance, administration, and purchasing, while France Telecom became involved with expanding and modernizing the network, and Southwestern Bell was responsible for strengthening systems and marketing, which were its forte. Typically, 50–100 foreign experts came to work in the privatized telecommunications firm.

17. In 1990–91, the connection charge in Argentina for a commercial user was US$2,632, with a waiting period of almost two years! By December 1994, that charge had declined to US$750.

18. The better concession agreements laid out specific goals for network expansion, quality of service, and public service that the concessionaire had to meet; they set difficult rather than easy targets, and imposed penalties for nonfulfillment; their pricing rules motivated the concessionaire to cut costs and become efficient; and they ensured that the government would have access to the information required for judging compliance and for regulating the sector. The Jamaican concession fell short on many of these criteria: it set no specific targets for expansion or quality, provided for no penalties for nonfulfillment other than revocation of the license, and guaranteed a high, real, after-tax rate of return of 17.5–20 percent. In Argentina, many aspects of the postprivatization regulatory environment were unclear, and targets for expansion and quality were very easy. On the other hand, Mexico and Venezuela fashioned concession agreements that were cleverer and more challenging.

19. In Argentina, a further rebalancing of rates was widely expected after the May 1995 elections (author's interviews in Buenos Aires, March 1995).

20. However, in Argentina and Mexico, the privatized firm was allowed to provide cellular service only one or two years after its competitor in the region had begun doing so.

21. Argentine telephone privatization illustrates how public commitments to furthering competition were progressively abandoned as the privatization unfolded (see chapter 4). The original plan called for dividing the national telephone company into several regional companies before privatization, separating local service from long-distance service, permitting free entry into long-distance service (immediately) and into all basic services (within five years), and ending all cross-subsidization. However, as negotiations proceeded, most of these commitments were abandoned to ensure a quick, successful sale.

22. Within months of privatization, the Menem administration passed the Law on Convertability (April 1991), which forbid indexation in all contracts, including those negotiated in the past by the government. The privatized companies and the government had to negotiate new pricing rules to replace the indexation formula accepted at the time of privatization.

23. Managers of a state-owned firm are less likely than private managers to believe that their monopoly privileges will be terminated at a future date, and even if they did, their capacity to cope with that eventuality is limited. Sensing that, potential entrants are unlikely to make the advance investments necessary

to take on the incumbent state enterprise, which would reinforce the government's suspicion that the private sector is unwilling to invest in risky, capital-intensive sectors. Conversely, with privatization, the logic can work in the opposite direction (as discussed in chapter 3).

24. However, it is quite possible that, if prices could have been raised as sharply as they were after privatization, the state enterprises could have expanded the network at rates comparable to those of the privatized firms, at least in Mexico.

25. This is not to say that the performance contract is a useless device— merely that the regulatory contract between the government and a private firm seems to have more teeth than a similar contract with a state enterprise.

26. For an excellent discussion of the relation between country conditions and alternative approaches to telecommunications regulation, see Levy and Spiller (1994).

27. Willig (1994) makes a similar point about how privatization reduces the scope for opportunistic behavior by government.

REFERENCES

Abdala, Manuel A. 1994. "The Divestiture of ENTel (Telecommunications Services in Argentina)." Paper prepared for the Cofinancing and Financial Advisory Services, Privatization and Private Sector Development Group, World Bank, Washington, D.C.

Adam, Chris, William P. Cavendish, and Percy Mistry. 1992. *Adjusting Privatization: Case Studies from Developing Countries*. London: Queen Elizabeth House.

Aharoni, Yair. 1982. "State-Owned Enterprise: An Agent without a Principal." In *Public Enterprise in Less-Developed Countries*, ed. Leroy P. Jones et al. Cambridge: Cambridge Univ. Press.

Alexander, Myrna, and Carlos Corti. 1993. *Argentina's Privatization Program*. Washington, D.C.: World Bank.

Ambrose, William, Paul R. Hennemeyer, and Jean-Paul Chapon. 1990. *Privatizing Telecommunications Systems: Business Opportunities in Developing Countries*. Discussion Paper 10. Washington, D.C.: World Bank.

Austin, James E., Lawrence Wortzel, and Jeffrey F. Coburn. 1986. "Privatizing State-Owned Enterprises: Hopes and Realities." *Columbia Journal of World Business* 21 (3): 51–60.

Clare, Ken, and Ravi Ramamurti. 1994. "Project Performance Audit Report on Road Transport and Telecommunications Sector Adjustment Loan (ME-3207)." Washington, D.C., World Bank.

Galal, Ahmed, Leroy P. Jones, Pankaj Tandon, and Ingo Vogelsang. 1994. *Welfare Consequences of Selling Public Enterprises: An Empirical Analysis*. New York: Oxford Univ. Press.

Gerschenkron, Alexander. 1962. *Economic Backwardness in Historical Perspective*. Cambridge: Harvard Univ. Press.

Gonzalez Fraga, Javier. 1991. "The Argentina Privatization in Retrospect." In *Privatization of Public Enterprises in Latin America*, ed. William Glade. San Francisco: ICS Press.

Hachette, Dominique, and Rolf Lüders. 1993. *Privatization in Chile: An Economic Appraisal.* San Francisco: ICS Press.

Jones, Leroy P. 1982. Introduction to *Public Enterprise in Less-Developed Countries,* ed. Leroy P. Jones, with Richard Mallon, Edward S. Mason, Paul N. Rosenstein-Rodan, and Raymond Vernon. Cambridge: Cambridge Univ. Press.

Kelly, Janet. 1988. "Venezuela: Letting in the Market." In *The Promise of Privatization,* ed. Raymond Vernon. New York: Council on Foreign Relations.

Levy, Brian, and Pablo T. Spiller. 1994. "Regulation, Institutions, and Commitment in Telecommunications: A Comparative Analysis of Five Country Studies." In *Proceedings of the World Bank Annual Conference on Development Economics.* Washington, D.C.: World Bank.

Mallon, Richard D. 1994. "State-Owned Enterprise Reform through Performance Contracts: The Bolivian Experiment." *World Development* 22 (6): 1–10.

Nellis, John. 1991. "Contract Plans: A Review of International Experience." In *Privatization and Control of State-Owned Enterprises,* ed. Ravi Ramamurti and Raymond Vernon. Washington, D.C.: World Bank.

Ramamurti, Ravi. 1992a. "The Impact of Privatization on the Latin American Debt Problem." *Journal of Interamerican Studies and World Affairs* 34 (2): 93–125.

———. 1992b. "Why Are Developing Countries Privatizing?" *Journal of International Business Studies* 23 (2): 225–49.

———. 1993. "Teléfonos de México: The Privatization Decision." *Case Research Journal* 13 (2): 43–67.

Ramamurti, Ravi, and Raymond Vernon, eds. 1991. *Privatization and Control of State-Owned Enterprises.* Washington, D.C.: World Bank.

Sader, Frank. 1993. *Privatization and Foreign Investment in the Developing World: 1988–1992.* Washington, D.C.: World Bank.

Shirley, Mary, and John Nellis. 1991. *Public Enterprise Reform: The Lessons of Experience.* Washington, D.C.: World Bank.

Tandon, Pankaj. 1994. "Teléfonos de México." In Galal et al.

Taylor, Robert, and Eloy Vidal. 1994. "Fast Turnaround for Venezuela's Telephone." *Lessons.* Washington, D.C.: World Bank.

Vernon, Raymond. 1971. *Sovereignty at Bay: The Multinational Spread of U.S. Firms.* New York: Basic Books.

———, ed. 1988. *The Promise of Privatization: A Challenge for American Policy.* New York: Council on Foreign Relations.

Vickers, John, and George Yarrow. 1988. *Privatization: An Economic Analysis.* Cambridge: MIT Press.

Vuylsteke, Charles. 1988. *Techniques of Privatization of State-Owned Enterprises.* Vol. 1. *Methods and Implementation.* Washington, D.C.: World Bank.

Wellenius, Bjorn, Peter A. Stern, Timothy E. Nulty, and Richard D. Stern, eds. 1989. *Restructuring and Managing the Telecommunications Sector.* Washington, D.C.: World Bank.

Werneck, R. 1991. "The Uneasy Steps toward Privatization in Brazil." In *Privatization of Public Enterprises in Latin America,* ed. William Glade. San Francisco: ICS Press.

Willig, Robert D. 1994. "Public versus Regulated Private Enterprise." In

Proceedings of the World Bank Annual Conference on Development Economics. Washington, D.C.: World Bank.

World Bank. 1993. *Argentina's Privatization Program: Experience, Issues, and Lessons.* Washington, D.C.: World Bank.

———. 1994. *World Development Report.* New York: Oxford Univ. Press.

I.   TELECOMMUNICATIONS

2. Pioneering Telephone Privatization

JAMAICA

Alvin G. Wint

In 1985, the Jamaican government began negotiations with the British telecommunications firm Cable & Wireless (c&w) with the objective of reducing the government's role in the nation's telecommunications sector. These negotiations culminated in a May 1987 decision to merge the domestic telephone company (Jamaica Telephone Company, or JTC), in which the government had a majority shareholding, with Jamaica International Telecommunications (JAMINTEL), the international telephone company that was a joint venture between the government of Jamaica and c&w. These companies became subsidiaries of a newly formed holding company: Telecommunications of Jamaica (TOJ). By July 1989, the Jamaican government had sold sufficient shares in the TOJ, both to c&w and to the Jamaican public, that control of the company passed to c&w, and the privatization operation was complete: the first completed privatization transaction of the four telecommunication privatizations reported upon in this volume.

Yet many questions remained. In privatizing the telecommunications industry, the Jamaican government sold its holdings in an industry it had gone to great lengths to acquire little more than a decade earlier. Indeed, the People's National Party administration that sold the final tranches of shares in the TOJ was led by Michael Manley, whose earlier PNP administration had nationalized the domestic segment of the industry in 1975.

What factors led to such a dramatic turnaround? Had the state failed in its efforts to manage this industry? Was this part of a new economic strategy pursued by Jamaica? Or was the government seeking to extricate itself from a short-term financial emergency. In addition, questions emerged regarding the manner in which the company was

49

privatized. Why was there no competition in the bidding process, for example? And what of the terms of the privatization, including the associated regulatory framework, that were granted to the lone multinational with whom negotiations were held. Were these terms as attractive as they appeared? And if so, why?

This chapter seeks to address the above questions. It examines the factors that motivated the government of Jamaica to privatize the country's telecommunications industry. It also focuses on the manner in which the privatization transaction was conducted, the motivations of the principal purchaser, the nature of the regulatory regime that was put in place alongside privatization, and the results of the privatization.

The Motivation for Privatizing Telecommunications

The factors that led the Jamaican government to privatize the country's telecommunications industry appear to be a combination of political and economic factors.

Political Factors

One perspective on the privatization of the telecommunications industry is that it was a direct outcome of the changes in the political philosophy of the Jamaican government over the period 1972–80. In 1972, the PNP replaced the Jamaica Labour Party (JLP), which had been in power since independence. The PNP came to power advocating a democratic socialist philosophy and very quickly moved to an alignment with socialist countries in other parts of the world. An important component of the Manley government's philosophy during the 1970s was the need to place the "commanding heights" of the economy in the hands of the government.

The companies most aggressively targeted for nationalization were large companies with high market power within the country. The JTC clearly fit this profile, as did other companies: Barclays Bank, the second largest commercial bank, was nationalized in 1977; Caribbean Cement Company (CCC), the monopoly supplier of cement, was also nationalized in 1977; and major companies in the critical bauxite and alumina industry were nationalized in the latter part of the 1970s. Accordingly, in pursuit of its policy, the PNP government nationalized the JTC in 1975.

The socialist philosophy of the Manley administration was in sharp contrast to the market-oriented philosophy of Jamaica's other major political party, the JLP, headed by Edward Seaga. Seaga had voiced strong opposition to the nationalization program of the PNP and vowed that his party would reverse these nationalizations if returned to power. In 1980, after eight successive years of a two-term, Manley-led, PNP administration, the JLP did replace the PNP. The JLP immediately began moving

Jamaica toward a more market-oriented development path, in which the private sector would take over many of the operations that the government had been performing. It was in this spirit that the Seaga administration began a privatization program, which eventually came to include the privatization of the telecommunications sector.

The general privatization program began shortly after Seaga came to power in October 1980. In 1981, the new administration established a public-private divestment committee to recommend candidates for divestment to the cabinet. The United States Agency for International Development (USAID) paid for foreign and local technical assistance to this committee. Based upon the recommendations of this committee, several small companies were privatized during the 1981–84 period.

The privatization process was accelerated in 1984, when a new organization, the National Investment Bank of Jamaica (NIBJ), was created. This organization, designed to be the government's merchant bank, was mandated to concentrate on private investments through joint ventures and the divestment of state-owned enterprises (NIBJ, *Annual Report 1989*). The NIBJ was also advised to target several core firms, since the Seaga administration was determined to return such firms to the private sector. Thus the NIBJ was the agency that arranged the privatization of Barclays Bank (whose name had been changed to National Commercial Bank after nationalization and which, by 1987, had become the nation's largest commercial bank) and the CCC. Both of these companies were privatized by the public offering of stock. In December 1986, 30.6 million National Commercial Bank (NCB) shares, representing 51 percent of the voting stock of the company, were sold via public offering, netting about J$90 million (US$16.4 million). In June 1987, the CCC was privatized, also by public offering; 78.69 million CCC shares, representing 78 percent of the voting stock of the company, were sold to the public, netting about J$157 million (US$28 million) for the government of Jamaica. These privatizations, in each instance, represented the largest offering of stock on the Jamaican stock exchange to date (Leeds 1991).

The privatizations of these large companies set the stage for the privatization of the telecommunications sector. Even though special circumstances surrounded the privatization of telecommunications, this privatization was clearly part of a structured program of privatization that moved gradually from the privatization of small companies, such as Southern Processors, a small food-processing establishment in rural Jamaica, to the privatization of one of Jamaica's largest companies, Telecommunications of Jamaica. In all of these privatizations, political ideology clearly played an important role.

The ideological nature of the privatization program was emphasized in a 1986 report on the reasons for privatization, which was presented to the cabinet by Prime Minister Seaga. His objectives were, first, to improve the efficiency of the economy through private ownership and to involve a large number of citizens in the free-market system and, second, to reduce the fiscal deficit and to accumulate foreign exchange (ibid., 89). The ideological nature of the program was reinforced by the reaction of Manley's opposition party. Manley declared that the privatization of NCB was "an act of ideological aggression" (ibid., 96) and threatened that his government would buy back all shares as soon as it was returned to power. Similarly, one of the leading spokesmen of the PNP declared that the CCC privatization was a "sordid transaction that never should have been permitted" (ibid., 106).

Another factor that suggests that ideology rather than economics was at work at the outset of Seaga's privatization program is the fact that the Seaga administration sought to privatize the best-performing state-owned enterprises, rather than weak companies that were a drain on the government budget. Seaga himself stated, "So far as I am concerned, you must take the best enterprises you have and just do the deed if you want to accomplish objectives such as ours" (ibid., 89). In the case of the telecommunications sector, for example, both the JTC and JAMINTEL had long records of profitability. In the five years immediately preceding privatization, for instance, the JTC's real return on average ordinary stockholder's equity after taxation was 5.85 percent, rising to 8.22 percent in 1987, just prior to the privatization.[1] Similarly, JAMINTEL had a consistent record of profitability and had declared a dividend in every year but one since its creation in 1971.

This is not to suggest that the companies did not have their share of problems during the days of government ownership. The JTC, in particular, faced operating problems. As Table 2-1 suggests, growth in the network was erratic and unspectacular over the 1975–87 period, especially given the demand for services. A report by the World Bank's International Finance Corporation (IFC), based upon 1988 data, points out that, at current rates of installation, a potential Jamaican telephone subscriber would have to wait twenty years for a connection (Ambrose et al. 1990). Indeed, as in many developing countries, this statistic does not fully reflect the severity of the problem of inadequate telephone services, since it only takes into consideration individuals who placed their names on a waiting list for a telephone. Prior to the introduction of telephones in rural Jamaica, it would have taken an act of unparalleled optimism for a resident in most areas of rural Jamaica to apply for a telephone.

Economic Factors

Short-term economic objectives also played a role in privatization, including that of the telecommunications sector. As was true of many

Table 2-1. Telecommunications of Jamaica, Performance, 1971–1993

Year	Number of Main Lines (thousands)	Growth (%)	Main Lines/ 100 people[1]	Number of Employees	Employees/ 1,000 Main Lines[2]
1971	35.0	n.a.	n.a.	—	—
1972	36.5	4.3	1.87	—	—
1973	38.2	4.6	1.95	—	—
1974	42.3	10.7	2.11	—	—
1975	47.8	13.0	2.34	—	—
1976	50.0	4.6	2.40	—	—
1977	52.0	4.0	2.47	—	—
1978	54.0	3.8	2.54	—	—
1979	54.0	0.0	2.51	—	—
1980	54.0	0.0	2.48	—	—
1981	55.0	1.8	2.68	—	—
1982	59.2	7.6	2.85	—	—
1983	62.4	5.4	2.89	—	—
1984	67.0	7.3	2.94	—	—
1985	69.8	4.2	2.98	1,855	27
1987[3]	76.7	9.9	3.19	2,199	29
1988	85.2	10.8	3.55	2,799	33
1989	90.0	5.9	3.67	3,166	35
1990	106.0	17.7	4.20	3,401	32
1991	132.0	24.5	5.17	3,736	28
1992	168.0	27.3	6.58	4,150	25
1993	209.0	24.4	8.36	4,165	20

Source: TOJ, various years.

[1] These figures compare with 5.2 in Mexico, 9.6 in Argentina, 7.5 in Venezuela, 0.5 in India, and 51 in the United States.

[2] These figures compare with 10 in Mexico, 14 in Argentina, 11 in Venezuela, 96 in India, and 0.2 in the United States.

[3] In 1987, the fiscal year-end for both companies was changed from December to March. The period represented by these data is the fiteen-month period from January 1986 to March 1987.

n.a. = not applicable.

— = not available.

developing countries, the Jamaican economy suffered severely during the 1970s and 1980s. Increased oil prices, a high propensity to import consumer goods, stagnant prices for Jamaica's traditional agricultural products and its bauxite, capital flight during the late 1970s, especially, high debt service obligations from prior loans, and inadequate revenue collection all placed severe strains on the economy.

These strains were exacerbated by a variety of social programs the Jamaican government had put in place since the mid-1970s. The economic trends and social programs of the period combined to put tremendous pressure on Jamaica's balance of payments and central government fiscal budget during the 1970s and 1980s. In response to the country's deteriorating financial situation, the World Bank and the IMF placed pressure on Jamaica to reduce its budget deficit as a condition for a second structural adjustment loan from the World Bank in 1983 (these institutions played a similar role in other countries' economies; see Ramamurti 1992). Consequently, part of the benefits that accrued from privatization, and many would say part of the reason for privatization, was the short-term fiscal and foreign exchange support that the sales of these assets would generate for the government.

Jamaica's current prime minister, P. J. Patterson, who succeeded Michael Manley in 1992 and who was in opposition at the time of the privatization of the NCB and the onset of the TOJ privatization, provided support for an economic explanation for the country's privatization program.[2] He suggested, for example, that in the case of the NCB privatization the impetus for privatization was the "government's compelling budgetary needs" and that the "TOJ privatization was the result of the government's immediate need for foreign exchange" (*Jamaica Daily Gleaner,* July 7, 1992). Clearly, this statement does not eliminate the possibility that there were ideological reasons for privatization. But it is plausible, and in fact likely, that privatization occurred because of the combination of political philosophy and short-term economic need that held sway in the mid-1980s.

The Process of Privatizing the Telecommunications Industry

In preparation for privatizing the telecommunications sector, the Jamaican government restructured the industry. The JTC, the government-owned (90% shareholding) monopoly supplier of domestic telecommunication services, and JAMINTEL, the joint venture between the Jamaican government (51%), and C&W (49%), which had a monopoly on international telecommunication services, became subsidiaries of the TOJ. This latter holding company was created in May 1987, with the Jamaican government owning 83 percent of its shares, C&W, 9 percent, and the public, the remaining 8 percent.

Although the privatization of the TOJ began as part of the Seaga government's broader privatization program, it was also a very different case of privatization than that of any other company. First, it represented by far the largest privatization undertaken in Jamaica's history. In contrast to the preceding privatizations of large companies, such as the NCB and the CCC, the sale of the Jamaican government's 83 percent share in the TOJ generated US$155.8 million, or about six times the proceeds received from the divestment of its shares in the CCC (see table 2-2).

Privatization also spanned two different political administrations, beginning with Seaga's JLP administration and completed, surprisingly, by the Manley administration that came to power in February 1989. The new Manley administration bore little resemblance to the administra-

Table 2-2. TOJ Stock, Sales of Government Holdings

Date Shares Were Sold	Number of Shares Sold	Buyer of Shares	Price of Shares (J$)	Proceeds from Shares J$m	Proceeds from Shares US$m	Percentage of Government Shares Sold	Percentage of Government Shares Remaining after Sale
July 23, 1987	102,336,848	c&w	1.00	102.3	18.6	11	72
October 2, 1987	183,479,960	c&w	1.00	183.5	33.4	19	53
September 28, 1988	126,500,000	Public	0.88	108.5	19.7	13	40
July 13, 1989	193,136,730	c&w	1.20	231.8	42.1	20	20
November 16, 1990	193,136,730	c&w	1.74	336.1	42.0	20	0
Total				962.2	155.8		

Source: TOJ, various years.

tion that held power from 1972 to 1980. Michael Manley claimed to have recognized the futility of an economic philosophy that sought to shelter the Jamaican economy from international competition, and he moved, with even greater alacrity than the previous JLP administration, to integrate Jamaica into the global economy through trade and investment (Manley 1990). Indeed, the new Manley administration may have believed that there was no better way to signal its new economic philosophy than by completing, with a flourish, the privatization of a company that the earlier Manley administration had nationalized.

Further, possibly because of these characteristics, this privatization was not handled by the government's principal privatization entity, the NIBJ. The negotiations were conducted largely in secret, with only a few key players involved, and the negotiating team for the government of Jamaica was headed by Mayer Matalon, chairman of the JTC.[3] In addition, both Edward Seaga and Michael Manley, during their respective terms in office, were personally and intimately involved in the details of the privatization of the telecommunications sector.

Stages in the Privatization Process

The actual privatization of the telecommunications sector took several years. Preparation began in 1985, when the government began negotiations with c&w, the British telecommunications firm that had been involved in telecommunication operations in Jamaica since 1870. These negotiations culminated in the May 1987 decision to create the TOJ as a holding company that would establish corporate objectives for the group, coordinate the acquisition and allocation of resources, and arrange financing.

During the creation of the TOJ, the remainder of the privatization program began to be mapped out in the shareholders' agreement. The government agreed to divest shares so that c&w would own 20 percent of the TOJ. The transfer of the shares necessary to accomplish this ownership restructuring took place in July 1987. On October 2, 1987, the government transferred additional shares to C&W, bringing that company's shareholdings up to 39 percent of the stock of the TOJ.

On September 28, 1988, there was a public offering of stock in the TOJ, increasing the public's share holding from 8 to 21 percent of the outstanding shares. With the 39 percent of shares held by C&W, this transfer of 13 percent of shares to the public raised the private sector's share to 60 percent, marking the transfer of majority ownership in the company from the government to the private sector. But with its 40 percent shareholding, compared to C&W's 39 percent, the Jamaican government continued to control the company. Indeed, the government stated in 1988 that "the current intention of Government is not to reduce its shareholding below the 40% level" (Telecommunications of Jamaica 1988).

Despite this intention, on July 13, 1989, the new government of Michael Manley's "reformed," more market-oriented, PNP sold an additional 20 percent of its shares in the company to C&W, reducing its holding of the company's stock to 20 percent. The final 20 percent of government shares were sold to C&W on November 16, 1990. At this point, C&W owned 79 percent of the shares in the TOJ, while the public owned 21 percent, and the Jamaican government owned no shares in the country's monopoly supplier of domestic and international telecommunications services (see table 2-2 for the sales of government shares in TOJ and the proceeds received therefrom).

The Public Offering

The September 28, 1988, offering was the third time in as many years that the Jamaican government had engaged in a public offering of stock as part of a program of privatizing a core company; the earlier offerings were the NCB stock offering in 1986 and the CCC stock offering in 1987. The manner in which the third offering was arranged built upon the perceived strengths and weaknesses of these two prior offerings.

The strategy was to ensure widespread public participation in the offering to deflect any political criticism of the privatization. To achieve widespread participation, the stock would have to be priced low enough to ensure full, or near full, subscription to the offering and the offering would have to be heavily publicized. Richard Downer of Price Waterhouse, who was involved in both the NCB and CCC privatizations, spearheaded all aspects of the program, including a market and public relations campaign similar to those he used in these privatizations. The privatization team sought to ensure widespread ownership by, once again, allowing employees of the company to have preferential access to the company's shares: 2 percent of TOJ's stock, or 21.1 million shares, was reserved for TOJ employees. Further, 51,000 residential customers of the JTC received priority treatment in the purchase of up to 1,750 shares each, for a total of 89.25 million shares, or 8.5 percent of the stock.

One of the most difficult issues was determining the price at which the stock should be offered to the public. Again, the experience of the prior privatizations played an important role: the NCB stock offering was 170 percent oversubscribed, and the stock traded at a 67 percent premium the day following the public offering; the CCC offering several months later was about 30 percent undersubscribed, and the stock traded at a discount of about 20 percent the day following the offering. In the case of the TOJ, the decision was made to sell 126.5 million shares. Given the undersubscription of the CCC shares, it was decided to price these shares at a level that would be more likely to ensure full subscription. The price finally chosen was J$0.88 per share, a discount of J$0.12 below the J$1.00 par value of the shares and also a discount below the book value of the shares, which was J$1.19. At the time of the offering, the company had an earnings per share of J$0.22, leading to a price/earnings ratio of four. The price of J$0.88 ensured that, even though many more TOJ shares were being offered than CCC shares (126.5 million vs. 107 million) the additional capital to be absorbed by the stock exchange would be far less (J$111 million vs. J$214 million). Further, the fourteen local financial institutions agreed to underwrite the shares and to take up to half of the offer.

The Motivation for Sales to Cable & Wireless

The principal purchaser of the Jamaican government's shares in the TOJ was the foreign investor C&W. The motivation for the sale of shares to C&W might reasonably be examined along two fronts. We have pursued the ideological basis behind Jamaica's privatization program, but ideology does not explain why such a large component of shares in the nation's monopoly supplier of telecommunications services was sold to a foreign investor. It seems clear that the Seaga administration first began negotiations with C&W because of its desire to obtain access to the technology, capital, and expertise required to modernize the nation's telecommunications infrastructure. C&W, in addition to providing the necessary deep pockets and the modern technology and expertise, also had the advantage of a long history of operations in Jamaica and amicable relations with the Jamaican government. Recall that at the onset of negotiations, C&W held 49 percent of the long-distance company JAMINTEL, with the Jamaican government owning the remaining 51 percent of that company. Senior managers of JAMINTEL and the JTC believed that it was principally the JTC's need for capital that pushed the government to create an attractive investment opportunity by merging the companies (NIBJ 1992, 38).

One can only speculate, however, on why the Jamaican government did not open up the purchasing process to bids from other suppliers. Instead, the entire transaction was shrouded in secrecy, and the sale of the first two tranches of shares to C&W (the amount required to bring its share to 20% and the amount that brought the company's share to 39%—see table 2-2) was presented to the public as a fait accompli. There was no public debate and only limited disclosure prior to the agreement of sale.

In many respects, it seems clear that the Jamaican government drifted into privatization, rather than deciding from the outset to sell a dominant majority of the shares in both telecommunications companies to a private company. Had the decision to privatize been made in the latter vein it is more likely that the transaction would have been opened to multiple bidders. Given the incremental nature of the privatization transaction, however, it is less surprising that it was not opened for bidding and that, instead, the Jamaican government gradually sold its shares to a long-standing telecommunications partner.

Additionally, there is the question of why the government did not consider opening up even the international segment of the sector to competition. Two reasons have some merit: first, the Jamaican market is relatively small and would not attract the same degree of interest as the larger markets of many other developing countries. Jamaica's total number of lines in 1990, for example, was approximately equivalent to the number of lines added in six months in larger developing countries like Venezuela. Having said that, however, it is important to note that the merit of this argument loses force daily with changes in telecommunications technology. The introduction of microwave, satellite, and cellular technology reduce significantly the economies of scale that obtains in telecommunications, especially when compared with an era in which all telecommunication traffic flowed through wires and cables. Clearly, if the Jamaican government accepted this argument for not allowing competition in the international segment of the industry, or even in the domestic segment, it was operating upon outmoded assumptions of the nature of technology in the telecommunications industry.

The second reason, also of dubious merit, is that competition in the international segment would reduce the willingness of any investor to subsidize domestic telephone charges with international charges. Such subsidization had long occurred in the Jamaican telecommunications industry, and the government seemed to have no intention of reversing that policy. Cross-subsidization kept the cost of local telephone calls very low, with no price increases between 1984 and 1993. Monthly telephone rental in 1993 cost as little as US$2 per month for basic telephone services.[4] In 1991, 77 percent of TOJ revenue came from international calls, both outgoing and incoming. No private investor would be likely to invest in the international segment of the telecommunications industry in a country the size of Jamaica unless local services were priced at their full cost. Thus, the statement that a monopoly over long-distance and domestic services was necessary for a successful cross-subsidization policy is true, but this simply begs the question of whether or not cross-subsidization is appropriate in the first instance. Some Latin American countries, profiled in other chapters in this volume, decided that a policy of cross-subsidization with its attendant economic distortions was an inappropriate policy. In its privatization of the telecommunications company ENTel, for example, the Argentine government explicitly moved away from a policy of cross-subsidization.

The sale to C&W of the remaining blocs of government shares probably resulted from different motivations. Edward Seaga, prime minister during the sale of the first two tranches of shares, maintained that his government "intended to maintain its 40% share holding in the company."[5] It is widely held that when the new PNP administration came to power the need for foreign exchange to pass an IMF test led the government to sell the remaining blocs of shares. C&W was again the obvious candidate to purchase these shares.

The Foreign Investor's Perspective

The C&W motivation to purchase the government's shares in the TOJ can be readily explained on financial grounds based upon attractive regulatory agreements, to be discussed henceforth, and also upon price adjustments in telephone services that the company was able to negotiate with the Jamaican government. In April 1987, just before the incorporation of the TOJ, the government gave permission for a 55 percent increase in the nominal price of outgoing overseas calls. This nominal price increase represented a real increase for that year of about 48 percent (in 1987, inflation in Jamaica stood at about 7%). Prior to the 1987 increase, the price of international calls had remained stable between 1971 and 1979, increased marginally in 1979, and increased significantly in 1985. The 1987 price increase meant that the per minute rate from Kingston to New York was about US$1.10.[6] International rates continued to increase gradually up until 1993, with an increase approximately every six months. As a result of these increases, in 1993 the per minute rate from Kingston to New York was US$1.25, compared with a price of about US$0.85 per minute for a call in the opposite direction.

In addition to the favorable regulatory and pricing regime, c&w was able to negotiate with the government of Jamaica, the company was also quite comfortable about operating in the Jamaican environment based upon its many years of operations in the country. Given its lengthy experience in Jamaica, c&w was well placed to evaluate the risks and opportunities involved in doing business in Jamaica's telecommunications sector. The risks involved in doing business in a telecommunications industry in a developing country are of a particular type. In developing countries with the types of penetration of telecommunications that existed in Jamaica, and in a situation where a government was willing to grant a monopoly, there are virtually no business or commercial risks. But there are significant risks associated with government regulations and the likelihood of its expropriation of assets. Investments, once made, are sunk, and the investor becomes subject to the regulatory system.[7]

The "lumpy" nature of telecommunications investments makes the industry somewhat analogous to the extractive industries that moved to developing countries in such numbers after World War II. In those cases, the bargains between multinational corporations and host governments negotiated prior to the commitment of lumpy investments had a tendency to obsolesce after the investments were made.[8] Recognizing the similarities between these types of investment may have led c&w to place an even higher premium on negotiating with a government that it felt it understood and with which it had a history of cordial relations.

There was another important motivation for c&w. The company was in the midst of a multiyear program to gain a position in telecommunications markets around the world. Between 1986 and 1990, for example, the company purchased interests in telecommunications companies privatized in the Caribbean (Jamaica, Barbados, St. Kitts and Nevis); the South Pacific (Fiji, Vanautu, Solomon Islands); Sub-Saharan Africa (Sierra Leone); and the Middle East (Bahrain).[9] In light of the company's global ambitions, Jamaica quite possibly was more important than the size of its market would suggest. It complemented other Caribbean acquisitions, but it was better placed than some of these acquisitions to become a regional telecommunications hub. c&w's control of the local and international telecommunications companies in Jamaica was also complemented by the company's majority shareholding in Jamaica Digiport International, a company licensed to offer teleport facilities in the country's free zones.

c&w's familiarity with Jamaica, the attractive regulatory regime, and the strategic fit that a telecommunications operation in Jamaica offered probably made the investment in the toj highly attractive to c&w.

The Results of the Privatization

Privatization can be evaluated on at least two levels. At the transaction level, success can be defined as concluding the transfer of ownership from the public to the private sector smoothly and fairly. When, for example, the NCB offering was oversubscribed, Prime Minister Seaga declared the privatization a "fabulous success" (Leeds 1991, 101). Success, in this regard, views the fair and smooth transfer of assets from the public to the private sector as an end in itself. Such a view requires an ideological faith in the inherent superiority of the private sector over the public sector in managing the assets of the privatized entities.

By this yardstick, the TOJ privatization was a success. The transfers to C&W seem to have been handled relatively easily, although very few details of the actual negotiations have come to light. The offering of stock to the public also went smoothly. Not unexpectedly, given the degree to which the offering was underwritten, the commitment of the underwriting financial institutions, and the attention the government paid to pricing, the offering was oversubscribed by 20 percent: 11,114 people applied for 152,379,450 shares, although only 126,500,000 were offered for sale. Only two of the institutions that underwrote the offering held shares in the company in 1992, and neither institution's shareholding exceeded 0.7 percent of the total number of shares outstanding.

The government seemed to have correctly priced the shares, because when the stock opened for trading one month later it opened at J$0.90 per share. The stock stayed in the range of J$0.90 to J$1.10 per share (about US$0.20) through December 1, 1988 (*Jamaica Daily Gleaner* and *Financial Gleaner*, various editions). The stock continued to trade at about J$1 per share for about two years even in the midst of a significant "bull" market on the Jamaican stock exchange. The stock's performance strengthened in Jamaican dollar terms after 1991 but showed no significant real appreciation. In September 1993, the stock traded at a price of J$5.50 (US$0.22).

At another level, privatization can be viewed, not as an end in itself, but rather as a means to other ends, such as improving the efficiency of the privatized entity, increasing the capital invested in the sector through private financing, or generating funds, including foreign exchange, for the government. In terms of the latter two financial objectives, the Jamaican government received about US$156 million in proceeds for the sale of its stock in the TOJ. A financial analysis of the privatization suggests that this represented a fair value for the company, given the value of its assets and its prospects for future earnings (Spiller and Sampson 1992, 41). The price the government received per main telephone line also compares favorably with the prices received in the sale of other telecommunications companies in the region. With an average of about 83,000 main lines over the period of privatization and sale proceeds of about US$155.5 million, the price per main line was about US$1,873. This compares with a price per line of US$2,900 in the sale of Venezuela's CANTV, US$1,653 in the sale of Mexico's TELMEX, and US$800 in the sale of Argentina's ENTel.

In addition, investment in the telecommunications sector increased significantly after the privatization. In the four-year period prior to privatization, net investment in fixed assets for the JTC and JAMINTEL averaged US$16 million per year. In the four years after privatization, investment averaged US$72 million. The investment in fixed assets resulted from a multiyear capital development program designed to modernize and expand the telecommunications network. An important component of this modernization was the conversion of the network to a digital network. This goal was achieved by 1992, when the chairman boasted that "Jamaica is one of the few countries in the world with a fully digital network" (TOJ 1992, 5). Other elements of the capital development program included the installation of fiber-optic equipment, the replacement of coin-operated phones with credit card phones, the burying of cable lines underground, the introduction of cellular telephones, the introduction of an "international call authorisation system" (ICAS) to eliminate unauthorized calls, and the installation of small switches (640-line capacity) in many rural districts (thirty-three such switches were installed in 1991–92, seventeen in 1992–93, and twenty-seven were planned for 1993–94).

The extent of the network expansion is reflected in the increase in main lines detailed in table 2-1. From an expansion rate of about 3,000 lines per year in the 1970s and 1980s, the company added 26,000 main lines in 1991, 36,000 main lines in 1992, and 41,000 main lines in 1993. At that rate of expansion, and given the current waiting list for telephones (albeit not a useful indicator of true demand), a potential subscriber could get a telephone in one and a half years, in contrast to the twenty years reported by the IFC based upon 1988 data. Additionally, there is some evidence that the sector became more efficient after privatization. The number of main lines per employee, for example, increased during the period immediately prior to privatization and during the privatization transition period but declined consistently thereafter (see table 2-1).

The changes in investment outlays and in levels of efficiency are not solely related to ownership structure. Other critical variables have to be considered as measures of the success of privatization.

Table 2-3. TOJ Financial Indicators, 1988–1993

Financial Indicator	1988	1989	1990	1991	1992	1993
After-tax profits and depreciation (cash flow; US$m)	28.1	57.7	55.0	60.5	34.6	78.4
Capital investment during the year (US$m)	25.1	45.6	84.9	116.7	50.9	100.0
Cash flow as a % of investment	111.7	126.5	64.7	51.8	67.8	78.4
Long-term debt (US$m)	28.2	42.8	101.2	154.1	143.6	156.5
Change in long-term debt (US$m)	—	14.6	58.4	52.9	–10.5	12.4
Cash flow and change in long-term debt as a % of investment	—	158.5	133.6	97.2	46.3	90.8

Source: TOJ, various years.

The Interaction of Ownership, Competition, and Regulation

As indicated in chapter 1, while the ownership of a company in an infrastructural industry may have an effect on its efficiency and its investment outlays, two other variables are also likely to have an effect: the extent to which the company faces competition, immediately or prospectively, and the nature of the system by which it is regulated.

Regarding increased investment outlays in the Jamaican telecommunications sector, the change to private ownership may have been the catalyst that led to increased investment, although as table 2-3 indicates, these outlays were financed largely by internal resources and increases in long-term debt. This corresponds to the situation in other countries, such as Mexico, where most new investment was also financed internally through funds generated from increases in telephone tariffs (see chapter 3). In both Jamaica and Mexico, about 75 percent of postprivatization capital investment was self-financed. Clearly, C&W also believed that a regulatory regime was in place that would allow an attractive return on investment and that was sufficiently stable to allow the company to commit long-term capital. Thus, the change in the regulatory regime in 1988 was critical to increased investment outlays in this sector.

One way in which a regulatory change can complement the privatization of a telecommunications company is to force the new private owners to take into account the national development objectives of the country. Regulation thus substitutes for public ownership as the means to the end sought by the government. The Jamaican government encouraged the new TOJ to take into account the country's development objectives by stipulating network expansion and by allowing the company to earn an attractive return on its investment in the licenses negotiated in 1988 (Telephone Act 1988). These licenses—the All Island Telephone License and the Telecommunications of Jamaica Ltd. (telegraphic services) Special License—allowed the company "exclusive rights to sell and supply domestic and international telephone services for public and private purposes in all parts of the Island of Jamaica for a period of twenty-five years from Sep. 1, 1988, with provision for renewal for another period of 25 years" (ibid., 4).

From the perspective of improving national development through an efficient nationwide communication network, the license required the company to provide "an adequate, safe, reliable and efficient service by modern standards to all parts of the Island of Jamaica at reasonable rates so as to meet the growing demands of the Island and to contribute to economic development. The company should make regular improvements to its exchange, local distribution, and trunk network system as promptly as is feasible in order to make telephone service available to all parts of the Island of Jamaica" (ibid., 4, 10).

Implementation of these provisions required the company to undertake formal development programs in consultation with the government. The company had to submit to the minister of public utilities and transport within three months of the end of each financial year a report on the implementation of the formal development programs that had been planned at the beginning of the financial year. Notably, the license did not include explicit expansion goals in the manner in which such goals were explicitly introduced in concessions in other Latin American countries, such as Mexico, Venezuela, and Argentina, as reported elsewhere in this volume. Indeed, as the Mexican case indicates, not only were specific goals outlined with regard to expansion and modernization, but the concession agreement negotiated with TELMEX also included financial penalties if the company failed to achieve the prescribed targets.

Nor did the Jamaican license stipulate any acceptable service indicators. In the privatization of Argentina's ENTel, for example, call completion rates, failure per 100 lines, repair delays, and installation delays were all specified in the concession agreement. In contrast, the Jamaican license stipulated that "the company shall maintain standards of service which shall be no lower than those prevailing immediately before the date of the license" (ibid., 7). This does not sound like a clarion call to increase service quality or a support of increasing efficiency in the telecommunications sector as a rationale for privatization.

Further, the enforcement provisions of the Jamaican license were relatively weak. The Jamaican government could revoke the company's license only if it did not comply with the provisions of the license. Failing that, the only opportunity for license revocation was that, two and one-half years prior to the expiration of the license, the minister could notify the company in writing that the government intended to acquire the telephone operations of the company. Were such an acquisition to take place, the price to be paid to the company would reflect the fair market value of its assets, with no allowance or deductions for compulsory purchase or goodwill.

Although the government tried to use the "stick" of license revocation or nonrenewal in making the company pursue national development objectives in the absence of competition, this was a very weak stick. The only credible threat of intervention appeared to exist just before the expiration of license. But twenty-five years is an extremely long time from the perspective of corporate decisionmakers, and mechanisms for revoking the license if the company did not comply with provisions, such as development of the network, were relatively unspecific and would undoubtedly not have compelled a company to engage in a significant development program. In reality, once it decided upon exclusivity in the license, the only element within its control that the government could use to promote development of the country's telecommunications network was the "carrot" of financial incentives, via price increases.

The financial incentives were primarily monopoly rights, cross-subsidization, and price rises. Under the license, the company would be regulated using rate of return on shareholders' equity calculations. The real after-tax (and after-preference-dividend) rate of return on equity permitted under the license was between 17.5 and 20 percent. This represented a real rather than a nominal rate of return, because shareholder's equity was increased every year to reflect both increases in inflation and the depreciation of the Jamaican dollar, which combined to increase the replacement cost of the firm's physical assets. The company was allowed annual adjustments in telephone rates in order to stay within the boundaries of the permitted rate of return.

Since rates of return were based upon accounting shareholders' equity, this created an incentive for the company to reinvest earnings rather than distribute them in the form of dividends, especially if the company was approaching the upper bounds of profitability. The distribution of dividends would reduce retained earnings, leading to lower accounting equity and, therefore, rates of return higher than those that would obtain were profits reinvested rather than distributed. Investment might be anticipated, also, by the fact that the profit boundary was sufficiently high to make this investment option attractive when compared to the opportunity cost of c&w's non-Jamaican capital. (Indeed, one might add that these real returns were sufficiently high that they probably compared well with the cost of anybody's capital anywhere.)

Regarding rate of return calculations, however, the Jamaican license once again differed significantly from the concessions negotiated in Mexico, Argentina, and Venezuela. In all three of these countries the governments involved applied the price cap model *(RPI - X)* popularized in the privatization of British Telecom. In this model, the telecommunications companies could increase the prices of telecommunications services by the amount of inflation less an adjustment for technological improvements and cost reductions in the industry over time and volume *(X)*. As the chapters devoted to these cases indicate, the *X* factor was 2 percent for Argentina and 3 percent for Venezuela and Mexico, following prescribed "honeymoon" periods in all three cases. Such a rate of return model has the advantage that it provides greater incentive for the regulated company to seek efficiency in its operations.

The high real rates of return the Jamaican license offered could increase the amount of capital available for expansion only if the company could anticipate that invested capital would generate these returns. The assurance of return was provided through the absence of competition and also through an "understanding" between the Jamaican government and the TOJ that there would be no increase in domestic telephone rates for five years but that the permitted rate of return could be met by subsidizing domestic rates with international rates.[10] And there were indeed no changes in the real prices for domestic telephone services, but there were regular increases in the prices for international telephone services.[11] These increases were, in part, a result of the depreciation of the Jamaican dollar. But the increase in per minute cost of a call from Kingston to New York from US$1.10 in 1987 to US$1.25 in 1993 indicates that there was also a gradual increase in the price of international telephone services.

The subsidization of domestic rates by international ones would be particularly effective in the case of Jamaica. Jamaicans are one of the world's most footloose people; it is estimated that as many Jamaicans live overseas as in Jamaica, with over half of that number concentrated in nearby North America. Subsidization allows expansion of the telephone network to the poorest Jamaicans in rural sections of the island, who are likely to have relatives overseas whose telephone calls lead to payments from international communications companies to the TOJ. These payments more than compensate for low domestic user charges. The TOJ could profit from each rural phone installed even if the user never made a telephone call and monthly user charges were very low.

Subsidization also provided political support for privatization and for foreign ownership of privatized assets. Indeed, increases in public support for the privatization may well have resulted from the subsidization program. Even though the public would not necessarily recognize the term *subsidization*, they would realize that their local telephone calls and monthly telephone rental were inexpensive. In March 1990, only 36 percent of the population supported the government's divestment of TOJ shares, with primary support coming from middle-income voters and members of the political party (JLP) that initiated the agreement between the government and C&W. By July 1991, however, public support had increased to 54 percent, most of it from low-income voters and supporters of the political party (PNP) in office when the final transfer of shares from the government to C&W took place (Stone 1992).

Thus, the postprivatization regulatory regime appeared to succeed in providing financial incentives for the privatized company to increase investment in the telecommunications sector. Such an increase in investment would allow for improvements in both the scope and the quality of the telecommunications system, which would assist in the country's quest for development. But at what cost?

Lessons from Jamaica's Privatization of Telecommunications

The potential lessons for other developing countries that derive from the privatization of the telecommunications sector in Jamaica can be separated into those relating to how to conduct the actual privatization and those relating to how to accomplish the underlying objectives pursued through the privatization of a telecommunications company.

The Mechanics of Privatization

The TOJ privatization could have been conducted very differently. The manner in which the company was privatized suggests that the government drifted into privatization. Because of the gradual, relatively uncoordinated nature of the privatization transaction, the government foreclosed options that it could otherwise have exercised. It is unlikely that the government could have sold a controlling interest to a domestic firm or business group because of the high capital costs involved. Further, it is probable that the local stock market would have balked at a much larger public offering. This left foreign firms as the principal candidates able to purchase a controlling interest in the TOJ. The government could, however, have requested bids from other firms. It chose not to because of its existing, almost incestuous, relationship with C&W. The government's unwillingness to introduce actual or prospective competition at any stage in the privatization proceedings was one of the missed opportunities of this privatization effort.

In this regard, once again, the Jamaican experience differed from the privatizations of the other telecommunications companies reported on in this volume. Jamaica is the only one of the four cases examined that introduced neither actual nor prospective competition. Mexico introduced competition for value added services and for cellular and domestic services (immediately) and long-distance service (after seven years); Venezuela opened all services to competition immediately, except for the switch telephone service for which CANTV was given a nine-year monopoly, subject to the caveat that it allow its competitors to interconnect with its network; and Argentina allowed ENTel a five-year monopoly on local services while opening international, value added, and cellular services to immediate competition.

Interestingly, in the Jamaican case the scope of the monopoly provided to the TOJ was somewhat ambiguous because the 1988 license was based upon an 1893 telephone act that defined telephone services as wire-based transmission. The 1988 license, strangely, remained silent on whether the TOJ also had a monopoly on value added services, cellular service, and equipment connection. The company assumed, however, that it did, indeed, have such a monopoly.[12]

Attaining Development Objectives through Privatization

Several of the lessons of the Jamaican case relate to how governments can encourage a firm that has the potential to create many positive externalities for the country to engage in activities that make these externalities likely to surface in the absence of public ownership. In the case of the telecommunications sector in Jamaica, the externalities come from the efficient expansion and upgrading of the telecommunications network.

The Jamaican government tried to encourage desirable investment through a regulatory regime that went beyond government fiat and exhortation to provide unusual incentives for expansion. The regulatory regime, especially the exclusivity and the high rate of allowable returns that accompanied privatization, made capacity expansion likely (indeed, one might say that the new regulatory regime guaranteed such expansion) because the regulatory regime made it extremely attractive for the foreign firm to invest in capacity expansion in Jamaica. With these two features of monopoly status plus high returns, the Jamaican government provided C&W with an investment environment that was virtually devoid of business or commercial risk.

There are at least two sets of problems associated with the regulatory regime adopted by the Jamaican government. One is that the government may have given away too much. C&W might, for example, have settled for a license with a shorter period of exclusivity. It is not clear how strongly the government tested the company's resolve in this area. The company might also have settled for a lower rate of return than the generous 17.5 percent after tax real return promised by the government. Clearly, the Jamaican government considered itself to be in a very weak bargaining position. It felt that it was constrained in its ability to

alter the competition and regulatory variables in the direction of enforcing efficiency if it simultaneously desired the rapid expansion of the
telecommunications network. It faced difficult trade-offs: it presided
over a small country in which investments had been nationalized in the
past, yet the country desperately needed capital infusion and advanced
technology for its telecommunications sector. Given these circumstances, it was perhaps highly unlikely that any major telecommunications firm would have been willing to commit capital resources and state-
of-the-art technology absent assurances of high returns via an exclusive
license and an ability to charge prices that would enable it to earn these
returns on its committed resources. Indeed, c&w is reputed to have
strongly resisted regulatory formulas other than rate of return calculations. The company resisted, for example, the use of the *RPI- X* formula
that, as mentioned earlier, was used in the privatizations of telecommunications companies in Mexico, Argentina, and Latin America (Adams
et al. 1992, 147).

Yet, the government may nevertheless have underestimated its own
bargaining strength because of a lack of understanding of c&w's global
strategic thrust, the desire of many telecommunications companies
around the world to move into the growing, unsaturated markets of
developing countries, and the changing technology that allowed companies to enter these markets at significantly lower costs than those that
applied in yesteryear.

As a consequence, the country was left with a telecommunications
regulatory system that provided strong incentives for expansion of the
telecommunications network but weaker incentives for efficient telecommunications operations. With its monopoly status, the TOJ could
raise long-distance telephone rates as high as the market would bear in
order to meet its government-allowed profitability. In addition to concerns about inefficiency, the specter of constantly increasing long-distance rates and the ongoing subsidizing of domestic use by international
use also did not sit well with the country's avowed goal of moving to an
export orientation. This subsidization would, of course, penalize Jamaican firms seeking to tap into export markets.

The broader lesson from the Jamaican experience in this context,
therefore, reaffirms the validity of bargaining power models as a useful
conceptual base for understanding the nature of relations between host
governments and multinational corporations and for interpreting the
actions of host governments and multinational corporations. The Jamaican government gave c&w an extremely attractive position—a sweet-
heart deal, if you will—in the Jamaican telecommunications market.
But, given the government's weak negotiating position, this may have
been the price it had to pay to meet its objectives for a rapid expansion

of the telecommunications sector, part of Jamaica's quest for development and modernity. The truth may never be known, because the Jamaican government appears to have conducted insufficient investigations into conditions within the industry and into the strategies of the company with which it was negotiating.

NOTES

The author wishes to acknowledge the assistance provided during the research for this chapter by Cezley Sampson, director of the Mona Institute of Business and consultant on privatization, and Stephen Sterling, director of privatization at the National Investment Bank of Jamaica. Presenters and discussants at the conference leading to this volume also provided helpful comments, in particular, Ben Petrazzini and the editor.

1. Real versus nominal rates of return represent an important distinction in Jamaica, as in many other developing countries, because of the high rates of inflation and the associated depreciation of its currency. The JTC and TOJ return on shareholder's equity reflects real rather than nominal results, however, because the company annually revalues its physical assets to reflect the replacement cost of these assets. In so doing, the company uses U.S. telephone industry indexes for equipment purchased from abroad. The effect of these revaluations is to increase shareholder's equity via a capital reserve account.

2. After succeeding Michael Manley as president of the PNP and as prime minister, Patterson successfully led the PNP to victory over the opposition JLP in the 1993 national elections.

3. Matalon later became chairman of Telecommunications of Jamaica.

4. Value added features such as call waiting and call forwarding could be purchased at an additional cost of approximately US$2 per month.

5. National Investment Bank of Jamaica, Report, June 1992, 22.

6. For an analysis of rate increases between 1971 and 1991, see Spiller and Sampson 1992, fig. 4.

7. For a detailed discussion of the risks of "administrative expropriation" in the context of telecommunications companies, see Levy and Spiller 1993.

8. For the origins of the term "obsolescing bargain" and a discussion of its early application, see Vernon 1971.

9. For more details on C&W's global investment strategy, see Muller 1991.

10. It seems appropriate to call this an understanding rather than a formal agreement, since there appears to be no written record of an agreement and this issue does not appear in the 1988 license.

11. Indeed, the TOJ chairman made the policy of subsidization explicit: "Since 1984, there has been no increase in domestic telephone rates. The growth in the network that will be realised from the five-year development programme currently under way will contribute significantly to the Group's ability to maintain domestic rates at current levels" (TOJ Annual Report 1991, 9).

12. In 1993 a new telephone act was proposed from which a new license would be derived. This license would maintain the agreements negotiated in the 1988 license, including the term of exclusivity, which would continue to run for

twenty-five years from September 1, 1988. There was debate, however, unresolved at the time of this writing, as to the scope of services over which the TOJ should be granted a monopoly.

REFERENCES

Adam, Chris, William P. Cavendish, and Percy Mistry. 1992. *Adjusting Privatization: Case Studies from Developing Countries*. London: Queen Elizabeth House.

Ambrose, William, Paul R. Hennemeyer, and Jean-Paul Chapon. 1990. *Privatizing Telecommunications Systems: Business Opportunities in Developing Countries*. Discussion Paper 10. Washington, D.C.: World Bank.

Financial Gleaner (Kingston). Various issues.

Jamaica Daily Gleaner. Various issues.

Leeds, Roger. 1991. "Privatization through Public Offerings: Lessons from Two Jamaican Cases." In *Privatization and Control of State-Owned Enterprises*, ed. Ravi Ramamurti and Raymond Vernon. Washington, D.C.: World Bank.

Levy, Brian, and Pablo T. Spiller. 1993. "Regulation, Institutions, and Commitment in Telecommunications: A Comparative Analysis of Five Country Studies." In *Proceedings of the World Bank Conference on Development Economics 1993*. Washington, D.C.: World Bank.

Manley, Michael. 1990. *Politics of Change*. Rev. ed. Washington, D.C.: Howard Univ. Press.

Muller, Milton. 1991. *International Telecommunications in Hong Kong: The Case for Liberalization*. Hong Kong: Chinese Univ. Press.

IJB (National Investment Bank of Jamaica). Various years. *Annual Report*.

———. 1992. "Study of the Performance of Privatised Companies (June)." KPMG Peat Marwick & Partners, Kingston.

Ramamurti, Ravi. 1992. "Why Are Developing Countries Privatizing?" *Journal of International Business Studies* 23 (2):225–49.

Spiller, Pablo T., and Cezley Sampson. 1992. *Regulation, Institutions, and Commitment: The Jamaican Telecommunications Sector*. Washington, D.C.: World Bank.

Stone, Carl. 1992. "Putting Public Enterprises to Work: A Study of Privatization in Jamaica." Univ. of West Indies—Mona.

Telephone Act. 1988. Government of Jamaica, Kingston.

TOJ (Telecommunications of Jamaica). Various years. *Annual Report*. Kingston.

———. 1988. *Prospectus: Offer of Sale*. Kingston.

Vernon, Raymond. 1971. *Sovereignty at Bay: The Multinational Spread of U.S. Enterprises*. New York: Basic Books.

3. Telephone Privatization in a Large Country

MEXICO

Ravi Ramamurti

Prime Minister Margaret Thatcher of the United Kingdom demonstrated to the world that giant state firms could be privatized in industrialized countries, and President Carlos Salinas de Gortari of Mexico demonstrated the same for the developing world.[1] Teléfonos de México (TELMEX), the giant telephone monopoly, was at the heart of Salinas's $20-billion privatization program. TELMEX alone raised US$6 billion for the Mexican treasury, nearly four times the sum raised by the previous government through the privatization of 723 companies.[2] Not only was this large and complex privatization completed in just fifteen months, it attracted direct foreign investment from leading Western firms, such as Southwestern Bell of the United States and France Telecom, and portfolio investment from investors in the three major financial centers, New York, London, and Tokyo. The bargaining power of the Mexican government relative to private investors, especially foreign investors, and the skill with which its policymakers privatized TELMEX were in sharp contrast to the Jamaican situation described in the previous chapter.

This chapter considers four questions. Why did the Mexican government choose to privatize TELMEX? How did it overcome the barriers to privatization that have stymied efforts by other governments to divest far smaller firms? What were the motivations of foreign investors who participated in the privatization transaction? And finally, how is privatization likely to affect the short-run and long-run performance of the firm, keeping in mind that TELMEX's performance will depend not only on who owns it but also, perhaps even more, by the degree of competition in its market and the quality of regulation of the telecommunications sector (Vickers and Yarrow 1988).[3] On the last question, we explore specifically the interplay among ownership, competition, and regulation; that is, we ask how the act of carrying out privatization influenced government choices with respect to competition and regulatory policies.

The Motivations for Privatizing TELMEX

Two aspects to the Mexican government's decision to privatize TELMEX merit explanation. The first is why TELMEX found its way onto Salinas's "hit list" although there had been no talk earlier—at least in public—of divesting that firm and although privatizing telephone companies was not yet a fad in the developing world. The second point is why Salinas targeted TELMEX for privatization so early in his term of office. It is always difficult to identify the precise reasons that organizations do what they do, and so it is with the Mexican government and TELMEX. At best, official reasons provide a partial explanation; at worst, they are misleading.

It is easier to identify the reasons that did not motivate the Salinas government to privatize TELMEX. It can safely be asserted that TELMEX was not being targeted for divestiture because international agencies like the IMF and the World Bank were forcing Mexico to do so.[4] To be sure, the World Bank had been promoting privatization in all developing countries seeking structural adjustment loans, including Mexico, which first approached the Bank for such a loan in 1983. However, large, monopolistic firms like TELMEX were not viewed by the World Bank as candidates for sale, at least not at that time. Nor does it seem likely that external pressure was applied in the context of concluding the Brady deal on Mexico's foreign debt, since that deal was concluded before the TELMEX decision was even announced by Salinas. In the end, the World Bank did get involved in TELMEX's privatization through a telecommunications sectoral adjustment loan approved in May 1990, but the initiative for this loan as well as Salinas's privatization program seems to have come from the government of Mexico rather than the Bank. If anything, the pressure applied by the Bank while making this loan was reportedly to slow down the planned pace of privatization, not to accelerate it.[5] At least in Mexico, the World Bank's role in privatization was that of follower rather than leader.[6]

It is also clear that TELMEX was not privatized because it was poorly run or unprofitable, although Salinas did explain his decision by saying that "privatization will be the means for realizing the commitment to modernize Teléfonos de México." In fact, TELMEX was among the better run state firms in Mexico, possibly among the best run. The reasons for this were many, but somewhere on the top of the list was the fact it never

Table 3-1. Telephone Company Performance at Privatization, Comparative Data

Country	Main Lines/ 100 people	Employees/ 1,000 Main Lines	Waiting Time for Line (yrs.)	Main Lines with Failure (%)	Call Completion Rate (%) Local	Call Completion Rate (%) Long Distance	Days to Repair a Line	Dial Tone in 3 Secs. (%)
Mexico	5.2	10	2–3	10	92	90	4	97
Argentina	9.6	14	22	45	49	29	14	—
Brazil	5.5	11	—	5	39	—	2	84
Chile	4.6	8	—	7	97	93	3	95
Venezuela	7.5	11	8	—	49	31	—	—
Tanzania	0.2	69	11	—	—	—	—	—
India	0.5	96	—	13	—	—	—	—
Indonesia	0.4	50	8	17	—	—	—	—
United States	51	6.6	A few days	< 1	—	—	—	—
Japan	40	6.6	A few days	< 1	—	—	—	—

Source: Statistical Division, Comision Economica para America Latina (CEPAL), U.N. Industrial Development Organization (UNIDO), Baring Securities (1991), and other sources.

became a wholly government-owned firm; the Mexican government acquired 51 percent of the company's voting shares in 1972, and the rest was owned by Mexican citizens and institutions as well as foreigners. This ownership structure was the result of TELMEX's origin in the private sector—it emerged out of the merger of the two foreign-owned telephone companies that pioneered telephone service in Mexico, L. M. Ericsson of Sweden and International Telephone and Telegraph (ITT) of the United States. Consequently, the government shared seats on the board with private individuals, and the company's stock was traded not only on the Mexican stock exchange but in the over-the-counter (NASDAQ) market in the United States, as well.[7] After gaining control over the firm, the government retained most of the managers who had run the firm earlier. For thirteen of the eighteen years that TELMEX was controlled by the government, the same person, a highly respected manager, served as the firm's CEO. "In the beginning," said one long-time officer of the company, "nothing changed in the way the company operated." By the 1980s, however, TELMEX was suffering from many of the problems that afflicted other Mexican state enterprises: low prices, political interference, entrenched unions linked to the ruling party, and investment constraints tied to the government's need to restrain public sector borrowing and spending.

Even then, however, by many measures TELMEX's performance was not bad. The waiting time for a telephone connection in Mexico was two to three years, which was outrageous by the standards of rich countries but significantly better than the eight years it took in Indonesia and Venezuela and the twenty-two years it took in Argentina (see table 3-1). In Mexico, 10 percent of the lines were down at any time, compared to fewer than 1 percent in the United States and to 45 percent in Argentina. TELMEX was overmanned by the standards of rich countries by 50–60 percent, but its ratio of telephone lines per employee was not only higher than Chile's but also higher than British Telecom's. If the publicly reported numbers are to be believed, similar patterns are to be seen in other performance measures as well, such as the local and long-distance call completion rates and the number of days it took to repair a line (see table 3-1).[8] In Latin America in 1990, only Chile appeared to have a telephone system that worked better than Mexico's.

In the period of state ownership, TELMEX was always profitable and always paid dividends. From 1985 to 1989, return on sales averaged 23.6 percent and return on equity 12.8 percent (see table 3-2). The government's pricing rules were, in fact, designed to yield a 12 percent return on capital. Although residential rates were kept low for political reasons, national and international long-distance services, which were used mostly by businesses, were overpriced.[9] As a result, in 1989, the monthly rent for a residential telephone was less than US$2.50, and a local call cost less than one U.S. cent, while a seven-minute direct-dial call to the United States cost more than US$8.00.

With revenue per line at the US$400 level, compared with US$700 or more in the United States and the United Kingdom, and with demand growing faster than in the industrialized countries, TELMEX found itself unable to invest rapidly enough to meet demand, leading to a widening capacity gap, especially in the 1980s. While the government was reluctant to raise local telephone rates, it did not hesitate to raise indirect taxes on telephone service to giddying heights—an average of 60 percent of TELMEX's revenues in 1988. Ironically, at the time of its introduction in the 1960s, the telephone service tax was intended to be fully earmarked for investment in the telephone sector, but over the years the portion earmarked for reinvestment in the telephone sector went down even as the rate of taxation went up.[10] By 1989, more than half the telephone tax was diverted to the treasury for general expenses, so that telephone users were financing government programs in other sectors.

In the 1970s and 1980s, TELMEX invested whatever funds were available to modernize and expand the system at an average rate of 6 percent per year. By 1981, 99 percent of the exchanges were automatic; from 1982 on, only digital exchanges were added to the system, thereby raising the percentage of digital lines from almost zero in that year to 22 percent in 1989. In 1988, TELMEX introduced 800-number service for the first time and extended it to calls to and from the United States in the following year. However, it was slow in the use of fiber-optic transmission.[11]

If TELMEX's performance was not terrible, why did the Salinas

Table 3-2. TELMEX Financial Indicators, 1985–92 (US$m)

Financial Indicator	Actual					Projection		
	1985	1986	1987	1988	1989	1990	1991	1992
Income statement data (revenues)								
International long-distance service	478	515	564	710	907	861	992	1,116
National long-distance service	303	237	309	449	709	1,322	1,599	1,934
Local service	182	116	153	315	442	1,131	1,331	1,566
Other service	31	22	18	25	57	173	241	324
Total revenues	994	890	1,045	1,499	2,115	3,488	4,164	4,940
Net income after taxes	119	113	206	628	450	1,068	1,431	1,773
Balance sheet data (assets)								
Debt and other liabilities	1,586	1,658	2,156	2,612	2,892	3,757	4,199	7,230
Equity	1,454	1,445	1,573	3,211	4,107	4,117	5,427	4,330
Total assets	3,040	3,102	3,730	5,825	6,999	7,874	9,626	11,560
Sources of funds								
Cash flow from operations	404	308	385	449	833	1,520	1,907	2,383
Outside financing	452	504	1,064	699	638	575	524	256
Total sources	856	812	1,449	1,148	1,471	2,095	2,431	2,639
Uses of funds								
Investment in plant and equipment	576	499	531	746	955	1,741	1,917	2,130
Debt amortization	29	45	73	148	129	92	112	117
Other	251	268	845	254	387	262	402	392
Per-share data								
Earnings per share (US$/share)	0.06	0.04	0.06	0.16	0.11	0.25	0.34	0.42

Source: TELMEX. Projections for 1990–91 are based on a report by Baring Securities (1991) and assume that revenue per line will increase from US$450 in 1989 to US$661 in 1990 and US$700 in 1991. The number of lines in service was projected to grow at 10.4 percent in 1990 and about 12 percent in 1991 and 1992. Totals may not add to 100 due to rounding. The number of outstanding shares in all years was 4,257 million.

administration select it as one of the first firms to be privatized? The answer probably lies in a combination of three factors that, upon closer examination, are not fully consistent with one another. The first factor, which was perhaps the most important, was Salinas's conviction that Mexico had to transform itself from an inward-looking, state-dominated protected economy to an outward-looking, privatized, open economy that would take advantage of its location next to a large, rich neighbor. Actions taken by Salinas prior to or during the privatization of TELMEX, such as sweeping changes in trade, foreign investment, and industrial policies, indicate that his agenda was broader than the mere divestment of TELMEX. The fact that Salinas privatized so many other large state-owned enterprises after TELMEX suggests that if TELMEX had not been one of the first to go, it would surely have gone some time later in his term.

To explain TELMEX's number-one position in the divestiture lineup, one has to assume that to achieve the goal of economic transformation Salinas needed to send a clear signal to private investors at home and abroad that the country was embarking on a truly new course and that he believed that privatizing TELMEX would send just that kind of signal. Mexico's debt crisis and economic stagnation during the 1980s had turned off foreign investors, while the nationalization of several Mexican banks in the final days of the Lopez Portillo administration (1982) had strained the government's relations with the local private sector. Some dramatic action was necessary to indicate the beginning of a new era, to show Salinas's resolve and seriousness in reversing past policies.[12] One argument is that a reform-minded government may have to signal its commitment by overshooting, that is "by initiating reforms of a magnitude or at a pace that an uncommitted government would never attempt."[13]

In retrospect, it appears that the signal Salinas wished to send had to have three characteristics. First, it had to be loud, so that it would register above the din of international news. Second, it had to be quick, so that the economic turnaround could begin early in his term. And third, it had to show that the Mexican government was willing to let private investors earn high rates of return on their investments. The last condition required that the firm targeted for early privatization be a "plum" rather than a "lemon."

If the signal had to be loud, and drama was important, the state-owned enterprise selected for immediate privatization had to be big, and if speed was also important, the barriers to the big firm's privatization had to be low.[14] Of the big firms in government hands (e.g., the nationalized banks, the oil company, and the steel company),[15] TELMEX was an attractive choice because it was a profitable company with pent-up demand and enormous growth potential. Besides, the privatization of telephone service, unlike the oil industry, would not stir nationalistic passions; nor would it require any changes to the constitution, which required only Mexican, not state, control of telephone service firms. And TELMEX would surely be easier to price and sell because its shares were already being traded in Mexico and (lightly) in the United States. Having served from 1981 to 1986 as a government director on the board of TELMEX in the Miguel de la Madrid administration, Salinas was surely aware of these advantages. All that remained was to turn TELMEX into a plum, an activity that took up a lot of the privatizers' time between Salinas's announcement and the actual sale in December 1990.

Besides the signaling effect, the second factor that probably prompted Salinas to pursue large-scale privatization was the desire to reduce even further the government's budget deficit, which had fallen from 17 percent of gross domestic product (GDP) in 1982 to 10 percent by 1988. This factor was quite consistent with the goal of sending a signal to private investors, since both were better served by the privatization of a large, well-run firm rather than a small, poorly run firm—or even a large, poorly run firm.[16] The government did not seem to think that it could finance the US$2–2.5 billion per year that TELMEX was estimated to need to expand the system at the projected rate of 12 percent per annum, nor, apparently, did it believe TELMEX could raise that kind of money internally or on its own credit.[17]

Finally, the third reason for privatizing TELMEX—one that was emphasized in official pronouncements—was that it would improve the sector's performance. As noted earlier, TELMEX's performance left much to be desired, but other state enterprises might easily have been found that were in greater need of performance improvement. The government argued that privatization would enable TELMEX to expand faster while modernizing its network and services to include high-speed data transmission, fiber-optic links, mobile telephones, and digital-overlay networks. However, the precise reasons that privatization was necessary to bring about these or other improvements were never spelled out; given the poor reputation of state enterprises in general, perhaps such an explanation was considered unnecessary. Two days after Salinas's announcement about privatizing TELMEX, the Secretariat of Communications and Transport (SCT) announced ambitious targets that the new owners, whoever they might be, would have to achieve:

—The number of lines in service to be expanded at a minimum rate of 12 percent per annum until 1994; by 2000, telephone density to increase to ten per 100 population, compared to five per 100 population in 1989.

—All towns with a population of 500 or more to have telephone service by the end of 1994.

—The number of public telephones to be increased from 0.8 per 1,000 persons to 2 per 1,000 persons in 1994 and 5 per 1,000 in 1998.

—In towns with automatic exchanges, waiting time for a new connection to be six months by 1995 and one month by 2000.

—The quality of service to be improved as stipulated (see table 3-7).

The objective of improving TELMEX's performance through privatization, however, was not entirely consistent with that of sending a signal to private investors or of reducing the budget deficit. Some policies for improving TELMEX's efficiency, for instance, could conflict with the goal of ensuring a "successful" sale, which was critical for sending the right signal to the investment community, while other policies could conflict with the goal of selling the firm for the highest possible price. The actual choices made by the government revealed the relative importance of these goals.

Overcoming Barriers to Privatization

Selling any state enterprise involves two challenges. The first is freeing the enterprise from the clutches of its existing beneficiaries; the second is enticing private buyers to purchase the firm. Both challenges are heightened when the firm is a core enterprise, that is, large by national standards and enjoying high market power. In such cases, the stakes are high for all current beneficiaries, who have a greater incentive to resist privatization (Austin et al. 1986). At the same time, potential buyers may be unwilling or unable to raise the funds necessary to buy a core firm, while the prospect of continued government regulation, which is inescapable in these cases, adds to the investors' risk.

Persuading Existing Beneficiaries

In general, of all the beneficiaries of a state enterprise, workers and unions offer the fiercest resistance to privatization because they fear losing jobs, pay, and influence. TELMEX was no exception, inasmuch as its employees were among the best paid in Mexico and employment in the company had consistently grown faster than the size of TELMEX's network since the government had taken control of the firm.[18] The telephone workers' union (STRM) exerted a great deal of influence on the internal workings of the company, as did unions in other state enterprises.[19] The STRM recognized that privatization could change all this.

President Salinas seems to have become personally involved in securing the union's support for privatization, presenting workers with a carrot-and-stick offer. The carrot included a promise that no existing worker would lose his or her job as a result of privatization and that workers would receive a stake in the privatized firm. The first of these promises was enshrined in the six principles that Salinas said would govern TELMEX's privatization. The second was fulfilled in June 1990, shortly after a controlling interest in TELMEX had been sold to private investors. Workers paid the prevailing market price for 4.4 percent of TELMEX, financed by a soft loan of US$325 million from the national development bank.

The stick consisted of a veiled threat that if the STRM did not go along with the government's policy, TELMEX would be privatized anyhow, without any guarantees about the welfare of its workers. The threat must have been taken seriously because of the government's earlier handling of labor problems in Aeromexico.[20] Salinas had also taken tough, bold measures against powerful leaders of the oil workers union shortly after becoming president. The STRM leader, Francisco Hernández Juárez, may have reckoned that his future was brighter if he cooperated with Salinas than if he fought him.[21]

The carrot-and-stick combination yielded three concessions from the union: first, the union agreed to support the privatization of TEL-MEX with the safeguards promised by the government; second, it agreed to replace the STRM's fifty-seven labor contracts with TELMEX with a single contract for all unionized workers, along with a reduction in the number of job classifications from more than 500 to just 50; and third, it gave management the freedom to introduce new technology, including the freedom to redeploy workers. In a gesture to the union and Hernández, Salinas formally announced the government's decision to privatize TELMEX at the annual meeting of the STRM in September 1989, at which time workers voted unanimously to support the privatization.

A second source of resistance to privatization tends to be the firm's managers, who fear they may be replaced, and bureaucrats and ministers, who fear losing influence over a large, powerful enterprise. Such fears seem to have existed in the TELMEX case, but the prospect of resistance from any of these quarters was quickly crushed. Within a month of Salinas's announcement, TELMEX was transferred from the SCT to the Secretariat of Finance and Public Credit where a small but dedicated privatization unit was based. By 1989, this had become standard practice for privatizing firms in Mexico. In October 1989, the minister of finance replaced the minister of the SCT as TELMEX's chairman, and a new CEO, committed to privatization, was brought in. These moves reduced the risk of sabotage by TELMEX officials and simultaneously placed the firm's technical resources at the command of the privatizers.

In many countries the legislature is a source of some opposition to privatization, but this was not so at the time in Mexico, where this arm of government had limited powers relative to the executive. Besides, Salinas chose to privatize TELMEX within the bounds of existing laws and regulations for the telephone sector. The Mexican constitution permitted private provision of telephone service, unlike satellite service and telegraph, which were reserved for the state. The rules allowed up to 49 percent of a telephone service company to be owned by foreigners, and Salinas chose not to change that. All that was necessary was to amend the stipulation in TELMEX's articles of association that at least 51 percent of the company's stock had to be owned by the state.[22] In June 1990, the necessary changes were voted on at a special meeting of shareholders.

With respect to consumers, the government seems to have made the reasonable assumption that business users would welcome privatization because it could lead to better service and shorten the waiting time for new connections. Since the service they used most, long distance, was already overpriced, privatization might even help them if it reduced or eliminated the subsidization of local service by long-distance service. At any rate, business users were reportedly more concerned about the availability of service and its quality than about price. As one executive quipped: "The most expensive telephone service is the one you don't have!"

Residential users, on the other hand, were likely to fear that privatization could lead to higher prices. Here, the government seems to have gambled that residential users would not mind paying more provided the quality of TELMEX's service improved. Therefore, Salinas's six principles included at least two that assured consumers that privatization would lead to faster expansion of the telephone system and "radically improved service." The SCT also laid out specific targets for rural service, public telephone density, waiting time for new connections, waiting time for repairs, and quality of service. On each of these measures, the privatized firm was expected to show significant improvement.

Within three months of Salinas's announcement, in December 1989, the SCT permitted TELMEX to raise rates substantially: residential users faced increases in the monthly rent from about US$3 to US$3.50, and the charge per local call went from less than one U.S. cent to more than ten U.S. cents. Long-distance rates were also raised (see table 3-3 for price data converted into U.S. dollars). As a result, TELMEX's annual revenue per line increased by 47 percent, from US$450 in 1989 to US$661 in 1990. Then, on December 31, 1990, within days of transferring control over the firm to the new owners, the government authorized a further rate increase, which took TELMEX's revenue per line to US$744, so that prices in Mexico on most services were as high as, or substantially higher than, those in the United States (see table 3-4). Opposition parties and consumers grumbled about the sharp increase in prices, but

Table 3-3. TELMEX Tariffs for Regulated Services, 1987–94 (constant 1987–94 US$)

Regulated Service		For Year Ending December 31[1]					January 1, 1992	January 1, 1994
		1987	1988	1989	1990	1991		
Residential service								
Installation	(US$)	98.00	276.00	254.00	225.00	358.00	485.00	543.33
Purchase of securities[2]	(US$)	256.00	300.00	276.00	244.00	0.00	0.00	0.00
Monthly rent	(US$)	1.65	2.58	2.37	3.52	4.83	6.81	12.30[3]
Metered service per 3-min. local call[4]	(US¢)	0.60	0.94	0.87	10.50	11.00	12.70	14.24
Commercial service								
Installation	(US$)	217.00	498.00	458.00	405.00	614.00	840.00	941.52
Purchase of securities	(US$)	341.00	400.00	369.00	325.00	0.00	0.00	0.00
Monthly rent	(US$)	2.87	4.48	6.18	9.86	12.85	17.43	24.88
Metered service per 3-min. local call[4]	(US¢)	0.60	0.94	1.30	10.50	11.00	12.70	14.24
Domestic long-distance call[5]	(US$)	0.54	0.75	1.03	1.79	2.27	2.57	2.65
International long-distance call[6]	(US$)	7.98	8.33	8.36	6.22	7.26	7.69	10.89

Source: Goldman Sachs (1992); TELMEX.

Note: Tariffs are converted from data in nominal Mexican pesos (M$) into US$ at the following exchange rates: US$1 = the following old pesos: 1,474 (1987), 2,325 (1988), 2,526 (1989), 2,861 (1990), 3,038 (1991), 3,096 (1992), and 3,300 (1994).

[1] Average of rates in effect at the beginning of each month during the period.

[2] Amounts received from the sale of securities to new customers in exchange for priority in installation. Effective January 1, 1991, this scheme was ended.

[3] For 1994 alone, the monthly rent shown is that applicable to users paying the highest rate in the Mexico City region. (Monthly rents varied from zone to zone within the country.)

[4] For residential customers, this charge applied to local calls in excess of 150 per month through March 1991 and 100 per month thereafter. Commercial customers were permitted 300 free calls per month in 1987, none in 1988 and 1989, 90 at a reduced rate in 1990, and none beginning January 1, 1991.

[5] Charge for a 5-minute direct-dial call over a distance of 450 km. at daytime rates.

[6] Charge for a 7-minute direct-dial call from Mexico City to New York, at daytime rates, for the portion of the call from Mexico City to the U.S. border (except for 1994). The charge to the customer included an amount for the U.S. portion of the call; for 1987 through 1989, the charge was the average peso equivalent of US$8.61 (at the official exchange rate); for 1990 the charge was the average peso equivalent of US$6.30. However, the figure shown for 1994 ($10.89) is the total charge to the customer for the call, which is substantially lower than the total charge of US$16.97 in 1989 and US$12.52 in 1990.

in the Mexican context there was little else they could do. When consumers registered their protest by simultaneously taking their telephones off the hook, a company spokesman reportedly warned that if telephone lines were burned as a result, it would take forever to fix them. So much for consumer protest!

Enticing Private Buyers

The second aspect of the privatization process—enticing private buyers to invest in the company—consumed most of the privatizers' time. The

Table 3-4. TELMEX Prices for Service November 1991, Comparative Data (US$)

Service	TELMEX	Pacific Bell (U.S.)	Southwestern Bell (U.S.)	Ratio of TELMEX to U.S. Companies
Installation				
Residential	374.00	35.00	38.00	10.20
Commercial	641.00	71.00	88.00	8.06
Monthly rent				
Residential	7.60	16.00	16.80	0.46
Commercial	17.80	14.40	22.90	0.95
Metered service per 3-min. call (USȼ)	10.90	8.00	8.00	1.36
Domestic long-distance call[1]	0.44	0.31	0.37	1.29
International long-distance call to U.S.[2]	0.92	0.96	0.98	0.95
International long-distance call to other foreign country[3]	2.64	1.55	1.50	1.73

Source: SCT and interviews.

[1] Direct-dial, 400 km. distance, charge per minute.

[2] Direct-dial call from Mexico City to a particular region of the United States, charge per minute. Rates shown for Pacific Bell and Southwestern Bell are for the same call in reverse direction.

[3] Direct-dial call to unspecified country, charge per minute. Rates shown under U.S. companies are for calling the same country from the United States.

many actions taken on this front were designed, or so it seems in retrospect, to reduce the risks and to increase the potential return to prospective buyers. In other words, the government worked hard to turn TELMEX into a plum for investors. TELMEX was a reasonably attractive company to begin with. It was fairly well run and profitable. Its future promised real growth of 12 percent per year for at least five more years. It had one million people on the waiting list for new connections. Demand for long-distance service was booming as the Mexican economy began to open up and trade with the United States expanded. To be sure, the company had excess workers, but this was nothing that three or four years of growth at 12 percent could not solve.

The Mexican government desired, nevertheless, to make the firm more attractive to prospective buyers, a desire that was to influence the privatizers at every turn. Perhaps the single most important step the government took in this regard was to raise prices sharply before privatization. TELMEX's profits increased from US$206 million in 1987 to US$628 million in 1988 and US$450 million in 1989. Just as significant as the overall increase was the fact that rates were rebalanced. Most of the increase occurred in local service and domestic long-distance service; international rates were lowered, partly to placate U.S. authorities, who were complaining that calls to the United States originating in Mexico were much more expensive than those originating in the United States. By raising rates for the part of the business that was a natural monopoly (that is, local service), the government enhanced TELMEX's ability to respond to competition, if any, in long-distance service. The price of TELMEX shares rose more steeply in the Mexican stock exchange in response to the tariff revision than it did either when privatization was announced by Salinas or after control of the firm was actually turned over to the new owners.

To soften the blow to consumers, the government simultaneously announced that the punitive telephone tax on users, ranging from 22 to 70 percent depending on the type of service, would be replaced by a tax-deductible 29 percent telephone tax on TELMEX. However, the company could avoid paying the telephone tax altogether if it reinvested its profits in its own business. In 1990, this amounted to a pure transfer from the government to the company of US$643 million,[23] while a World Bank report estimated that the price-cum-tax reform increased the value of TELMEX by US$15 billion.

The third incentive offered to prospective buyers was to give TELMEX a continued monopoly status in national and international long-distance services for a period of six years, even though competition would readily have appeared in 1989 had it been permitted. Government officials involved described a struggle between the Secretariat of Commerce and Industrial Development, which favored opening up the service to competition, and the privatizers in the Finance Ministry, who feared that without exclusivity in long-distance service TELMEX might not be attractive to private investors. In fact, during prebid discussions, prospective buyers of TELMEX strongly preferred that the federal microwave network owned by the communications ministry be consolidated within the firm. The regulating agency (SCT), they argued, ought not to be simultaneously a competitor of TELMEX. After heated debates within the government, and only days before the TELMEX sale, the federal microwave network was sold to TELMEX for US$300 million. The company thus became an even more powerful player in Mexico's telecommunications industry.

The revised license agreement for TELMEX also permitted the firm to diversify into related and unrelated businesses, such as value added services, Yellow Pages, equipment manufacture, installation and maintenance services, public branch exchanges (PBXs), and so on, as long as these activities were carried out through separate subsidiaries (see Amendment to Concession of Teléfonos de México 1990). The only exclusion was television service. TELMEX was also granted the only national license for cellular telephone service, with the sole condition that it could not enter any region until a competitor had already done so. On many of these issues, the Secretariat of Commerce and Industrial Development preferred to restrict TELMEX, while the privatizers in the Secretariat of Finance and Public Credit preferred to enlarge the firm's scope. When the matter went to Salinas for resolution, he seems to have come down on the side of the privatizers. In the same spirit, the government chose not to divide TELMEX into regional companies (as in Argentina) or along types of service (long-distance service versus local service, as in Chile). Jacques Rogozinski, the official mainly responsible for carrying out the privatization, said the government was worried that if the firm were divided, some parts would be much less attractive than others and, more important, that the division would create legal, accounting, and administrative nightmares that could delay the privatization of TELMEX by a few years.[24] Salinas had told the privatization team that TELMEX ought to be privatized by June 1990; at the request of the team, he extended the deadline to the end of the calendar year. The transaction was, in fact, consummated on December 20, 1990.

In terms of reducing the risk to potential buyers, perhaps the most essential element in the government's plan was restructuring equity capital so as to reduce the amount of money a private consortium would have to offer to obtain control over the company. The gist of what the government did was to concentrate the voting power in 40 percent of the company's shares, thereby reducing the percentage of total equity that a controlling investor had to buy from 51 percent to just 20.4 percent. Further, the government ruled that the 20.4 percent bloc could be owned entirely by Mexicans or by a trust controlled by Mexicans; in other words, foreign investors could own up to 49 percent of a trust that purchased the controlling interest without violating Mexico's foreign investment rules. Therefore, if foreign partners could be found, a Mexican group could expect to control TELMEX by buying barely 10 percent of TELMEX's total equity. Mexican law requires that any investor owning 10 percent of the equity in a company be allowed to nominate one director to the board; with scarcely that level of investment, the Mexican group that controlled TELMEX would be able to nominate nine members to TELMEX's eighteen-member board.

The government also reduced other risks for prospective buyers. The risk of competition, as noted earlier, was eliminated for a period of six years in the one area in which it was a real threat—long-distance service. Oddly enough, entry was freely permitted for local service, where the barriers to entry were enormous and the likely returns very low. To be sure, the government allowed competition in areas such as cellular service, value added service, and equipment supply, but in 1989, these activities accounted for only 5 percent of TELMEX's sales.[25]

In addition, the government eliminated the risk of a hostile takeover of TELMEX for ten years after privatization by restricting the rights of members of the controlling consortium to sell their shares. For instance, a foreign company investing in TELMEX through a Mexican-controlled trust was barred from selling its shares for five years and even thereafter had to sell them to Mexicans in the trust. Again, this seems to have been done to entice Mexican bidders.

Finally, the government eliminated the risk that telephone rates might be excessively low by adjusting prices upward well before privatization. The government took this unpopular step on its own watch, rather than permitting it to happen after the new owners took over. Equally important, the government ruled that until 1996 TELMEX would have the freedom to automatically raise tariffs on a basket of services by an amount equal to the increase in consumer prices. In 1997 and 1998, the basket as a whole could be increased by three percentage points less than the inflation in the retail price index (the so-called *RPI-X* formula). After 1998, rates would be regulated to yield a fair return on capital. This pricing formula was much more generous than the British Telecom (BT) formula after which it was modeled. The BT was required from the beginning to raise rates by inflation less 3 percent because of the anticipated economies of scale in telephone service provision; by 1993, BT's price cap was set at 7.5 percent below retail price inflation.[26]

Five Mexican groups, fourteen foreign telecommunications firms (including seven from the United States), and three U.S. banks were prequalified to submit bids. The Mexican government was keen on having local groups team up with foreign firms that had technical expertise in telecommunications. Accordingly, bidders were required to have direct knowledge or access to knowledge of the telecommunications industry. In the end, three bids were received (see table 3-5), and Grupo Carso, in alliance with Southwestern Bell and France Telecom, was selected as the winner. Grupo Carso, like other Mexican groups, was highly diversified, with interests in tobacco, mining, metallurgy, paper, restaurants, and copper and copper alloys—none of which, except copper, had even a remote relationship to telephone service.

Why Foreigners Invested in TELMEX

TELMEX attracted US$1.5 billion in direct foreign investment from Southwestern Bell and France Telecom and another US$4 billion in foreign portfolio investment. How can this level of foreign interest in 1989–90 in a Mexican telephone company be explained?[27] The question presupposes that the response of foreigners was surprisingly strong, which it was, if the following factors are kept in mind.

First, the Mexican plan for privatizing TELMEX limited foreign ownership in voting shares to 49 percent or less, with no single foreign investor

Table 3-5. TELMEX Bids Received, November 1990

Bidder	Price Offered per Share[1]	Total offer (US$m)	Percentage of Capital	Payment Conditions
Gentor Group	US$1.58	700.0	10.4	US$125m immediately and US$575m in 6 months
Acciones y Valores, Telefónica de España, and GTE (U.S.)	US$1.95	1,687.2	20.4	US$250m immediately and US$1,437m in 6 months
Grupo Carso, Southwestern Bell, France Cables et Radio	US$2	1,760, including US$26m in dividends	20.4	US$975m immediately, US$759m in 6 months, and US$26m in dividends receivable in 6 months on shares purchased

Source: Privatization Unit, Ministry of France, Government of Mexico.

[1]Per equivalent A or AA share before dilution.

being allowed to own more than 10 percent. Was it reasonable to expect foreign firms to invest several hundred million dollars without any prospect of controlling the firm? Any foreign firm that chose to do so would have to accept being the junior partner in a consortium led by local partners, who would almost certainly have no technical expertise in telecommunications and with whom the foreign firm probably had never before done business. It was also unlikely that local partners would give de facto control of the firm to their foreign partners through a side agreement after investing sums that would be monumental by the standards of the local private sector. Secondly, telecommunications firms in industrialized countries, especially the United States, had little or no experience with foreign direct investment at the time, let alone experience in Mexico, although some European firms, such as C&W (UK) and France Telecom, owned significant shares in the telecommunications firms in former British and French colonies (Ambrose et al. 1990). Finally, foreign manufacturers of telephone equipment, who might have believed that a stake in TELMEX could help promote equipment sales in Mexico, were disqualified at the outset by the Mexican government to prevent the obvious conflict of interest that would ensue.[28]

These barriers to foreign investment explain why the Mexican government bent over backward to make TELMEX appealing to potential buyers. Besides the many steps taken by the government to make TELMEX a relatively low-risk, high-return firm, Mexico's decision to exempt foreign investors from taxes on capital gains and dividends must have helped. The government also did an excellent job in selling TELMEX to foreign investors through promotional visits to key financial centers and by inviting foreign firm representatives to visit TELMEX. In 1990, scores of executives from foreign telephone companies were buzzing around TELMEX's offices and facilities, gathering information.

Two other factors probably motivated Western telephone companies to seek foreign investment opportunities.[29] One was the fact that domestic markets in the industrialized countries in the West were growing at rates much lower than that projected for Mexico. The other was the fact that many of these companies were spinning off cash from domestic operations that they could not reinvest in the domestic market to earn returns comparable to those promised by a firm such as TELMEX. Besides, some firms, such as the Baby Bells, faced restrictions on diversification at home but greater latitude in foreign operations.

As it turned out, the binding constraint on attracting bids for TELMEX was not the number of foreign firms interested in the firm but the number of local investors willing and able to team up with them. The government's criteria for prequalification ensured that only large, financially strong Mexican firms would participate, while foreign investors were required to have a minimum size and to have experienced a minimum level of growth in the past. The government also left it to local investors to select the foreign partners with whom they wished to team. The local partner thus had the upper hand in negotiations with foreign firms since the former were far fewer in number.

In the end, foreign firms seem to have been lured to Mexico by the enormously high returns that TELMEX promised, with payback periods in months rather than years. However, Southwestern Bell had special reasons to bid for TELMEX. Its service territory in the United States bordered Mexico, and calls to and from Mexico accounted for a substantial portion of its revenues. With the prospect of a North American Free Trade Agreement that could further deepen ties between the United States and Mexico, Southwestern Bell officials were reportedly very keen to own a piece of TELMEX. Southwestern Bell is believed to have spent in excess of a thousand person-weeks in the period before the bid, sizing up TELMEX, meeting with key officials, including Salinas, and assessing which of the local firms likely to bid had the best prospects of winning. "If they had been allowed," said one TELMEX official, "they would have bought the whole company themselves. They were really bullish about TELMEX." Southwestern Bell was the only member of Grupo Carso that chose in December 1989 to purchase options for an additional 5 percent of TELMEX's nonvoting shares. As a result, Southwestern Bell owned nearly twice as many shares as Carlos Slim, head of Grupo Carso, although half of the shares were nonvoting. Between the time Southwestern Bell paid for the option and the time those options were exercised a year later, the price of TELMEX stock had more than doubled.

Indeed, with financial returns from TELMEX being that high, both Southwestern Bell and France Telecom seemed content to assume a low-key position within the firm. To underline the fact that TELMEX was controlled by Mexicans, both foreign firms maintained small offices at a location separate from TELMEX's multistory corporate headquarters and projected the image of being mere technical consultants to the Mexican owners. In reality, however, the two foreign firms together nominated seven directors to TELMEX's board.[30]

The Impact of Privatization on TELMEX's Performance

In theory, changing ownership can affect performance in three ways (see figure 1-1). The first and most direct way is through differences in the way a firm is managed and the goals it pursues because of the change in ownership. The second, indirect, way is through variations in the degree of competition it faces in input and output markets, variations that are somehow linked to privatization. The third, also indirect, way is through alterations in the quality of government regulation of the firm, alterations that, again, are somehow linked to or associated with privatization.

The Impact of Ownership Change

There is ample evidence in the TELMEX case that the change in ownership alone affected the firm's behavior, even though the new owners had brought in only seven executives to TELMEX within the first year of privatization: the chairman, the president, and five people in the purchasing, labor relations, and finance departments. However, the new owners pushed more aggressively than previous managements for cost reduction in areas such as inventory management, labor productivity, purchasing, and overhead.

TELMEX's workforce, which had grown at 8 percent per year in the 1980s, stopped growing in 1989, even though the network expanded at more than 12 percent per year from 1990 to 1993 (see table 3-6). As a result, the number of lines per employee, a standard measure of labor productivity in the telecommunications industry, rose from 95.2 in 1989 to 151.5 in 1993, representing a cumulative improvement of 46 percent in the three years following privatization. The annual savings on salaries and benefits because of the increase in labor productivity probably amounted to US$685 million before taxes and US$445 million after taxes.[31] Corporate staff departments were also consolidated and some senior management positions were eliminated.

Purchase agreements with the two companies that supplied most of the equipment to TELMEX—L. M. Ericsson de Mexico and Alcatel de Mexico—were reopened and renegotiated to yield significantly better terms for the company under the threat of switching to foreign suppliers. Although the Mexican government had signed a five-year supply

Table 3-6. TELMEX Performance, 1988–1993

Performance Indicator	1988	1989	1990	1991	1992	1993
Lines in service						
Annual increase (thousands)	288.0	460.0	508.0	670.0	729.0	867.0
Percentage increase	7.0	10.5	10.5	12.5	12.1	12.8
Total lines (thousands)	4,387.0	4,847.0	5,355.0	6,025.0	6,754.0	7,621.0
Lines installed						
Annual increase (thousands)	354.0	535.0	705.0	759.0	711.0	975.0
Percentage increase	7.4	10.4	12.4	11.9	9.9	12.4
Total lines (thousands)	5,152.0	5,687.0	6,392.0	7,151.0	7,862.0	8,837.0
Telephone density						
(lines/100 people)	5.6	6.1	6.6	7.2	8.0	8.7
Number of employees						
(telephone service only)	49,995	49,203	49,912	49,488	48,937	48,771
Lines per employee	85.5	95.2	104.2	117.7	133.3	151.5
Capital expenditures (US$m)	1,080.0	987.0	1,831.0	1,967.0	2,352.0	2,282.0

Source: TELMEX.

agreement with these companies just before privatization, the new owners extracted large price concessions under the threat of delaying orders until the last year or two of the contractual period (Moffett 1992). As part of the same strategy, in 1991 the American Telephone and Telegraph Company (AT&T) was brought in as a new supplier of equipment and awarded a large fiber-optic contract. The 20–25 percent reduction in equipment prices thus obtained probably saved the company US$150 million per year, not counting any savings that may have been achieved in other areas of capital expenditure.[32]

Internal incentive systems were also altered; for instance, a stock-option scheme was introduced for senior managers. Senior executives who had been with the company for many years noted that decisionmaking had been speeded up as well.

On the revenue side, despite the price hikes, the volume of local, domestic long-distance, and international calls grew rapidly, aided in part by the faster growth of the network after privatization. As a result, for 1991, TELMEX's net profit after taxes was US$1.7 billion, compared with a projection of US$1 billion, while in 1992 and 1993 it was in the range of US$2.5 billion. Despite being the twelfth-largest telephone company in the world, TELMEX's stock market capitalization placed it second in the world, next only to British Telecom.

An important question is whether privatization was necessary to expand the Mexican telephone network (see table 3-6). There is historical evidence that the TELMEX system did, in fact, expand at double-digit rates before privatization (for example in 1989). The private sector was responsible for the supply of equipment, its installation, and the construction of facilities even before privatization; apparently, TELMEX had the organizational capacity to supervise that process at rates much higher than the 5–6 percent at which the Mexican network expanded in the decade before privatization. In the 1980s, TELMEX had been constrained by the funds available to finance growth, and this did change after privatization, not because the firm was able to tap into new sources of capital but because higher prices (and to a much lesser extent, lower costs) yielded the firm vast amounts of internal funds. For instance, in 1992 and 1993, TELMEX's capital expenditure was US\$2.35 billion and US\$2.28 billion, respectively, sums more than double those in 1988 and 1989 (see table 3-6). However, even in 1992 and 1993, TELMEX's capital expenditure represented only 70 percent of its net profit after tax plus depreciation, indicating just how cash-rich the privatized firm had become.

It seems plausible that even as a state-owned enterprise TELMEX would have been able to expand the Mexican network at comparable rates provided telephone tariffs had been increased as sharply as they were at the time of privatization. But the question with a less clear-cut answer is, Could tariffs have been raised as sharply as they were in the absence of privatization? Supporters of TELMEX's privatization would argue that they could not have been; that is, the government could not have gotten away with the huge price increases of 1989 and 1990 without the promise of privatization. The public would not have believed that a state-owned TELMEX would use the higher prices to expand and modernize the system or to improve the quality of service. On the other hand, opponents might argue that the prices of some other crucial products, such as gasoline and electricity, were raised markedly by the Salinas administration even though state-owned enterprises in those sectors were not privatized.

One area in which privatization clearly did not have impressive results was in improving the quality of service. Although in the aggregate, averaging across all regions and months, TELMEX claimed to have exceeded the quality targets laid out in the concession agreement (see table 3-7), it consistently failed to do so on individual performance measures, such as the percentage of failing lines, and in the large, congested market of Mexico City, where 40 percent of all lines were located (see table 3-8). For instance, at an aggregate level, the percentage of lines under repair had decreased from 10 percent at the time of privatization to 9 percent in 1992, compared with the target of 7 percent, but in the Mexico City region, that proportion was as high as 11.3 percent in 1992 and 9.2 percent in 1993. Indeed, during the rainy season in 1992, as many as one in six lines in the Mexico City region was out of order at any time.

The company also failed consistently to meet the target for improving

Table 3-7. TELMEX'S Quality of Service, 1990–1994 (%)

Peformance Indicator	1990 Actual[1]	1991 Target	1991 Actual	1992 Target	1992 Actual	1993 Target	1993 Actual	1994 Target
Service continuity index (ICON)[2]	80.20	83.42	86.27	86.19	89.53	87.07	90.89	87.95
Lines with failure	10.00	8.00	9.43	7.00	9.12	6.00	7.53	5.00
Same-day line repair	45.00	48.00	52.94	50.00	68.81	50.00	74.10	50.00
3-day line repair	82.00	86.00	90.96	90.00	93.23	91.00	93.60	92.00
Service quality index (ICAL)[2]	91.08	91.66	92.36	92.38	93.68	92.82	95.93	93.64
Dial tone in 4 secs.	97.00	97.00	98.46	97.00	99.26	98.00	99.65	98.00
Local calls, 1st try	92.00	92.00	93.45	94.00	95.65	94.00	97.19	95.00
Long-distance calls, 1st try	90.00	92.00	92.46	92.00	94.24	92.00	97.82	93.00
Special operators answering in 10 secs.	90.00	90.00	83.11	91.00	83.62	91.00	83.64	92.00
Public telephones in service	87.00	88.00	90.84	89.00	91.73	90.00	95.16	91.00

Source: TELMEX.

[1] Preprivatization benchmark. TELMEX officials question the reliability of these numbers.

[2] ICON and ICAL are composite measures of service quality consisting of the elements listed under each.

operator service; here, if the data are to be believed, service actually deteriorated relative to 1990. In 1992, consumers registered more than a million complaints each month about TELMEX's service, motivated in part by their higher expectations from a privatized firm that was charging high prices. As one observer put it, "Consumers are complaining that they have to pay First World prices for Third World service!"

Privatization and Competition

The second source of performance improvement was the indirect impact privatization had on competition within the sector.[33] In the short run, the outcome was at best neutral or negative; that is, privatization did not increase competition within any segment of the sector, while it weakened it marginally in others.

In output markets, the manner in which TELMEX was privatized made the firm an even more entrenched player than before. Had it not been privatized, competition might have been permitted in long-distance service, or cellular telephone service might have been reserved for the private sector (thus keeping TELMEX out of that segment). However, in its eagerness to make TELMEX attractive to buyers, the government made TELMEX the exclusive provider of long-distance service for six years and also handed it the only national license for cellular telephone service. To be sure, fringe businesses, such as value added services, were opened up to competition at the time of privatization (SCT 1990), but the chances are that this would have happened even without privatization. In some key areas—for example, long-distance service—one could argue that privatization probably locked out competition even more

Table 3-8. TELMEX's Quality of Service in Greater Mexico City, 1992 and 1993 (%)

	1992			1993		
Performance Indicator	Target	Annual Average	Worst Month	Target	Annual Average	Worst Month
Service continuity index (ICON)	86.19	84.24	81.54	87.07	86.23	81.40
Lines with failure	7.00	11.26	16.18	6.00	9.24	10.96
Same-day line repair	50.00	60.59	50.15	50.00	63.02	49.40
3-day repair rate	90.00	86.70	79.30	91.00	88.58	78.20
Service quality index (ICAL)	92.38	92.66	91.48	92.82	94.60	92.98
Dial tone in 4 secs.	97.00	99.38	98.82	98.00	99.40	99.05
Local calls, 1st try	94.00	92.55	89.60	94.00	93.60	90.73
Long-distance call, 1st try	92.00	94.54	93.50	92.00	97.30	94.26
Special operators answering in 10 secs.	91.00	81.52	77.64	91.00	75.37	67.16
Public telephones in service	89.00	90.34	86.66	90.00	96.45	95.07

Source: TELMEX.

forcefully than might have been the case if the firm had remained state owned. Certainly, the decision to consolidate the federal microwave network within TELMEX would probably not have occurred without privatization.

Further, the manner in which TELMEX was privatized prevented hostile takeovers of the company; that is, the market for corporate control was not allowed to operate for at least a decade. Likewise, the labor union's power and role, although diminished, was still strong, and the promise not to lay off anyone reduced the scope for trimming the workforce or for shedding poor performers.

The outlook in the longer term, however, is quite different. The threat of opening long-distance service to competition in 1997 was taken very seriously by the company. Therefore, TELMEX was moving aggressively to upgrade its long-distance system so that it could hold its own as prices fell in the future. The same threat would probably have been less credible if TELMEX had not been privatized. Besides, in the telecommunications industry, technology is evolving in a manner that is likely to make competition stronger rather than weaker in the future, including possibly in local service. In a sign of things to come, in October 1993, Bell Atlantic of the United States paid US$1.04 billion to acquire a 42 percent stake in a private Mexican company, Grupo Iusacell, a budding cellular service company. The *Wall Street Journal* described the deal as "a pricey bid [by Bell Atlantic] to play a role in breaking Teléfonos de México's monopoly on local service" (Kneale 1993).

By 1994, private participation had expanded in several segments of the industry, although TELMEX was by far the largest player. Among the private players were nine firms offering cellular telephone service to 392,000 customers, forty-two companies providing paging services to

136,000 users, fifteen companies providing trunking service to 23,000 users, about twenty providers of value added services, five private companies with public teleports, and one cable television consortium (made up of five private television companies). In addition, large companies such as BANOBRAS operated private networks within Mexico. Most of these firms emerged after the new telecommunication regulations were issued in 1990. Although public telephone service provided exclusively by TELMEX accounted for 80 percent or more of the telecommunication sector's total revenues, many of the newer services were growing at faster rates. Thus, even if the sector reforms did not end TELMEX's dominant position, they did produce a nucleus of private firms that could some day challenge TELMEX.

In mid-1994, as the end of TELMEX's exclusivity period began to approach, private firms sought signals from the government about the precise nature of competition that would be permitted after 1996. In particular, they were interested in knowing if TELMEX's monopoly right to provide long-distance service would be continued or ended. To the Mexican government's credit, it recognized that, for competition to materialize in long-distance service in 1996, concessions would have to be granted about two years earlier, that is, some time in 1994. Accordingly, the following issues were under debate within the government in mid-1994: Should entry be completely open after 1996 or should it be restricted and, if so, to how many firms? What obligations for network expansion ought to be imposed on the new concessionaires? How should concessionaires be selected, especially if a public auction is not used? What rules should govern interconnection between the new entrants' networks and TELMEX's network? And what public service obligations ought to apply to TELMEX after 1996?

As of May 1994 it appeared that the government was unlikely to permit free entry into long-distance or local service, that a limited number of concessions would be issued, and that the new entrants would be required to help expand the basic network. Once the additional concessions are awarded and competition within the sector is strengthened, the reforms made in 1990 will be cemented and will probably be irreversible.

In sum, it seems fair to conclude that the threat to open up the Mexican market to competition would not have been very credible in 1990—either to TELMEX or to potential private entrants—had TELMEX not been privatized. While this is pure speculation, it is on speculative issues such as this that any verdict on the merits of privatization may ultimately rest.

Likewise, hostile takeovers will become possible by the year 2000, thus preventing the incumbent management from becoming too complacent. And through attrition, early retirements, and selective hiring (after excess labor is first absorbed through growth), the company may be able to improve the quality of its workforce as well. In 1993, the STRM approved a new labor contract that limited wage increases to 9.8 percent, as advised by the government, and included a new productivity-based incentive scheme. In addition, once competition is introduced into the sector, the union may have to show greater flexibility than it did in the years immediately following privatization. The company's management believed that additional productivity gains were waiting to be exploited, especially in the two classes of employees whose services can be reduced if the union cooperates: telephone operators, of whom there were 10,000 even as late as 1993, and repairmen, of whom there were several thousand. Perhaps competition will produce the change in union attitudes and work rules that privatization was apparently unable to produce.

Privatization and Regulation

In the short run, privatization probably had a positive impact on the quality of regulation in the Mexican telecommunications sector. When TELMEX was state owned, the government's role as regulator was blurred with its role as owner. Ownership gave the government so much room to intervene, starting with the right to appoint CEOs, that the rules governing TELMEX did not have to be spelled out formally or explicitly; they could be made up as required and changed as convenient. Not surprisingly, the concession agreement under which TELMEX operated up to 1989 used vague language and simply referred the company to the government on all kinds of matters.

Privatization forced the government to develop a more complete concession agreement, one that was nearly four times as long. Now all power was vested with the company unless the government specifically took some of it away for a good reason. (Earlier, all power had resided with the government unless the government explicitly gave some of it to the enterprise.)

The government sought a number of inputs to draft the new concession. Government officials visited several countries to compare alternative approaches to regulation; in the end, they used an approach similar to Britain's but with some important differences. Experts from TELMEX helped draft aspects of the agreement, while other experts were hired by the firm to study specific aspects (such as the merits of dividing TELMEX before privatization). Still other experts were funded through a technical assistance loan from the World Bank or hired by the local adviser to the government, Banco Internacional.[34] All this expertise was used to draft a concession agreement that was clever and comprehensive. It clearly stipulated some of the privatized firm's obligations, for example, in the areas of rural service, rates of expansion of the network, public telephones, and system modernization. It also stipulated precise standards of service that the company had to achieve and included financial penalties for failing to do so. Further, it specified the conditions under which TELMEX could diversify and the rules under which it would have to provide access to the local network to future competitors (that is, the rules for interconnection). It is doubtful that all these steps would have been taken without privatization. Performance contracts, which come closest to establishing a formal regulatory relation between governments and state enterprises, have proved to be hopelessly weak at getting either party to honor its commitments (Nellis 1991).

In the longer term, however, the concession agreement is likely to become obsolete as unanticipated events occur and prompt the government to change some goals or targets. The difficulty of writing comprehensive contracts that cover all contingencies is well recognized in the regulation literature (see, e.g., Sappington and Stiglitz 1987). In the future, will the government be able to muster the expertise and resources that it did in 1989–90, when TELMEX was being readied for privatization? My guess is that it will not. Unfortunately, Mexico chose not to strengthen the SCT when it privatized TELMEX, despite urging by the World Bank. A few peripheral activities being carried out within the SCT were privatized, while others were transferred to the new government agency, TELECOMM, but the idea of turning the SCT into a well-staffed, autonomous regulatory agency following the British model for OFTEL was not pursued for a number of reasons.[35] First, the idea was reportedly resisted by the SCT, possibly because doing so would have compounded the ministry's loss of power following the privatization of TELMEX. Second, creating an autonomous regulatory agency for telecommunications may have created similar demands from other ministries at a time when Mexican officials were intent on reducing the size of government. In the end, the government seems to have opted to create one high-powered Fair Competition Commission, as required under NAFTA, with jurisdiction over all sectors. Third, a strong regulatory agency may have made TELMEX less attractive to prospective buyers, a point made in a World Bank review of the sector:

> Progress in developing SCT regulatory capacity has been slow. . . . It is evident that there was no clear consensus on the part of the Mexican authorities on the need for strengthening this regulatory capacity. Fears were expressed that a strong SCT might conspire against the adequate development of the private sector. The Bank might have taken a stronger stance regarding this issue, but given the overriding importance of a successful TELMEX sale, and the drafting of the regulations, at that time, in 1990, it did not seem appropriate to delay the loan. (World Bank 1993, 13)

For these reasons, the SCT suffered from a shortage of policy-level staff even in 1994. More than half its staff in the telecommunications section consisted of administrative personnel. One official estimated that the SCT had only about twenty experts truly capable of handling complex, regulatory issues; if history is any guide, about half of those experts would leave the ministry when Salinas's term ended in late 1994.

A privatized TELMEX is likely to protect and maximize its interests more aggressively than it did as a state-owned firm, while the government will be ill equipped in terms of expertise and staff to haggle with the company. The nature of that struggle was illustrated over the matter of service quality. Customer dissatisfaction with TELMEX's service, especially in the Mexico City region, on matters such as frequent line failures, delays in repairing lines, and errors in billing, translated into pressure on the SCT to find a solution. It was not until public discontent with TELMEX found its way into the political arena that the SCT responded: in 1993, based on TELMEX's quality of service during 1992, the SCT ordered TELMEX to credit every customer in the Greater Mexico City region one month's worth of rent, which reportedly cost the company about US$75 million. Nonetheless, the SCT did not receive high marks for enforcing the quality targets and sanctions prescribed in the concession agreement. For instance, by mid-1994, it had still not conducted an independent audit of TELMEX's quality reporting system, and some government officials expressed reservations about the reliability of information obtained from TELMEX.

The subject of interconnection policy presents a different example. Here, the SCT charged TELMEX with the responsibility of proposing the rules that should apply for interconnecting with its network if and when competition is permitted in long-distance service. Not surprisingly, TELMEX proposed rules that would make life difficult for potential competitors. However, the SCT shared TELMEX's proposals with those potential entrants, including the association of Mexican cellular companies (from which TELMEX was deliberately excluded). By so doing, the SCT was able to pit TELMEX's expertise and interests against those of its potential competitors in long-distance service. TELMEX's access to expertise from its foreign partners was offset by equally impressive expertise to which its potential competitors had access, including firms such as GTE, Telefónica de España, and Bell Atlantic.

The SCT's differing experiences with regard to regulating quality of service and designing interconnection policy shows how critical competition—or potential competition—can be in easing the regulator's task. The SCT's need for in-house expertise was greatly reduced when competing private parties could be pitted against one another to hammer out a policy. Even on the matter of quality of service, it was the threat of competition after 1996 that seems to have finally focused TELMEX's attention on that problem. In 1993, as public outrage against the company mounted and the government's commitment to permitting competition in long-distance service after 1996 solidified, TELMEX replaced or modernized three times as many lines as it had done in the previous two years and aggressively upgraded the external plant. The company also announced that by the year 2000 it would replace 2.8 million lines, or nearly half of all lines in operation when TELMEX was privatized, and it assigned special operators to take consumer complaints over the phone, created new centers where bills could be paid, and launched a public relations campaign to improve its image.

As the threat of competition was even stronger with respect to business users, TELMEX paid more attention to their needs. Business users interviewed by the author expressed satisfaction with TELMEX's new fiber-optic overlay network and noted that after privatization the company had become much more responsive to their needs.[36] One internal survey conducted for TELMEX by a third party reportedly found that 70 percent of the hundred largest users felt that the company's service had improved since privatization, 20 percent thought it had neither improved nor worsened, while 10 percent felt it had become worse.[37]

On the whole, although privatization did not produce a spectacular improvement in quality of service in all areas, it certainly brought the question of quality into focus and led to the establishment of a system to monitor and enforce quality standards, neither of which is likely to have happened in the absence of privatization.

Lessons from the TELMEX Experience

From a practical standpoint, the TELMEX case offers many lessons for policymakers in developing countries. Above all, it demonstrates that telephone companies can be privatized in developing countries through a creative packaging of the deal. Local and foreign investors can be found, especially in the form of portfolio investment, to a degree unimaginable a few years ago. While this may seem obvious in the mid-1990s, it was hardly obvious to the Mexican policymakers who privatized TELMEX.

The TELMEX case also illustrates the tactics by which support can be built for telecommunications privatization. Worker support can be garnered by a promise of no layoffs, which does not impose substantial long-run costs because of the potential for growth in such firms. In addition, workers can be offered a side payment in the form of subsidized sales of shares in the privatized firm. Moreover, the TELMEX case offers pointers on how governments can realize a good price for their firm. These include the strategy of raising prices before privatization rather than after (if prices are to be raised at all), of selling the government's shares in tranches rather than all at once (as happened in the United Kingdom in many cases), of restructuring the firm's labor, legal, and financial affairs before privatization, and of reducing uncertainty for buyers by clarifying, up front, the rules of the game.

Another conclusion to be drawn from the TELMEX case is that successful privatization requires a great deal of planning. Mexican officials did not privatize without first clearing out several policy cobwebs that hampered the industry. Although Mexico's privatizers were working under a very tight time constraint imposed by Salinas, they took more time and pains to clarify the policy environment before privatization than did their Argentine counterparts.[38]

Further, the TELMEX case underscores the need for effective regulation after privatization. As noted earlier, privatization provided the impetus to take a fresh look at all aspects of the firm's regulation and to spell out explicitly the conditions under which the privatized firm would have to operate. What it did not do as well was to strengthen the institutional capacity for regulation, despite urging by the World Bank. This failing will adversely affect the quality of regulation in the longer run, as the "wisdom" captured in the concession agreement of 1990 begins to become obsolete. Fortunately, however, as the risk of poor regulation increases, so does the disciplining force of competition, aided by trends in technology that seem to be entirely on the consumer's side. Therefore, the long-run outcome for Mexico could well be a strong, modern telecommunications firm whose markets become increasingly contestable, if not competitive.

The Mexican experience points to some potential traps that other countries might want to avoid. One is to avoid giving the privatized firm too many privileges in order to ensure a quick and successful sale. Another is to keep the exclusivity period for long-distance service as short as possible.[39] The greatest gains in Mexico are likely to be realized with the onset of competition. A third pitfall is that of granting price increases entirely independent of improvements in the quality of service, especially for residential users. In this regard, countries should probably strengthen the systems for measuring quality well before privatization is implemented. A fourth lesson is to consider setting up the regulatory agency as an autonomous entity, funded by a levy on the industry, and staffed with well-paid, well-trained experts. Finally, if the government truly wants to maximize its proceeds from privatization, it might want to consider selling control to foreign investors, although in that case the government's influence over the owners will probably be less than it would if control resided in the hands of national investors.[40]

In considering the transferability of the Mexican experience to other developing countries, one must distinguish between industry-specific, firm-specific, and country-specific factors. In terms of the first set of factors, the telecommunications sectors of most developing countries, like that in Mexico, have been plagued by capacity shortages, obsolete technology, and inefficiency but offer enormous potential for growth and upward price adjustments, making them particularly attractive to private investors.

In terms of firm-specific factors, however, TELMEX enjoyed two advantages that may or may not be true of other state-owned telecommunications firms. First, by the standards of the public sector, TELMEX was a fairly well-run company, even though in its last decade as a state firm its performance had begun to deteriorate. Second, it was probably easier to price and sell the firm because, before privatization, its shares were being traded in Mexico and the United States.

In terms of country-specific factors, Mexico had certain advantages that other developing countries may not enjoy. The most important of these was the very strong commitment to privatization and deregulation at the highest levels of the Salinas administration. Without such commitment, implementation would have faltered. Second, senior civil servants in Mexico charged with privatization and economic reform were extremely talented and well trained. Countries without that kind of administrative capacity are likely to find it difficult to privatize and regulate large, monopolistic firms. Third, the private sector in Mexico is sufficiently well developed to buy and run giant enterprises. Countries with weak domestic private sectors may have to rely heavily on foreign investors to privatize the sector. Fourth, there were no legal or constitutional obstacles to turning control over TELMEX to the domestic private sector. And, finally, Mexico's large size and proximity to the United States probably made TELMEX particularly attractive to foreign investors.

Notwithstanding the special circumstances in Mexico, both privatization and deregulation are ideas that many developing countries can adopt for their telecommunications sectors. Other countries also can learn from the experience of countries like Mexico that have pioneered telecommunications privatization. However, the precise strategy used will vary according to national circumstances.

For multinational companies (MNCs), the TELMEX case indicates that the privatization and deregulation trend sweeping the world creates opportunities for profitable growth. For instance, Southwestern Bell's paper profits on its investment in TELMEX in 1991 (around US$1 billion) exceeded its profits from all its operations in the United States. At the same time, these deals carry their risks, such as the need to work in complex partnerships with local companies and other telecommunications MNCs, the likelihood of conflicts with regulators, the possibility of being thrown out once the MNC has transferred some of its expertise to local firms, and the gamble of engaging in a practice (foreign direct investment) that is new for many telecommunications firms (such as the Baby Bells in the United States). However, from the foreign investor's perspective, if the payback period is as short as it was in the Mexican case, the worst-case scenario cannot be very bad, while the best-case scenario can be enormously profitable.

Conclusions

This chapter began with three questions: Why was TELMEX privatized? How were the barriers to its privatization overcome? And what were the consequences of changing its ownership?

The privatization of TELMEX was motivated by several goals. Although improving the firm's performance was among them, in practice it was less important than two other goals: (1) using the privatization of TELMEX to send a signal to local and foreign investors that Mexico was embarking on a new economic strategy, and (2) using the sale proceeds to reduce the country's fiscal deficit and public indebtedness. From the government's point of view, TELMEX was an attractive candidate for early privatization because of its relatively good performance and attractive future prospects, not because of its relatively poor performance and dismal future.

Even though Mexican policymakers may have wanted to use privatization to improve TELMEX's performance, when push came to shove, they had to compromise on that goal in order to sell the company. Once the government had publicly committed to privatizing TELMEX, it became imperative for those charged with implementing the policy to make sure the sale was a "success," which came to mean selling the firm quickly, for a good price, to qualified buyers. Failing to find a buyer for TELMEX or selling at a low price would have embarrassed the Salinas government, invited charges of corruption and incompetence, and potentially derailed the new government's economic reform program. Therefore, the privatizers had to make TELMEX very attractive to potential buyers, even at the risk of giving the firm too much protection or too many privileges. Consequently, TELMEX was sold intact rather than in parts, it was granted hefty, unconditional price increases before privatization, it was granted exclusive rights for long-distance service for six years, it was granted the only national license for cellular service, and so on. The government also minimized the risk that inflation would erode the firm's prices, that competition would eat into future margins, that the government could administratively expropriate future profits, or that the buyers could be ousted by corporate raiders. The result was a package offering very high returns and relatively low risks—in short, TELMEX was a plum.

Does this mean that the privatization of TELMEX was nothing more than the transfer of a stream of rents from the state to the private sector? The answer is a clear no. Privatization made a real difference but not necessarily for the reasons one might have expected.

To be sure, private ownership produced significant internal changes, especially by way of cost reduction and improvements in labor productivity. Yet the TELMEX experience points to two important aspects of privatization. First, some of the internal improvements that followed privatization would probably not have occurred if certain changes in the competitive and regulatory environments had not also occurred. Conversely, many of those changes in the competitive environment and in regulation would probably not have occurred without privatization. Thus, the real significance of privatization lies not so much in its direct effects but in its subtler interactions with competition policy and regulation (see figure 1-1).

For instance, the post-privatization increase in labor productivity almost certainly would not have occurred without privatization. But even with private ownership, this might not have occurred in the same degree if the government had used the rate-of-return method of price regulation rather than the *RPI–X* method, which offered the incentive to reduce costs without fear of expropriation by regulators.

Among the regulatory reforms that might not have been made without privatization were the raising and rebalancing of prices or the preparation of a new comprehensive concession agreement. Senior Mexican officials maintain that the long overdue price adjustments, especially for local service to residential users, would not have been possible without privatization. Whether or not one agrees with this assertion, it illustrates the linkages that exist between ownership and regulation. So does the assertion that a comprehensive concession agreement containing promises on behalf of the government and commitments on behalf of the new owners would not have worked if the state were both owner and regulator of the telephone company. Thus, in the short run at least, privatization improved the quality of regulation of the sector.

However, all the indirect effects of privatization were not positive. As discussed earlier, in the short run, privatization froze out competition to a greater extent than would have been the case if TELMEX had remained state owned because of the need to make it a plum for investors. On the other hand, in the longer term, privatization will result in more competition in the sector because the government's threat of introducing competition in basic services in 1996 is more credible both to TELMEX and to potential entrants because the government is no longer a direct participant in the industry.

From a theoretical standpoint, the main conclusion from the TELMEX case study is that ownership, competition, and regulation are not independent policy variables but a set of loosely connected tools whose important interactions are only beginning to be understood.

NOTES

The author is grateful to several people in Mexico who helped with this research. Among them were Dr. Jacques Rogozinski, formerly head of the Privatization Unit, Secretariat of Finance and Public Credit; Joaquin Munõz and Emilio Carillio Gamboa, former CEOS of TELMEX; Carlos Casasús, former finance director of TELMEX; Adolfo Cerezo, Carlos Kauachi Kauachi, and Oscar de Leon of TELMEX; Jorge Silberstein of the Secretariat of Finance and Public Credit; Carlos Mier y Teran and Laura Elisa of the Secretariat of Communications and Transport; Richard Atterbury, president of Southwestern Bell International Holdings; Christian Chauvin, president of France Cables et Radio de Mexico; Raul Robledo of Banco Internacional; and Gabriel Martinez of the Secretariat of Commerce and Industrial Development. Most interviewees requested anonymity and are, therefore, not cited by name.

1. Although Argentina's privatization program under President Menem paralleled Mexico's and was even more ambitious in scope, Mexico's state firms were bigger in size and were privatized with more sophistication, making Mexico, more than Argentina, a model for other developing countries.

2. The value of the hundreds of state enterprises privatized by the Miguel de la Madrid administration (1982–88) was only US$471.2 million (see "Salinas Privatization" 1992).

3. For a more detailed description of the context within which the TELMEX privatization occurred, see Ramamurti 1993.

4. External pressure from foreign debtors and international agencies like the World Bank and the IMF seems to have been an important reason why many developing countries pursued privatization in the 1980s; see Ramamurti 1992.

5. World Bank official, interview with author, Washington, D.C., August 1994.

6. An internal report of the World Bank notes that "in this [telecommunications] program, the Bank clearly followed what the Mexican Government had already under way and provided, through consultants, some technical advice on specific issues and was able to establish a high-level dialogue on the general nature of the reforms."

7. In 1988, TELMEX was the only Mexican stock trading in the United States.

8. What these numbers do not reveal is that getting a faulty line repaired within three to four days still required numerous visits and complaints as well as the payment of bribes to TELMEX employees.

9. In all these areas, TELMEX was the only licensed provider of service.

10. It was by "loaning" the proceeds from the telephone service tax to the

privately owned TELMEX that the government began to acquire control over the firm. Subsequently, much of that debt was converted to preferred stock, on which TELMEX paid a tax-deductible dividend. In 1972, those shares were turned into common shares, giving the government a controlling interest in TELMEX.

11. Although first introduced in 1981, optical fiber accounted for less than 1 percent of the transmission capacity in 1990.

12. In his retrospective view of the TELMEX privatization, Tandon (1994) reaches the conclusion that the sale of TELMEX played a part in reversing Mexico's economic malaise.

13. The quote is from Haggard and Webb (1993, 159), who are paraphrasing Rodrik (1989). They go on to say, "When a program is implemented slowly, confidence in it deteriorates as anticipated benefits fail to emerge. The government retreats with its credibility diminished and in the next round must take even bolder action to signal its commitment."

14. In the 1990s, with governments scrambling for funds, a capital-intensive industry was an attractive candidate for privatization, unlike in the 1950s and 1960s, when the same industry would have been ripe for nationalization. See, for instance, Jones and Mason (1982), who argue that state-owned enterprises tend to be in significantly more capital-intensive industries than private firms.

15. In 1982, banks were added to the list of sectors reserved for the state in the country's constitution (along with oil, nuclear power, electricity, telegraph, and satellite communications). Therefore, denationalizing banks would require a constitutional amendment, which could take an unpredictable amount of time.

16. Our reason for considering deficit reduction a less important goal than the signaling investors is the fact that Salinas continued to privatize enterprises even after the budget deficit had turned into a surplus.

17. The 12 percent rate is based on an internal report produced by TELMEX in 1988–89.

18. According to former and current directors of TELMEX interviewed by the author, at least 30 percent of the company's workforce was redundant, especially telephone operators.

19. For instance, management had to select people to fill openings at the worker level from slates drawn up by the union.

20. In 1988, the Mexican government had overcome union resistance to the restructuring of the national airline, Aeromexico, by filing for bankruptcy and creating a new firm, which bought the old firm's assets and rehired a third of the original workforce (see chapter 8).

21. Hernández was rumored to be interested in becoming the next head of Mexico's largest labor federation. Given the ruling party's power and influence over all aspects of society, including labor unions, Salinas's support could propel his career forward. In retrospect, that theory was supported by Juárez's growing influence in the Mexican labor movement after 1990.

22. Shares reserved for the state were designated AA and had to account for at least 51 percent of total equity at all times, as per the bylaws adopted when TELMEX became a state-controlled enterprise in 1972.

23. Tandon 1994, notes that this "transfer" would continue indefinitely into the future.

24. If TELMEX had been divided geographically, the southern part would have been much less attractive to buyers than the northern part, which was booming.

25. For technical reasons, cellular service had to be a duopoly, and in this segment, as noted earlier, TELMEX was the only firm with a national license.

26. According to Gillick (1992, 730), in 1989, the BT formula was changed to $RPI - 4.5$ percent; in 1991, to $RPI - 6.25$ percent; and in 1993 to $RPI - 7.5$ percent.

27. For a discussion of foreign investment in the telecommunications sector, see Thompson 1992.

28. Had this been allowed, L. M. Ericsson de Mexico (Sweden) or Alcatel de Mexico (France) might have been very interested, since both already had plants in Mexico that had supplied almost all of TELMEX's past requirements for equipment.

29. For a more detailed discussion of the foreign investor's motivations, see chapter 12.

30. Until August 1993, a representative of the SCT was to serve on TELMEX's board. In addition, the government was allowed to nominate one director as long as it owned 5 percent or more in nonvoting stock.

31. The calculations are based on average salaries and benefits per employee of more than US$30,000 in 1993.

32. Switching and other equipment supplied by the two Mexican suppliers, Alcatel and Ericsson, accounted for about 30 percent of TELMEX's annual capital spending of US$2.2 billion. A 20–25 percent reduction in their prices translates into an annual savings of about US$150 million.

33. Note that we are exploring here how privatization affected the status of competition in the industry, not the impact of competition on TELMEX's performance.

34. For instance, McKinsey & Co. conducted a detailed assessment of future growth possibilities, including the effect of pricing on demand for various services by various types of customers.

35. The U.K. experience indicates that an effective regulatory agency will be small, well-staffed, and autonomous. Comparing the U.K.'s Office of Telecommunications with the Federal Communications Commission in the United States, Gillick (1992) notes that the former had a staff of 134 and a budget of US$12 million, compared with a staff of 1,795 and a budget of US$116 million in the latter.

36. Banco Internacional and Bolsa Mexicana de Valores, interviews with author, Mexico City, May 1994.

37. TELMEX officials, interviews with author, Mexico City, May 1994.

38. In the Mexican case, the privatizers seem to have begun planning for TELMEX's privatization soon after Salinas took office, even though the president's public announcement was made nine months later. Therefore, Mexican privatizers had more time to prepare than one would think at first glance. On the Argentine experience, see chapter 4.

39. When Peru privatized its telephone company in 1994, the exclusivity

period was only five years, despite the much higher political and economic uncertainties in that country compared to Mexico. Of course, Peru had the advantage of riding on the coattails of the Mexican and Venezuelan telecommunications privatizations.

40. Mexican officials interviewed observed consistently that local investors understand better the government's compulsions, have a greater commitment to the long-term welfare of the firm, are more amenable to government influence because of other investments in the country, and are more likely to reinvest their profits in Mexico.

REFERENCES

Ambrose, William, Paul R. Hennemeyer, and Jean-Paul Chapon. 1990. *Privatizing Telecommunications Systems: Business Opportunities in Developing Countries.* Discussion Paper 10. Washington, D.C.: World Bank.

"Amendment to the Concession of Teléfonos de México, S.A. de C.V. 1990." 1990. Official English translation. Mexico City.

Austin, James E., Lawrence Wortzel, and Jeffrey F. Coburn. 1986. "Privatizing State-Owned Enterprises: Hopes and Realities." *Columbia Journal of World Business* 21 (3): 51–60.

Baring Securities. 1991. *Teléfonos de México: Mexico's Telecommunications Giant.* Boston.

Gillick, David. 1992. "Telecommunications Policies and Regulatory Structures: New Issues and Trends." *Telecommunications Policy* 16 (9): 726–31.

Goldman, Sachs, & Co. et al. 1992. *Prospectus for Teléfonos de México S.A. de C.V.* New York.

Haggard, Stephen, and Steven B. Webb. 1993. "What Do We Know about the Political Economy of Economic Policy Reform?" *World Bank Research Observer* 8 (2): 143–68.

Jones, Leroy P., and Edward Mason. 1982. "Role of Economic Factors in Determining the Size and Structure of Public Enterprises in Developing Countries." In *Public Enterprise in Less-Developed Countries,* ed. Leroy P. Jones, with Richard Mallon, Edward S. Mason, Paul N. Rosenstein-Rodan, and Raymond Vernon. Cambridge: Cambridge Univ. Press.

Kneale, Dennis. 1993. "Bell Atlantic Will Invest $1.04 Billion for 42 Percent of Mexican Cellular Concern." *Wall Street Journal,* Oct. 12.

Moffett, Matt. 1992. "Teléfonos de México Makes a Promising Start on a Daunting Task." *Wall Street Journal,* Feb. 19.

Nellis, John. 1991. "Contract Plans: A Review of International Experience." In *Privatization and Control of State-Owned Enterprises,* ed. Ravi Ramamurti and Raymond Vernon. Washington, D.C.: World Bank.

Ramamurti, Ravi. 1992. "Why Are Developing Countries Privatizing?" *Journal of International Business Studies* 23 (2): 225–49.

———. 1993. "Teléfonos de México: The Privatization Decision (A) and (B)." *Case Research Journal* 13 (2): 43–67.

Rodrik, Dani. 1989. "Promises, Promises: Credible Policy Reform via Signalling." *Economic Journal* (Journal of the Royal Economic Society) 99 (Sept.): 756–72.

"Salinas Privatization Yields 20.3 Billion Dollars." 1992. Notimex (Mexican News Service), Dec. 30.

Sappington, D. E. M., and J. E. Stiglitz. 1987. "Privatization, Information, and Incentives." *Journal of Policy Analysis and Management* 6 (4): 567–82.

SCT (Secretariat of Communications and Transport). 1976. *Concession Agreement for Teléfonos de México.* Mexico City: Director General of Telecommunications.

Tandon, Pankaj. 1994. "Teléfonos de México." In *Welfare Consequences of Selling Public Enterprises: Case Studies from Chile, Malaysia, Mexico, and the U.K.*, ed. Ahmed Galal, Leroy P. Jones, Pankaj Tandon, and Ingo Vogelsang. New York: Oxford Univ. Press.

Thompson, Samme. 1992. "Telecommunications Privatizations and International Capital Markets." *Telecommunications Policy* 16 (9): 732–37.

Vickers, John, and George Yarrow. 1988. *Privatization: An Economic Analysis.* Cambridge: MIT Press.

World Bank. 1993. *Mexico: Road Transport and Telecommunications Sector Adjustment Loan Project Completion Report.* Report 12623, Country Operations Division I, Latin America and the Caribbean Regional Office. Washington, D.C.: World Bank.

4. Telephone Privatization in a Hurry

ARGENTINA

. . . .

Ben Petrazzini

On September 3, 1946, foreign private companies were forced to sell their telecommunications firms in Argentina to the country's government, headed by Juan D. Perón. Forty-four years later, on November 8, 1990, another Peronist government, this one headed by Carlos Menem, sold the state telephone monopoly back to foreign investors.

Although telecommunications sector reform spread globally beginning in the late 1980s, its roots and outcomes differed from country to country. In industrialized countries, restructuring arose mainly to satisfy the needs of corporate users, who became increasingly aware that cheap, sophisticated, and reliable telecommunications services were vital for global operations in an information economy. In developing countries, changes in the sector were generally part of economic adjustment programs aimed at improving the government's fiscal position and the country's economic growth.[1] In Latin America, Argentina was the third country, after Chile and Jamaica, to carry out a sweeping privatization of its state-owned enterprises. After failed attempts by previous administrations to sell some of the government's larger enterprises, the government of Carlos Menem, in 1990, transferred to the private sector the first large public utility, Empresa Nacional de Telecommunicaciones (ENTel). This first stage of the Argentine privatization occurred at a time of economic turmoil and political instability. Hyperinflation and opposition to the program affected the pace and nature of the reform, as reflected in the compressed sales timetable, the purchase price, the inability to open the Argentine telecommunications market to competition, and the initial tariff levels.

This chapter examines the emergence of the Argentine telecommunications industry, its performance under state ownership, and the forces leading to its hasty privatization in 1990. It also examines the bargaining process, the impact of that process on each segment of the market, and the government's policies toward deregulation and competition. Finally, the chapter assesses the consequences of ENTel's privatization on consumers, workers, and investors.

Background

As with many other developing countries, Argentina's telecommunications needs were initially provided by branches of foreign-owned telephone companies. Thus, the roots of the telecommunications industry were both foreign and private.

The Era of Private Foreign Ownership

The nationalization of Argentine telecommunications in 1946 ended more than sixty-eight years of private control. The country's first telephone connection was made in Buenos Aires on February 12, 1878, by two Argentinians who pioneered the construction of the first Argentine telephone system based on descriptions of Alexander Graham Bell's invention (figure 4-1)[2] The production, installation, and operation of the telephone system were totally in Argentine hands until 1881, when foreign corporations competed for a place in Argentina's emerging market. Only three (one Belgian, one British, and one American) survived competition in the incipient, unregulated market. Ferocious competition among the companies, including the physical destruction of installed equipment, led them to seek an accord, and by 1882, they had merged into the Unión Telefónica (UT).[3] The UT put the only Argentine-owned company out of business and became an unregulated private monopoly.[4] After the first year of operation, the UT's prices rose while service declined. In 1887, consumers, upset with the poor quality and high prices, created the Sociedad Cooperativa Telefónica. By offering similar services but at lower prices, the Sociedad grew and rapidly expanded its penetration. Within two years, of the 9,097 users, 6,731 were still with the UT, while 2,366 had signed up with the Sociedad.

In the mid-1920s, International Telephone and Telegraph (ITT) entered the Argentine market at a time when the Sociedad was facing financial problems. With huge capital investments that enabled it to provide improved service, ITT quickly attracted many customers and was able to purchase the troubled Sociedad in 1927 and the UT in 1929. The new company continued its operations under the UT name.

The lack of federal regulations enforcing universal service coupled with the profit motive of the private companies resulted in a concentra-

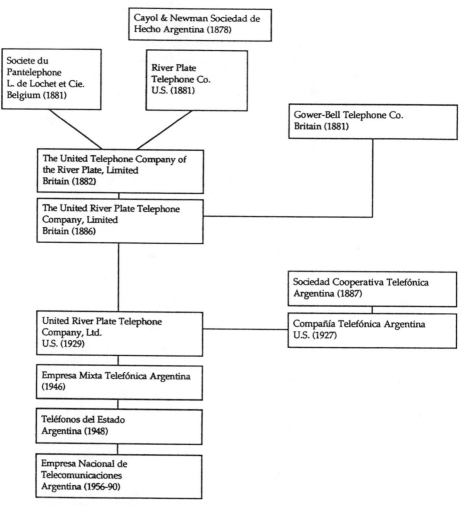

Figure 4-1. The Corporate History of ENTel.
Source: Tesler (1990).

tion of service in the Buenos Aires region and left much of the rest of
Argentina without telephones. In response, two systems developed during the 1920s: a private one under the control of the Swedish telephone
company, Ericsson, and a public one in the form of local cooperatives,
which operated in those areas where Ericsson chose not to participate.
By 1941, the market had grown to nearly half a million subscribers served
by forty-three companies.[5]

As early as the 1930s, the sector had grown complex and politically sensitive enough to trigger government concern. In 1936, Presidential Decree 91698/36 signaled the initiation of state intervention and the regulation of Argentine telecommunications. At that time, the UT was charging extra for connections and certain services while disconnecting customers who did not comply. The government declared the charges illegal and required the UT to reduce its rates and reconnect those customers who had been cut off. However, the government was too weak institutionally and politically to coerce the company to obey, and the UT continued its illegal operations until 1939, when it was forced to change its practices by an order of the country's supreme court.

The Origins of State Ownership

The scenario shifted radically in 1945 when a new populist government, led by General Juan D. Perón, launched a decade of state expansion and intervention in the domestic economy. On September 3, 1946, the government bought the assets and controlling shares of the UT, which were still owned by ITT. A few days later, Congress ratified the decision with the promulgation of Law 12864.[6] President Perón explained the logic for the acquisition of the telephone company as follows: "Telephone and telegraph services are essential for the economy and the defense of the country. They constitute the nervous system of the nation. It was an anachronism, [and] it was incompatible with [the] sentiments of national sovereignty and the level of domestic development, that this nervous system was not the property of the Argentine nation" (Donikian et al. 1990, 31).

Initially, ownership was mixed, with the government, employees, and local private investors holding interests in the firm, which operated as Empresa Mixta Telefónica de Argentina (ETMA). Parallel with the industry's economic and defense role, a new conception developed of telecommunications as a public service requiring the close supervision of the state.[7] A few months after ETMA began operations, Perón attacked the company's private investors, arguing that they were interested only in political control and not in contributing financial resources for the development of telecommunications. With the justification that telephones were "an essential public service," the government nationalized the company on March 18, 1948, under the name of Teléfonos del Estado.[8] From 1948 to 1952, the state bought and incorporated into Teléfonos del Estado a variety of public and privately owned telecommunications companies operating in the interior of the country.[9] By 1969, thirty-one private companies had been incorporated into the state enterprise. In 1956 Teléfonos del Estado changed its name to Empresa Nacional de Telecommunicaciones (ENTel), which continued to expand its operations nationwide. By the early 1970s, it controlled 92 percent of the market.[10]

Table 4-1. ENTEL Performance, 1950–1990

Year	Number of Lines Installed (thousands)	Number of Lines in Service (thousands)	Annual Average Growth (%)[1]	Number of Employees	Lines/ 100 People
1950	701	—	—	—	—
1960	1,074	—	5.32	—	—
1970	1,481	—	3.78	—	—
1976	1,808	1,678	3.67	—	6.8
1977	1,825	1,692	0.94	—	6.7
1978	1,901	1,728	4.16	—	6.9
1979	2,102	1,797	10.50	—	7.5
1980	2,205	1,879	4.90	—	7.8
1981	2,341	1,992	6.16	45,761	8.1
1982	2,492	2,124	6.45	45,441	8.5
1983	2,550	2,245	2.32	47,833	8.6
1984	2,601	2,357	2.00	48,158	8.6
1985	2,699	2,462	3.76	47,088	8.8
1986	2,843	2,605	5.33	46,261	9.2
1987	2,917	2,711	2.60	46,876	9.3
1988	3,264	2,858	11.89	46,857	10.3
1989	3,437	3,057	5.30	46,040	10.7
1990	3,458	3,096	0.61	42,908	10.8

Source: SIGEP (1983–90).

[1] Lines installed compared to previous year.

— = not available.

ENTel's Performance under State Ownership

From the mid-1940s to the mid-1950s, an official policy of infrastructure development quickly expanded the number of lines. The expansion of the network slowed during the 1960s and into the mid-1970s, with an average of 46,520 new lines installed each year, but it speeded up again from 1979 to 1988, when an average of 147,400 lines were installed annually. Despite this uneven network development, the 3.4 million installed lines in 1989 gave Argentina an average of 10.7 lines per 100 inhabitants (table 4-1), which was quite low compared with some developed countries but was much higher than the Latin American average in 1990 of 6.7 lines per 100 inhabitants (ITU 1992).[11] However, Argentina's main telecommunications problem was not so much the number of lines in service but the quality of service and the company's overall performance. Although it could be argued that ENTel's continuing decay was an inescapable part of Argentina's economic deterioration, the company management's poor commercial and entrepreneurial spirit was undeniably a factor. As a public service that served a variety of social, political, and economic goals, telecommunications was never viewed as a business that ought to turn a profit.

The management of the company was strongly tied to domestic politics and, hence, to the country's political pendulum. The chief exec-

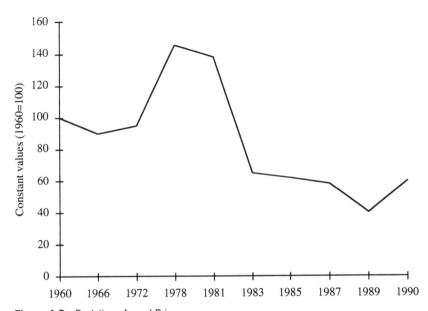

Figure 4-2. Evolution of ENTel Prices.
Source: SIGEP, cited in Hill and Abdala (1993).

utive and other senior managers were appointed by the Argentine president and were vulnerable to waves of political change that periodically swept the political scene. From the late 1950s to the late 1980s, twenty-eight different executive directors headed ENTel under twelve different presidents.[12] And government agencies often issued policies that contradicted one another. For example, the Ministry of Economy set ENTel's budget, the Ministry of Labor set salaries, the Secretariat of Industry made equipment purchasing decisions, the Secretariat of Communication crafted telecommunications policies, and the Ministry of Services and Public Works decided on broader public service policies—not to mention the fact that often the Ministry of Economy or the country's president set telephone tariffs based on the political needs of the moment. Furthermore, ENTel's high degree of politicization adversely affected its pricing structure, thus denying it funds for expansion and maintenance of the system. Its tariff structure and revenue mechanisms were designed to meet social needs, to subsidize welfare programs or industrial development programs, to control inflation, and so forth. Tariffs fell in real terms throughout the 1980s, with a steep fall after the mid-1980s. In August 1989, tariffs reached their lowest point since 1960, dropping 830 percent in real terms from the same month in the previous year (see figure 4-2 and table 4-2).

Tariffs set on political grounds and insensitive to cost indicators or

Table 4-2. ENTel Local and Domestic Long-Distance Charges, January 1988–December 1992

Date	Charges (1992 pesos/minute)	
	Local	Domestic Long Distance
January 1988	0.0156	0.3634
July 1988	0.0201	0.4683
January 1989	0.0188	0.4380
July 1989	0.0030	0.0699
January 1990	0.0117	0.2726
July 1990	0.0204	0.4753
November 1990	0.0280	0.6524
March 1991	0.0268	0.6244
July 1991	0.0233	0.5428
January 1992	0.0217	0.5056
July 1992	0.0202	0.4706
December 1992	0.0196	0.4566

Source: ENTel, Telefónica, and Telecom.

profit criteria had a considerable impact on ENTel's financial performance. While the company had showed a profit ever since the mid-1940s, low tariffs, high taxes, and the rapid expansion of debt due to exchange rate fluctuations left ENTel operating in the red for most of the 1980s (table 4-3).[13] The fiscal crisis of the 1980s and the subsequent sharp reduction of foreign loans to Latin American countries eliminated a key financial resource, damaging even further the company's ability to operate and expand. In 1985, for example, 90 percent of the company's debt was in foreign currency; by 1989, while the total debt had reached US$1.2 billion, the share of foreign loans was still 51 percent of the total (SIGEP 1990, 10).

Economic constraints and the lack of development plans resulted in a long waiting list for telephone connection. While the waiting list for new connections in 1941 stood at an equivalent of 2.2 percent of customers with telephone service, that proportion jumped to 29 percent in 1946, and to a steady average of approximately 40 percent throughout the 1960s and 1970s. During those years some customers waited twelve to fourteen years for telephone installation. Moreover, many never even bothered to sign up. In 1985, a new expansion program called Megatel was established, under which customers financed the installation of new lines by paying connection charges in advance. During the three years following this plan, the waiting list fell to 24 percent of those with telephone service.[14] By 1990, when the company was privatized, the average time for new connections had dropped sharply but was still an unacceptable four years.

Unfortunately, in the late 1980s, although the waiting list shrank, so

Table 4-3. ENTel Financial Indicators, 1956–1990
(millions of 1992 pesos)

Year	Annual Sales	Net Profit after Taxes	Revenue/ Line	Rate of Investment
1956–60	117.52[1]	34.94	138.76[2]	—
1961–65	156.99	48.11	149.73	—
1966–70	179.95	57.73	150.74	—
1971–75	242.07	21.43	159.02	—
1976	323.11	2.36	138.25	—
1977	321.08	79.17	189.74	—
1978	379.99	159.86	219.96	—
1979	317.53	58.07	176.74	—
1980	330.70	31.90	176.07	—
1981	360.41	-8.77	180.96	—
1982	306.73	-350.79	144.33	—
1983	276.85	-367.50	123.40	—
1984	325.63	-591.18	138.08	—
1985	392.15	-221.81	159.35	—
1986	396.37	-113.77	152.10	—
1987	334.92	-138.08	122.89	350
1988	210.32	10.24	—	450
1989	181.46	-292.57	—	250
1990	—	—	—	270

Source: ENTel, SIGEP, and Fucade.

[1] Data for previous years were, 1946–50 (71.23), 1951–55 (105.84).

[2] Data for previous years were, 1946–50 (143.32), 1951–55 (151.76).

— = not available.

did the quality of service. With network equipment dating from the 1930s, a rapid shrinkage of maintenance crews, and few new investments, half of local calls and three-quarters of long-distance calls failed to go through.[15] In 1989, 46.6 percent of the lines were out of service, requiring an average of approximately eleven days to be fixed (ENTel 1990). The maintenance staff was reduced by more than 40 percent in the 1980s, while administrative and executive positions rose by 35 percent. And compared to the workers-to-lines ratio of leading companies in the world, ENTel was considerably overstaffed. This excess of labor led to poor productivity by international standards (table 4-4). In 1981, for example, there were fifty-one installed lines per employee. Following a hiring freeze in 1985 and an increase in the number of connected lines, the ratio improved by 1989 to 75 lines per employee.[16]

During the 1980s, ENTel's labor force fluctuated around 47,000 employees. Most were affiliated with one of four labor unions, which strongly influenced ENTel's management and operation: they negotiated contracts for all employees, participated in the purchase of new technologies, and influenced the selection of personnel.[17] Unions also won ENTel employees a reduced working week of only thirty-five

Table 4-4. Performance of Six Telecommunications Companies, 1989

Company	Number of Lines (millions)	Number of Employees	Lines/ Employee	Lines/ 100 People
Southwestern Bell (U.S.)	12.11	58,190	208	50
France Telecom	26.98	156,451	173	48
British Telecom	25.01	245,700	102	44
TELMEX (Mexico)	5.27	49,518	105	6
CTC (Chile)	0.68	7,500	91	6
ENTel (Argentina)	3.44	46,040	75	11

hours. Equipment acquisition and network development were also affected by politics. Each new government canceled existing contracts and negotiated new ones with new providers.[18] It was widely believed that ENTel paid up to three times the international price for hardware, with obvious payoffs for the companies, their managers, and government officials.[19]

In the year and a half prior to privatization, several of ENTel's performance indicators worsened sharply. For example, the number of out-of-service customer lines increased by 65 percent. Most installation and connection projects suffered delays that exceeded historic averages, and the number of new lines installed in 1990 fell sharply. Finally, the debt of the company jumped from US$1.29 billion in December 1989 to US$2.14 billion a year later (SIGEP 1990).

Some argue that the company's deteriorating performance resulted from a conscious decision of the government to prove to the public that ENTel needed to be privatized. Others argue that ENTel's managers were preoccupied with privatization negotiations and failed to give adequate attention to day-to-day operations. Performance may have also declined because workers and second-level managers opposed privatization and did not cooperate with the newly appointed administration. Whatever the reason, the erosion of the company's performance affected privatization in two significant ways. First, it reduced the interest of potential buyers in ENTel and lowered the price received for the company. Second, it led the government to set "easy" targets for the new owners in the postprivatization period.

Early Privatization Attempts

The military regime that governed the country between 1976 and 1983 made the first attempts to reduce the state's role in the economy.[20] Laying the blame for poor economic performance on an overextended state, the military regime developed a reform program that set privatization of key state enterprises as a goal. But long-standing struggles among government factions drove the project to a dead end. The state remained virtually intact and even expanded its economic and social role in this period (Boneo 1985, 31). The devastating 1982 economic crisis and military defeat in the Malvinas (Falkland) war marked the beginning of the end for the military regime.

In 1983, a new democratic government headed by Raúl R. Alfonsín of the Radical Party took office. While initiating a new set of welfare policies, this government also announced a plan to "rationalize" the state. From 1985 to 1987, a variety of small companies were reprivatized.[21] In the telecommunications sector, structural economic factors played an important role in setting in motion reform programs. But the pressure for reform came not only from structural conditions but also from concrete demands from certain sectors of the Argentine business community. The banking sector was particularly involved in demanding regulatory reforms that would allow them to establish private data and voice services in the area of Buenos Aires, where most financial institutions are located. In March 1988 a group of fourteen private firms announced the creation of Privatel, a telecommunications company that, with the technical support of Bell South International, would serve the needs and demands of the business sector. This initiative, which never flourished, came at the same time that the government announced the signing of an agreement with Telefónica de España for the partial privatization of ENTel.

In the early stages of the state reform program, when the government sold small companies that were facing financial problems, there was no opposition to the official plan. However, when the government announced plans to sell two of the largest state enterprises—ENTel and Aerolíneas Argentinas—the Peronist Party, the unions, and local telecommunications equipment suppliers successfully blocked further reforms in the public sector. The lack of strong official commitment to the project also weakened support from domestic private capital, thereby strengthening the opposition forces. When the next president, Carlos Menem of the Peronist Party, took power in July 1989, ENTel was still owned by the state, under the same organizational and regulatory status that it had in 1983.

ENTel's Privatization under Menem

Carlos Menem's election rhetoric appealed to traditional Peronist values, which called for a central role for the state. Yet, upon stepping into office, he implemented a very different agenda, of which privatization was a core policy.[22] In September 1989, the president formally announced that telecommunications would be the first large public utility to be put on the auction block. The government's main goal was to "demonopolize and deregulate telecommunications services to make them more efficient for the benefit of the users" (Decree 731/89; see Argentina 1989). Despite this official claim of pragmatic efficiency, it was widely accepted that the underlying forces driving privatization were macroeconomic in nature. Argentina was confronting its worst-ever hyperinflation, a deepening fiscal crisis, negative economic growth, and the prospects of social disruption. Prices rose 75.5 percent in May, 174.5 percent in June, and reached an unprecedented 196.6 percent in July, the month in which Menem came to power. Real wages for industrial workers dropped by as much as 42.5 percent compared to the same period in the previous year, while unemployment rose to 7.7 percent. In the second quarter of 1989, GDP fell by 9.5 percent, while the public sector deficit stood at an estimated 10 percent of GDP.

In an effort to maintain control, Menem put together a coalition of powerful social actors. Against all expectations, he appointed as minister of economy—the key political position in the country next to the president—a top executive of the largest Argentine multinational corporation. Under this new leadership, privatization regained momentum and flourished. In the telecommunications sector, Menem appointed as ENTel's *interventora* Maria Julia Alsogaray, one of the most outspoken and active representatives of the Unión de Centro Democrático (UCD).[23] A privatization team was formed with UCD members and other individuals personally connected to Ms. Alsogaray. At the same time, three consulting commissions—one economic, one legal, and one technical—were created in the Ministry of Public Works and Services, under the control of minister Roberto Dromi. The economic and legal commissions comprised professionals from the private sector. The technical commission had members from both the private sector and ENTel and collaborated with external consultants on telecommunications reform. Nonetheless, the small team of political appointees, headed by Ms. Alsogaray, took the lead and controlled the process. They became the principal crafters and interlocutors in the sale of ENTel.[24] The minister of economy and the minister of services and public works participated mostly in the concluding phases.[25]

The work of the privatization team was enhanced by the expertise of foreign and local consulting and professional firms. In November 1989, Morgan Stanley & Company and Banco Roberts were appointed as financial advisers; Coopers & Lybrand and Hartenech & Lopez provided technical advice; and Deloitte, Haskins & Sells, Touche & Ross, and Ruival, Otone & Asociados, helped with the financial evaluation of ENTel.[26] A local law firm served as the legal adviser and was responsible for drafting the sale contracts and the regulatory framework—known as *pliegos*. International financial institutions also contributed in a less formal fashion with advice and financial support. The creditor banks, for example, granted in a timely fashion the waiver needed to lift the outstanding mortgages on Argentine state firms, and the World Bank supported the process with strategic advice and some financial support, such as loans to finance the early retirement of some workers.

The Original Plan

The sale of ENTel spearheaded an overarching program to put Argentina on the "fast track" to a private, market economy, and its success was central for the survival of Menem's neoliberal project. As Ramamurti points out in chapter 3, a successful privatization requires a great deal of planning, but in Argentina the new privatization team's mandate was to sell the company in just fourteen months. This small group of new state officials had to quickly develop a plan to demonopolize, liberalize, and deregulate the sector. In 1989, the central administration proposed the following package:

—*Divest ENTel.* The company would be divided into several regional operating companies.

—*Liberalize the telecommunications market.* Value added and international telephone service would be open to competition from the outset.[27] Local basic telephone service would be a protected private monopoly during the first five years following divestiture, but afterward competition would be allowed in all basic services.[28]

—*Attract foreign direct investment.* Sixty percent of the company would be sold to private investors. The remaining 40 percent would be divided among ENTel workers (10%), local telephone cooperatives (5%), and the national and international stock market (25%). ENTel would be sold for cash, with little or no participation of debt-equity swaps.

—*Eliminate subsidization.* The subsidization by long-distance service of local service would be ended, with expansion of the public network being dependent on investment by the new owners. And subsidies to other sectors of the economy, through taxes on telephone services, which stood at 31.58 percent of the tariff, would be terminated.

—*Tailoring the origin and nature of capital.* Efficiency would be achieved by tailoring the conditions for buyers so that only private foreign operating companies with extensive experience in the field could apply. Specifically, the privatization team wanted to exclude European state-owned telephone companies and to attract the Baby Bells of the United States.

To achieve many of the above goals, a major task would be attracting foreign direct investment, which came to be regarded by top state officials as one of the few viable strategies to jump-start Argentina's sinking economy.[29] However, due to political and economic instability, Argen-

tina was regarded as risky by the international financial community, and
ENTel was rated very poorly vis-à-vis other telecommunications companies being privatized around the world.

Menem's privatization team was mindful of the role to be played by
foreign investors in the sale of ENTel and of the threats to foreign investment created by the turbulent domestic political environment. They
were also cognizant that the failure to privatize ENTel would jeopardize
Menem's entire economic program. In the administration's view, the
path to success required (1) the insulation of the process from broad
political participation, while allowing private investors a role in the
design of the privatization, and (2) an offering attractive enough to
override the poor image of the company and the country. Thus, the Menem administration had to overcome potential opposition to privatization and then prepare ENTel for sale.

Overcoming Domestic Opposition

The lesson from the Alfonsín administration was that the government
had to insulate itself from domestic pressure and concentrate power in
the hands of the president.[30] Blocking the participation of opposition
parties and the Argentine Congress was key to this. Profiting from the
weaknesses of the Radical Party and disorientation within his own party,
Menem passed two laws in Congress that became central to the success
of the reform process: the Economic Emergency Law and the Public
Sector Reform Law. The latter, in particular, concentrated power in the
executive branch (Law 23696, art. 9.11; see Argentina 1989). Subsequently, the privatization of ENTel was done almost entirely through
presidential decree. Potential influences from more traditional, welfare-
state-oriented sectors of his own party were blocked by a "protective
belt" of presidential advisers drawn mostly from the UCD and a few
selected Peronists.[31] As the author of state reform and privatization, the
Radical Party was inhibited from resisting the new program.

The labor movement constituted the principal political opposition
to privatization (even though, by the late 1980s, Latin American labor
unions were not as powerful as they once were).[32] President Menem
weakened this opposition by luring some labor leaders into government
positions and marginalizing others. For example, Julio Guillan, the head
of the telephone workers union (FOETRA), was appointed secretary of
communication. Although some groups in the union supported Guillan
in his new position, others strongly opposed what they saw as the coop-
tation of their leadership. Guillan's acceptance of the appointment generated a schism in the telephone workers movement. In August 1990,
when the telephone workers union organized a national strike and dis-

connected Argentina from the world, Menem called in the army to operate the system and fired more than 400 workers.[33] That was labor's last meaningful resistance to ENTel's privatization.

Representatives of domestic and international private capital were on the whole supportive of Menem's new policies. Historically, relations between the business community and the Argentine government had gone through cycles, with business supporting some military and conservative governments while generally opposing President Alfonsín's welfare policies. Business leaders viewed Menem's election as heralding a return to traditional populist policies but were surprised when he chose several prominent figures from the business community to design and implement his new economic program.[34] Thus, in the first year of his administration Menem gathered solid support from powerful national and international actors and weakened the equally powerful domestic opposition.

Restructuring ENTel for Sale

While battling the opposition, the government and the privatization team had to prepare ENTel for sale. The restructuring consisted mainly of crafting new regulations, building a different institutional framework, and reforming the financial practices of the company and the sector in general.

Regulatory and Institutional Restructuring Unlike such privatization in other countries, there was no attempt by the Argentine government to develop a new regulatory framework for the sector prior to the sale of ENTel. Apart from dividing the company into two regional operating entities, no other major legal, administrative, or financial changes were made. The country's constitution, foreign investment law, and national telecommunications law (Law 19798; see Argentina 1972) remained untouched, with the exception of a ruling that any norm that contradicted the *pliegos* or the contracts would be considered invalid. Speed was the main reason for not undertaking any major regulatory or organizational changes.[35]

The Division of ENTel In an effort to build a competitive market in the future, the government proposed breaking ENTel into five regional operating companies, replicating ENTel's five administrative regions.[36] International consultants, however, saw no economic or technical basis for the idea. A new scheme was designed to divide Argentina into a northern, southern, and greater Buenos Aires region (Decree 731/89, art. 2; see Argentina 1989). Feedback from potential international investors, however, revealed that serious bidders were likely only for the Buenos Aires area, in which 59.2 percent of the national traffic was concentrated. Consequently, ENTel was ultimately divided into just two regions. The north included thirteen provinces and the northern part of

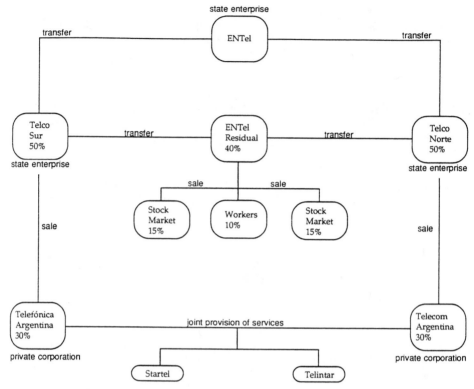

Figure 4-3. ENTel's Divestiture Scheme.

Buenos Aires, and the south included nine provinces and the remainder of Buenos Aires.[37] In the government's view, this was the only way to make ENTel attractive while splitting the company for competitive purposes. The competitive argument was grounded in the notion that, by dividing the company into two regional operating companies, a sort of "competition by comparison" would be created. The government also believed that the existence of two firms would help to develop a competitive environment once the period of exclusivity was over.

The division of ENTel into two regional companies led to the formation of four companies in all (see figure 4-3). Telco Norte would provide basic services to the northern region; Telco Sur would provide basic services to the southern region; Proveedora de Servicios de Valor Agregado, or Startel, would provide all value added services and be jointly owned by the companies that controlled the northern and southern areas; and Servicios Internacionales, or Telintar, would provide national and international long-distance services and would also be jointly owned by the two regional companies. Forty percent of ENTel's shares would remain in the hands of the government—as ENTel Residual—until they were sold in the stock market. The organizational split was accompanied by new legislation that explicitly called for the continued subsidization of local service by long-distance service (Decree 62/90, art. 7.8.5; see Argentina 1990).[38]

Market Liberalization Reflecting the general free-market orientation of the new administration, value added services, domestic services, and international long-distance services were to be opened to third providers. In this way, long-distance and value added services would follow the trend started by equipment providers and cellular telephony. The equipment market was liberalized in 1987, and in 1988 the government granted a license to a telecommunications provider other than ENTel to operate cellular telephone services in one of the two Buenos Aires frequency bands. Basic local telephone service, however, was to remain a monopoly for five years, after which it would be opened to multiple providers (Decree 731/89, art. 10; see Argentina 1989). By December 1989, the government felt confident that it could achieve its goals. Fourteen companies showed interest in acquiring rights for the provision of basic services, and four were potential bidders for international services. But after exploring carefully the economic and political climate of the country, the conditions set by the government, and the unclear and often contradictory regulatory framework, seven companies withdrew from the process.[39]

Witnessing the retreat of prospective buyers in the prequalification stage, the Argentine government realized that it would not be easy to achieve liberalization unless the deal was made more attractive to potential investors. New reforms were introduced to the *pliego,* limiting the competitive outlook of the initial project and preserving a protected market. The five years of exclusivity in basic services was extended to ten years. The first two years were granted for corporate adjustment to the new business environment, the following five years for the operation of the service, and an extension of three years would follow if the companies achieved the goals established by the government. Value added and information services remained open to competition for a short time, but by early 1990, domestic long-distance service and international service were included in the monopoly basket, and only the least profitable services—cellular naval radio communication, national telex, and national data transmission—were open to competition (Decree 62/90, art. 9.11; see Argentina 1990). Cellular telephony and national data transmission were not part of the deal, since they had been liberalized in 1987 and 1988, respectively.[40]

By combining the privatization of ENTel with the broad restructur-

ing of the Argentine telecommunications sector, the fate of most telecommunications services was tied to the bargain. It is unclear whether
or not this was done intentionally in order to offer extra profits to
potential buyers. Nonetheless, in 1993, the privatized companies controlled and monopolized most of Argentina's telecommunications
services.

Financial Restructuring No restructuring of the company's finances
preceded ENTel's sale. The only major financial issues that the government tackled prior to the sale were related to the company's debt, the
initial tariff levels, and the mechanism through which to increase them.
In this sense, Argentina differs somewhat from Mexico.

At the time of privatization, ENTel owed approximately US$2,149
million to domestic and foreign creditors.[41] When Menem came into
office, the company's debt amounted to only US$1,287 million; the other
US$862 million accrued during Alsogaray's administration of ENTel.
Contracts signed with domestic equipment providers for the provision
of lines and switching equipment were a main source of this new debt.[42]
Since the government announced at the beginning of the privatization
process that it would take over all but US$380 million in outstanding
debt, the newly acquired debt actually enhanced the attractiveness of
ENTel in two ways. First, it derailed opposition to privatization by ENTel's
local equipment providers, who were able to clinch new business deals
just before ENTel was divested. Second, it enhanced ENTel's value by
including in the firm's assets a stockpile of expensive telecommunications equipment.

The last and most problematic task was the updating of telephone
tariffs. As in Mexico, at the time of privatization, tariffs were at their
lowest of the decade. To attract foreign investors, tariffs had to be raised
to match or surpass international rates of return.[43] In February 1990, the
government started updating telephone charges by increasing rates for
local and long-distance services by 50 percent in real terms.[44] In April
and July 1990, tariffs in real terms were raised again by 120 percent and
70 percent, respectively.

By November 8, 1990, when ENTel was ready to be sold, the government assumed that the issue of initial tariff levels had been fully settled.
However, the representatives of the winning consortia—Telefónica de
España and STET–France Cables et Radio—threatened to withdraw because, in their view, telephone rates were "insufficient to ensure a profitable operation." The issue quickly became an open struggle between
the government and the foreign companies. The government refused to
allow rates higher than US¢3.8 per pulse, while the potential buyers of
ENTel demanded US¢5.6.[45] The government finally granted an increase of 27 percent over previous charges, bringing the initial tariff

under private operation to approximately US¢4.8 per pulse, a 60 percent increase over the previous monthly rate (see huge increase between July 1989 and November 1990 in figure 4-4). This resulted in particularly high long-distance rates, but, as shown below, the charge for a three-minute local call was still lower in Argentina than in many other countries, including Mexico (figures in U.S. dollars):[46]

Japan	0.08	Germany	0.14
United States	0.10	Britain	0.24
Mexico	0.10	Argentina	0.07
France	0.11		

After the price increase, the head of international services of France Cables et Radio declared happily that "with the tariffs we have negotiated, the project will be profitable from the outset, at the same level as the best telephone companies" (ENTel 1990).

The initial tariff level was not the only crucial issue renegotiated shortly before the transfer. The other was the pricing regime, which had also appeared to be settled. In great haste, the government and the potential owners of ENTel decided on a new mechanism for updating tariffs. Originally, the government adopted a rate-of-return formula that guaranteed future operators a minimum rate of return of 16 percent on a rate base of US$3.2 billion.[47] The rate base was not calculated using ENTel's operating assets but was an artificial number designed to yield US$500 million in profits, a sum deemed necessary to grow and modernize ENTel at a reasonable rate. A valuation by the National Development Bank that set ENTel's assets at US$1.9 billion provided Congress with the required evidence to charge that the rate base was highly inflated. Under pressure from both the opposition parties and his own party, Menem pleased Congress and reduced the rate base from US$3.2 billion to US$1.9 billion.

A few weeks before the transfer of the companies, a new pricing mechanism was agreed to by the government and the new owners. The new regime followed the *RPI − X* model, with supplementary adjustment regulations to compensate for unexpected changes in the levels of the exchange rate and domestic consumer prices. For the first seven years, *X* was set at 2 percent, and if the period of exclusivity was extended to ten years, for the three remaining years *X* would be set at 4 percent.[48] Telephone tariff increases were to be based on the domestic consumer price index, unless the dollar or the domestic consumer prices rose more than 25 percent while the other variable remained fixed. In that case, the new rates were to be adjusted according to a combined formula, with 40 percent based on the dollar and 60 percent based on domestic consumer prices. Abdala (1992, 88) argues that both the

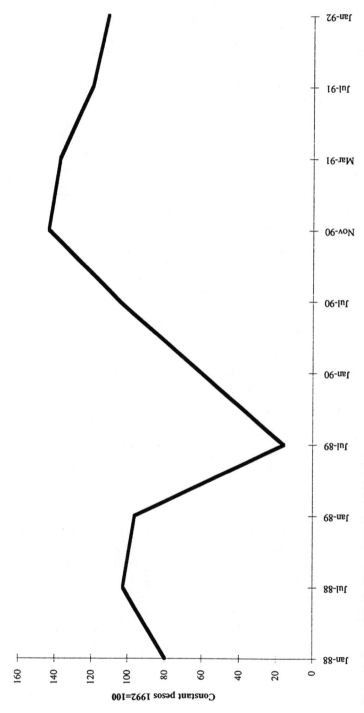

Figure 4-4. ENTEL Tariffs (Selected Months 1988–1992).

companies and the government benefited from the *RPI – X* regime—because after privatization the companies earned an average rate of return on fixed assets of 28.5 percent, and the companies' higher profits meant that the government's tax revenues were also higher. In short, both buyers and the government benefited from the new pricing rules at the expense of consumers.

The new owners enjoyed a further round of tariff increases that was not visible to consumers. Prior to privatization, the state applied a tax on telephone services equivalent to 31.58 percent of the tariff, which was used to finance the national pension fund. Following privatization, the tax was incorporated into the tariffs. Although telephone users scarcely noticed the change, the retired population suffered the loss of an important source of finance. Since the elimination of the tax needed congressional approval, and it was probable that the issue would result in intense controversy, the executive branch reduced the percentage of the tax to 0.001 percent—a reform that could be carried out simply by presidential decree!

Selling ENTel

Selling ENTel called for the resolution of two other issues: the amount to be paid and the terms of payment. Argentina's huge fiscal deficit and desperate need for foreign currency led some state officials to claim initially that they would accept only cash for the company. However, the Ministry of Economy, which was more aware of the sentiments of the international financial community, argued that permitting a debt-equity swap in the first stages of privatization would send a positive signal to international investors. This was the only way to regain credibility abroad and thus open up new lines of foreign credit. By December 1989, it was clear that the Ministry of Economy's view would prevail.[49] With the debt-for-equity swap as the primary method of payment, the government set the following rules for the purchase of 60 percent of each half of ENTel: a minimum of US$214 million in cash,[50] US$380 million in Argentine foreign debt payable over a three-year period, plus as much additional debt as each consortium wished to offer, subject to a floor of US$3.5 billion.

Attracting North American companies was crucial to the government's privatization plan. Aside from the quality of services and technical expertise of U.S. firms, government officials thought that American corporations could offer a better financial deal, while European state-owned telecommunications firms were questionable due to issues of sovereignty and national integrity. Therefore, legislation was written that indirectly excluded state-owned telephone companies from participating in bids. But Argentina was in no condition to be choosy about which foreign investors could buy ENTel. Economic and political conditions in the country as well as the small size and poor features of the Argentine market compared to the twenty-five other telephone companies scheduled for privatization eroded ENTel's attractiveness. Even before the bidding process was begun, it was announced that European state-owned enterprises could participate without any restrictions.

The search for bidders was complicated by the fact that the debt-swap requirement forced international financial institutions into the bidding consortia. The technical and financial requirements for the sale of ENTel led to the formation of bidding consortia that in most cases comprised a foreign telecommunications firm, an international commercial bank, and a local economic group with good political connections.

Initially, various foreign telecommunications companies—including BellSouth, Bell Atlantic, General Telephone and Electronics (GTE), Nynex International, US West, Cititel, Continental Telephone (all U.S. firms), STET (Italy), Telefónica (Spain), Cable & Wireless (England), France Cables et Radio (France), and Siemens (Germany)—showed interest in purchasing ENTel and formed consortia with financial institutions holding Argentine debt. Consortium members were attracted to ENTel for several reasons, including the fact that, as one executive of Bell Atlantic put it, "this was an attractive deal with excellent future profits." For financial institutions, the swap program allowed them to convert shaky debt into more promising equity investments.

In a further effort to lure foreign capital to Argentina, the government sought feedback on the design of the Argentine program from foreign telephone companies and international financial institutions.[51] Unfortunately, this approach boomeranged. Rather than increasing the confidence of potential investors, it generated insecurity and scared away some of the companies that the government most wanted to attract.[52] The desertion of a significant number of telecommunications firms due to the frequent changes in the rules weakened the government's bargaining power and made it a little too willing to accede to the demands of the remaining bidders.

By June 1990, only three of the original bidding consortia remained: one led by Telefónica, another led by STET and France Cables et Radio, and a third led by Bell Atlantic. Of those, the last did not qualify because the *pliegos* required that foreign telephone companies contribute at least 10 percent to the bidding consortium's equity, and Bell Atlantic was barred under U.S. rules from investing more than 4.9 percent. Desperate to accommodate the only remaining American company, the government bent the existing regulations once more and reduced from

10 percent to 4.9 percent the minimum percentage required for a tele-communications company to participate in a bidding consortium. In fact, Bell Atlantic did not contribute any capital to the consortium, since its 4.9 percent participation was in exchange for in-kind contribution as manager of the firm in Argentina.

On June 28, 1990, the Menem administration was finally able to announce that Bell Atlantic had won the bid for the northern area, and Telefónica de España for the southern.[53] But the complex and shifting process of privatization held yet another unpleasant surprise. Bell Atlantic withdrew its bid at the last minute when its financial partner, Manufac-turers Hanover, was unable to acquire the required amount of Argentine debt.[54] Pressed by these unexpected circumstances, the government finally granted the northern region to the STET–France Cables et Radio consortium. Each consortium now controlled 30 percent of the former ENTel, while the remaining 40 percent was divided between ENTel workers (10%), the national and international stock markets (25%), and telephone cooperatives (5%).[55]

The sale brought the Argentine state US$214 million in cash (US$114 million for the south, and US$100 million for the northern region) and US$5.029 billion in debt and interest at face value (Telefónica paid US$2.720 billion and STET–France Cables et Radio paid US$2.309 bil-lion). Based on the price of Argentine debt in the secondary market at the time (approximately 19% of the face value), the total price paid for the company came to US$955 million. Compared to privatized com-panies in other developing countries, Argentina received the lowest price per line in service: Telekom Malaysia realized US$3,357 per line, followed by CANTV of Venezuela with US$2,900 per line, Teléfonos de México with US$1,653 per line, and Telecommunications of Jamaica with US$1,873 per line, while ENTel raised only US$800 per line.

The STET–France Cables et Radio consortium—operating under the commercial name of Telecom Argentina—also included the Morgan Bank and the local economic conglomerate Compañía Naviera Pérez Companc (table 4-5).[56] The southern region was purchased by Com-pañía de Inversiones en Telecomunicaciones (Cointel) and operated by the Telefónica consortium, under the commercial name of Telefónica de Argentina. The consortium comprised Telefónica de España, Citi-bank, and a local company, Techint (table 4-6).[57] After the purchase, Citibank unloaded some of its shares in the international financial market.

In summary, the sale of ENTel brought considerable changes not only in the profile of the telecommunications sector but also in the distribution of wealth in the country. Argentine telecommunications came to be controlled by three foreign companies—which in turn were

Table 4-5. Telecom Argentina and Telefónica de Argentina, Distribution of Shares (percentage)

Company	Percentage of Shares
Initial distribution, Telecom Argentina	
France Cables et Radio	30
STET	30
Compañía Naviera Pérez Companc	30
J. P. Morgan Bank	10
Initial distribution, Telefónica de Argentina	
Citibank	57
Telefónica de España	33
Techint	10
Redistribution of Telefónica de Argentina's shares after privatization	
Citicorp Venture Capital	20.00
Banco Rio (Cayman)	14.56
Telefónica International Holding	10.00
Techint	8.31
Banco Central, S.A. (Spain)	7.04
Comercial del Plata	5.00
Banco Hispano Americano	5.00
Manufacturers Hanover	4.33
Bank of Tokyo	4.16
Bank of New York	4.16
Zurich Ltd.	4.16
APDT	4.03
Arab Banking Co.	3.41
Republic New York Financiera	1.50
Centrobanco (Panama)	1.42
Vanegas Ltd.	1.25
Banco Atlantico, S.A.	0.75
Bank of Nova Scotia	0.60
BFG	0.30

Source: Telefónica de Argentina.

controlled by their home-country governments—with significant partici-pation by equipment suppliers to the former ENTel. ENTel's sale also con-tributed to the further concentration of Argentina's productive system in a small number of hands. As of 1992, for instance, the Pérez Companc group controlled 30 percent of Telecom and, through financial institu-tions such as Banco Rio, controlled another 15.26 percent of Telefónica de Argentina. Indeed, the Pérez Companc group was the largest Argentine buyer of the country's state-owned enterprises, accounting for fully 28.57 percent of the funds raised by the government's privatization program. The Techint conglomerate was the second largest local investor in the privatization program, providing 17.39 percent of the funds raised by the government. Together, the two groups were responsible for buying almost half of all assets sold through privatization.[58]

Table 4-6. Telecom Argentina and Telefónica de Argentina, 1988–1990 Achievements, 1991–1996 Goals

Criterion	1988	1990	1991	1992	1993	1994	1995	1996
Annual network growth (%)	11.9	1.8	4.2	8.2	7.7	6.2	3.7	2.8
Number of additional lines	347,000	63,000	150,052	209,962	306,636	264,274	167,094	135,102
Number of additional public phones	—	—	2,360	3,708	5,962	5,632	4,218	3,924
Local call completion rate (%)	47	49	53	63	70	74	78	85
Long-distance call completion rate (%)	23	30	36	47	60	64	72	80
International call completion rate (%)	—	40	41	42	45	47	50	55
Failure rate/100 lines (%)	—	47	45	43	41	39	35	30
Days to repair faulty line	10	11	10	8.5	7	6	5	3
Installation delay (months)	—	48	36	24	12	8	6	4

Source: Decree 677/90 issued April 11, 1990. Boletín Oficial de la Republica Argentina, Buenos Aires, Argentina.

— = not available.

The New Structure of the Argentine Telecommunications Sector

ENTel, like TELMEX in Mexico and CANTV in Venezuela, was transferred to private owners on the condition that a variety of expansion and quality goals would be met after privatization (Decree 62/90, art. 10.1.8; see Argentina 1990). However, those goals were widely criticized for their laxity (see table 4-6).[59] Compared to Mexico, for example, Argentine requirements were extremely modest. While Mexico required a network growth of at least 12 percent a year in the first four years after privatization, Argentina required a growth rate of only 6.5 percent—dropping to 2.8 percent in the period from 1995 to 1996. While Mexico aimed to reduce the line failure rate to 5 percent by 1996, Argentina set a goal of 35 percent for 1995! While Mexico set a maximum delay of six months for new connections by 1994, the target in Argentina was eight months. While Mexico required the installation of digital networks in twenty-two cities and the construction of a 9,000-mile fiber-optic network, Argentina did not explicitly set any targets for digitization. And, finally, while Mexico established a variety of universal service goals to be achieved by 1994—such as the provision of basic telephone services in towns with more than 5,000 inhabitants and the availability of at least one telephone booth in all towns with more than 500 inhabitants—Argentina did not set any goals in these areas. The government did establish some sanctions, ranging from warnings and fines to possibly even the revocation of the license, to ensure that the companies complied with whatever goals were set in the concession agreement (Decree 62/90 and 677/90; see Argentina 1990; see also chapter 13).

The rules for interconnection, which are crucial when a telecommunications market is liberalized, were not spelled out precisely. During the period of exclusivity, Telecom and Telefónica were required to allow interconnection to the public network of independent local networks, including the small cooperatives in the interior of the country that accounted for 1 percent of the market. However, existing national data firms, which operated in competition with Startel, were not allowed to interconnect with the public network during the first seven years after privatization (a period that could be extended to ten years). After the exclusivity period, Telecom and Telefónica were required to interconnect any new market entrant on terms equal to those offered to their own long-distance and value added companies, but the price and conditions for interconnection were to be agreed upon by the parties. A regulatory authority would hear complaints from new entrants concerning those terms and could act without being called upon if prices or conditions were not "reasonable" or "equitable." However, the slow judicial process in Argentina promised to make things difficult for new entrants.

The enactment and enforcement of this regulatory framework called for a competent regulatory agency. As regulated and unregulated services began to mix, regulation and state intervention needed to expand rather than diminish. Argentina had little experience with the regulation of private utilities. Although in theory the Secretariat of Communication was responsible for telecommunications policy, control of the telephone company was dispersed among various government agencies, leading to an unstable and unpredictable environment. To rectify the situation, the government established in June 1990 the National Telecommunications Commission (Comisión Nacional de Telecomunicaciones, or CNT) (Decree 1185/90; see Argentina 1990). Prior to the creation of the CNT, the Secretariat of Communication was dismantled and its personnel were fired. However, the CNT was constituted by former employees of the Secretariat of Communication. In December 1991, the secretariat was revived under the new Ministry of Economy and Public Works, but this time with the status of an undersecretariat. The CNT board comprised five members, appointed by Argentina's president.[60] At the time, the agency was staffed by fifty highly qualified professionals and support personnel, all with high salaries and considerable autonomy in their day-to-day tasks. In January 1992, President Menem replaced the members of the board with an *interventor* and four *subinterventores;* the intervention brought renewed vitality to the institution.

The CNT's main function was to "apply, interpret, and enforce laws, decrees, and other norms in the telecommunications sector" (Decree 1185/90, art. 6; see Argentina 1990). Despite this overarching regulatory authority, the CNT's role was restricted to monitoring compliance with the concession, resolving conflicts among the companies and between the companies and its consumers, and setting standards for equipment. Conspicuously missing was the authority to fix tariffs, which was left under control of the executive. The CNT's budget was financed by a levy of 0.5 percent of the net sales of the regulated firms. In practice, however, the Ministry of Economy and Public Works controlled the funds and provided CNT only limited access to them.[61]

The Early Impact of Privatization

The sale of ENTel and the general reform of the Argentine telecommunications sector affected socioeconomic groups, such as consumers, labor, and service providers in diverse ways.

Consumers

In many countries, the privatization of state telecommunications firms and the liberalization of these markets changed the traditional arrangements that govern the provision of such services. A key transformation was the ending of subsidies of local rates by long-distance and international rates.[62] In Argentina, however, tariffs increased sharply for both local and long-distance services. After a year of operation, under pressure from the business community, the government requested a 3 percent reduction in the price of national long-distance service, with an offsetting hike in local tariffs. This adjustment was expected to inflict a loss of approximately US$145 million for each company over a five-year period. Although there was no contractual obligation to accept this new arrangement, both Telefónica and Telecom complied with the request—and for a good economic reason. Since the *pliegos* were imprecise about the terms for offering the second band of cellular telephony to Telefónica and Telecom, and considering that the CNT had rejected the right of the companies to a cellular service license, both firms yielded on the tariff issue in exchange for licenses for cellular service (Hill and Abdala 1993, 29).

Privatization and liberalization also had mixed consequences for telephone penetration. The fact that new private telecommunications enterprises are profit maximizers and seek market expansion (with total control of profits for reinvestment) would lead one to expect fast growth of the telephone network. But, although the *pliego* required the continuance of cross-subsidies to expand basic residential services, the tariff restructuring of 1992 showed that pressure from large users made this difficult.

The impact of privatization on the quality of service has been difficult to measure. The Communication Commission of the National Chamber of Deputies (CCD) argued that, although the concession set a ten-day limit for repairing faulty lines, in 1991 it still took as long as six months in some instances. On another issue, the CCD noted that, at the end of 1991, there were 45,000 telephones out of operation, which was 30 percent more than before privatization. However, Telecom and Telefónica published information showing that the number of out-of-order units had dropped from 90,000 to 11,000 in one year. Furthermore, the companies claimed to have exceeded the goals established in the *pliegos* for the installation of new lines.[63] According to reports from the companies, in the first two years of operation, Telefónica added approximately 343,000 new lines and Telecom added about 273,000 new lines, compared to an average of 98,000 lines added per year by ENTel in the five years before privatization. Telefónica argued also that it had increased the digitalization of its network from 18 percent in September 1991 to 24 percent a year later (Medina 1991, 10; and Hill and Abdala 1993, 32).

Public opinion polls, such as one carried out by Estudios y Políticas, revealed widespread disappointment with the initial performance of the privatized firms. A May 1991 poll showed that 66 percent of the respondents perceived no improvement in the service after privatization, 21 percent reported worse service, and only 8 percent believed there had been an improvement.[64]

Workers

Privatization had a mixed impact on ENTel workers. Their rights shrank, but their wages rose, they became part owners of the company, and they did not lose a large number of jobs in large numbers as some had predicted.[65] Prior to the sale of ENTel, the government had changed the workweek from thirty-five to forty hours, seniority and job guarantees were abandoned and temporary employees were freely recruited, management was given flexibility in allocating jobs, labor's role in the running of the company was reduced, and meetings and assemblies by workers were curtailed. The government also strove to reduce the number of union affiliates, thereby dismantling the political base and bargaining power of the workers. Telecom and Telefónica also implemented voluntary retirement plans, which saw the departure of approximately 5,000 workers, or 10 percent of ENTel's labor force. Interestingly, Telecom and Telefónica rehired a considerable number of those workers as contract employees. In this way, the companies obtained skilled labor while reducing their costs, such as pension contributions, vacation time, health insurance, and other fringe benefits. This maneuver also reduced the number of unionized employees.

Foreign Investors

Foreign telecommunications firms and financial institutions that invested in ENTel were among the main winners of the reform process. Due to the sharp increase in telephone rates, the new firms earned rates of return over fixed assets ranging from 24 to 33 percent (Abdala 1992, 86). For the first two years of privatized operation, Telefónica de Argentina and Telecom Argentina announced total revenues of US$2.76 billion and US$2.11 billion, respectively. The 30 percent of ENTel's shares held by the government were sold in two stages. In December 1991, the government sold the 30 percent it owned in Telefónica for US$837 million, and in March 1992 the same percentage of shares in Telecom Argentina were sold for US$1.2 billion. Thus, the value of Telefónica shares went up 3.6 times compared to the price the consortium paid for its 60 percent stake, while those owned by Telecom went up 4.5 times. In 1993, based on a stock market valuation of US$4.27 billion, Telefónica ranked seventeenth among all companies in the developing world, while Telecom placed twenty-second, with a capitalization of US$2.93 billion ("Top 100" 1993, 57).

From the perspective of foreign telecommunications firms, privatization also enabled them to diversify out of their saturated domestic markets into Argentina's potentially high-growth market. They also enjoyed the advantages of early entry, with a good chance of retaining a monopoly position in most segments of the market even after the expiration of the exclusivity period. However, the companies faced their share of problems in managing the consortia. For instance, in the STET–France Cables et Radio consortium, some members also had interests in telecommunications equipment firms. Equipment procurement generated friction and changes in top management during the early months, paralyzing the company.[66] Telefónica had an easier time in this regard, since its major investors had complementary activities.[67]

The influential presence of international banks and financial institutions was linked to the prominent role assigned to debt-equity swaps in the sale of ENTel. As a consequence, 82 percent of Telefónica shares were owned by eighteen international financial institutions. Privatization benefited all Argentine bondholders. Within a few days of the announcement that ENTel would be sold, the price of Argentine debt in the secondary market rose from 12 cents per dollar of face value to 19 cents on the dollar. After the privatization of ENTel, it traded at approximately 35 cents.

Given the political and economic power held by the new consortia and the protective regulatory framework put in place, the state's ability to open the market to competition in the future is somewhat suspect. Regulators face difficulty in gaining access to information about the cost structure of private firms to avoid predatory pricing and dumping. Telecom and Telefónica—presumably future competitors—are partners in Telintar and Startel, and although the CNT has the power to penalize the companies in a variety of ways, there are no clear rules to discourage or prevent anticompetitive behavior and collusion. Telecom's president, Gian Paolo Mondini, admitted publicly that his company and Telefónica coordinated their strategies in matters such as tariff and investment policy.

Conclusion

As other students of the Argentine telecommunications sector note, one of the most remarkable aspects of ENTel's privatization was that it happened at all. Menem's initiative to sell the company followed two previously unsuccessful attempts. However, Menem's privatization program did not go through without resistance. The announcement of ENTel's sale produced strong opposition from various interest groups and political institutions. In this regard, Argentina's experience—as well as those of other developing countries—points to the fact that if privatization is to happen it has to be under conditions of high concentration of power in the executive. The policymaking process must be insulated from political pressure, and the management of the privatization must be centralized in an ad hoc agency that is staffed with political appointees outside the traditional bureaucracy.

The unprecedented economic and fiscal crisis of 1989 pushed the Argentine government to implement privatization quickly. In only fourteen months, Menem turned over to the private sector a large public utility that had operated for more than fifty years as a state monopoly. As a result, the company never underwent the kind of restructuring that was carried out on such firms in Malaysia and Mexico. In Argentina, both local and foreign advisers argued that restructuring the company prior to sale was politically infeasible and of dubious economic value.

The failure to prepare ENTel adequately affected its sale price, which was among the lowest paid for a telecommunications firm in a developing country. The low selling price was the consequence not only of inadequate corporate restructuring but also of a lack of transparency and predictability during the bidding process. The government assumed that granting interested parties the opportunity to bargain over the conditions of the sale would lure a large number of private investors. Instead, perceptions that the regulatory framework was unstable scared away many potential buyers and left the government with only a few bidders. As the list of competing bidders diminished, their demands on the government increased. As a result, much of the planned liberalization of the local telecommunications market fell by the wayside and the level of initial telephone tariffs had to be raised above original targets. Because Menem linked the fate of his new economic plan to the privatization process and in particular to ENTel's sale, the government was caught in a dilemma. To comply with its announced timetable, the government had to deal with the only remaining investors and their costly demands. The government thus gave up liberalization and a reasonable initial tariff in order to gain a sale. However, it is probably true that the privatization of ENTel may not have been feasible if a juicy package had not been offered to prospective investors.

The administration nevertheless kept to its original plan to divide ENTel into two regional operating companies. This was to be the foundation of "competition by comparison" during the period when the privatized companies enjoyed monopoly power in basic services and the basis of a competitive duopolistic market after basic services were opened up to competition. However, the postprivatization behavior of the companies suggested that the two firms were at least as likely to function as a cartel as they were as competitors. Furthermore, it was not clear whether a competitive market would ever emerge. The experience of industrialized countries such as the Britain, Japan, and the United States calls attention to the difficulties of achieving fair competition. Overcoming the competitive advantages that established providers enjoy vis-à-vis new entrants requires the presence of a strong and independent regulatory body. Such an institution is generally absent in most developing countries, and that was certainly the case in Argentina. The lack of autonomy, limited human and material resources, and restricted finances placed the Argentine regulatory agency, the CNT, at odds with the technically and politically difficult tasks assigned to it.

In terms of its impact on stakeholders, the privatization of ENTel had mixed results for workers and had clear benefits for the new owners. Workers lost some of their rights and privileges, but they gained from higher wages and ownership in the privatized companies. And they did not, as many had predicted, lose a large number of jobs. On the other hand, foreign investors who invested in the new companies reaped large gains, due to the sharp increase in the value of both companies' shares. For the average consumer, however, rates went up sharply, with little discernible improvement in the quality of service.

Although a balanced assessment of the Argentine approach to telecommunications privatization requires the passage of more time, it was already evident by 1994 that the rush to divest the sector under conditions of high economic and political instability resulted in a suboptimal and less-than-smooth transition. For that reason, the Argentine experience offers lessons to other countries not only about how to privatize their telecommunications sectors but also about how not to do so. Perhaps the rest of the world can benefit from Argentina's experience, even if Argentines themselves did not profit as much as expected from ENTel's hasty privatization.

NOTES

1. A survey by the International Telecommunications Union (ITU) shows that in most developing countries telecommunications reform was tied to structural adjustment programs (Becher 1991).

2. For more history on the telecommunications sector in Argentina, see Tesler 1990, and Mulready 1956.

3. Until the 1940s, the Argentine state was a passive, noninterventionist institution that believed in laissez faire, market-driven policies.

4. In fact, for almost forty years, the UT operated without a proper concession. When the error was discovered in the mid-1920s, the government demanded that it be given a seat on the company's executive board in exchange for
legalizing the concession.

5. The UT controlled 89.42 percent of the market, Ericsson had 6.29 percent, and local cooperatives had 4.29 percent.

6. The government paid US$95 million for the UT, but the company contin-
ued under the managerial and technical control of ITT for an extended period
of time.

7. Given the growing role of the state in the telecommunications sector, the
government created the Ministry of Communications and the Secretariat of
State Telephones in 1949, both under the control of the General Administration
of Posts and Telecommunications.

8. Decree 18885/48. The company operated under the Dirección de Teléfonos del Estado.

9. CAT was the only carrier that was not nationalized. When the Peronist
administration was overthrown in 1955, it was bargaining with the company
about the conditions for incorporating CAT into the state patrimony. Under the
new administration, the process was put on hold until 1959, when the negotiations were formally canceled.

10. The remaining 8 percent was split between CAT (7%) and local cooperatives (1%).

11. The United States had fifty lines per 100 inhabitants, France forty-eight
lines per 100 inhabitants, and Britain forty-four lines per 100 inhabitants.

12. The Instability of ENTel's top managerial positions diluted any sense of
responsibility and commitment on the part of managers, who viewed their participation in ENTel as a transitory stage in their careers, a phenomenon discussed at length by Aharoni 1986. And ENTel was not unique: between 1940 and
1980 the average tenure was 13.7 months for ministers, 12.2 months for secre-
taries of state, and 14.1 months for provincial governors (Oszlak 1990, 12).

13. According to ENTel management, if the company had managed its foreign exchange exposure like private firms and if taxes had not gone up, the
company would have reported profits of approximately 14 percent of income in
that period (Garutti 1990, 23).

14. Through Megatel, more than half a million new lines were installed. At
the same time, the imposition of a $600 connection charge reduced the number
of people requesting new service (Coloma et al. 1992, 250).

15. The accepted standards for call completion for local and long-distance
calls are 95 and 85 percent, respectively.

16. Even though the number of employees remained stable, overtime work
increased dramatically to the equivalent in 1989 of 10,610 additional workers, or
24 percent of the company's personnel.

17. The contracts are called convenios colectivos de trabajo (collective working agreements).

18. The telecommunications equipment industry in Argentina was dominated for several decades by two branches of transnational companies: Com-

pañía Standard Electric Argentina (CSEA), a branch of ITT, and Equitel, a branch of Siemens. In the late 1970s, CSEA was bought by Equitel, and a new company, the Argentine-Japanese consortium Pecon Nec, entered the market as the second major equipment provider. Despite the existence of this duopolistic market structure, other suppliers, such as the French Alcatel, the Italian Telletra, and a variety of small local companies, were able to grab a share of the market at different times (Herrera 1989).

19. The privatized companies purchased equipment from ENTel's traditional suppliers at almost half the prices paid in the past.

20. For a study of privatization initiatives during the military regime, see Fontana 1985.

21. Further details on the Alfonsín privatization program can be found in Gonzalez Fraga 1991 and Arango de Maglio 1990.

22. In his campaign for the presidency, Menem argued that his government would not privatize state-owned enterprises but would make them efficient. Once in power, in a book published to support state reform, the new president argued in a chapter entitled "Incommensurate Growth of the State" that the state had failed in its entrepreneurial role and that, therefore, the main state enterprises should be privatized (Menem and Dromi 1990, 108).

23. An *interventor* in the Argentine political system is a direct appointee of the president to a particular institution to solve an institutional crisis affecting the entity. *Interventores*, for that reason, are temporary executive directors with special powers. The UCD is a party of free marketers, traditionally opposed to Peronist welfare policies.

24. The strategy of giving responsibility for the sale of ENTel to the new head of the company had both pros and cons. On the positive side, there was direct access to information and to the management of the company, which made the company as a whole more responsive to the sale requirements. On the negative side, the close involvement with the firm led to recurrent conflict with some managers and workers, which presented an unfavorable picture to prospective buyers (Waterbury 1992).

25. In this sense, the Argentine privatization differs from similar state reforms in other developing countries. In Mexico, for example, the sale of TELMEX was managed from the Ministry of Finance, or, more precisely, the Unidad de Desincorporación, an office created for the sale of all state-owned enterprises.

26. Although the valuation of ENTel was initially assigned to Banco Nacional de Desarrollo (Banade), due to lack of time and trained personnel, Banade transferred the task to Deloitte, Haskins & Sells.

27. According to the government's definition, value added service includes all services other than those defined as basic service (Decree 62/90, art. 8.5; see Argentina 1990).

28. Basic services are defined by Argentine legislation as the provision through the public network of all voice messages, be they local, regional, or international (Decree 62/90, art. 17.1; see Argentina 1990).

29. After the 1982 debt collapse, loans from international banks completely dried up, and foreign direct investment dropped by 62 percent from its average

in the previous decade. As the possibility of further loans from international financial institutions diminished sharply, Latin American countries struggled to recover traditional forms of capital inflows, mainly through foreign direct investment (Petrazzini 1993b).

30. For the development of an institutional and political explanation for the divergent outcomes in telecommunication privatization initiatives in developing countries, see Cowhey 1991 and Petrazzini 1993a.

31. By the time Menem became president he was already the head of the Peronist Party. This position, which controlled the political and financial power of the party, gave Menem significant power over rebellious groups and enough leverage to derail intraparty opposition.

32. This opposition differed considerably from that of the Mexican telephone union, which was willing to bargain with the government (see chapter 3).

33. A previous strike led by the union in April 1990 did not have much impact either on the government or on the workers.

34. The first economic program during the Menem administration was called the "BB plan," in reference to Bunge & Born, the multinational company that designed the economic program and contributed from its ranks the first two economic ministers of the Menem government.

35. Heightened by the failures of the Alfonsín administration, instability in the political environment left Menem with a very short honeymoon period in which to implement drastic reforms in the public sector. In Argentina's potentially disruptive environment, opposition could have arisen at any moment.

36. The five divisions reflected the five regions into which the country was divided as a result of the military's control of the telecommunications system.

37. Most other nations that privatized their telecommunications services, such as Chile, Malaysia, Mexico, New Zealand, and Venezuela, sold their companies intact.

38. The official argument was that the public network was not "mature enough" to develop without subsidies. Argentina and Jamaica are among the few countries that preserved cross-subsidization after privatization (on Jamaica, see chapter 2).

39. A careful analysis of the privatization decrees by SIGEP (Sindicatura de Empresas Públicas) in March 1990, showed a variety of serious contradictions. For example, Decree 62/90 demanded a variety of conditions for a company to qualify for the bidding process; however, article 3.1.11 allowed each prequalified company to be substituted by a subsidiary, even when the new entrant did not comply with the conditions required in the first. Article 3.2.2 prohibited rejected bidders from filing complaints against the prequalification process; yet, articles 3.10 and 5.8.1 determined that losing companies had up to five days to file complaints against the prequalification process (SIGEP 1990). By April 1990 only the following seven firms were still interested in ENTel: Nynex, GTE, Bell Atlantic (all from the United States), Telefónica (Spain), STET (Italy), Cable & Wireless (U.K.), and France Cables et Radio (France).

40. The regulation did not allow free entry into the sector and prohibited existing companies from expanding operations to include international service.

41. ENTel's total debt was divided in the following way: US$832 million local commercial debt, US$474 million of foreign commercial debt, US$103 million of local financial debt, US$444 million of foreign financial debt, and US$296 million of obligations to the state or other state enterprises (SIGEP 1990).

42. Apparently, ENTel was transferred with an inventory of 200,000 lines and a wealth of other equipment scheduled to be installed in the future.

43. For details on the Mexican tariff reform, see chapter 3 and Tandon 1994.

44. To offer guarantees to prospective buyers, planned tariff hikes prior to the transfer of ENTel were included in the legislation (Decree 62/90, art. 12.2; see Argentina 1990).

45. President Menem, who was in Rome at the time, sent a strong message to the companies by asserting that the Italian government guaranteed that, "as far as STET is concerned, there are no problems or objections." But the two consortia knew that they were the only bidders left in the process and that Menem's political project was very much tied to the success or failure of ENTel's privatization. Therefore, they not only consistently pushed to achieve the desired rates but did so in a coordinated way. Soon after the rate conflict started, the telephone companies formed a cartel, and representatives of STET–France Cables et Radio warned the government that if Telefónica was left out of a tariff settlement they would not sign the contract.

46. Figures are based on Takano 1992; chapter 3, this volume; and author's estimates. Calculations were as follows: for long distance, the rate per pulse (US¢4.8) was multiplied by an index based on distance. The maximum charge was based on distance of 840 kilometers (minimum charge, three minutes), which added up to US$2.55. For an international call from Buenos Aires to New York, the tariff was an average of US$2.95 per minute, while the same call in the reverse direction was US$0.87 per minute.

47. Due to the lack of precision in privatization legislation it was never clear whether the 16 percent rate of return was a guaranteed rate or a fixed rate that the new companies' profits could neither exceed nor fall below.

48. The new pricing regime took into consideration that the contracts required the firms to gradually reduce connection charges to US$100 by the end of the decade. In 1990, these charges were approximately US$1,000 for residential users and US$1,500 for business users.

49. This was one of the issues that Congress strongly resisted in the privatization plan. The majority of both the Radical and Peronist parties were against the idea of taking debt as a payment for ENTel. For some time, Congress actively tried to change the terms of the *pliego*, but the executive stood firm and imposed its criteria.

50. A cash ceiling was set in order to push bidders to offer as much debt as possible.

51. Although this mechanism made the process quite transparent to future investors, it raised suspicion about possible government corruption in the process. In the end, probably because of its political significance and public visibility, no major scandal erupted relating to ENTel's sale.

52. Interestingly, the only companies remaining were those of Latin origin (Spain, Italy, and France), and Pacific Bell, whose management staff for Latin America was of Latin origin.

53. Three consortia bid for the northern region, while only Telefónica and STET–France Cables et Radio bid for the southern. Telefónica won in both areas, offering US$2.408 billion for the northern region and US$2.834 billion for the southern region. According to the *pliegos*, the second bidder in the region with the lower value could become the winner by improving its offer. Bell Atlantic, which had originally offered US$2.337 billion, improved its bid by offering US$2.409 billion and was granted the northern region of the country. STET–Cables et Radio offered US$2.447 billion for the southern region and US$2.200 billion for the northern region. The bidding prices included 50 percent ownership of Telintar and Startel.

54. Bell Atlantic requested an extension on the payment deadline, and the government conceded on the condition that the contracts were signed on time. However, Manufacturers Hanover wanted an extension on the date for signing the contract, a concession that Menem's administration was not willing to make since it had a guarantee from STET–France Cables et Radio consortium that it would take over Bell Atlantic's position under the conditions required by the government.

55. The 5 percent reserved to telephone cooperatives was later included in the public offering.

56. Brief profiles of the three partners follow. STET (Societa Finanziaria Telefonica) was part of the Italian firm, Institute for Industrial Reconstruction (IRI). This telecommunications holding company controlled a variety of enterprises in the sector. In Italy, it provided services through a subsidiary that had 123,000 employees, operated 22 million lines, and provided value added and data services. France Cables et Radio was the international branch of the state-owned France Telecom, a powerful conglomerate that provided domestic and international telecommunications services throughout France. It had 154,000 employees, operated 28 million lines, provided value added services through the 5.6 million terminals of videotext, and operated the world's largest data-switched packet network. Finally, Compañía Naviera Pérez Companc was one of Argentina's most powerful economic groups. The consortium owned eighty companies, with operating profits in 1992 of more than US$2 billion, including a large stake in Pecom-Nec, an Argentine-Japanese telecommunications equipment producer that had close commercial relationships with ENTel.

57. The main investors were Telefónica de España, owned by a variety of domestic investors (43.9%), several foreign investors (22%), and the Spanish government (34.1%), which controlled the firm; Citibank, one of Argentina's main international creditors and a significant player in debt negotiations as the head of the Committee of Argentine Creditors; and Techint, an Italian multinational based in Milan, with 18,000 employees in Argentina, with annual profits of US$1.35 billion, and operating in several economic sectors, including oil, steel, and construction.

58. According to one report, Pérez Companc, along with other local eco-

nomic conglomerates, such as Techint, Benito Roggio, Astra, Sociedad Comercial del Plata, Bunge & Born, Socma, Loma Negra, and Bridas, and a few large international commercial banks, such as Citibank and Morgan, controlled 414 enterprises, accounting for approximately 50 percent of Argentina's GDP (Seoane and Martinez 1993, 79).

59. The goals were modest primarily because ENTel's performance at the time of transfer was so poor. Private owners merely needed to meet the modest levels of ENTel's performance in the year prior to the sale.

60. Presidential appointment of CNT's top officials is a double-edged strategy. On the one hand, it insulates the selection process from political controversy and harmonizes the actions of the agency with the policies of the government. On the other hand, by minimizing the participation of key political institutions, such as Congress, the appointment lacks legitimacy.

61. Part of those funds were used to repay the public debt and not to expand services, as required in the decree that created the CNT (Hill and Abdala 1993, 30).

62. In the United States, for example, local telephone rates rose by 53 percent since the breakup of AT&T, while long-distance and international charges fell by 40 percent. This tariff restructuring benefited a limited number of users. According to 1988 figures, only 10 percent of residential users spent more than US$25 a month on long-distance calls, and only 14 percent of business users spent more than US$50 (Horwitz 1992, 25).

63. As of 1994, these figures of network expansion had not been audited by the CNT.

64. To gain popular support in the preprivatization period, the government created high expectations about the virtues of private ownership. A year-and-a-half into private ownership, the companies had not been able to meet those expectations.

65. The 10 percent of shares set aside for workers were transferred to them in December 1992 for $16.6 million, which was to be paid out of the dividends earned by the shares. This price was the same as that paid by the consortia, not the prevailing market price in December 1992.

66. After several months of conflict, the French representative who headed Telecom was replaced by a manager from STET.

67. Citibank was in charge of the financial aspects, Telefónica provided the management, and Techint supervised installation services.

REFERENCES

Abdala, Manuel A. 1992. "Distributional Impact of Divestiture in a High Inflation Economy: The Case of ENTel Argentina." Ph.D. diss., Boston Univ.

Aharoni, Yair. 1986. *The Evolution and Management of State-Owned Enterprises.* Cambridge: Ballinger.

Arango de Maglio, Aida. 1990. "Radicalismo y Empresas Publicas (1983/1989)." *Realidad Economica* 97:29–54.

Argentina. 1972, 1989, 1990. *Boletin Oficial de la Republica Argentina.* Buenos Aires.

Becher, Ernst. 1991. *Restructuring of Telecommunications in Developing Countries: An Empirical Investigation with ITU's Role in Perspective*. Geneva: International Telecommunications Union.

Boneo, Horacio. 1985. *Privatizacion: Del Dicho al Hecho*. Buenos Aires: El Cronista Comercial.

Coloma, German, Pablo Gerchunoff, and María Rosa Schappacasse. 1992. "Empresa Nacional de Telecomunicaciones." In *Las Privatizaciones en la Argentina*, ed. Pablo Gerchunoff. Buenos Aires: Instituto Torcuato di Tella.

Cowhey, Peter. 1991. "The Political Economy of Telecommunications Reform in Developing Countries." Paper prepared for the seminar, Implementing Reforms in the Telecommunications Sector, World Bank, April.

Donikian, Luis, Raul Arri, Vito di Leo, and Roberto Varone. 1990. *Teléfonois: De la Politica Nacional al Saqueo Privatista*. Buenos Aires: Foetra.

ENTel. 1990. *Telecom Highlights International*. Nov. 21. Buenos Aires.

Fontana, Andres. 1985. "Fuerzas Armadas e Ideologia Neoconservadora: El Redimensionamiento del Estado en la Argentina (1976–1981)." In Boneo, ed., *Privatizacion*.

Garutti, Humberto. 1990. "La Privatizacion del Servicio de Telecomunicaciones en la Argentina." Paper prepared for the Tercera Reunion de la Comisión Técnica Permanente I: Servicios Públicos de Telecomunicaciones, Montevideo.

Gonzalez Fraga, Javier. 1991. "The Argentine Privatization in Retrospect." In *Privatization of Public Enterprises in Latin America*, ed. William Glade. San Francisco: ICS Press.

Herrera, Alejandra. 1989. *La Revolución Tecnológica y la Telefonía Argentina*. Buenos Aires: Legasa.

Hill, Alice, and Manuel A. Abdala. 1993. "Regulation, Institutions, and Commitment: Privatization and Regulation in the Argentine Telecommunications Sector." Working Paper. World Bank, Washington, D.C.

Horwitz, Robert. 1992. "Regulation of Parastatals." Economic Trends Research Group, Cape Town.

ITU (International Telecommunications Union). 1992. *Yearbook of Common Carrier Telecommunication Statistics*. Geneva.

Medina, Romeo. 1991. "Teléfonos: La Espera Sigue." *Clarin* 10 (Nov. 13).

Menem, Carlos, and Roberto Dromi. 1990. *Reforma del Estado y Transformacion Nacional*. Buenos Aires: Ciencias de la Administracion SRL.

Mulready, Ricardo. 1956. *Breve Historia de la Telefonía Argentina (1886–1956)*. Buenos Aires: Ricardo Mulready.

Oszlak, Oscar. 1990. *La Reforma del Estado en la Argentina*. Buenos Aires: CEDES.

Petrazzini, Ben. 1993a. "The Politics of Telecommunications Reform in Developing Countries." *Pacific Telecommunications Review* 14 (3): 4–23.

———. 1993b. "Foreign Direct Investment in Latin America's Privatization." In *Latin America's Turnaround: Privatization, Foreign Investment, and Growth*, ed. Paul Boeker. San Francisco: ICS Press.

Seoane, Maria, and Oscar Martinez. 1993. "Argentina S.A." *Noticias* (Jan. 3): 79.

SIGEP (Sindicatura de Empresas Publicas). 1983–90. *Annual Report.* Buenos Aires.

————. 1990. *Nota SIGEP.* Buenos Aires.

Takano, Yoshiro. 1992. *Nippon Telegraph and Telephone Privatization Study: The Experience of Japan and Lessons for Developing Countries.* Discussion Paper 179. Washington, D.C.: World Bank.

Tandon, Pankaj. 1994. "Teléfonos de México." In *Welfare Consequences of Selling Public Enterprises: An Empirical Analysis,* ed. Ahmed Galal, Leroy P. Jones, Pankaj Tandon, and Ingo Vogelsang. New York: Oxford Univ. Press.

Tesler, Mario. 1990. *La Telefonía Argentina: Su Otra Historia.* Buenos Aires: Rescate.

"Top 100 Emerging-Market Companies." 1993. *Business Week,* July 12.

Waterbury, J. 1992. "The Heart of the Matter? Public Enterprises and the Adjustment Process." In *The Politics of Structural Economic Adjustment,* ed. Stephan Haggard and Robert Kauffman. Princeton: Princeton Univ. Press.

5. A Planned Approach to Telephone Privatization

VENEZUELA

. . . .

Antonio Francés

Venezuela's telecommunications firm, the CANTV, was created in 1930 as a private company and acquired by the government in 1953. In the following decades, the Venezuelan government channeled significant funds to expand the telecommunications network. By 1980, a telephone density of eight subscribers per 100 inhabitants had been reached, similar to that in other Latin American countries but low by world standards. In the 1980s, the CANTV's expansion came to a standstill, while demand grew, service deteriorated, and inefficiency and corruption increased. By 1990, the CANTV's telephone network was in poor shape.

The CANTV's record as a state enterprise was symptomatic of the Venezuelan public sector's evolution between 1950 and 1990. The abundance of oil resources led to massive state participation in heavy industry and utilities. Most enterprises created in this process were inefficient and experienced prolonged crises and mounting foreign debt. In February 1989 the newly installed government of Carlos Andrés Pérez negotiated a structural adjustment program with the International Monetary Fund that envisaged the privatization of several state enterprises, including the CANTV. An extraordinary opportunity emerged to shift Venezuela's communications system into high gear. By 1991, the CANTV had been privatized, with the sale of 40 percent of its shares to a consortium led by GTE of the United States and 11 percent to employees of the company.

In the very first year after privatization, service was expanded, quality was improved, substantial investments were made, and a degree of competition was introduced into Venezuelan telecommunications services. Although lasting results remained to be seen, Venezuela's experience in telecommunications contrasted sharply with its experience in other sectors, such as water and airlines, where privatization yielded ambiguous results at best.[1] Unlike Argentina or Jamaica, Venezuela proceeded with the privatization of its telecommunications firm in a relatively planned manner. Venezuela also benefited from the fact that it could learn from the experience of the countries that preceded it along that path.

The CANTV before Privatization

Created as a private enterprise in 1930 under a concession granted by the Development Ministry, the CANTV's predecessor company was the most successful among several private firms that operated telephone services in Venezuela. Yet by 1946 the firm had to compete with the Communications Ministry, which began to offer long-distance telecommunications services. In 1953, the Venezuelan government purchased virtually all shares, but at the time the company was highly indebted and unable to invest in needed plant expansion. In 1965 the government transferred to the CANTV all Communications Ministry telephone facilities, granting it a twenty-five-year concession and converting it into the state agency for developing telecommunications services other than telegraph.

In the 1950s and 1960s, the CANTV introduced automatic dialing, installed a long-distance network, which helped integrate the country, and continued to acquire all other private telephone companies. In 1973 the CANTV became a national telephone monopoly. The period from 1965 to 1980 was the CANTV's heyday. Led by young engineers trained at the Communications Ministry's Planning and Development Office, the CANTV automated national long-distance service, laid submarine cables to North America and Europe, and installed the Camatagua ground satellite station. These were years of presidential ribbon cutting and development euphoria.

During the 1980s the CANTV management fell into the hands of political appointees. Equipment purchase decisions were slow and tied to political favoritism. Expansion came to a standstill, and service penetration stalled at 8.2 lines per 100 inhabitants. Demand satisfaction remained around 50 percent, and service deteriorated. Politicized staffing and promotion practices undermined morale: two-thirds of the CANTV employees held administrative jobs and only one-third performed technical tasks, in sharp contrast to ratios typical of well-administered telephone companies (tables 5.1 and 5.2). A mismatch of equipment

Table 5-1. CANTV, Preprivatization Performance Indicators, 1987–1990

Performance Indicator	1987	1988	1989	1990
Number of lines installed (thousands)	1,717	1,770	1,870	1,943
Subscriber lines in service (thousands)	1,374	1,427	1,433	1,456
Public telephones in service (thousands)	27	30	32	31
Lines/100 people	8.2	8.3	8.1	8.2
Residential lines (thousands)	963	1,003	997	1,006
Commercial lines (thousands)	411	425	436	450
International calls, minutes per line	96	101	107	113
Local calls completed (%)	52.8	52.4	48.7	49.4
Domestic long-distance calls completed (%)	36.7	33.5	30.7	29.4
International long-distance calls completed (%)	20.2	23.2	18.7	22.0
Hours telephones are out of service/year	46.1	42.3	51.0	93.5
Hours Telex is out of service/year	24.0	24.0	24.0	23.0
Telephones repaired within 72 hours (%)	81.0	85.1	83.5	72.3
Full-time employees	15,873	16,569	16,469	18,944
Part-time employees	1,183	1,344	2,987	917

Source: CANTV.

Note: Data are for year ending on December 31.

Table 5-2. CANTV, Preprivatization Performance Indicators, Comparative Data

Company	Access Lines (millions)	Number of Employees	Lines/ Employee
Bell Atlantic (U.S.)	17.48	78,100	255.6
NTT (Japan)[1]	52.45	276,650	189.6
France Telecom[2]	26.98	156,451	172.5
Telefónica de España (Spain)	12.60	75,455	167.0
TELMEX (Mexico)	5.27	51,218	106.4
British Telecom[1]	25.01	245,700	101.8
Teléfonos de Chile[2]	0.67	7,500	90.5
CANTV (Venezuela)	1.48	19,861	74.9

Source: Baring Securities (1991).

[1] As of March 1990.

[2] As of December 1990.

brands and models rendered maintenance difficult. The poor training and low morale of the majority of the technical personnel, in surroundings where political and personal criteria determined the opportunities for advancement, further affected maintenance. In addition, the lack of management continuity increased the power of trade unions. In the 1980s the CANTV had five presidents, with an average tenure of two years. The recruitment and promotion of nonprofessional personnel were largely controlled by the unions. Corruption began to spread at all levels, from the purchasing and contracting decisions to the installing and repairing of telephones. International calls by third parties, charged to unsuspecting subscribers, were often carried out with staff complicity. In 1989, for the first time, the company showed losses; again in 1990,

Table 5-3. CANTV, Preprivatization Profits and Losses, 1987–1990 (millions of US$)

Item	1987	1988	1989	1990
Operating revenue	562.1	686.3	354.8	438.7
Operating expenses	349.3	533.7	302.9	344.8
Operating profit	212.8	149.9	51.9	93.9
Other income and expenses	–7.2	–37.7	–160.0	–173.9
Net income before taxes	205.6	112.2	–108.1	–80.0
Provision for taxes	104.3	40.1	0	0
Net profit after taxes	101.3	72.1	–108.1	–80.0

Source: CANTV.

Note: Figures in bolivars were converted to U.S. dollars at the following average exchange rates (bolivars per US$): 14.50 (1987), 14.50 (1988), 39.125 (1989), and 47.44 (1990).

it showed losses, mostly due to the financial burden of servicing an external debt of over US$650 million (table 5-3).

In the meantime, a revolution had taken place in the telecommunications world. Microelectronics and computer developments led to telephone network digitalization and an explosive satellite communications expansion. Applying laser technology to fiber optics as a means of transmission allowed network transmission capacity to multiply a thousandfold. However, the most important changes were not technological. The decision to dismember AT&T, the world's largest telephone monopoly, and the decision of the British government to privatize British Telecom, one of the world's largest public telephone companies, caused a true commotion in an industry that was used to being tranquil and stable. At the same time, countries like Hong Kong, Japan, Malaysia, and New Zealand privatized their telephone companies. In Latin America, Chile, Argentina, and Mexico followed (Wellenius et al. 1989; Ambrose et al. 1990). It was not long before Venezuela felt compelled to follow the example of its Latin American neighbors.

Economic Reforms

The government of Carlos Andrés Pérez assumed power on February 2, 1989, and found the country almost devoid of foreign reserves and with no international credit. Consumer prices were regulated and goods were scarce. The new government immediately undertook a severe economic adjustment program. Within a short time, controls on prices and interest rates were eliminated, exchange rates were unified and floated, and the price of gasoline was increased. In February 1989, a letter of intent was filed with the International Monetary Fund, allowing bridge credits to be obtained, opening the way for external debt renegotiation. Pérez acted quickly but largely on his own, with no political support from his own party and only lukewarm backing from business. In 1989, inflation hit a rate of 81.5 percent and GNP decreased by 10.6 percent.

The restructuring of state companies, many of which showed losses, formed an essential part of the structural reform program complementing the economic adjustment program. In the Eighth National Plan (1989–94), the privatization of state enterprises was to be a priority.

On August 1, 1989, a privatization commission was created, targeting first a chain of government-owned hotels, which were considered easy to privatize. Nevertheless, this process was frustrated by pressure from trade union groups expecting to acquire these properties at a low price. The first successful privatization effected by Pérez's government was the Banco Occidental de Descuento sale in October 1991, which became a pilot case. Then, in March 1990, a Restructuring Commission for Public Sector Companies was created. A US$400 million World Bank loan was granted for restructuring public enterprises such as the CANTV, CADAFE (electricity), INOS (water), and INP (ports).

A World Bank report produced in February 1990 showed that the CANTV suffered from several problems, including low service quality, low demand satisfaction, and distorted tariffs. The need to improve both management and human resources was emphasized (Gonzalez Valle et al. 1990). At the cabinet level, privatization began to be perceived as the definitive solution for the CANTV's problems. However, the CANTV's management at the time supported restructuring within the public sector. Even under government ownership, the CANTV had maintained its private company character, which allowed the state to sell its shares to private parties without too many legal changes. A ruling by the public attorney (Ruling 179, July 31, 1990) established that, by selling 40 percent of the shares and placing 11 percent in trusteeship, the CANTV would become a fully private company. Consequently, it became evident that the privatization of the CANTV was legally feasible even without the passage of a privatization bill by congress.

Changes in the Telecommunications Sector

The government's decision to privatize the CANTV was followed by key new appointments. Roberto Smith, fresh from the task of formulating the Eighth National Plan, was appointed transport and communications minister, and Fernando Martínez Móttola, the chairman of the Public Enterprise Restructuring Commission, was appointed president of the CANTV. The newly formed restructuring team for telecommunications held a series of meetings with the World Bank mission and established basic guidelines. In preparation for privatization, an immediate action program was designed within CANTV to improve service, including the installation of 120,000 new phone lines per year, a reduction in service complaints, and improved attention to customers. The installation program fully met its goal, further service deterioration was prevented, and partial improvements in customer service were made.

Starting in August 1990, the CANTV president and his team held meetings with both workers and trade union leaders. A "zero layoff" policy was proposed, even though the previous administration had suggested the need to reduce the staff from 13 to 6 workers per 1,000 lines, which would have required laying off 10,000 workers. It was emphasized that accelerated plant growth following privatization would help cut worker rates per 1,000 lines and avoid the need to reduce staff. The CANTV's new leadership assigned top priority to labor contract negotiations, traditionally one of the tasks most feared by the company's management. These negotiations were completed in a record time of twelve months, before the end of 1990. By negotiating overall proposals and counterproposals, instead of clause by clause, the process was speeded up and greater transparency was offered. The discussion drafts were informally shared with the workers.

In Venezuela's open, democratic, and very contentious political environment, a favorable public opinion was deemed essential to achieve the privatization of public enterprises. Most political parties rejected privatization, and statist and nationalist sentiments were strong among intellectuals. However, telephone service was so bad that everyone agreed something had to be done. Many claimed that restructuring under state ownership would be enough. An opinion survey carried out in October 1990 showed that the public favored the privatization of the CANTV. The battle for public opinion was one of the hardest in the entire process; but by anticipating criticism, the privatizing group gained the initial advantage. When the final public confrontation arose in October and November 1991, the CANTV's privatization was considered by most as a remedy that ought not to be postponed (Francés 1993).

The privatization process was carried out by the Telecommunications Restructuring Group (TRG), created by decree on October 11, 1990, and attached to the Transport and Communications Ministry. The following stages of reform were envisaged: the preparation of a sector development plan, followed the introduction of a new telecommunications law, the installation of a new regulatory agency, the opening up of value added services to competition, and finally, the restructuring and privatization of the CANTV. The TRG was attached to the ministry but in practice reported to the president of the CANTV, Martínez Móttola, who reported to the minister. The Venezuelan Investment Fund (FIV), which was to be the government's privatization agency, was actively involved in the initial and the final stages of the CANTV privatization process.

The allocation of one of the two bands reserved for mobile cellular service served as a trial run for the privatization of the CANTV. Mobile cellular telephony service in Venezuela dated back to 1986, when the first system operated by the CANTV was initiated. By December 1990, this system had 7,455 subscribers. After 1988, some international operating companies had shown interest in obtaining a concession for mobile cellular telephone service in competition with the CANTV. It was decided to grant that concession through a competitive process to be handled by the TRG. The success of this process would be a key factor in gaining public trust for the CANTV's privatization. Following traditional practice, the awarding process was divided into two stages: preselection of participating companies and the bidding stage itself. Of the thirty-nine companies seeking prequalification, ten were prequalified, and seven of these submitted bids in January 1991. The highest bidder was Telcel, an association in which Bell South participated with 40 percent, Comunicaciones Telefónicas with 30 percent, Banco de Oriente with 15 percent, Belfort, Baquero & Sánchez (BBS) with 8 percent, and Racal Telecom of the United Kingdom with 2 percent. The acknowledged transparency of the awarding process and the high amount offered for the concession (US$107 million) lent credibility to the TRG and to the privatization process.

The Privatization Strategy

Those managing the process of privatizing the CANTV, such as Gerver Torres (FIV), Roberto Smith (MTC), and Fernando Martínez, were aware of the severe time and political constraints they faced. In December 1992, elections for mayors and state governors would take place. Accordingly, they felt it would be advisable for the privatization process to be concluded in 1991, in order to avoid turning it into an election issue. On the other hand, the politicians' position regarding the process continued to be ambiguous; it was expected that as the electoral process advanced, political opposition would increase.

COPEI, the main opposition party, supported privatization wholeheartedly. At the end of 1990, the MAS and Causa R, both minority leftist parties, openly opposed privatization, while Acción Democrática (AD), the ruling party, was divided. The chairman of the Privatization Commission in the Chamber of Deputies, Raúl Matos Azócar (AD) maintained a reserved attitude regarding the privatization of the CANTV.[2] The AD and COPEI together had enough votes in Congress to produce a solid majority, but the AD could manage a bare majority in coalition with smaller nonleftist parties.

Given the political circumstances, outright privatization seemed risky, and so other alternatives began to be explored, including the use of a management contract and the leasing of the CANTV to a private firm with an option to purchase. The TRG thought that leasing the company would allow control to be transferred to a reputable private operator, thus permitting the CANTV's expansion plans to be launched immediately, while the sale of shares could be carried out after the 1993 elections. By February, political acceptance had been achieved for the leasing plan, with the option to buy a 30 percent share after two years. In February 1990, this was formally announced by the transport and communications minister and the presidents of the FIV and the CANTV. Ten percent of shares would be sold to the company's workers ("This Semester" 1991). In effect, this allowed the TRG to turn over to the next government the hard decision of selling the CANTV's shares.

The complex issues involved in the lease-with-option-to-buy alternative became apparent as the policymakers began to think through the details. Who would own the newly installed plant in this scenario? How would investment be financed? Would the old CANTV plant be progressively retired? What would happen to existing CANTV employees? What about their contractual rights? Would the lessor have a separate contract with its own employees? How long would the CANTV survive as a legal entity? At that point, both the TRG and the FIV reopened the idea of selling the CANTV's shares directly and immediately. The main opposition party, COPEI, seemed ready to support this option, provided the plan provided for improvements in service quality, plant expansion, employment guarantees for CANTV labor, reasonable tariffs, rural and public telephone service, and equity participation by labor ("Eduardo Fernandez" 1991, p. 22). Public opinion seemed to be moving in favor of privatization by the day. In one survey, nearly 80 percent said they believed public services would improve with privatization ("People of Caracas" 1991).

By April 1991, direct sale appeared to be a politically viable alternative. Ildemaro Martínez of COPEI and Carmelo Lauria of the AD, the new party links to the process, understood the complexities involved in the leasing alternative and helped explain this to other party leaders. Meanwhile, groups opposed to privatization, particularly in Congress, continued to warn that privatizing the CANTV would hurt the nation's sovereignty and security. At that critical juncture, the ruling party's leadership endorsed the idea of privatizing the CANTV's ownership. In April 1991, the president of the republic approved his party's decision.

Meanwhile, thirteen international companies[3] presented their credentials on the basis that they satisfied the following prequalification criteria:

Service requirements pertaining to operations in the foreign firm's home market

—Six million or more installed lines

—At least 24 percent of local switchboards digitized

—More than 65 percent of incoming international calls completed successfully

—No more than one month to install a new line

—Sixteen hours or less to repair line faults

Financial requirements

—Gross annual income more than US$5 billion

Information submission requirements

—Letter of intent stating desire to participate in CANTV

—Audited financial statements for the previous three years

—Documents of the company or consortium describing rules of operation, constitution, and the like

—Service indication certificates issued by the respective national regulatory bodies

—Annual reports for the previous three years

Of the thirteen companies, Ameritech, GTE, Bell Canada, Bell Atlantic, France Telecom, Nippon Telephone, Southwestern Bell, and US West fully met the requirements ("Eight Companies" 1992). PTT Telecom, Telefónica de España, Cable & Wireless, STET, and Detacom failed to fulfill at least one of the established requisites. The international response was perceived by Venezuelan officials as very encouraging.

The Conditions Sheet and the Negotiation Process

In July 1991, the Memorandum of Sale, prepared by the investment banks, Lehman Brothers, and S. G. Warburg, was released.[4] The following week, the first versions of the documents of sale were handed out to prospective purchasers for their suggestions.

A data room containing all relevant information was opened to prospective purchasers. It started functioning by the beginning of May. In addition, operator visits were organized to the company's facilities all over the country. Visits could be made to additional facilities by operator request. In August, road presentations were made to top managers of the participating operating companies at their headquarters, including Ken Foster of GTE and J. V. Raymond Cyr of Bell Canada. The Venezuelan government encouraged formation of consortia comprising national and international companies. Each consortium had to include at least one prequalified operator, to assume its leadership. This operator was to have the consortium's statutory control. No firm could participate in more than one consortium, and telecommunications equipment manufacturing companies were excluded from participating as consortia leaders.

By August 1991, it had become known that two consortia, would present bids. Bidders were allowed to own up to 40 percent of the CANTV. The following list (from TRG) shows the percentages that each company bid for:

Consortium 1

Bell Atlantic	37.5
Bell Canada	37.5
Suma Corporation	12.5
Banco Provincial	6.25
Finalven	6.25

Consortium 2

General Telephone and Electronics (GTE)	51.0
American Telephone and Telegraph (AT&T)	5.0
Compañía Nacional Telefónica de España	16.0
Compañía Anónima La Electricidad de Caracas	16.0
Banco Consorcio Inversionista Mercantil (CIMA)	12.0

The first included Bell Atlantic and Bell Canada as equal partners, along with Banco Provincial and Finalven, two Venezuelan financial institutions, and the owner of one of two private television networks in Venezuela. The second consortium was led by GTE, a company that was in the process of moving away from manufacturing electronic and telecommunications equipment to providing telecommunications services. GTE's international strategy included expansion into Latin America, and it successfully operated the telephone company of the Dominican Republic, although it had failed to win the contest for TELMEX of Mexico. AT&T, a key member of GTE's consortium, had long been interested in the long-distance market in Venezuela. GTE's other partners included Telefónica de España, which already owned telephone companies in Argentina and Chile and was keen to expand in Latin American; Electricidad de Caracas, which was one of the most efficient electric utilities in Venezuela and had plans to enter data transmission services using its own network of urban conduits; and Banco Mercantil, which was a well-known Venezuelan financial organization.

Legal experts recommended the FIV as the most suitable governmental agency to handle the sale of CANTV shares. Therefore, the government transferred to the FIV US\$500.16 million in long-term loans and accumulated interest owed by the CANTV to foreign creditors. Likewise, the CANTV's debt and accumulated interest of 4.75 billion bolivars owed to the Ministry of Finance was transferred to the FIV. The CANTV's equity capital was increased from 1,617.5 million bolivars to 36,901.8 million bolivars. The FIV paid for the share increase by submitting the debt cancellation certificate to the CANTV and assuming possession of 95.66

percent of the company's shares. The state, through the Ministry of Transport and Communications, retained the remaining 4.33 percent. These actions strengthened the CANTV's financial situation and paved the way for the share sale, which the FIV was authorized to carry out according to its bylaws.

The Concession Contract

Under the 1940 Telecommunications Law, the state has the authority to provide telecommunications services through private concessionaires. However, following the examples of countries like Mexico, which rewrote the concession agreement between the government and the state enterprises *before* privatization, the Venezuelan government worked on a revised concession agreement for the CANTV. Moreover, the two prospective buyers were invited to give their feedback on the draft concession agreement. Negotiations were held in Caracas between the representatives of each consortium and the TRG, which was assisted by national and international law firms. Negotiations were conducted separately with each consortium, but any modification agreed to with one was automatically offered to the other. As a result, contracts were being drafted almost daily, and as many as eighteen revised drafts were produced. The government's aim was to have all contracts ready and signed by the consortia before the bidding, thus minimizing the need for further negotiations after selection of the winner. Although the concession agreement hammered out through this process and signed by the government and the CANTV in October 1991 was to be revised later by Congress, its main provisions at that time included the following:

—The CANTV received permission to install and operate four types of services for a period of thirty-five years, extendable by another twenty years.

—Switch telephone service would be provided exclusively by the CANTV for nine years for towns with over 5,000 inhabitants.

—Public telephone service, telex, data networks, private networks, and rural and remote telephone service would be offered under free competition. The CANTV was required to interconnect its competitors' services to the switched telephone network as necessary (except private networks).

—Value added services were to be opened up to competition.

—Mobile cellular telephone service (b and b) was to be opened up to competition.

Tariffs

In Venezuela as in other countries, over the years the real tariff for telephone service had fallen dramatically (the following discussion is

Table 5-4. CANTV Tariffs, Residential and Commercial, 1990 and 1992
(current bolivars)

Tariff	Residential		Commercial	
	1990	1992	1990	1992
Connection charge	3,500.00	6,700.00	7,000.00	17,100.00
Monthly rent	45	50	112.50	560.00
Digitization charge	0	60	0	300
Charge per extra pulse	0.50	0.84	0.57	1.23
Number of free pulses	200	100	0	0

Note: Tariffs are as of December 31 of the year. Average exchange rates were US$1 = 47.44 bolivars in 1990 and US$1 = 69 bolivars in 1992.

based on Francés 1993, 250–68). For instance, in 1991, the monthly rent for a residential telephone with 200 free pulses was only 45 bolivars (US$0.78, at the prevailing exchange rate), which was less than one-eighth of the real monthly rent in 1970. Cross-subsidization was extensive: in 1991, the monthly rent for a commercial telephone with no free pulses was 112.5 bolivars (US$1.96), more than double the residential rate, but this too had fallen sharply in real terms since 1970. In 1990, additional pulses were priced at only US$0.01 for residential users and US$0.012 for commercial users. Long-distance rates, too, had fallen sharply in real terms from 1970 to 1990.

Following the examples of Argentina, Jamaica, and Mexico, Venezuela raised tariffs significantly at the time of privatization, especially for nonresidential users (table 5-4). For commercial users, connection charges rose to US$246, monthly rent rose to US$8.10, a digitization charge of US$4.30 per month was added, and the charge per pulse was increased to US$0.017. Although these adjustments were much less drastic than in Mexico, they did serve to raise the CANTV's annual revenue per line from US$247.60 in 1989 to US$559.60 in 1992.

The tariff scheme adopted for the telephone service tried to balance user interests and network expansion needs. Tariffs for services subject to competition were to be set by operators, under broad guidelines from the regulatory agency. Other tariffs were regulated according to the price cap method, or the *RPI – X* method, developed in the United Kingdom. The productivity improvement factor *(X)* was to be applied quarterly, beginning January 1997, with an initial value of 0.75 percent for long-distance and international service and zero for other services. After the year 2000, rates would be fixed by the Ministry of Telecommunications.

Three baskets of services, each with a number of subgroups, were defined.[5] Income ceilings were applied to each basket and group, using a formula similar to the one adopted in Mexico. Ceilings were based on the wholesale price index, which usually increased less rapidly than the consumer price index in Venezuela.[6] Nevertheless, basic rental and local use charges were to increase during the initial years as a consequence of the tariff rebalancing process. This process was to begin in 1994 and included the progressive elimination of the subsidy of local service by long-distance service, in preparation for the opening up of the switched telephone service in 1999. Rebalancing was to follow an exponential formula that delayed increases until quality improvement had been achieved. By the year 2000, tariffs for each service were expected to reflect costs. National and international long-distance calls were expected to be cheaper in real terms than in 1993, while basic residential rent and local calls were expected to become more expensive. The basic residential rent would increase from approximately US$2 in 1992 to US$7 by the year 2000.

Taxes

Venezuela's income tax law, which was modified in 1991 independently of the CANTV's privatization, reduced the maximum corporate tax rate from 50 to 30 percent. A special tax of 5 percent of revenues of telecommunication services was established in the concession contract, along with a 0.5 percent duty to be paid to the ministry. As a government-owned company, the CANTV had been exempt from local taxes.

The Expansion Plan

The CANTV was committed to carrying out an ambitious expansion plan from 1992 to the year 2000. This plan was included as Annex A of the concession contract. It established yearly goals, by region, for the installation of new digital switching lines, replacement of old switching lines, and installation of public telephones. Demand was expected to be met fully by the year 2000. Total lines in service were to increase from 2 million in 1991 to 4.5 million in 2000. Six hundred and forty thousand old lines were to be replaced by digital ones. In the peak year, 450,000 new lines were expected to be installed. The CANTV's highest installation rate prior to privatization was less than 200,000. The number of public telephones in service was expected to total 85,000 by the year 2000 (table 5-5).

The Service Quality Plan

Service standards to be met by the year 2000 were set at levels prevalent in North America in 1991 (table 5-6). These goals, however, were considered by some to be overly ambitious. Quality of service, particularly in Caracas, was very poor. Waiting time for installation of new orders was as

Table 5-5. CANTV Expansion Goals in the Concession Contract, 1992–2000

Year	Additional Digital Lines	Total Lines	Public Telephones in Service
1992	169,500	2,196,240	45,000
1993	260,900	2,382,140	50,000
1994	300,000	2,607,140	55,000
1995	390,000	2,922,140	60,000
1996	470,000	3,317,140	65,000
1997	470,000	3,712,140	70,000
1998	450,000	4,087,140	75,000
1999	280,000	4,292,140	80,000
2000	220,000	4,437,140	85,000

Source: Concession contract, Annex A.

Table 5-6. CANTV Quality of Service, Actual, 1991 and 1992, and Targets for 1992 and 2000

Criterion	1991[1]	1992 Target	1992 Actual	2000[2]
Dial tone in 3 seconds (%)	—	78	90	98
Local calls completed (%)	48	52	53	68
Long-distance calls completed (%)	31	38	39	68
International calls completed (%)	19	25	33	65
Response time for operator services (sec.)	—	10	<5	5
Failures repaired in 24 hours (%)	43	52	57	70
Failures repaired in 48 hours (%)	58	70	78	90
Billing complaints (%)	1	<15	1	1
Customer satisfaction (%)	—	>15	51	98

Source: CANTV.

[1] December, actual.

[2] Target.

— = not available.

long as eight years. In Caracas, certain exchanges were virtually unreachable. At peak hours, it was sometimes necessary to wait several minutes to obtain a dial tone. It was not unusual to wait months to get a telephone repaired, and bribes were commonly used to speed up the process.

The concession contract established the regulatory conditions that would apply to the CANTV. They included the approval of rates and expansion plans, the monitoring of service performance, the achievement of contractual goals, the rules to apply at times of national emergency, and information reporting requirements. Regulatory responsibility was transferred from the Ministry of Transport and Communications to a new agency, the Comisión Nacional de Telecomunicaciones (Conatel), which was created in November 1991.

The Shares Sales Contract

The CANTV sale was to be governed by a number of restrictions. First, whoever purchased the CANTV could not sell those shares until January 1997 and had to retain 30 percent ownership until January 1999 and a 20 percent ownership until January 2001. Second, the lead investor in the consortium had to retain a 51 percent controlling interest in the consortium until January 2001. Third, any transfer of shares between members of the consortium would be subject to approval by the Ministry of Transport and Communications. And finally, four categories of shares were to be established: class A shares would belong to the consortium; class B would belong to the Republic of Venezuela; class C shares were to be placed in a trust to be sold to CANTV employees; and class D shares were available for purchase by other parties. No class D shares existed at the time of sale. Any sale of class A, B, or C shares to private parties would automatically render them class D shares. A total of 1,000 million shares were issued, of which 400 million were class A, 490 million were class B, and 110 million were class C, with a value of 286 bolivars (US$4.70) each. The vote of class B shares was required for decisions such as dissolving or merging the company or for selling its assets.

Until January 2001, the CANTV's president and four directors, as well as their deputies, were to be named by the owners of class A shares. Until January 2001, two directors and their deputies were to be named by the owners of the majority of class B shares. Thereafter, the Venezuelan government would name one director and his or her deputy, regardless of the number of shares it owned. Two directors and their deputies were to be named by the CANTV's employees.

Last-Minute Maneuvers

Two last-minute maneuvers were to occur before the bids were opened on November 15, about two weeks behind schedule. The first related to congressional approval of the concession contract and the second related to employee ownership in the company.

Although some experts believed that congressional approval of the concession agreement between the government and the CANTV was not required, other experts argued otherwise.[7] In the end, the government seems to have regarded such approval as legitimizing and stabilizing the privatization process, although as feared it gave the opposition parties an opportunity to attack the whole idea. MAS, the socialist party, suggested that at least the basic network should remain in the hands of the state and argued that selling the CANTV to a foreign company would result in excessive tariff increases and place basic services beyond the reach of the country's middle class, not to speak of the very poor ("MAS

Opposed" 1991; "Middle and Poor Class" 1991). MAS, was joined in its general opposition to the privatization plan by the Causa R party, which further demanded that the concession agreement ought in fact to be enshrined into law by Congress ("Agreement or a Law?" 1991). However, the ruling party (AD), with the support of the principal (right-of-center) opposition party, rejected the idea of enacting a law but agreed to refer the matter to a Bicameral Commission ("CANTV Concession" 1991).

Although the political process was tightly managed by the government, the Bicameral Commission introduced seven modifications to the concession contract: one of these gave greater powers to the ministry in framing rules for interconnection, the second redefined the conditions regarding the use of private lines, the third clarified that in the event of a breach of contract the rules established earlier for the oil industry would apply to the CANTV as well, the fourth clarified the rules for economic compensation, and the fifth redefined the rules for arbitration. While amendments of this sort pleased the Bicameral Commission and strengthened national sovereignty over the affairs of the CANTV, they upset potential investors like GTE and Bell Atlantic, especially on the subjects of "economic compensation" and "arbitration."[8] The GTE, in particular, was reportedly very upset by these unilateral modifications; it considered withdrawing from the process but was persuaded by government officials not to do so. To allow time to sort out these complications, the government delayed the date for submission of bids by two weeks, to November 15, 1991.

In those two weeks, the concluding steps were undertaken at a frenetic pace. First, a cabinet meeting chaired by the country's president unofficially approved the final amendments to the concession contract ("Last Night at Miraflores" 1991). Next, at an extraordinary cabinet meeting those amendments were officially approved. The following day, the transport and communications minister and the chairman of the CANTV signed the corresponding supplement to the concession agreement, subject to congressional approval. On November 4, the Executive Committee of the AD approved the concession contract by a wide margin, and the agreement was forwarded to the Congress, where a few more clauses were modified to satisfy the Bicameral Commission's objections.[9] On November 7, 1991, the Bicameral Commission approved the final report by a vote of fifteen in favor and two opposed and turned the matter over to the full Congress ("Congress Admitted" 1991). The MAS and Causa R benches used every dilatory tactic within their reach to delay approval, including filing a judicial appeal against the privatization process ("Protection Resource" 1991). However, the Civil Court declared the appeal for protection inadmissible and ratified the legality of the process followed ("CANTV: Protection" 1991). President Pérez, on his part, described those opposed to the plan as "old people from the past" ("CAP" 1991). Finally, on November 13, 1991, two days before the opening of bids and after an eight-hour debate, the entire chamber approved the concession agreement. A last-ditch attempt by the opposition parties to declare the contract a matter of "national interest," which would have forced a postponement of the opening of bids, was defeated in the Senate by a 42–2 vote and in the Chamber of Deputies by a 136–18 vote ("AD-COPEI Pact" 1991).

But while the legislative process was being wrapped up, the deal made with the CANTV's labor unions on employee stock ownership began to unravel. The idea of allowing for employee share ownership in the CANTV was actively supported by the labor unions as well as the ruling party (AD). From the outset, it was agreed that employee participation would be voluntary, that the amount of shares for which each employee would be eligible would depend on his or her seniority and salary level, that financing would be arranged to help workers buy shares, and that they would be represented on the board of directors. Employees were offered 110 million shares, or 11 percent of the stock, at a price of 284 bolivars each.

In September 1991, the national federation of labor (CTV) announced its support for the CANTV's privatization ("The CTV Decided" 1991). The umbrella trade union organization also created two commissions to participate in the CANTV privatization process. However, three days prior to the opening of bids, the CTV leaders declared that the privatization process was a "fraud," since employees and workers lacked the ability to pay close to 13 billion bolivars (US$200 million) in nine years ("CTV: CANTV" 1991). They threatened to request another postponement of the bid opening if a satisfactory employee share participation agreement could not be achieved ("CTV May Request" 1991). On November 15, one hour before the opening of bids was scheduled, a labor share participation agreement was signed between the CTV and the FIV that sweetened the plan even further: workers were given ten years to pay for their shares, free of interest, through payroll deductions of up to 10 percent of salary. After ten years, the shares were to be redeemed and any outstanding debt on them condoned.

With that last-minute headache resolved, the government was ready to accept and open bids on November 15, 1991, in the auditorium of Venezuela's central bank. The Bell Atlantic consortium bid US$1,407 million for 40 percent of the CANTV, while the GTE-led consortium bid US$1,885 million, or fully 34 percent higher. Fernando Martínez had the opportunity to refute the criticism that the CANTV would be sold for next to nothing and that the winner had been predetermined. The tumultuous ceremony at the central bank was followed by further cele-

brations in the Miraflores Palace.[10] On December 6, 1991, the sales
contract was signed with the GTE-led consortium, funds were transferred
into a New York account of the Venezuelan Republic, and the biggest
step in CANTV's privatization was completed.

Preliminary Results

Although it was too soon in 1994 to evaluate the results of the CANTV
privatization, there were several points on which government officials
could be satisfied about the whole experiment. For one thing, the state
had successfully transferred control of the company to the winning
consortium by selling 40 percent of the shares, while keeping 49 percent
and placing 11 percent in a trusteeship to be sold to company employees.
The selling price, in dollars per line, was probably the highest price paid
for a telephone company privatization until then.[11] The winning consortium consisted of some of the world's leading telecommunications companies, and the Venezuelan partners were equally luminous. The same
could be said of the consortium that lost the bid.

But more importantly, CANTV's telephone plant expansion plans for
the first few years surpassed the line installation goals stipulated by the
government. Instead of aiming to install 170,000 lines in 1992 and increasing that number steadily to 470,000 in 1996, as required by the
concession contract, the CANTV decided it was both feasible and profitable to install 354,000 lines in 1992 and 450,000 lines in 1993. Total lines
to be installed by 2000 remained the same, 4.5 million, but further
increases would be considered if the demand materialized. According to
plans submitted by the CANTV (table 5-7), telephone density would reach
eighteen lines per 100 inhabitants in the year 2000, a level equal to that
of Portugal in 1993 but still below that of South Korea (twenty-four lines
per 100 inhabitants) and Spain (twenty-eight lines per 100 inhabitants).
Likewise, digitization would rise from 20 percent in 1991 to 80 percent
by the year 2000.

Along several dimensions, the actual results for 1992 and 1993 were
as good as or even better than the targets set for the CANTV in the concession agreement (table 5-8).

However, the winning consortium did face difficulties in its dealings
with unions, despite the fact that salaries more than doubled after privatization and the value of the employees' shares in the CANTV had
grown substantially. The unions were accustomed to an antagonistic
relations with the company's management and strove to maintain their
power. Labor strikes occurred in 1992 and 1993 at the time of contract
negotiations. The radical party (Causa R), which fiercely opposed privatization, controlled the CANTV's unions in Caracas and was trying to

Table 5-7. CANTV Long-Term Expansion Plan, 1991–2000

Criterion	1991	1992	1993	2000
Number of customers (millions)	1.5	1.8	2.1	4.4
Number of public telephones (thousands)	31.7	45.0	50.0	85.0
Lines/100 people	8	9	11	18
International circuits	2,010	2,767	3,418	8,000
Digitization (%)	20	36	46	80

Source: CANTV.

Table 5-8. CANTV, Concession Contract Targets and Actual Performance, 1992 and 1993

Program	Target		Actual	
	1992	1993	1992	1993
Line expansion and modernization program	210,600	335,900	413,000	453,000
New customers	a	a	210,000	251,000
New public telephones	13,400	5,000	13,400	5,060
Replacement of public telephones	a	a	10,000	12,000

Source: CANTV.

aNot specified in concession contract.

expand its influence. Causa R also capitalized on the fears and resentments of the many redundant or unqualified employees of the CANTV, even though the company was not permitted under the concession agreement to make drastic payroll reductions.

From a user's point of view, a perceptible improvement was evident in international and in national long-distance telephone service between the main cities (see table 5-6). Operator-attended services improved substantially, such as for operator information or repair assistance. On the other hand, even in 1994 the quality of local service in Caracas had improved only slightly, much like TELMEX's experience in the Mexico City region (chapter 3). Also, the time to repair failures and make new connections was still unacceptably long and subject to extortion attempts by employees. However, improvement in these areas were expected as the CANTV initiated an anticorruption campaign, asking the public to report abuses by company employees. Users also benefited from the broader range of telecommunications service that became available because of deregulation of the sector in conjunction with the privatization of the CANTV. These included value added services, which combine telecommunications with data processing and mobile satellite services, and cellular telephony, where Telcel, the CANTV's competitor, had more than 100,000 subscribers by the beginning of 1993.[12]

The government also granted eight concessions and seventeen per mits to operate private telecommunications networks, thus allowing entry by some of the major international long-distance service companies into the country, particularly in data networks. Private network investment in 1992 was US$30 million, and its impact on improvement in telecommunications service was visible even by 1993. In addition, the government granted eight concessions for trunking services, five for value added services, and one for mobile data service. These services were to enter into operation once the corresponding service regulations and the conditions for interconnection with the CANTV's basic network were approved.

The buying consortium was able to capture what seemed, at least until 1993, an attractive opportunity. The investment fit nicely with the GTE's expansion strategy, building on the experience in the United States and the Dominican Republic. Telefónica de España was also able to continue its expansion into Latin America, while AT&T obtained a toehold in a market it had been trying for years to enter. At the time, its local partner, Electricidad de Caracas, had projects under way in the data transmission business, and the investment in the CANTV seemed to offer it a useful connection with the dominant firm in the sector.

As in the United Kingdom and Argentina, the Venezuelan government, in September 1991, created an autonomous regulatory agency, Conatel, under the Ministry of Transport and Communications, which began functioning a few months before the CANTV's privatization. It had a seven-member advisory council, a general director reporting to the minister, and a technical staff. The core of Conatel personnel came from the TRG. The success achieved in the sector's privatization and liberalization granted this team enough prestige and legitimacy to exercise a leading role in the telecommunications sector. Conatel's tasks as a regulating entity were divided into those relating to the sector's liberalization and those relating to compliance with ongoing concession agreements. The CANTV was required to submit its annual expansion plans to Conatel up to the year 2000. In 1992, Conatel and the CANTV agreed on the methodology to be applied for measuring service quality. Conatel was also responsible for overseeing the application of the corresponding service regulations, particularly those regarding interconnection among competing service networks.[13] Finally, Conatel established a system for tracking customer complaints.

The Outlook for Competition and Regulation

In developing countries, the basic network continues to require substantial investment to achieve an acceptable telephonic density. In Venezuela, for instance, the CANTV was expected to have to invest US$10 billion to achieve a density of twenty main telephones per 100 inhabitants. More than half the funds necessary for achieving this were expected to come from internal sources, notably from domestic and international long-distance service, which were priced well above marginal costs. The nine-year exclusivity period granted to the CANTV in its concession contract was intended to shelter it from competition in these lucrative segments.

At the same time, it was already clear by 1994 that competition was beginning to nibble away at the fringes of the CANTV's power in areas such as cellular service and private data networks. The concession contract permitted the CANTV to provide under competition every telecommunications service "existing or to be invented." However, in areas other than basic service, the CANTV's competitors could hope to take the lead. For instance, in cellular service, by 1993 the CANTV's sole competitor, Telecel, had signed on two subscribers for every one signed on by the CANTV, leading to a total of 150,000 cellular users within a space of three years. On the other hand, the granting of concessions for some other services, including value added services and public telephones, had been delayed by lengthy negotiations between Conatel, the regulatory agency, and the CANTV regarding the terms of interconnection, not unlike those witnessed in Mexico. It was obvious that the CANTV had every incentive to try to delay the entry of competitors. In the future, the CANTV will also have the advantage of operating a modern fiber-optic network, which was under construction in 1993.

Another potential source of competition were private network operators offering national and international voice and data circuits. Concessions were granted to operators intending to provide this service on a commercial basis, either by renting transmission capacity wholesale from the CANTV or by installing their networks and then leasing them to users. The latter provision did not exist in other Latin American countries where telecommunications had been privatized and was strongly resisted by the two competing consortia during the contract negotiations phase. The target market for private circuit operators was the 400 large companies that accounted for the bulk of the CANTV's long-distance revenues. Connection of private circuits to the switched telephone network was forbidden but difficult to monitor and, in practice, was widespread, according to CANTV sources. Furthermore, some companies obtained concessions for several services, such as private networks, trunking and value added, raising for the CANTV the specter of rival integrated networks in the future. These potential competitors would be spared the burden of developing and operating underground local networks and could rely, instead, on microwave links to customer premises.

In summary, competition could benefit consumers by spurring the

CANTV to offer improved services at lower rates, but it could also divert away resources that might otherwise have been used to expand the basic network.

The preceding considerations highlight the role of the regulatory body in achieving a balance between expanding the basic system and injecting competition into the market. It was often argued that competition in telecommunications was a luxury that Venezuela could ill afford, but the government's approach was also influenced by the following arguments in favor of competition. First, competition would mute the political opposition to privatization, which claimed that privatization would merely turn a public monopoly into a private, foreign-controlled monopoly. Second, competition could be used to attract multiple investors into the sector. And, finally, the experience of developed countries, in particular the United States and the United Kingdom, suggested that competition was the wave of the future.

By introducing competition, Conatel's task was made far more difficult, and it became vulnerable to criticism from all sides, thus weakening its institutional standing and even threatening its survival. Paradoxically, the introduction of competition—even if only slightly—increased rather than decreased the need for a technically sound, politically independent, and corruption-free regulatory body. Conatel faced enormous challenges in negotiating the terms of competition for new services that would satisfy the CANTV as well as the other concessionaires. The CANTV argued that Conatel was permitting excessive competition and detracting from CANTV's rights under the concession agreement, while other operators felt that Conatel was not doing enough to protect them from the CANTV's enormous power. Both sides used experts to support their respective positions, drawing to Caracas experts from the GTE, on the CANTV's behalf, as well as from the MCI, Sprint, and other international operators, who were partners of the CANTV's local competitors. Although Conatel's own experts were highly motivated and well trained, they were not much of a match for the resources the multinational firms deployed. Indeed, delays in resolving issues regarding competition led the provisional Venezuelan government that held office in the second half of 1993 to postpone the sale of the government's remaining holdings in the CANTV.

Conatel survived virtually intact the first change in government in May 1993, when President Carlos Andrés Pérez was forced out of office under charges of corruption, but only because of the intense lobbying by private firms and industry associations against a change in Conatel's leadership. (A bill proposing legal autonomy for Conatel and granting its head a fixed-term appointment was not approved by Congress.) However, Conatel was less lucky when the administration changed one more time, in February 1994, when parties opposed to the CANTV's privatization came into office. Under the new president, Rafael Caldera, the director general of Conatel was replaced by a political appointee, calling into question the future course of regulation. At the time of writing, it was unclear if this change in Conatel's leadership would lead to the exodus of its core technical staff, a group that in the Venezuelan context could not be replaced easily.

Despite the developments in 1994, the privatization of the CANTV is unlikely to be reversed because a future government is unlikely to be able to find the money required to buy back the privately owned shares, and outright expropriation seems out of the question, given its international and foreign policy implications. However, since the government and the workers still owned a combined 60 percent of the CANTV's shares in 1994, a government hostile to the CANTV and to the sector's privatization could try to change the bylaws of the company to regain control of the firm. Another point of attack could be the quarterly rate revision by the CANTV that requires Conatel's approval. Repression or delays in the granting of rate increases could be viewed by the CANTV as a breach of the concession contract, leading to lawsuits or legal arbitration.

If Conatel manages to survive reasonably unscathed the political ups and downs that seem inevitable in Venezuela, and if future governments recognize the importance of telecommunications for the country's development, the original plans for expanding and modernizing the sector through the year 1999, when the CANTV's exclusivity period ends, may be realized. However, it is more likely than not that deviations will occur from the scenario envisaged at the time of the CANTV's privatization.

Lessons from the Venezuelan Experience

In retrospect, the Venezuelan telecommunications restructuring process was surprisingly smooth and successful. This success was due not only to good planning but also to favorable circumstances. Venezuela was fortunate that the privatization of the CANTV was guided by high-caliber technocrats and that the TRG worked as a cohesive group. These officials also benefited from World Bank support and international expertise. The experience of awarding the concession for the second mobile cellular telephony service proved useful as a practice run for the CANTV's privatization. Venezuela also adopted a relatively open and systematic approach to setting the conditions of the sale, the evaluation of bids, and so on. Unlike the Jamaican case, described in chapter 2, officials in Venezuela used a transparent approach and paid attention to public opinion and the media. And unlike the Argentine case described in chapter 4, the CANTV's performance improved rather than worsened in the time up to privatization. Finally, Venezuela was wise to create a separate regulatory agency for telecommunications, although in 1994 the future role and status of that agency were clouded by political uncertainty.

In addition, one must recognize that the Venezuelan economy's growth potential probably made the CANTV a highly desirable telecommunications company in which to invest. In 1991, while CANTV was being sold, the Venezuelan economy was showing clear signs of vitality and expansion. One cannot help wondering what the sale price might have been if the privatization had taken place in 1992, soon after two unsuccessful coup attempts, or in 1994, when economic conditions deteriorated dramatically. Potential buyers might have used a higher discount rate, thus bidding a much lower price. The speed of the privatization process, criticized by some as being excessive, appears in retrospect to have been all too appropriate.

When we compare the Venezuelan telecommunications privatization with other similar processes in Latin America, including those examined in the three previous chapters, the Venezuelan case must be judged a qualified success. First, the price paid per installed line was one of the highest, at US$2,900 per line versus US$1,900 per line in Mexico. At the same time, Venezuela did not fall into the trap of seeking too high a selling price, as was the case in Puerto Rico. Second, some political and labor problems were avoided, thus preventing open conflicts or important delays, as happened in Argentina, although labor held a higher share of equity than in Argentina or Mexico and also had a seat on the board. Third, the clear definition of the conditions of the sale before the submission of bids probably reduced uncertainty for the buyers and increased the price realized by the government. Fourth, the prequalification of operators and the condition of placing the leadership of the buying consortium in the hands of a ranking international operator brought about a clearer control structure and better access to international technology and experience than was achieved elsewhere. Fifth, similar to Mexico and Argentina, an expansion and service quality improvement program was established. Also, a method to periodically review rates was established, as in Argentina, Chile, and Mexico. Sixth, nonbasic services were opened to competition, as in Chile and Mexico, thus limiting the monopoly of the basic network operator. Seventh, as in Mexico, only part of the shares were sold at the outset and the state kept 49 percent to be sold later. Eighth, a regulatory agency, separated from the communications ministry, was created, similar to the one created in Argentina.

In summary, the restructuring process of the telecommunications sector in Venezuela took advantage of the experience in Latin America and elsewhere, as well as the regulatory experience of the United States, the United Kingdom, and other industrialized countries. At the same time, by adding innovations of its own, Venezuela broadened the range of ideas and alternatives, which other developing countries could consider when privatizing their own telephone monopolies. Yet, Venezuela illustrates the difficulties of regulating sectors such as telecommunications under conditions of political uncertainty and instability, even when a measure of competition is injected into the sector and the regulatory agency is created as a quasi-independent entity. Further, the political and economic instability that hit Venezuela in 1993 and 1994 underlines the importance of macroeconomic conditions in determining the long-run results from privatization. In the end, those conditions will probably account as much for the CANTV's performance as who owns the enterprise.

NOTES

1. On the Venezuela airlines, see chapter 9.

2. Matos Azócar was the planning minister (Cordiplan) between 1984 and 1986, during Jaime Lusinchi's government.

3. Ameritech, Bell Atlantic, Bell Canada, Cable & Wireless, France Telecom, Detacom, GTE, Nippon Telephone, PTT Telecom Netherland, Southwestern Bell, STET, Telefónica de España, and US West.

4. The Memorandum of Sale described the nature of the proposed transaction and contained information about the country and its economy, the telecommunications sector, and the CANTV.

5. Basket 1 included all services except installation and monthly rent for residential subscribers, which were included in basket 3; basket 2 included interconnection charges.

6. Between January 1992 and July 1993 telephone tariffs rose by only 24% compared to a 50% increase in the consumer price index.

7. One adviser felt that congressional approval was not mandatory since the 1940 telecommunications law authorized the executive branch to grant concessions. However, two other advisers deemed such approval necessary, with one of them expressing the view that concession contracts signed with the CANTV in 1930, 1955, and 1965 had been adopted as laws by Congress. See "Government Presents Three Judgments" 1991.

8. In the original text, arbitration lacked any recourse of appeal. It was modified to allow appeals to the Venezuelan Supreme Court.

9. There were modifications of the economic stability clause, which did not guarantee company profitability but rather continuity of service during political changes or natural disasters, and clauses that gave television stations direct access to satellites and reiterated that all users should receive equal treatment in terms of quality of service, prices, and access.

10. The bid opening ceremony, attended by a good part of the country's

political and business elite, was extremely emotional. When the winning bid was announced, pandemonium broke out and it took close to twenty minutes to restore calm in the auditorium. The Miraflores ceremony was probably the high point of Carlos Andrés Pérez's presidency. Less than three months later, an attempted military coup and its aftermath signaled Pérez's rapid slide toward unpopularity and his eventual removal from office.

11. Considering that 2 million lines were installed by the end of 1991, it cost US$2,356 per line, or nearly US$2,900 per line in service, compared to US$1,900 in the case of TELMEX.

12. The growth of this service in Venezuela was among the fastest recorded in the world. Movilnet, an affiliate of CANTV, was slower to respond, although it too was expanding rapidly. In 1992 mobile cellular telephony investments reached US$292 million.

13. In 1993, the CANTV expressed concern about private circuit networks being used for transmitting switched telephone traffic. It claimed that high-speed data networks could be used for voice transmission, especially if concession holders were allowed to operate both private voice circuits and data networks.

REFERENCES

"AD-COPEI Pact Approved CANTV Privatization." 1991. *El Informador*, Nov. 14.

"Agreement or a Law? CANTV Provokes Legal Issue." 1991. *Reporte*, Sept. 27.

Ambrose, William, Paul R. Hennemeyer, and Jean-Paul Chapon. 1990. *Privatizing Telecommunications Systems: Business Opportunities in Developing Countries.* Discussion Paper 10. Washington, D.C.: World Bank.

Baring Securities. 1991. *Teléfonos de México: Mexico's Telecommunications Giant.* Boston.

"CANTV Concession Shall Be Presented in Agreement Form." 1991. *El Diario de Caracas*, Sept. 28.

"CANTV: Protection Resource Declared Inadmissible." 1991. *Economia Hoy*, Nov. 15.

"CAP: The Old People from the Past Are Opposed to Privatization." *El Nacional*, Nov. 15.

"Congress Admitted the Final CANTV Report." 1991. *Reporte*, Nov. 13.

"CTV: CANTV Privatization a Fraud." 1991. *Critica*, Nov. 13.

"CTV May Request Envelope Opening Postponement." 1991. *El Diario de Caracas*, Nov. 12.

"The CTV Decided to Support Privatization of CANTV." 1991. *El Universal*, Sept. 26.

"Eduardo Fernandez to the CANTV: People Are Insulted with the Poor Telephone Service Rendered." 1991. *2001*, Jan 30.

"Eight Companies Qualify as Potential CANTV Operators." 1992. *El Nacional*, Apr. 23.

Francés, Antonio. 1993. *¡Aló Venezuela! Apertura y Privatización de las Telecomunicaciones.* Caracas: Conatel-Ediciones IESA.

Gonzalez Valle, F., F. Garcia Ruiz, et al. 1990. "Informe para el World Bank sobre la Compañia Anónima de Teléfonos de Venezuela." Vols. 1 and 2. Madrid.

"Government Presents Three Judgments on CANTV Concession Contract." 1991. *El Universal*, Sept. 21.

"Last Night at Miraflores: AD-Government Analyzed the CANTV Privatization." 1991. *El Nacional*, Nov. 1.

"MAS Opposed to Total Transfer of CANTV to the Private Sector." 1991. *El Nacional*, Feb. 12.

"Middle and Poor Class Will Not Be Able to Meet High Telephone Cost." 1991. *El Espacio*, Mar. 24.

Ministry of Transport and Communications. 1991. "Contrato de Concesion entre la Republica de Venezuela, MTC y la Compañia Anónima Nacional Teléfonos de Venezuela." Caracas.

"People of Caracas Demand Privatization." 1991. *El Nacional*, Feb. 12.

"Protection Resource against CANTV Concession." 1991. *Economia Hoy*, Nov. 13.

"This Semester Operations Will Be Privatized." 1991. *El Diario de Caracas*, Feb. 3.

Wellenius, Bjorn, Paul A. Stern, and Timothy E. Nulty, eds. 1989. *Restructuring and Managing the Telecommunications Sector*. Washington, D.C.: World Bank.

II. AIRLINES

6. Ownership and Competition in Chile's Airline Industry

· ·

Ricardo Paredes-Molina and Ravi Ramamurti

Linea Aérea Nacional of Chile (LAN-Chile) is an interesting case for study because, over its six decades of existence, conditions in its market varied a great deal. For nearly the first thirty years, it operated as a state-owned monopoly in the domestic market and the sole Chilean carrier on international routes. Over the next twenty years, it shared the domestic market with a small private firm, Linea Aérea del Cobre (LADECO), in a market that, on the surface, was competitive but that in fact was rigged by the government in LAN's favor. For nearly a decade thereafter (1979–89), LAN operated as a state-owned firm in markets that were truly quite competitive, as Chile adopted an "open skies" policy similar to the one adopted in the United States. Finally, from 1989 onward, LAN operated as a privatized firm in a market that continued to be competitive. By 1993, that competition came mainly from other Chilean carriers, especially LADECO, and on international routes from large U.S. carriers like American Airlines and United Air Lines.

In other words, the Chilean experience serves as a natural experiment in which market structure, regulatory regime, and ownership changed systematically. This allows one to raise such questions as: How did LAN behave when it was a state-owned monopoly? How and why did a private competitor (LADECO) enter the industry when a state monopoly was already entrenched? What was the nature of competition in the resulting duopoly? Did the state-owned LAN and privately owned LADECO respond differently to the onset of competition under Chile's open skies policy? And, with market structure and regulation remaining more or less stable, how did privatization affect the behavior and performance of LAN?

177

To be sure, a single case study does not permit one to generate definitive answers to these questions, even if all the historical data were readily available, which was not the case. In fact, data on LAN were patchy for most of the years when Chile was under military rule (1973–89), even on basic variables such as sales, profitability, employment, and prices. Nevertheless, the study did yield some interesting hypotheses and findings.

Phase One: Era of Weak Competition (1929–1978)

In LAN's early years it operated as a state-owned monopoly. LAN's origin was not very different from that of other national airlines; it was started in 1929 by a military government to strengthen transport links within the country. Air links were particularly important in Chile's case, given the country's unusually long but narrow dimensions and its low population density. In particular, the military leaders of the time were keen to establish links between Santiago, the nation's capital, and Arica, the northernmost city in the country, which Chile had recently won from Peru in a bitter war.

LAN's primary task, as suggested by its original name, was to transport mail within the country.[1] Its goals, organizational structure, and methods of operation appear to have evolved in a manner similar to that of many state-owned enterprises. Although profitability was one of its goals, other goals, strategic and social, were also considered important. Similarly, although LAN was created as an autonomous enterprise outside the traditional government structure, like many state enterprises in Chile and elsewhere, it borrowed systems for planning, organizing, personnel management, and compensation from the government. For instance, the rules for hiring and firing employees or setting their salary levels were modeled after those of the civil service. Consequently, LAN began to exhibit the strengths and weaknesses often seen in state enterprises. On the one hand, LAN seems to have helped the government accomplish its main objective of transporting people and mail by air within Chile, especially to remote parts of the country, whether the icy south or the desolate north; it also became Chile's flag carrier on international routes. However, these gains were achieved without much regard for cost, quality of service, or trends in the marketplace. LAN is believed to have reported considerable losses in these years.

The organizational rigidity displayed by LAN seems to have reinforced the notion that it needed protection from competition. As a result, for most of the first thirty years of its existence, no other Chilean carrier was allowed to compete with LAN on domestic routes, and only after fifty years was another Chilean carrier allowed to enter the international segment. LAN's monopoly position was preserved by the Junta Aeronautica Civil (JAC), or the Chilean Aeronautical Authority, a five-person board appointed by the nation's president. It should be noted that the JAC had the authority, if it so wished, to permit other Chilean operators in the airline industry. Not until 1957 was that authority in fact exercised.

That year, Chile's airline industry began a new chapter with the birth of a small tourist carrier, later renamed Linea Aérea del Cobre (LADECO), the Copper Airline. Apparently, the government permitted this new airline not because its support for LAN was wavering but because LADECO was seen as augmenting LAN's role on a very limited scale and in a very limited area, namely the transport of copper workers from their homes to their mines in places such as Calama, Potrerillos, El Salvador, and Antofagasta. In addition, LADECO was permitted to serve a route to Puerto Aysen.

LADECO seems to have made the most of this limited opportunity by providing good service to copper workers, who became an increasingly powerful lobby in Chilean politics. Yet, for two decades after its creation, LADECO remained the junior player in the industry, picking up the crumbs falling off LAN's plate, as it were, and accepting a regulatory system in which LAN's interest came first. Until 1979, LADECO and LAN never competed on the same routes. Nor was LADECO able to seek the right to fly on more domestic routes, except those that LAN willingly gave up from time to time.

Yet, LADECO found its business expanding at a slow but steady rate, chiefly because LAN found itself dropping more and more routes over time. LADECO seems to have been able to make money on those routes because of its lower cost structure, notwithstanding the fact LADECO's scale of operations was one-sixth or one-seventh that of LAN. Besides higher overheads and excess employment, LAN seems to have suffered from having a heterogeneous, obsolete fleet of aircraft.[2] Moreover, since the tariffs of both airlines were fixed by the JAC, LAN's higher cost structure may have resulted in pricing rules that enabled lower-cost LADECO to earn attractive returns.[3]

By the early 1960s, LAN was receiving a government subsidy equal to about 60 percent of total costs, partly to cover operating deficits and partly to finance capital outlays. As LAN's dependence on government funds increased, its operating autonomy declined while the influence of the government's budget office grew; LAN became even less responsive to the needs of customers and markets, which further worsened its performance.

To break this vicious cycle of poor performance leading to lower autonomy and even worse performance, in 1964, the Christian Democratic government of Eduardo Frei brought in a new executive vice president, Eric Campaña, to turn LAN around. Over the next six years, Campaña made efforts to improve operational efficiency by reducing maintenance costs, using incentive schemes to increase employee productivity, and rationalizing the route structure. However, his most significant achievement seems to have been persuading the government to pass the National Airline Organic Law (Federal Decree Law 3 of 1969), which clarified LAN's obligations, privileges, and operational freedoms. The law spelled out LAN's obligation to meet the country's needs for air transport, including the operation of unprofitable routes, but it conceded that the government should compensate the firm out of the national budget for any resulting losses and provide the funds necessary to achieve the assigned goals. In terms of privileges, it exempted LAN from all taxes and duties but not from any incentives that may be offered to the airline industry, required that all public sector officials acquire tickets only from LAN when traveling for work, and that all public sector cargo be transported via LAN. In addition, the law required that LAN "must be consulted prior to the discussion and conclusion of international agreements on air transport or any other act . . . granting permission . . . to operate commercially in the country" (Hachette and Lüders 1993, 246). Under Campaña's leadership, LAN reportedly showed a profit for the first time in its history.

However, as in the case of so many state enterprises, that improvement turned out to be short-lived. With the election of Salvador Allende, a socialist, as president in 1970, the Chilean economic landscape was rapidly transformed. While the private sector was severely affected by the government's sweeping nationalization program, state firms were affected by price controls and by the government's effort to create jobs in those firms. Inflation soared to 500 percent per annum even though the prices of 3,000 items were pegged, the budget deficit rose to 25 percent of GDP, and customs duties averaged 105 percent. Within two to three years, employment in LAN doubled from 2,000 to about 4,000, and domestic airfares fell in real terms. However, under the government's multiple exchange rate system, LAN's foreign exchange revenues were converted to local currency at nearly four times the rate at which LAN's imports were converted.[4] This hidden subsidy seems to have kept LAN afloat during the Allende years.

Interestingly enough, Allende's sweeping nationalization program did not include LADECO, for reasons that appear to have been essentially political in nature. For one thing, LADECO's excellent service seems to have won the hearts of the powerful copper workers, who would have opposed LADECO's nationalization even though the copper industry itself had been nationalized by Allende. In addition, LADECO seems to have been financially connected with *El Mercurio,* the most influential newspaper in the country, which also opposed nationalization. At any rate, in retrospect, the Allende years seem to have weakened LAN's health while leaving LADECO relatively unaffected, thus continuing the long-term trend in which LAN's position declined relative to LADECO's.

The squeeze on LAN that began in the Allende period only worsened under the military junta of Augusto Pinochet, which overthrew Allende in 1973. The new government embarked immediately on a denationalization and economic austerity program that subjected state enterprises to a "hard budget" constraint and required them to cut employment by 20 percent and freeze wages. A new decree passed in 1974 (Supreme Decree 15 of 1974) also forbade the government to extend new subsidies to state firms. Consequently, when the government adopted a unified exchange rate system, LAN's hidden subsidy under the multiple exchange rate system ended abruptly, and the firm was forced to borrow to stay afloat. Since Minister of Economy J. L. Frederici had barred state enterprises from borrowing abroad in order to ease inflationary pressures, LAN was forced to borrow funds from expensive, domestic sources. To reduce its operating costs, LAN shrank its workforce from 4,500 to 2,000 but incurred high severance payments in the process.[5] It also terminated service on additional routes, which LADECO seems to have happily taken over. As a result, by 1978, LADECO's share of the domestic market had risen to a respectable 27 percent, up from only 17.8 percent in 1975, while LAN's had fallen to 73 percent (see table 6-1). Although still the leader in the market, LAN was badly wounded and was about to be wounded far more seriously when the Chilean government adopted an open skies policy in 1979.

In summary, LAN's history up to 1978 included many of the problems that so often afflict state-owned enterprise. It also included the many remedies that governments so often use to solve those problems: protecting the firm from competition, offering it special privileges, clarifying its goals, securing its manager's autonomy, or installing new leadership, and when these failed, taking a tough approach with hard budget constraints and a firm hand in dealing with demands from managers or labor. However, most of these remedies did not have the anticipated effects, and others were unsustainable even if they worked for a period, especially in the politically volatile conditions in Chile in the 1970s.

Note also that the degree of competition faced by LAN in the home market seemed not to be any greater after LADECO's creation than before it. Although on the surface, after 1957, two firms operated in the home market, the JAC approved tariffs, capacity, and routes for both LAN and LADECO.[6] Besides, the private firm was permitted to operate only in

Table 6-1. LAN and LADECO, Share of Domestic Air Passenger Traffic, 1975–1992

Year	Passenger-Kilometers (millions)				Share (%)		
	LAN	LADECO	Other	Total	LAN	LADECO	Other
1975	325	71		397	82	18	
1976	289	100		390	74	26	
1977	361	125		487	74	26	
1978	377	141		519	73	27	
1979	232	235	1	468	50	50	
1980	181	335	14	530	34	63	3
1981	306	408	44	759	40	54	6
1982	254	378	40	673	38	56	6
1983	208	306	35	550	38	56	6
1984	246	321	39	606	41	53	6
1985	272	306	27	605	45	51	4
1986	298	300	13	610	49	49	2
1987	315	355	13	683	46	52	2
1988	358	385	13	757	47	51	2
1989	412	408	12	832	50	49	1
1990	458	417	4	879	52	47	
1991	417	397	102	916	46	43	11
1992	610	513	54	1,177	52	44	5

Source: JAC.

Note: Blank cells indicate less than or equal to 1.

those markets from which the state enterprise willingly withdrew. From the government's point of view, the value of having a LADECO around may have been that the private firm was able to profitably serve those routes that the state enterprise was forced to discard.

It is also interesting that the pro-private-sector government of Pinochet was content to stop with the reprivatization of firms nationalized by Allende rather than go on to privatize firms like LAN that were performing badly under government ownership. The privatization of core enterprises such as LAN seems to have been an idea whose time had not yet come. Instead, the Pinochet government preferred to throw open LAN's market to unrestrained competition, ushering in phase two of our story.

Phase Two: Injection of Real Competition (1979–1986)

In March 1979 the Chilean government, which until then had severely restrained competition in the airline industry, moved with a vengeance in the opposite direction.[7] A year after the deregulation of the airline industry in the United States, Chile adopted an open skies law that was equally liberal in scope. The movement of passengers and freight in both domestic and international markets was opened at once to carriers of any nationality, although foreign carriers could operate in Chile only if Chilean carriers could do the same in the foreign carrier's domestic market (Decree Law 2564, art. 2). Pricing and capacity decisions were deregulated unless otherwise required in international agreements. All carriers were required to register their fares with the JAC. The law (art. 10) also eliminated all rules that favored LAN over existing or prospective private competitors so as to "create optimum competitive conditions among all companies" (Hachette and Lüders 1993, 247).

Short-Run Consequences (1979–1983)

The open skies law instantaneously removed the biggest obstacle to LADECO's expansion within the domestic market. In fact, the firm was promptly purchased by Grupo Cruzat, the largest and most dynamic business group operating in Chile.[8] Under new ownership, LADECO announced the largest investment and fleet modernization program in its history, buying five Boeing 727-200s in the ensuing months. For the first time, LADECO began to offer service on the same routes as LAN, charging lower prices and offering better service. Not surprisingly, LADECO's share of domestic traffic began to rise sharply, reaching 50 percent in 1979 and 63 percent in 1980! LAN was quickly reduced to the minor player in the industry, with a share in 1980 of only 34 percent. New entrants also appeared, but collectively garnered only 3 percent of the domestic passenger market (table 6-1).

In the domestic freight market, which was less than one-third as big as the passenger transportation market but growing faster, deregulation was to have dramatic effects. More than half a dozen new airlines appeared that collectively captured nearly half the volume in 1979, principally at LAN's expense, while LADECO managed to hold on to its pre-1978 share (see table 6-2). However, as the dust began to settle, many of the new freight operators were displaced by LAN and LADECO.

LAN's reaction to deregulation was in stark contrast to that of LADECO or the new entrants. Shorn of its special privileges and faced with competition from diverse national carriers in both the passenger and freight businesses, LAN's reaction was best described as that of a deer caught in the headlights. Other than matching LADECO's price cuts, which presumably was an administratively simple response, LAN seems to have been unable to react—to reduce, for example, its operating costs, expand and modernize its fleet, improve its service, or match the marketing tactics of its private rivals. And the reason for not being able to do any of these things was, very simply, its status as a state-owned enterprise. Deregulation may have altered the condition in LAN's market, but it did nothing to alter LAN's internal operating procedures, administrative mechanisms, or incentives.

Table 6-2. LAN and LADECO, Share of Air Freight Traffic, 1975–1992

| | Domestic Market | | | | International Market | | | | | |
| | | | | | | | | | Share (%) | | |
Year	Ton Kilometers (millions)	Share (%) LAN	LADECO	Other	Ton Kilometers (millions)	LAN	LADECO	Other	European	North American	South American
1975	12	72	24	4	74	36	1	3	41	10	9
1976	13	72	21	7	101	37	3	0	38	9	12
1977	14	81	19	0	129	39	3	3	39	5	12
1978	16	64	15	22	143	43	4	0	36	5	12
1979	16	32	19	49	161	32	4	17	31	4	11
1980	15	42	30	28	207	31	0	19	30	3	16
1981	21	45	30	25	243	26	1	22	33	3	16
1982	18	43	34	23	232	23	1	21	36	7	13
1983	17	46	34	20	212	25	1	15	41	9	9
1984	15	49	33	18	214	22	2	12	44	11	8
1985	13	49	39	12	204	25	1	14	40	12	8
1986	14	52	47	0	285	22	1	14	38	16	9
1987	14	53	46	1	326	28	2	16	33	13	8
1988	16	55	43	2	406	30	6	14	32	11	7
1989	16	57	42	1	537	29	8	19	32	7	5
1990	16	56	42	2	628	27	10	20	31	7	5
1991	16	50	48	1	672	28	8	21	28	10	5
1992	17	56	43	1	737	29	11	23	22	9	6

Source: JAC.

One example of LAN's inability to respond to the new market conditions was provided by Patricio Sepulveda, who was president of LAN through much of the postderegulation period. He explained that, while LADECO was briskly modernizing and expanding its fleet, LAN had great difficulty in getting the government's permission to lease just one DC-10 aircraft. After several months of paper pushing, LAN was permitted to sign a three-month lease for an aircraft; it then had to go through another round of paper pushing to extend that lease for a few months, even though it had benefited demonstrably from the first lease. Another example of organizational "stickiness" was LAN's inability to lower its costs by renegotiating labor contracts with unionized employees, especially its powerful pilots. LAN's pilots worked under terms and conditions similar to those offered to Chile's pampered air force pilots; for instance, LAN pilots, like their air force counterparts, could retire with a full pension after just ten years of service; consequently, many of LAN's pilots retired after the stipulated period but came right back to work for the airline, thus earning both a salary and a pension from the company. Pilots were also entitled to very liberal compensation schemes that were not easily altered: for instance, they were entitled to bonus payments after flying a certain distance, even though those rules proved overly generous with the advent of faster aircraft.

As a result of its organizational rigidities, LAN costs did not fall even though revenues were being hurt by falling tariffs. Iglesias and Paredes (1986) report that between 1979 and 1982, the average markup charged by LAN fell by 17.3 percent while those charged by the average International Air Transport Association (IATA) carrier remained unchanged. On the other hand, while the average IATA carrier's unit cost fell by 12 percent in that same period, LAN's increased by 16.7 percent.

From LAN's perspective, the only bright spot in the industry was the international segment, which other Chilean firms could not enter despite the open skies policy since foreign governments had to authorize those entries. Given the slow pace with which bilateral air service agreements could be amended and the reluctance of most other governments to liberalize their airline policies, LAN was well protected from new Chilean competitors, including LADECO. LADECO's share of international passenger traffic rose to just 2.6 percent in 1980 and 5.2 percent in 1984, while LAN's fell by only 2.3 percentage points in the first two years (table 6-3). However, by 1984 LAN's share of international traffic had fallen by almost ten percentage points compared to the period before open skies. That decrease came about not because of LADECO but because of foreign carriers, which were free to expand service or cut tariffs on service to Chile without seeking the Chilean government's approval or offering reciprocal concessions to LAN.[9] Ironically, most of those competitors were state-owned airlines that enjoyed sheltered domestic markets and other privileges once available to LAN. Among the main gainers were European carriers, while privately owned American carriers, such as Pan Am and Eastern Air Lines, were too busy adjusting to deregulation in the U.S. market to worry about minor opportunities in the U.S.-Chilean market.

At any rate, LAN's financial woes worsened sharply in the open skies era, as its volume of business shrank, yields fell, and costs rose.

Medium and Longer-Term Consequences (1983–1986)

If in the short-run LAN's response to deregulation was dismal and LADECO's was impressive, the opposite seems to have been the case in the years that followed. So far as LAN was concerned, its financial condition became so bad in the aftermath of deregulation that the government was forced to take drastic action. From 1981 to 1983, LAN's monthly losses averaged US$2.8 million, calling for government transfers of US$42 million in 1982 and US$52.3 million in 1983. LAN's debt to the banks grew to US$60 million, its debt-to-equity ratio topped 3:1, and it had negative working capital. In the first half of 1984, the government had to transfer another US$70 million to the company. As losses soared, LAN

Table 6-3. Share of International Air Passenger Traffic, Comparative Data, 1975–1992

Year	Passenger Kilometers (millions)							Share (%)					
	LAN	LADECO	Other Chilean	European	North American	South American	Total	LAN	LADECO	Other Chilean	European	North American	South American
1975	532	0	0	495	233	171	1,431	37	0	0	35	16	12
1976	505	0	0	497	295	239	1,536	33	0	0	32	19	16
1977	588		0	571	385	348	1,891	31	0	0	30	20	18
1978	675	14	0	491	493	414	2,087	32	1	0	24	24	20
1979	788	49	9	608	590	528	2,572	31	2	0	24	23	21
1980	842	76	0	764	619	590	2,891	29	3	0	26	21	20
1981	876	112	0	1,014	671	613	3,285	27	3	0	31	20	19
1982	670	83	0	958	634	554	2,899	23	3	0	33	22	19
1983	613	96		809	512	440	2,470	25	4	0	33	21	18
1984	637	140		840	557	493	2,667	24	5	0	32	21	18
1985	605	151		802	514	546	2,619	23	6	0	31	20	21
1986	747	151		817	553	587	2,855	26	5	0	29	19	21
1987	864	182		908	644	692	3,290	26	6	0	28	20	21
1988	1,070	251		940	676	834	3,770	28	7	0	25	18	22
1989	1,206	345		1,000	646	1,024	4,222	29	8	0	24	15	24
1990	1,200	419		1,110	781	1,187	4,699	26	9	0	24	17	25
1991	1,189	555		1,300	1,085	1,350	5,479	22	10	0	24	20	25
1992	1,384	729	1	1,442	915	1,477	5,950	23	12	0	24	15	25

Source: JAC.

Note: Blank cells indicate less than or equal to one.

curtailed service, which further worsened its financial results. In 1983, one report declared LAN technically bankrupt.

With the need for drastic action beyond the pale of doubt, the government supported the decision of LAN's president, Patricio Sepulveda, to close down the company and start up a new one that would take over the old LAN's assets and routes but not its debts. With the demise of the old LAN, all labor agreements with pilots and other staff also terminated automatically. In 1984, the new LAN rehired only those persons it truly needed, under terms and conditions set by the market. Employment was cut to less than half, and generous severance payments were offered to those who were let go. Adopting an innovative arrangement, many former workers were encouraged to form supplier companies that offered services to the new LAN on a contractual basis, usually at substantially lower rates than what those services had cost the company earlier. Even cabin crews were hired on a contractual basis and paid according to the number of hours of service provided.

Although Sepulveda killed the old LAN and created a new LAN, the new company's legal status, including its right to operate international routes under existing bilateral agreements, was the subject of some dispute because the new LAN had not been formally created by an act of the government. However, according to Chile's 1980 constitution, the state was prohibited from starting new companies in areas where the private sector was already active unless three-fourths of the legislature voted to override that proscription. At the time, the powers of Chile's suspended legislature were exercised by the commanders in chief of the armed forces, that is, of the navy, the air force, the army, and the police. Within this group there was disagreement on whether LAN ought to be bailed out or allowed to fold up and disappear. Some members reportedly saw bankrputcy as a healthy event in a market economy, while others argued that to shut down LAN would worsen Chile's recession and unemployment, both of which were already bad at that time. Also, some military officers were reportedly unhappy with the thought of allowing a "strategic" enterprise created more than fifty years earlier by one military government to become bankrupt during the tenure of another military government. While this debate raged on for the better part of a year, the new LAN operated "illegally."

Eventually, the committee of commanders in chief authorized the creation of a new LAN, including government funding of it, with the passage of a special law in 1985. The new LAN was permitted to take over the old LAN's routes. To maximize managerial autonomy, the new LAN was created as a joint stock company controlled by CORFO, the state holding company, which assumed US$56 million in the old LAN's debt in exchange for 98.7 percent of the new LAN's equity.[10] In addition, CORFO paid US$4.3 million in severance compensations for the dismissal of about 1,000 workers, US$2.2 million to suppliers, and an additional US$4.3 million to finance other operational expenses. The new LAN's goal was also explicitly declared as profit maximization. Sepulveda cut the number of management levels and rationalized the fleet. According to one estimate, the total cost to the government of the restructuring process, including transfers, subsidies, and write-offs, was US$133 million.[11]

After 1985, with a new organizational structure, LAN started an aggressive strategy to recover its market share. Apart from receiving traffic permits for the twelve international routes it had before, the company also opened new routes, increased frequency of flights (mainly to the United States and Argentina), and launched special programs to regain market share, such as offering executive class seating and a promotional program for children.[12] In 1987, LAN bought three Boeing 767s, which added significantly to its fleet size. LAN's market share rose from 37 percent of the domestic market in 1983 to 45 percent in 1985 and 48.8 percent in 1986. Likewise, in the international segment, LAN's market participation increased from 23 to 28 percent in these two years (table 6-3).

Meanwhile, as LAN's fortunes were improving, LADECO's took a turn for the worse. Following Chile's economic crisis of 1982, Grupo Cruzat, like many other diversified business groups in the country, went bankrupt and had to be taken over by the state.[13] The goal of the government intervenor was to clear up the financial situation caused by the enormous amount of cross-lending that had been going on within the group. Once LADECO's finances were cleared up, it was offered for sale to the private sector, and in 1986, LADECO returned to the private sector under a new set of owners. Then, for the first time in history of Chile's airline industry, two large, financially healthy firms operated in the sector with similar goals and organizational flexibility, even though one was state owned and the other private.[14]

The Privatization of LAN (1986–1989)

In June 1986, about a year after the formal creation of the new LAN, the idea of privatizing the firm gained ground. Since 1984, the Pinochet government had been privatizing several state enterprises, and LAN seems to have found its way onto the divestiture list by the end of 1985 even though privatization was not seriously envisaged when the new LAN was created.[15] Initially, the government's intent was to sell a minority interest (30%) in LAN to private investors, a decision that may have been encouraged by LAN's rising sales and profits after reorganization (see table 6-4). Having publicly announced its intention to partly privatize

Table 6-4. LAN Financial Indicators, 1984–1992

Financial Indicator	1984	1985	1986	1987	1988	1989	1990	1991	1992
Assets (US$000)	7,437	57,878	78,417	91,112	99,317	110,606	203,997	199,497	214,251
Liabilities (US$000)	127	20,206	32,404	40,679	47,025	54,154	159,561	146,933	155,857
Equity (US$000)	7,310	37,672	46,013	50,433	52,292	56,452	44,436	52,564	58,394
Sales (US$000)	17,500	33,051	144,856	156,771	183,032	213,067	243,403	261,055	309,388
Variable costs (US$000)	-10,598	-18,625	-89,332	-97,853	-118,022	-138,624	-174,271	-173,705	-118,022
Sales and administrative costs (US$000)	-9,290	-11,166	-48,953	-53,299	-61,068	-74,443	-69,132	-87,350	—
Operating profits (US$000)	-2,388	3,260	6,571	5,619	3,942	2,564	2,493	2,206	1,875
Net profits (US$000)	-2,264	2,629	5,882	4,117	7,859	6,399	-8,456	3,472	1,174
Long-run liability/total liability	0.00	1.75	8.99	7.29	9.59	10.16	54.93	62.33	54.89
Profits/equity (%)	-30.97	6.98	12.78	8.16	15.03	11.34	-19.03	6.61	0.32
Profits/assets (%)	-30.44	4.54	7.50	4.52	7.91	5.79	-4.15	1.74	0.88

Source: CORFO files.

— = not available.

LAN, the government then became intent on selling LAN's shares one way or another, even if that called for divesting a controlling interest in the firm.[16] By 1988, the Pinochet government's calculus seems to have been affected by the fact that in the October 1988 plebiscite the public rejected an extension of the Pinochet administration. By then, Pinochet was anxious to privatize as many firms as possible before turning power over to a democratically elected government in October 1989. Presumably, his government wanted to shrink the state enterprise sector as much as possible before leaving office.[17] Thus, the government's determination and motivation to privatize LAN evolved over time.

Before turning to the question of how privatization affected LAN's behavior, we briefly examine how the privatization transaction was structured and executed (see Cominetti 1992).

The First Attempt

As the government considered alternative ways of selling a minority interest in LAN, one possibility was to offer its shares to institutional investors, such as Chilean pension funds, which had purchased the shares of other privatized firms, such as Endesa, Chilgener, and the Chile Telephone Company. However, pension funds were barred from investing in firms that had been in existence for fewer than three years, which was technically the case for the new LAN. A second possibility was to sell shares to LAN's workers, a practice that had become common in the government's second wave of privatizations.[18] Here again, employees of the new LAN had not accumulated much money in their retirement accounts to pay for the shares. Nevertheless, since there seemed to be no other option, in 1988, the government sold 16 percent of the company to LAN's workers (a worker with at least six months of service was eligible). Not only was the price charged low (US$0.15 per share), but the government had also to find a way to finance the workers' purchase, which it did through a state-owned bank.[19]

Then, in August 1988, CORFO invited bids from national and international firms for 32.7 percent of LAN, which, along with the workers' shares, would put a total of approximately 49 percent in private hands. Bidders had to be prequalified based on their financial, technical, and marketing expertise. The minimum price was set at US$0.27 per share. The terms of reference also stated that down the road buyers could buy an additional 11 percent from CORFO or inject fresh capital into the firm so as to reduce CORFO's participation to 40 percent.

Only three firms prequalified: the European Bank for Latin America (EBLA); Guiness Peat Aviation (GPA), an aircraft leasing firm; and LADECO. The Chilean Antitrust Commission ruled that LADECO could not participate in the auction, as that would be detrimental to competition. For the same reason, the Antitrust Commission ruled that, should EBLA's offer be accepted, it would have to sell its participation in ICAROSAN, which in turn owned 12.5 percent of LADECO. Thus, only GPA survived the prequalification process, and its bid of US$0.151 per share was below the minimum acceptable price. Recognizing that private investors seemed uninterested in LAN unless they could obtain a controlling interest, the government passed a new law that permitted CORFO's participation to fall as low as 40 percent.

The Second Attempt

In March 1989, CORFO placed another invitation for bids, this time for 51 percent of LAN and at a marginally higher minimum price of US$0.28 per share.[20] The new owners were barred from selling their shares for one year. This time, three firms were prequalified: ICAROSAN, AEROPASUR (a company owned by LAN's workers), and a joint venture among Forestal Quiñenco, Air New Zealand Ltd. Scandinavian Airline System (SAS), and EBLA did not seek prequalification this time around. Among the firms that were prequalified, ICAROSAN submitted the highest offer, US$42.3 million, which translated into US$0.475 per share, fully 70 percent higher than the book value per share.

CORFO rejected AEROPASUR's bid of US$39 million only reluctantly, since a larger worker participation would have been attained if AEROPASUR were involved. However, the workers' bid had three weaknesses. First, their bid was 7 percent lower than ICAROSAN's. Second, AEROPASUR's bid was regarded as overleveraged, since the bid was backed by a loan from the Security Pacific Bank, with the shares themselves serving as collateral (a leveraged buyout). Third, the Security Pacific Bank, which intended to make the loan by swapping Chilean government debt for local currency debt under the country's swap program, was ruled ineligible to participate in that program.[21]

But ICAROSAN's bid also had weaknesses. First, AEROPASUR alleged that EBLA and SAS, both of which had not been prequalified, were partners in ICAROSAN's bid. Although this was not completely accurate, it is true that SAS had guaranteed a loan of US$29 million extended by Morgan Guaranty of the United States to Guillermo Carey, the head of ICAROSAN, in return for which Carey gave SAS the option to buy shares in LAN at a later date.[22] It is also true that EBLA owned 49 percent of ICAROSAN, but as required by Belgian law, the bank was permitted to be only a passive investor. Second, the Antitrust Commission insisted once again that ICAROSAN could participate in LAN's ownership only if Carey sold his holdings in LADECO. When Carey divested his holdings in

LADECO, CORFO had no good reason to reject what seemed like an attractive offer. Although some officials in LAN and CORFO reportedly had misgivings about the business plan drawn up for LAN by Guillermo Carey, others argued that the government had no business worrying about what the new owners did with LAN. In September 1989, barely three months before the democratically elected government of President Patricio Aylwin took office, CORFO sold 51 percent of LAN's stock to ICAROSAN.

Phase Three: The Postprivatization Period (1989 Onward)

As many expected, soon after winning the bid, ICAROSAN sought the government's permission to bring in additional partners. Specifically, Carey proposed selling 35 percent of LAN's stock to SAS. After satisfying itself that minority foreign ownership would not damage LAN's status as a Chilean carrier under the provisions of Chile's bilateral agreements,[23] the Pinochet government authorized the sale of 30 percent of LAN's stock to SAS (even though the terms of LAN's privatization had expressly prohibited the new owners from selling their holdings for one year).

However, the deal with SAS was not consummated formally until December 1989, eight days after Aylwin assumed office as president of Chile in a democratic election. That delay was prompted by the fact that SAS was owned by the Scandinavian states of Denmark, Norway, and Sweden, all of which opposed Pinochet's authoritarian rule and were not willing to permit SAS to invest in LAN until power in Chile had actually been transferred to a democratic government.[24] And, from a purely commercial standpoint, SAS's board may have preferred not to invest in LAN until the new government's policies towards privatization and the role of foreign investment in the sector were clarified.[25] Thus, SAS's strategy seems to have been to lock in the LAN deal through Carey during the Pinochet administration while waiting until later to assume a direct equity stake. However, even after ICAROSAN transferred 30 percent of LAN's equity to SAS, making it the single largest shareholder in LAN, SAS chose to give Guillermo Carey full powers to run the airline on a day-to-day basis.

Why was SAS, which paid US\$25 million for 30 percent of LAN, content to be a passive partner? The answer seems to lie in two factors. For one thing, senior managers at SAS seem to have been highly impressed by Guillermo Carey, his entrepreneurial spirit, his knowledge of the Chilean market, and his contacts within the country. At the same time, SAS seems to have been vague about its reasons for investing in LAN. Underlying SAS's interest in LAN was the notion of turning the Scandinavian airline into a megacarrier, a term widely used at the time in industry circles to describe an airline with strategic alliances in every major region of the world. SAS already had alliances in the United States and Asia but lacked one in Latin America. Since it had failed to buy Aerolíneas Argentinas after several months of frustrating negotiations with the Argentinian government (see chapter 7), and since it had not been able to buy a piece of one of Brazil's large airlines, SAS seems to have decided to zero in on LAN. After all, by the standards of Latin American carriers, LAN was in pretty good shape after its 1984 restructuring, and Chile was probably seen as the Latin American country most friendly to foreign investors. However, having secured a stake in LAN, SAS management did not wish to manage the Chilean carrier on a day-to-day basis, although plans were drawn up to integrate certain aspects of the operations of LAN and SAS. SAS and Carey reportedly signed an administrative agreement in London delegating full powers to Carey to run LAN.

To help finance the expansion plans, Carey persuaded SAS and CORFO that the company's equity capital ought to be increased. In April 1990, existing shareholders were invited to invest additional funds in the company to expand LAN's capital by 10 percent. CORFO tried to use this opportunity to make former LAN employees, who had been let go during the 1984 restructuring, part owners of the new LAN. However, by August 1990 it was clear that neither Sociedad de Turismo San Lorenzo, an investment firm owned by former LAN workers, nor AEROPASUR, the investment firm owned by LAN workers, would be able to come up with the money to pay for their share purchases. And since CORFO was prohibited from making fresh investments in LAN, the portion of LAN's equity owned by SAS and ICAROSAN rose while that owned by AEROPASUR and CORFO fell (table 6-5).

With that, the new management started a very aggressive expansion policy. A US$550 million fleet renewal program was launched, much of it financed by debt (see table 6-4). LAN bought two Boeing 767-200 ERs and leased one Boeing 767-200 ER and two Dash 300 ERs for use on international routes. For domestic routes, the company leased three BAE 146-200s, enabling it to add five new destinations—La Serena, Los Angeles, Valdivia, Osorno, and Coyhaique. The expansion of the fleet and the introduction of night discounts increased LAN's domestic market share from 39.4 to 43.6 percent in only one year. However, the expansion program led to a fare war with LADECO, which reduced domestic yields by 10 percent, although tariffs on international routes rose by 5 percent. Finally, the new management sharply increased its administrative overheads (table 6-4); in less than a year the number of LAN employees increased from 1,635 to 2,125.[26] Apparently, Carey was currying favor with union leaders and workers, whose support he may have been seeking because of the one seat they had on the board.

Table 6-5. LAN Ownership, 1984–1991 (%)

Owner	1984	1985	1988	1989	1990	1991
Chilean government	100.0					
CORFO		98.7	83.7	31.8	21.7	25.6
AEROPASUR			15.0	15.0	13.5	11.3
ICAROSAN				51.0	16.6	19.5
Scandinavian Airlines System					41.2	41.2
CAP		1.3	1.3	1.3	1.3	1.5
Others				0.9	5.7	0.9

The expansion program initiated after privatization proved to be overly optimistic. The Persian Gulf crisis only worsened matters. One expert estimated that a company like LAN only needed three Boeing 767s on long-haul routes, one Boeing 707 for the Easter Island–Tahiti route, and five smaller aircraft for domestic services. However, LAN was committed to five additional Boeing 767s, at a monthly lease payment per aircraft of US$800,000. Carey's fleet acquisition decisions translated into an annual commitment of US$48 million, which in light of the slower than anticipated growth in demand was easily big enough to bankrupt the company. Between January and September 1990, in its very first months as a private carrier, LAN lost US$7.6 million. If the trend continued, LAN's net loss for the year could have exceeded US$10 million, compared to a profit of US$6.4 million in the previous year—a reversal of US$16 million in just one year. Only a part of the fall could be ascribed to the oil shock that increased the cost of jet fuel by US$2 million. By far, the bigger causes were LAN's imprudent fleet acquisition and employment policies.

In July 1990, the Chilean government, through the executive vice president of LAN, contacted Jan Carlzon, the CEO of SAS, and informed him about LAN's dire situation. SAS's senior controller, who was despatched by Carlzon to study the problem, recommended Carey's removal. In October 1990, about a year after privatization, CORFO and SAS united to oust Carey and appointed Juan Luis Moure as chairman of the board.[27] Carey promptly filed a lawsuit against SAS charging that it had violated his London agreement with the Scandinavian airline.

SAS then dispatched a team of four persons to attempt yet another turnaround of LAN. The new management reduced the frequency of domestic flights, cut such flights as the nonstop service to New York, reduced employment by more than 300 workers between September 1990 and February 1991, and froze wages. However, the most important problem to be solved was the reassignment of surplus aircraft, including those scheduled for delivery in the near future. In the end, LAN managed to sublease one Boeing 767-200 to Royal Brunei Airlines for ten months and then to Aeromexico, which also subleased another aircraft. Two Boeing 767-300s were subleased to Transbrasil. In each case, LAN continued to be responsible for paying the lessors during the first eighteen months of the five-year subleases in the event of default. Estimates of the total cost of restructuring LAN, including the penalties imposed by the aircraft leasing company and the costs of reducing the number of employees, amounted US$53 million. Much of that cost was booked in 1993 (US$30 million) rather than in 1991 or 1992.[28] Despite that, LAN reported a net loss after taxes of US$8.4 million in 1990.

Thus, the immediate impact of privatization was to worsen LAN's performance, largely because the new management's plan for the company was overly ambitious. To be sure, the onset of the Persian Gulf War worsened matters, not because it led to a decline in traffic but because it boosted the price of aviation fuel.[29] In 1990, even though LAN was now a private company, the state came to its rescue once again: the Chilean air force paid US$16 million for two Boeing 707s with a market value of only US$6 million, thus extending to LAN an implicit subsidy of US$10 million. At the same time, the government reportedly persuaded local private banks to extend subsidized loans to LAN to help tide it over its financial problems.[30]

The postprivatization performance of LAN can also be seen in terms of the price of its stock compared to that of other privatized firms and the Chilean market as a whole. While the market index (SPI) increased by more than 200 percent in real terms between July 1989 and the last quarter of 1993 and an index for privatized firms increased by 400 percent, LAN's stock fell by about 50 percent by 1991 and barely returned to its preprivatization value after SAS took over the management of the operations.

Conclusions

We distinguish three periods in this analysis, the first running from 1929 to 1978, the second following the adoption of the open skies policy and ending with the privatization of LAN (1979–89), and the third representing the postprivatization years (1989 onward). What do we learn from these periods about the interplay between ownership, competition, and regulation?

In the first period, the Chilean government's approach to the airline sector was typical of that found in many developing countries, including those covered in other chapters of this volume. The industry was dominated by a state-owned carrier that was expected to fulfill a strategic role and enjoyed special privileges, including protection from competition. State ownership and monopoly seemed to go hand in hand: the fact that the monopoly was state owned may have been viewed as eliminating the risk that monopoly power would be abused; on the other hand, the inefficiency and losses suffered by the state enterprise appear to have encouraged the government to protect its market power. In this period, the government made a number of attempts to improve LAN's performance, but any improvements registered were not sustained over time, especially as governments changed. LAN continually required new forms of protection and subsidy.

In 1957, a small but important dent was made in LAN's monopoly power with the creation of a second national company, privately owned LADECO. However, in the first twenty years of LADECO's existence, the private firm was not allowed to compete directly with LAN on any route, and prices for both airlines were set by the regulatory agency (JAC). In this period, LADECO might accurately be described as a scavenger, collecting the crumbs falling off LAN's plate. Over the years, more and more crumbs were to fall off LAN's plate, and LADECO seems to have held on to all routes it so obtained. And, as we noted earlier, LAN's inefficiency may have proved a boon for LADECO, inasmuch as the tariffs set by the JAC for the private airline might have been influenced in some degree by the state-owned airline's cost structure.

The second period (1979–89) began with an exogenous policy change favoring deregulation of the sector, undoubtedly rooted in General Pinochet's commitment to free-market principles. How else is one to explain the reversal of government policies that historically protected LAN's interests more vigorously than those of the consumer? Yet, it is interesting that even the Pinochet government did not attempt to privatize LAN, although hundreds of firms nationalized by his socialist predecessor, Salvador Allende, were denationalized (or reprivatized). Perhaps the idea of selling off firms that had traditionally been in the public sector did not cross the minds of Pinochet's advisers.[31] Alternatively, deregulation may have seemed a politically easier step than privatization.[32] At any rate, Chile became one of the few countries to deregulate its airline sector long before privatizing its flag carrier.

That experiment was to demonstrate an interesting relation between ownership and competition. Vickers and Yarrow (1988) argue that the degree of competition in a firm's market is a more important determinant of a firm's efficiency than ownership per se, but in fact, when state-owned LAN was subjected to competition it seems to have registered hardly any efficiency gains, at least not within the first five years of deregulation. The reason for that, of course, was that the open skies policy changed conditions in LAN's market dramatically but did nothing to change LAN's internal decision making systems or incentives. Consequently, in the medium term, LAN neither reduced its costs, nor improved the quality of its service, nor matched LADECO's marketing tactics. All it seems to have done was match LADECO's price cuts, which, from an administrative standpoint, were easy to implement. However, deregulation did expose LAN's weaknesses and inefficiencies for all to see, thus putting pressure on the government to do something about the company. Even if LAN did not quickly adjust to its new environment, deregulation had the important effect of showing the world how critical it was that an adjustment be made.

That adjustment came fully five years into deregulation, when LAN was drastically restructured; apparently, things had to get a lot worse before they could get better. The restructuring addressed some of the main sources of LAN's organizational rigidity, and LAN's employment levels and labor contracts were drastically altered—in addition, of course, to financial restructuring, which sharply reduced the firm's debt servicing burden. The new LAN proved to be an aggressive competitor, gaining market share at the expense of national and foreign competitors. The question of whether those performance gains would be sustainable—or would dissipate within a few years, as some observers of state enterprises argue (see Kikeri et al. 1992)—could not be studied because LAN was privatized five years after it was restructured.

In 1989, the third and most recent phase of LAN's history began, when LAN's ownership and control changed but market structure and regulation remained more or less unchanged. Once again, surprisingly, the immediate impact was largely negative: a profitable LAN turned into a highly unprofitable firm in the very first year after privatization because of an overambitious expansion plan, similar to the one launched by Aeromexico after it was privatized (see chapter 8).

There are at least two interesting aspects to LAN's postprivatization period. First, privatization did not solve the problems associated with state ownership. Carey gained control over the firm by investing only US$1 to US$2 million of his own money, and it was rumored that he may have profited personally by signing an excessive number of aircraft leases. One would have thought that having SAS as a major investor in the consortium would have prevented errors in judgment or mala fide decisions. On the other hand, one must also note the speed with which LAN's problems were attacked in 1990 once they were discovered. In short, if LAN had been state owned it probably would not have expanded as ambitiously as it did in 1990, but it probably also would not have taken remedial steps as quickly as it did in 1990–91.

Second, even after privatization, the state had an important residual role in this sector. One role stemmed from the state's continued holdings in LAN, which even as of 1993 had not been divested despite several attempts in that direction. Another was that of regulator of the industry, responsible not only for negotiating international agreements but also for supervising conduct within the privatized sector. Chile was somewhat unique in Latin America in having a reasonably well developed anti-monopoly law, which not only obstructed LADECO's bid to buy LAN in 1989 but investigated charges of collusion between the two in the post open skies period. A final role, which perhaps was unintended at the time of LAN's privatization, was the government's apparent obligation or commitment to keep LAN alive because of its political, strategic, or symbolic significance. Thus, when LAN was on the verge of bankruptcy under private management, it was the government that initiated Carey's removal and arranged disguised subsidies and financial assistance to save the airline. The LAN experience shows that as long as a government feels compelled to ensure the survival of its national airline—or any other privatized firm, for that matter—the argument that private firms, unlike state enterprises, operate under the threat of bankruptcy will not hold water.

The LAN experience also suggests that governments need to think about the sequence in which reforms are implemented. Specifically, in what order should governments restructure a state enterprise, deregulate its sector, or privatize that firm? Theoretically, these three measures can be sequenced in six different ways.[33] Of those, three can be eliminated as infeasible if one assumes that the state will have to restructure a state enterprise before being able to privatize it—that is, that private buyers will not touch it until the state has cleaned up the mess it created. Of the remaining, feasible, options, the Mexican government seems to have pursued the following sequence: restructure first, then privatize, and, finally, deregulate (see chapter 8). The advantage of this sequence is that the state enterprise is organizationally readied for competing before deregulation sets in; disadvantages include the fact that all governments may not be able to restructure their troubled enterprises at will and the risk that governments may find themselves unable to deregulate a sector after a firm in that sector has been privatized, especially if the buyers were promised protection from competition at the time of privatization.[34] An alternative sequence would be to restructure first, then to deregulate, and finally to privatize. The advantage of this sequence, once again, is that the state enterprise is readied for competition before deregulation, but by delaying privatization, the government takes the risk that the state enterprise may fetch less money after its rent-seeking opportunities have disappeared. A final alternative is to follow Chile's example, to deregulate first, then to restructure, and finally to privatize. The main advantage of this sequence, as noted earlier, is that the premature introduction of competition can cause an a state enterprise's performance to become intolerably bad, thus allowing the government to take the politically difficult action involved not only in restructuring but, possibly, in privatization as well.

We conclude with a brief look at the broad question of why LAN's privatization, like the three other airline privatizations studied in this volume, was much more problematic than most of the telecommunications privatizations studied in this volume. The answer seems to lie in three aspects that distinguished the airline industry from the telecommunications sector. The first, and perhaps most important, factor was the monopoly power that was part of the privatization transaction in every telecommunications sector but was absent in every airline privatization studied in this volume. Second, every airline privatization was constrained by the need to place control over the airline in national hands so as not to lose the airline's standing in bilateral agreements. Consequently, clear and complete control could not be transferred to a reputable foreign operator, as it was in some of the telecommunications cases. Finally, the airline industry faced market prospects that were decidedly inferior to those of the telecommunications sector. Not only was demand growth slower in the airline industry than in the latter industry in many developing countries, it also followed a more volatile pattern. In addition, there was surplus capacity on a global basis in the airline industry in the late 1980s and early 1990s, which made that period an unfavorable time for privatizing airlines: witness the very limited interest shown by foreign airlines during the privatizations of LAN, VIASA, and Aerolíneas Argentinas.

Therefore, the conclusion from the LAN study and others in this volume is that the interest private investors will show in a privatization transaction as well as the gains from privatization are likely to vary considerably across industries and sectors.

NOTES

The authors are indebted to Eric Campaña, president of LAN in the period 1964–70 and a director on the board of LAN in 1993, for providing a wealth of useful data, and to the following for their invaluable help: Patricio Sepulveda, president of LAN from 1981 to 1989; Colonel José Martinez, executive manager of CORFO from 1983 to 1990; José Luis Ibañez, president of LADECO; and Rudi Schwab, general manager of LAN in 1993. Patricia Briceño, Jennifer Jacobs, and Maria Eugenia Torres rendered efficient research assistance. The usual disclaimers apply.

1. LAN's original name was Linea Aero Postal, or Airmail Line.

2. Economies of scale in the airline business in matters such as purchasing, operations, and maintenance are believed to hinge on having a homogeneous fleet.

3. It is not unusual to find that, when a state-owned firm and a private firm

operate in an industry in which prices are controlled by government, the higher cost structure of the state-owned firm results in regulated prices that allow a more efficient private enterprise to earn attractive margins and returns.

4. At the time, the central bank used forty different exchange rates. LAN's rate for converting foreign revenues to local currency was US$1 = Ch$0.2, while LAN's imports were converted at US$1 = Ch$0.046. To get an idea of the magnitude of the implied subsidy, if similar distortions had existed in 1991 the company's profits for the year would have been 60 percent higher and return on equity would have been 9 percent instead of 6 percent.

5. As with most other cost data, we were unable to obtain reliable estimates of the magnitude of severance payments. However, we did hear from one source that the cycles of hiring and firing that LAN went through over its lifetime cost it US$150 million, a figure that seems to us to be on the high side.

6. The JAC derived its authority to regulate tariffs, capacities, and routes under Law 241 of 1960, according to Hachette and Lüders (1993), 244.

7. For a discussion of the sweeping nature of the privatization program in Chile in the 1980s, see Sigmund (1990).

8. The Cruzat Group owned some of the largest companies in the country, including the Banco de Santiago (banking), Copec (oil distribution), Compañia de Cervecerías Unidas (beer monopoly), and firms in the fish meal and real estate industries (Paredes and Sánchez 1993).

9. Both LAN and LADECO complained to us that Chile's open skies policy started out by making too many unilateral concessions to foreign airlines, most of which enjoyed sheltered positions in their home markets, unlike Chilean carriers.

10. Since under Chilean law a joint stock company had to have at least two shareholders, another state enterprise controlled by CORFO was asked to buy a very small (1.3%) stake in the new LAN.

11. Among losses acknowledged were US$11 million in untraceable accounts receivable; apparently the invoices involved had illegible signatures scribbled across them.

12. The twelve routes are Belgium, Bolivia, Brazil, Canada, France, Germany, Paraguay, Peru, Spain, United States, Uruguay, and Venezuela.

13. It is difficult to arrive at definitive conclusions about the relative performance of LADECO as a private firm. While it is true that LADECO did not do better than LAN during the recession, this may be due to the effect of the high leverage that the whole Cruzat conglomerate had over LADECO.

14. There is no evidence that the government intervenor tried to turn LADECO's miseries into a source of competitive advantage for LAN.

15. For an extensive review of the Chilean privatization process, see Hachette and Lüders (1993) and Muñoz (1993).

16. The law under which the new LAN was created in 1985 stipulated that CORFO should own at least 67 percent of the stock. Therefore, to sell a controlling interest in LAN the government had to amend that law.

17. Opposition parties declared that privatizations carried out by Pinochet after the October 1988 plebiscite vote against the Pinochet regime would be annulled ("Guillermo Carey" 1989).

18. The second wave consisted of firms sold in the 1984–89 period and is distinguished from the reprivatizations that occurred soon after Allende was overthrown (1974–76). For more on this, see Hachette and Lüders (1993), 45–65. Among the state enterprises that workers bought shares in were the electricity (Chilgener) and steel (CAP) companies.

19. Workers were expected to pay 10 percent of the price at once and the balance within six months, which was later extended to one year. Eventually, the state-owned bank, Banco del Estado, extended a loan to an investment corporation, AEROPASUR, with the shares serving as collateral.

20. The reference price was set on the basis of a study by the Shearson-Lehman Co.

21. According to the rules, only firms that did not operate in the country were eligible to participate. The Security Pacific Bank did not pass this test.

22. Carey reportedly admitted, if "I had gone alone, there's no way I could have got that much money, but SAS said [to Morgan Guaranty], 'This is a good project with good potential'" ("Guillermo Carey" 1989).

23. The head of the International Aviation section of the U.S. Department of Transportation reportedly ruled that, as long as LAN's ownership and control remained in Chilean hands, a stake of 30–35 percent could be sold to foreign investors. Since the U.S.-Chile route was the most valuable part of LAN's international flights, advance consultation with U.S. officials would prevent any disputes down the road about LAN's rights under existing U.S.-Chile bilateral air service agreements.

24. However, all aspects of the deal between Carey and SAS were concluded in the final days of the Pinochet administration.

25. Indeed, during the election campaign, the opposition parties had threatened to undo all privatizations, including that of LAN, which were completed by the Pinochet government after the October 1989 plebiscite. However, after assuming office, the Aylwin government did not follow through on that threat.

26. As stated earlier, since 1985, LAN had contracted workers from independent firms created by former LAN workers. Carey reversed that highly profitable policy by rehiring many laid-off workers, which raised LAN's operating costs in 1990.

27. In April 1991, Moure was nominated by SAS to fill one of the seats on the board allotted to it. He became chief executive of LAN with full powers. At the same time, Rudy Schwab, a Scandinavian, was appointed general manager. The reorganization may have been prompted by the desire to ensure that LAN was regarded as being controlled by Chileans rather than foreigners.

28. In part, this explains why in 1991, ICAROSAN and SAS reportedly attempted to sell their holdings in LAN. This operation did not succeed, partly because the Chilean Antitrust Commission would not permit Iberia, the Spanish airline, which had an interest in LADECO, to invest in LAN as well.

29. Even though many international airlines fared badly in 1990 and 1991, demand for airline travel in Chile, in both the domestic and international segments, grew in these years (tables 6-1 and 6-3).

30. Among the other things LAN did to ease the financial crunch was to sell a Boeing 737-200 to Aloha Airlines for US$15 million.

31. After all, it was only in the 1980s that Britain began to sell off giant state enterprises and to set the example that many other countries, including Chile, were to follow.

32. A number of countries, particularly in Asia, have preferred to deregulate and liberalize sectors in which state enterprises have been dominant rather than privatize those enterprises.

33. The combinations for restructuring (R), privatizing (P), and deregulating (D) are: R-P-D, R-D-P, P-D-R, P-R-D, D-R-P, and D-P-R.

34. For example, the Argentine government seems to have promised the buyers of Aerolíneas Argentinas sole designation on all international routes for ten years after privatization (see chapter 7). In addition, in every telecommunications privatization studied in this volume, restructuring and privatization were accompanied by promises or legal commitments to restrain competition in the market for some time.

REFERENCES

Cominetti, R. 1992. "Notes on the Privatization Process of LAN." Economic Commission for Latin America and the Caribbean (ECLAC), Santiago.

"Guillermo Carey, LAN-Chile's New Owner, Gets Set to Branch Out at Home and Abroad." 1989. *Latin Finance*, Nov. 22.

Hachette, D., and R. Lüders. 1993. *Privatization in Chile: An Economic Appraisal*. San Francisco: ICS Press.

Iglesias, A., and R. Paredes. 1986. "The Open Skies Law in Chile." Working Paper. Univ. of Chile—Santiago, Dept. of Economics.

Kikeri, Sunita, John Nellis, and Mary Shirley. 1992. *Privatization: The Lessons of Experience*. Washington, D.C.: World Bank.

Muñoz, O., ed. 1993. *After Privatizations: Towards a Regulatory State*. Santiago: CIEPLAN.

Paredes, R., and J. M. Sánchez. 1993. "Economic Groups in Chile." ECLAC, Santiago.

Sigmund, P. 1990. "Chile: Privatization, Reprivatizion, Hyperprivatization." In *The Political Economy of Public Sector Reform and Privatization*, ed. E. N. Suleiman and John Waterbury. Boulder: Westview.

Vickers, John, and George Yarrow. 1988. *Privatization: An Economic Analysis*. Cambridge: MIT Press.

7. A Privatization Nightmare

AEROLÍNEAS ARGENTINAS

··

Robert Grosse

Under extreme and continuing pressure from the huge external debt burdens of the Latin American countries during the late 1980s, governments in the region began to reach for market-based solutions such as debt-equity swaps to convert loans into equity investments, conversions of loans into long-term bonds at lower principal values, and even outright sale of national assets to generate funds for redeeming the debts (Grosse 1991). This last response produced a wave of sell-offs of state-owned firms, following the lead of European countries (especially Great Britain) earlier in the decade (Hemming and Mansoor 1988; Kay et al. 1986).

Although the governments in Chile and Mexico led Latin America's surge of privatizations, the government of President Raul Alfonsín in Argentina began a process of economic liberalization and privatization in that country that rivaled the most open policies anywhere else. One of the first steps in that process, after opening up tariff and financial barriers to competitive business, was the initiation of a long series of sales of major government-owned companies, from telecommunications to oil, and including some of the largest and most important firms such as ENTel, the national telephone company (1990), SEGBA, the Buenos Aires electric power system (1992), YPF, the national oil company (1993), and Aerolíneas Argentinas, the national airline (1990).

This chapter examines the privatization of Aerolíneas Argentinas, as it was carried out through sale of controlling ownership of shares to the Spanish airline, Iberia. Both government and company perspectives are analyzed, to demonstrate the continued bargaining relation between them and to show the interplay of interests and constraints that affected this process.

The privatization of Aerolíneas Argentinas is a noteworthy experience because it points out key problems and areas for careful negotiation that will arise in other privatizations, especially large-scale ones in highly concentrated industries in developing countries. It also demonstrates that there are no simple solutions for privatizing firms in such capital-intensive and globally oversupplied industries as airlines, steel, and automobiles. In many ways, the Aerolíneas case portrays the many things that can go terribly wrong in a privatization transaction.

A number of critical issues should be tackled in empirical analyses of privatizations, in response to the centrality of these issues in conceptual analyses. For example, the social (or nonfinancial) benefits and costs to Argentina of the sale of Aerolíneas need to be compared to the private benefits and costs of this sale to the buyer, Iberia. Since governments need to take into account such concerns as income distribution and economic structure as well as political reaction to the privatization, they will value this transaction differently than the company purchasing the state-owned firm. The buyer will be concerned with the economic viability of the venture, based on future cash flows generated and on the ability to realize those flows in the home country's currency. While neither of these measures can be fully carried out ex ante, both can be discussed in some detail with the evidence that has accumulated thus far in the present case. The strategies of Iberia and the Argentine government must be judged in light of these different goals.

As a first step toward evaluating the two sides' strategies, consider the situations of Aerolíneas Argentinas in Latin America and Iberia in Europe at the end of the 1980s. Table 7-1 gives the two airlines' financial positions for the year 1989 on several dimensions.

Note that, depending on the measure, Aerolíneas was the second or third largest carrier in Latin America at the time, while Iberia was the seventh largest carrier in Europe. Both airlines were in weak financial conditions due to increasingly fierce competition in the industry and to recessionary economic conditions, in Latin America in the late 1980s and in Europe at the beginning of the 1990s.[1]

Each side's strategy is considered in the context of the bargaining relation between the Argentine government and Iberia, which can be described as follows. The Argentine government possessed ownership of Aerolíneas, which in turn possessed a desirable route structure in Latin America and between Latin America, Europe, and North America. Iberia possessed a desirable route structure in Europe, a cultural and language bias in favor of Latin America, and greater access to financial resources than Aerolíneas. The Argentine government was looking for a purchaser of Aerolíneas that could bring in financial resources and build the carrier into a more competitive Latin American airline. Iberia

Table 7-1. Aerolineas Argentinas and Iberia, Financial and Physical Indicators, Comparative Data, 1989

Carrier	Revenues (US$m)	Profits (US$m)	Freight-Ton- Kilometers (million)	Passenger- Kilometers (million)	Load Factor (%)
Latin America					
Aerolíneas Argentinas	757	25	199	8,319	67
Aeromexico	366	2	6	5,474	69
Avianca	—	—	80	3,619	
Mexicana	744	13	118	10,538	63
Varig	1,866	10	1,016	16,415	71
VASP			114	4,638	
Europe					
Aeroflot	—	—	2,760	228,974	—
Air France	60	6	3,279	36,815	—
Alitalia	3,811	-174	1,108	17,920	64
British Airways	7,726	348	2,186	64,300	72
Iberia	—	—	737	21,119	—
KLM	2,623	235	1,999	25,030	—
Lufthansa	6,700	73	3,905	36,169	—

Source: *Air Transport World* (June 1990), 76–78; Pilling (1992), 47.
— = not available.

was looking for a partner to expand its international routes to position itself to compete with other European carriers in the 1990s and beyond. Both sides wanted to build Aerolíneas into a successful international competitor, with strong links to Europe and North America. Based on the bargaining resources, relative stakes, and similarity of interests of the two sides, the privatization process developed over the years.

A Brief History

Aerolíneas Argentinas was founded as a government-owned airline in 1950 under the government of President Juan Perón. Aerolíneas combined the routes, airplanes, and other assets of a number of regional airlines that had served Argentina before that time; these private airlines had been nationalized in the late 1940s and then pooled into the newly formed Aerolíneas in 1950.

From that time onward, Aerolíneas was the national flag carrier of Argentina in international aviation and the largest airline in the domestic market.

A few small private airline companies were formed over the years, but only Austral (established in 1970) became a factor in the domestic passenger and air cargo service. Austral was founded by a group of Argentine businessmen to provide an alternative to Aerolíneas in the domestic airline market. It was managed aggressively and reasonably successfully for most of the 1970s. Under the military government that took power in 1978, Austral was nationalized and became a companion to Aerolíneas in the hands of the Ministry of Transportation. After operating in this manner for almost a decade, Austral was reprivatized by the government of President Raul Alfonsín in 1987. Austral was sold to a group led by Enrique Pescarmona, which had businesses in capital equipment, agriculture, and other sectors, both in Argentina and abroad. From the beginning of its newly privatized life in 1987, Austral looked to international routes as a part of the strategy for long-run survival and profitability.

The process that led to Iberia's acquisition of controlling interest in Aerolíneas Argentinas began in the mid-1980s. The government of President Alfonsín had committed itself to a process of economic rationalization, to be pursued among other ways through the partial or total sell-off of poorly performing state-owned companies. In negotiations with the World Bank in the context of dealing with the government's overwhelming foreign debt, a commitment was made in 1986 to begin the privatization of major companies, starting with Aerolíneas and ENTel.

The government holding company that controlled Aerolíneas (the Directory of Public Enterprises, or DEP) held negotiations in 1987 with several European carriers that were looking for cooperative agreements for both technical assistance and route linkages. In February 1988 it was announced that a minority interest in the airline would be sold to Scandinavian Airline Systems (SAS). This announcement presupposed the approval of both houses of the Argentine Congress, which was required for any sale of government-owned properties such as Aerolíneas.

The initial SAS Memorandum of Understanding, signed in February 1988 (by Aerolíneas President Horacio Domingorena, Public Enterprise Director Horacio Losovitz, Minister of Public Works Rodolfo Terragno, and SAS President Jan Carlzon), called for a sale of 40 percent of Aerolíneas to SAS for US$204 million, of which US$100 million would be paid immediately upon congressional approval for 20 percent of the airline. The government would have retained 51 percent of the shares and given 9 percent to Aerolíneas employees, and SAS would have retained the right to buy the other 20 percent within three years. The government of President Alfonsín, and especially Minister of Public Works Terragno, were strongly committed to achieving the privatizations of both Aerolíneas and ENTel during their term in office, which was scheduled to end in December 1989. Under this agreement, SAS, via Aerolíneas, would retain the sole right to provide international air transport from Argentina, the same right that Aerolíneas possessed at the time. That is, operating under the name Aerolíneas Argentinas, the privatized firm (to be controlled by SAS) would remain the Argentine flag carrier, with monopoly rights to serve foreign destinations and with the right to be included in any bilateral agreement on new routes with foreign governments.

This proposed agreement with SAS subsequently was challenged by a rival bid from a consortium led by Enrique Pescarmona, president of Cielos del Sur (parent of Austral Airlines). This group negotiated with two European partners, Swissair and Alitalia, to put together a combined offer for Aerolíneas. To try to thwart the government's efforts to sell Aerolíneas to SAS—which would keep Austral out of international routes by leaving the monopoly with Aerolíneas—the Pescarmona group presented a formal bid to Terragno in July 1988 and carried out a press campaign to inform the public about their counteroffer. The process of pursuing congressional approval for the SAS agreement continued through the rest of the year, with the Cielos del Sur bid never being formally considered but always arising in the debate.

As the year progressed, opposition to the sale arose from both opposition political parties (presidential elections were forthcoming in May of 1989) and from unions representing Aerolíneas workers. Three of the airline's five unions were linked to the Peronist Partido Justicialista, in opposition to Alfonsín's Unión Cívica Radical. PJ presidential candidate Carlos Menem in turn made the deal with SAS into a campaign issue, along with criticism of President Alfonsín's economic policies in general. This politicized debate of the intended partial privatization lasted through the year. By the end of the year, Congress was sufficiently polarized against the deal that approval was clearly not forthcoming. SAS withdrew its offer in December 1988. The Pescarmona group was never able to obtain full financial and other information from the government to finalize its bid, and ultimately Swissair withdrew from the consortium after months of unsuccessful efforts. The Argentine government never formally considered this bid.

After national elections in May 1989, President Carlos Menem took office (in July) and quickly moved to expand the privatization effort.[2] He opened the way for sale of the national telephone company, ENTel, and for a renewed effort to sell Aerolíneas. In addition, his leadership team put together an entire package of privatization initiatives, with percentages to be sold, timetables, and other details for the sale of such major state-owned companies as the national oil company (YPF) and the Buenos Aires electric power company (SEGBA). While not all of the timetable had been met by the end of 1993, most of the major privatizations had been carried out and additional sales were under way or in planning (Oppenheimer 1993; Alexander and Corti 1993).

The renewed attempt to sell Aerolíneas encountered renewed difficulties for one key reason: the company was in poor financial shape (losing more than US$10 million per month in 1990). At the same time, the global airline industry was similarly in poor shape, with losses being realized by many if not most of the major international carriers.[3] While the first round of discussions of cooperation agreements in 1988 had attracted initial statements of interest from half a dozen airlines, the second round produced only Austral (in the consortium with Iberia) as a viable candidate for acquiring controlling interest in Aerolíneas. Several other consortia, including Varig with Citibank, American Airlines with Chase Manhattan Bank, and Alitalia began information gathering, but none of them ultimately chose to make a bid.

Negotiations between the government (led by Public Works Minister Roberto Dromi) and Iberia (led by President Miguel Aguiló) came to an initial conclusion with the bid of June 1990. Iberia offered to buy 30 percent of Aerolíneas directly, its banking partners from Spain (Banco Central Hispano, Cofivacasa, and Banesto) would buy 19 percent, a group of Argentine partners including Austral would buy 36 percent, Aerolíneas employees would receive 10 percent, and the Argentine government would keep 5 percent of the total shares. The Argentine partners included Enrique Pescarmona, owner of Cielos del Sur (parent company of Austral Airlines), who agreed to buy 17 percent of the privatized Aerolíneas. Also in the consortium were Amadeo Riva and Francisco de Vincenzo, both owners of construction companies, who each agreed to buy 8.5 percent of the firm. And finally, Alfredo Otalora, an Argentine doctor and investor, agreed to buy 2 percent of the privatized Aerolíneas. This produced a total of 36 percent Argentine investment, which would add to the government and employees' stakes of 15 percent, to give Argentine investors 51 percent of the total stock of the new company.[4]

Upon formal acceptance of the bid in November 1990, Iberia and its consortium contributed their agreed initial payment of US$130 million in cash, which was to be followed by an additional investment of another US$130 million in ten equal parts over the following five years, along with redemption of approximately US$2.1 billion of Argentine foreign debt to be purchased in the secondary market.[5] This was to purchase 85 percent of Aerolíneas, leaving 5 percent to the government and 10 percent to be held by the government for the workers. The payment was financed with a loan from the Spanish banks, and the loan then appeared on the books of the new Aerolíneas.[6]

Managerially, Aerolíneas was turned over to the new owners. Amadeo Riva became president, with Francisco de Vincenzo and Alfredo Otalora joining the board of directors. Iberia installed a management team of three executives from Spain: Manuel Estevez, Manuel Sanchez, and Salustiano Mandia. Iberia did not send a full team of strategic planners and other officers at this time; presumably, this was because a final agreement with the Argentine government had not been achieved. This failure to introduce large-scale change in Aerolíneas at the time of privatization has been criticized as a major strategic error, since the needed changes (such as rationalization of facilities and labor force reductions) were much more difficult to carry out later.

The sale separated Aerolíneas from two of its former businesses: duty-free stores in Argentina and ramp service for all airlines in Argentina. These parts of the government-owned Aerolíneas were sold separately to other purchasers. Both sales were highly profitable, but separating them from Aerolíneas left the airline in a less profitable position. This arrangement was not a surprise to the purchasing group, and their offer reflected the loss of these businesses. Nevertheless, the loss of these two income-generating assets made it more difficult for the privatized Aerolíneas to achieve profitability.

The privatization ultimately took four years, allowing sufficient time for potential buyers to examine most of the details. Examples in Europe (e.g., British Airways) and Mexico (e.g., Mexicana) were available as models for Aerolíneas. But the Argentine government apparently did not sufficiently learn from those examples to avoid problems with Aerolíneas Argentinas. The finalization of the privatization agreement was complicated and slow. In 1991 the ownership of the new Aerolíneas was restructured. Enrique Pescarmona left the consortium in March, selling Cielos del Sur to Iberia for US$30 million. His stake was divided between the two construction firms, which redistributed the Argentine shares to Devi Construcciones (now 17%), Riva, S.A. (also 17%), plus the holdings of the government, the workers, and Otalora. The total Argentine share remained at 51 percent.

In both 1991 and 1992, mounting losses at Aerolíneas required the partners to contribute more funds to the firm. Since the Argentine investors balked at these requirements, their shares were eroded as the Argentine government and the Spanish investors were forced to contribute the needed funds. By July 1992 another restructuring of the Argentine consortium resulted in the government taking over 28 percent more shares, leaving 10 percent with the workers and 8 percent in the hands of Alfredo Otalora and other Argentine investors. The Spanish shareholdings did not change: in September 1993 the ownership remained 30 percent Iberia; 19 percent Spanish banks; 43 percent Argentine government (including workers' share), and 8 percent Argentine investors.

A number of primarily financial disagreements between Spanish and Argentine participants surfaced over the first three years of the venture. In one major instance, the purchase of US$2.1 billion of Argentine foreign debt on the secondary market was initially estimated to cost about US$273 million (at US$0.13 per dollar of face value of the debt). After the original agreement of November 1990, but before the definitive agreement of April 12, 1991, the price of Argentine government foreign debt on the secondary market rose dramatically, to about US$0.38 per dollar of face value. Thus, after renegotiation the April 1991 agreement called for delivery of US$1.61 billion (face value) of foreign debt.

Iberia had purchased some of the debt at lower prices, but in the process of complying with the agreement was forced to buy much of the total at the high end of the range. This obviously raised the purchase price in pesetas by a huge amount. Iberia initially delivered, in May 1991, approximately US$841 million face value of the foreign debt, leaving about US$769 million face value outstanding. In a revised agreement with the Argentine government in July 1991, Iberia agreed to deliver, that month, US$210 million face value of debt and then offset some claims on Aerolíneas worth US$109 million. Together, these transactions lowered the outstanding balance to US$61 million market value owed in the form of foreign debt.

While the above description may appear reasonably clear, the negotiation of the foreign debt repurchase and the cancellation of this claim were quite complex and protracted. The Argentine government had achieved a strong bargaining position by this time (early 1991), after Iberia had paid US$130 million and had committed to additional financial outlays. Iberia, for its part, was largely committed to the venture and thus was forced to accept a higher purchase price than anticipated when the secondary market debt rose so significantly in value. Another noteworthy incident was the decision to lay off 775 workers in late 1992. This step led to worker protests against Iberia and threats by the Argentine government to renationalize the airline. While it was broadly agreed that such labor force reductions were needed for the airline to become competitive, Iberia had waited more than a year after the privatization to carry them out, which left workers in a much stronger position to oppose the cuts and Iberia in a much weaker position to enforce them. The firm's plans were ultimately upheld but only after a bitter public battle with the labor unions in late 1992.

The Bargaining Context

At the end of the 1980s, both Iberia and Aerolíneas Argentinas were in trouble. Both carriers operated relatively limited international networks in comparison with key rivals, and both served previously highly protected domestic markets. With the advent of increasingly broader open skies policies around the world, airlines were facing new competition from foreign carriers even in their domestic markets. The limited Spanish market was highly integrated with other European destinations, and the single-market initiative of the European Community threatened to allow the largest carriers (e.g., British Airways and Lufthansa) to move aggressively into other EC member country markets. The Argentine market was also relatively limited, and with increasing competition from North American carriers (American Airlines and United Air Lines) plus Varig (Brazil) and Iberia, Aerolíneas was similarly facing heightened competition.

Consider each partner's *bargaining resources* in this context. Iberia possessed a larger international route structure than Aerolíneas, with more planes in its inventory and greater financial resources to contribute. The Argentine government, on the other hand, faced a huge problem of servicing foreign debt, which required the generation of new sources of foreign exchange. The government was responding to this problem with a broad array of procompetition policies, in which a central piece was the privatization of state-owned companies. At the same time, Aerolíneas was one of the leading airlines in Latin America and so offered an attractive target for a foreign airline looking to establish a major beachhead in Latin America.

Thus, the key bargaining resources offered by the foreign airline company were both financial and geographical, in terms of routes. It was argued that Iberia possessed superior management to that of Aerolíneas and, thus, that technical skills would be brought in through the deal, as well. The government of Argentina offered mainly the access to Aerolíneas's routes and facilities. In addition, as a continued part owner of the privatized airline, the government could be expected to offer favorable regulatory treatment. Basically, the government controlled access to the market for airline service in Argentina, especially the designation of the national flag carrier airline, which Iberia sought as a means to extend its international route structure.

A second dimension of the bargaining relation was the *relative stakes* held by each side. At stake for Argentina's government were both the financial gain to be realized through privatization and the political gain of selling off inefficient firms and proceeding toward a modern, capitalist economy. At stake for Iberia was its future competitive position: without Aerolíneas it would be one of several weak carriers in Europe; with Aerolíneas, it would be the best-positioned European carrier in Latin America and an attractive potential partner for other international airlines looking for strategic alliances in Europe and elsewhere.

If Iberia failed to come to an agreement with Argentina's government, there were other alternatives for building a Latin American network linked to its European base. In fact, Iberia subsequently did pursue other Latin American carriers, buying controlling interest in LADECO in

Chile and in VIASA in Venezuela and negotiating for interests in additional carriers. At stake for Iberia, therefore, was the Argentine market and the ability to build routes through Argentina. For Argentina's government, the stakes were considerably higher. The failed agreement with SAS had already shown the government's weakness (albeit the previous government) in putting together a deal, and the economic situation of Aerolíneas had deteriorated continuously since 1988. If the Iberia bid were not accepted, the government had no additional bids to fall back on. The bidding process in 1990 had produced only the Iberia-Austral consortium interested enough to formalize its bid. Thus, the government had both an economic interest in seeing this particular deal through successfully and a political interest in demonstrating its ability to privatize its designated companies, as promised. A third and final dimension was the *similarity of interests* between the two sides. The more their interests coincided, the more likely a successful agreement could be reached and maintained. On this dimension, the two sides were fairly closely aligned in 1990: Iberia was interested in expanding in the Latin American market, while Argentina's government wanted to expand its economic ties with Europe. As partners in the partially privatized airline, both would seek profits in the new venture. Each side saw itself as being under pressure to achieve a successful agreement for strategic reasons.

However, it was still true that Iberia represented a foreign presence in a "national treasure" such as Aerolíneas. Nationalistic interests as well as interests of employees likely to be laid off were clearly opposed to an agreement. Likewise, Iberia (and its private sector partners) were disposed to pursue a more profitable strategy, while the Argentine government as part owner would still look to social as well as financial goals for the new company. Thus, the similarity of interests was far from complete.

The three key dimensions of this bargaining situation are shown in figure 7-1. According to this perspective, the initial bargaining conditions favored Iberia in the negotiations. The agreement reached in November 1990 clearly reflected these conditions, giving a very favorable treatment to Iberia, as shown at point AR_{90}.

The Obsolescing Bargain

Once Iberia's consortium had made the initial payment of US\$130 million in November 1990, the Spanish airline immediately became heavily committed to its venture with Aerolíneas. That is, with a 30 percent ownership interest in hand and more than US\$100 million already disbursed, Iberia was hostage to the situation. This kind of reversal of bargaining strengths has been called the obsolescing bargain (Vernon

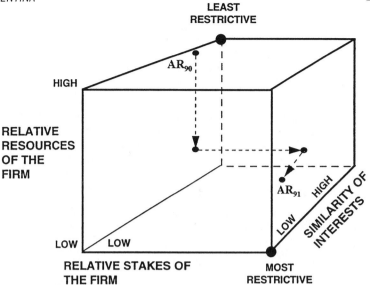

Figure 7-1. The Bargaining Relation between Iberia and Argentina's Government.

1977). While the Argentine government still maintained a large equity ownership in Aerolíneas, Iberia now had to both try to operate the company profitably and deal with the government as regulator (and partner). Iberia's initially strong bargaining position had become somewhat obsolete upon the signing of the agreement, because of the sunk cost of the investment. And as the two airlines began to coordinate their activities and share personnel, information, and facilities, Iberia became even more tied to Aerolíneas and, thus, subject to the Argentine government's possible intervention. Altogether, the bargaining positions of the two sides changed dramatically by the end of 1990.

Consider the situation in 1991, when the Argentine private sector partners had proven unable or unwilling to meet the financial commitments needed to preserve their shares in Aerolíneas. The negative cash flow of Aerolíneas required the partners to inject about US$10 million per month during the year. Iberia needed to move forward with the restructuring of the revenue-generating business of Aerolíneas, while the Argentine government needed to settle the ownership issue. Iberia had agreed to a share of 30 percent in Aerolíneas, and the decisions of its local partners had no bearing on this share. The government, however, wanted to receive the cash inflow promised by the other purchasers and to relinquish ownership down to its 5 percent target (plus custody of the 10% of shares held for employees of Aerolíneas). Thus, in dealing with Iberia's request to borrow funds from Spanish banks to pay the remaining US$130 million of the purchase price, Argentina's government was in a stronger position than it had been one year earlier.

While the government had improved its position upon receiving Iberia's payment in 1990, Iberia had not only been subjected to the obsolescing bargain but it also faced severe financial problems at home. The Iraqi invasion of Kuwait and subsequent Persian Gulf War led to drastic reductions in European air travel in late 1990 and 1991. Subsequently, Spain entered a severe recession, which reduced air travel significantly. Both of these events curtailed Iberia's revenues to the point that the airline lost more than US$100 million in 1991. Iberia had much more at stake in 1991 than it had only one year earlier.

The Argentine government itself had entered a more positive economic phase by 1991. Its economic stabilization policy had cut inflation from more than 1,000 percent per year in 1989 to less than 40 percent per year in 1990. A number of privatizations had been successfully carried out by that time and had generated important revenues for the government. At the same time, the confidence of Argentine investors had been restored in the country, and more than US$1 billion of flight capital was estimated to have returned to Argentina in 1991. In all, the economic picture was far more favorable at the end of 1991 than one year earlier, and the government had much stronger bargaining resources.

When the Argentine private sector partners in the privatization failed to comply with the need for new funds, the government had to reabsorb the shares of Aerolíneas and wait for a future opportunity to sell them in the market. Iberia was legally unable to take a larger share in the airline, nor was it able to dictate the terms of the restructuring. The bargaining situation had moved to approximately point AR_{91} in figure 7-1.

Continued difficulties plagued the Iberia-Aerolíneas venture (see table 7-2). The weakness of the Spanish market left Iberia with financial losses in both years. Aerolíneas likewise suffered continued financial problems.[7] These underlying problems made friction between Spanish and Argentine decisionmakers that much more severe. The 1992 decision by Iberia to lay off workers led not only to public protest and a threat by the government to renationalize the company but, subsequently, to a decision to fine Aerolíneas US$1 million. The fine was not carried out, but again the damage to Iberia's image was done.

Because both partners viewed their relation as more desirable than pursuing other alternatives, the bargaining seemed likely to continue into the future. As the situation moved more toward point G in figure 7-1, Argentina's government was likely to gain more and more bargaining strength. Iberia, on the other hand, needed to pursue a strategy to move the situation back toward point C, where its bargaining position was strongest.

Table 7-2. Aerolíneas Argentinas and Iberia, Financial and Physical Indicators, Comparative Data, 1992

Carrier	Revenues (US$m)	Profits (US$m)	Freight Ton Kilometers (million)	Passenger Kilometers (million)	Load Factor (%)
Latin America					
Aerolíneas Argentinas	910	−188.7	185	9,196	65
Aeromexico	1,020	−52.3	67	8,765	
Avianca	439	6.7	88	3,396	61
Mexicana	—	—	57	5,889	55
Varig	—	—	930	17,246	
VASP	—	—	170	4,519	
Europe					
Aeroflot	—	—	2,350	117,400	—
Air France	11,189	−617	3,972	55,504	67
Alitalia	4,240	−9	1,307	27,397	65
British Airways	6,390	370	2,653	69,730	—
Iberia	3,553	−264	588	23,836	66
KLM	4,273	68	2,407	32,297	—
Lufthansa	9,300	−230	4,400	48,100	—

Source: *Air Transport World* (June 1993), 76–78; Aerolíneas Argentinas (1991–92).

— = not available.

Outcomes

The privatization of Aerolíneas Argentinas was highly unsatisfactory through at least the first half of 1994, and it was an exception to the series of more successful privatizations carried out by the Argentine government in the early 1990s. Beyond the slightest doubt, global conditions in the airline industry, in which virtually all international carriers lost money in the early 1990s, contributed greatly to this outcome.

Looking at specific targets of privatization in this case, it is possible to measure a number of the results fairly clearly. The Argentine government sold 30 percent ownership of Aerolíneas to Iberia, and Iberia was given management control over the privatized firm. The Argentine government in 1993 owned 43 percent of Aerolíneas, intending to sell all but 5 percent (with another 10% held for the workers) as soon as the market would permit. Ownership would remain 51 percent in Argentine hands, so that Aerolíneas could receive treatment as the national flag carrier airline in international agreements. Aerolíneas was granted a ten-year monopoly, until November of 2000, on international routes from Argentina. Domestic routes could be contested, although (except for the fact that Austral was part of the privatized Aerolíneas) no domestic competitors for scheduled airline service existed in 1993. The international routes were heavily contested by foreign carriers such as Ameri-

Table 7-3. Measures of Efficiency and Performance at Aerolíneas Argentinas, 1989 and 1992

Performance Indicator	1989	1992
Revenues (US$m)	631.9	910.9
Number of Employees	10,791	8,417
Revenue per employee (US$)	58,558	108,221
Freight-ton-kilometers	18,432	21,979
Passenger-kilometers per employee	801,594	1,092,551
Load factor	66.6	64.5
Domestic	59.1	62.6
International	71.0	65.0
Earnings (US$m)	24.6	−188.7

Source: Air Transport World; Aerolíneas Argentinas (1991–92).

can Airlines, United Air Lines, Lufthansa, KLM, and British Airways. The privatization of Aerolíneas appeared to have little impact on an already highly competitive situation. The domestic routes could be contested in the future through either the sell-off of Austral or the creation of a new domestic competitor. The privatization of Aerolíneas did negatively affect the competitive situation, since Austral was taken from being a competitor to being a sister airline of Aerolíneas.

The efficiency of the airline under private (or at least foreign) rather than public management can be evaluated through measures such as passenger miles flown per employee or seat occupancy percentages before and after the privatization (table 7-3).

The results are varied. Passenger seat occupancy dropped importantly in international flights, although it improved in domestic flights. Profitability certainly dropped by 1992. Efficiency in the use of employees improved notably in passenger-kilometers flown as well as in freight-tons shipped. Passenger-kilometers per employee rose 36 percent between 1989 and 1992. Similarly, freight-ton-kilometers per employee improved by 19 percent in three years.

Another measure of efficiency is the pricing of airline service. On international routes, this pricing was largely determined by competition with American, Varig, United, and other international carriers serving Buenos Aires, a situation not affected significantly by privatization; that is, consumers of airline service faced fairly competitive conditions even before the sale of Aerolíneas. But on domestic routes, the operation of Austral as a subsidiary of Aerolíneas eliminated the possibility of competition, which could have produced more competitive pricing. This situation may change as additional domestic carriers are permitted to offer regular (noncharter) service on domestic routes or if Austral is sold to other investors, as has been discussed since the privatization of Aerolíneas. In summary, up to the end of 1993 the privatization of Aerolíneas

Argentinas had no significant impact on domestic or international prices of airline services.

The Argentine government, despite its political loss of face resulting from the poor economic results of the privatized Aerolíneas, probably benefited economically from the sale. Where before privatization the airline was costing the government an estimated annual subsidy of US$40 million, after that time the company was forced to operate on its own. In addition, the sale itself generated current income in 1990–91 of approximately US$260 million in cash and US$1,600 million in foreign debt retired (with an average market value of about US$450 million). These figures do not even include the additional sales of the ramp service and the duty-free shops, which were not included in the package sold to Iberia and its partners at privatization.

Of course, the story must include the government's remaining 43 percent interest in Aerolíneas as of mid-1993. This share cost the government large cash infusions in 1991 and 1992, as Aerolíneas was losing millions of dollars each month. Thus, a subsidy of sorts was still being paid, while the government was unable to sell its remaining shares of the airline (or until Aerolíneas started making money). The results for Iberia were largely negative through 1993. Because Aerolíneas did not earn a profit after privatization, Iberia realized only losses and the need to put more cash into the airline. While projections for the future show some prospect for profit after 1994, the immediate future is bleak and the medium-term future seems unlikely to produce the hoped-for earnings. The anticipated efficiencies from operating a Latin American system, including VIASA, LADECO, and Aerolíneas along with Iberia, had not yet been realized, so that the potential for some significant cost savings presumably remained. Thus, on financial grounds, the purchase of Aerolíneas appears to have been a major loss for Iberia.

Lessons

There is no question that, with hindsight, both Iberia and the Argentine government would dramatically rethink their strategies. But while management errors caused some key problems, regional and global competitive conditions in the airline industry contributed importantly to the poor initial results of this privatization.

One clear lesson learned by Iberia is to select local partners with greater attention to their commitment to financial underwriting.[8] The repeated restructuring of the local ownership of Aerolíneas cost enormous amounts of management time and effort, which would have been much better spent in running the airline. This lesson holds as well for the Argentine government, which gained negative political returns on this privatization, in contrast to the positive results from numerous other sales of state-owned companies during this same period.

A second lesson for the acquiring airline (Iberia) is that the obsolescing bargain so completely alters the terms of the bargain that the airline should build very careful details into its strategy and into the agreement to ensure continued advantage in the bargaining process. For example, the inability of Iberia to operate Aerolíneas immediately as a fully integrated part of its global organization failed to permit realization of economies of scale in many activities. Specific commitments to achieving such economies in reservation systems, maintenance facilities, and even management personnel would be needed to pursue these goals. The prolonged delay in obtaining the final agreement prevented Iberia from revamping Aerolíneas until more than a year after the original agreement.

As of 1993, Iberia needed to use strategy to move the bargaining relation back toward point C on figure 7-1. This strategy could include forming an alliance with another international airline, which could bring in more financial support, links to other routes, and superior technology to push Aerolíneas toward renewed profitability. A link with another airline would lessen the government's alternatives; it would have to co-opt another partner, thus raising the stakes for the government. Such an alliance could also add enough to Iberia's bargaining resources to recoup its advantage relative to the government. And finally, a solid strategy with an additional partner could enable Aerolíneas to achieve positive profitability, which would serve both company and government, thus reducing the tension of operating a money-losing venture.[9]

The government of Argentina needed a better plan for engendering competition among bidders for Aerolíneas at the outset of this process. With only one bid, the process was already biased toward problems. The valuation of Aerolíneas by internationally accepted auditors and a clear definition of the rules for postprivatization needed to be presented before the bidding.[10] Political conditions in Argentina, especially the government's commitment to sell Aerolíneas and ENTel, made such a deliberate process difficult to carry out, but the ex post results reveal the costs associated with adopting a hasty approach.

The story of the first three years of Aerolíneas as a privatized company was quite negative. If Iberia had in fact been able to construct a competitive route system and build alliances with other international airlines, then its Latin American strategy, of which Aerolíneas formed an integral part, could well have proven successful. Conditions in the global airline industry and in Europe after 1991 conspired against Iberia, but an economic upturn in Europe could provide the turning point to this otherwise dismal story. A 1993 study showed the possibility of the

profitable operation of Aerolíneas by 1994 under fairly reasonable assumptions about changes in strategy and economic conditions. Perhaps
then the Aerolíneas "nightmare" will have a happy ending.

NOTES

1. Aerolíneas was losing money on its airline operations, although its duty-
free shop and ramp services produced enough profits to generate an overall
profit of US$25 million in fiscal 1989 (Pilling 1992, 47).

2. The new government was scheduled to take office in December. However, Argentine law permits an earlier exchange of power. The Alfonsín government was so weakened by electoral defeat and continued opposition to its policies that President Alfonsín stepped down in July rather than continuing to the
end of his term.

3. The world airline industry was estimated to have lost US$2.4 billion in
1990. This situation was attributed to fierce competition in the United States
and Europe and to the Persian Gulf War. The war both reduced international air
travel and raised the cost of jet fuel from about US$0.60 per gallon in July to
US$1.40 per gallon in October ("1990 World Airline Report" 1991).

4. Dr. Otalora actually lived in Spain and was seen as an implicit partner of
the Spanish group, thus giving Iberia implicit controlling interest in Aerolíneas.

5. According to Aerolíneas financial statements, the first payment was made
on September 28, 1990, at Banco de la Nacion's New York office and approved by
Decree 2438-90 of the Argentine government (Aerolíneas Argentinas 1991–92).
For discussion of this secondary market in Latin American external debt, see
Aramburu and Grosse 1992.

6. This financing technique is common in leveraged buyouts, but it appears
to have caused an outcry against the Iberia consortium, which was accused of
"not putting up a penny" for Aerolíneas. Subsequent payments for the completion of the privatization also were paid with loans proceeds, and these loans also
appear as liabilities on the books of Aerolíneas.

7. On a stopover in Lima in early 1992, a local catering firm brought
cholera-infected food onto an Aerolíneas flight and a half dozen passengers
became ill. Numerous reservations were cancelled, and Aerolíneas's image was
damaged for many months.

8. Paradoxically, Iberia was brought in as a partner by Austral, then Austral's
owners dropped out of the consortium once Iberia had taken control.

9. The new partner would have to replace the Spanish banks as an investor
in Aerolíneas, since a majority of the airline must be held by Argentine shareholders to retain its flag carrier status.

10. A valuation had been carried out by Price Waterhouse before the SAS bid
in 1988, when Aerolíneas was valued at approximately US$510 million.

REFERENCES

Aerolíneas Argentinas, S.A. 1991–92. *Directors' Report and Financial Statements*. Buenos Aires.

Alexander, Myrna, and Carlos Corti. 1993. "Argentina's Privatization Program." CFS Discussion Paper 103. World Bank, Washington, D.C.

Aramburu, Diego, and Robert Grosse. 1992. "Determinants of Loan Prices in the Secondary Market for Latin American Debt." In *Recent Advances in International Banking and Finance,* ed. Sarkis Khoury. New York: JAI.

Grosse, Robert, ed. 1991. *Private Sector Solutions to the Latin American Debt Problem.* New Brunswick, N.J.: Transaction.

Hemming, Richard, and Ali Mansoor. 1988. "Privatization and Public Enterprise." Occasional Paper 56. International Monetary Fund, Washington, D.C.

Kay, John, Colin Mayer, and David Thompson. 1986. *Privatization and Regulation: The U.K. Experience.* Oxford: Clarendon.

"1990 World Airline Report." 1991. *Air Transport World.* June.

Oppenheimer, Andrés. 1993. "Sale of State-Owned Companies in Full Swing." *Miami Herald,* Mar. 29.

Pilling, Mark. 1992. "Aerolíneas Finds Its Own Identity." *Interavia Aerospace Review* (May): 46–48.

"Respuesta al Mayday." 1993. *Apertura* 42 (Apr.): 56–69.

Vernon, Raymond. 1977. *Storm over the Multinationals.* New York: Basic Books.

8. Divestiture and Deregulation

THE CASE OF MEXICO'S AIRLINES

. . . .

Pankaj Tandon

In a short period of about three years, Mexico's airline industry was completely overhauled. From a heavily regulated government duopoly, it was transformed into a completely free, entirely private, market. Both government airlines were privatized and a major deregulation was introduced. This was followed by significant new entry, some intense competition, and then a merger of the two newly privatized firms. An analysis of this market may therefore have lessons both for divestiture policy and for the economics of deregulation.

Background

Prior to 1988, the Mexican airline industry was dominated by the two government-owned airlines: Mexicana Airline and Aeromexico. Historically, both had been private airlines.

Mexicana Airline, founded in 1921, is the oldest airline in Latin America and the fourth oldest in the world.[1] In its early years, it was based in the port of Tampico. In 1926, all of its shares were acquired by Pan American Airlines. Pan Am obtained a concession from the U.S. Postal Service to transport mail between the United States and Mexico and inaugurated Mexicana's first international flight (Mexico City–Los Angeles) in 1935. Over the next three decades, Mexicana steadily expanded its system. In 1967, Pan Am sold its interest in the airline to a group of Mexican investors, led by Cresencio Ballesteros, a construction industry figure. The airline then embarked on a program to modernize and rapidly expand its fleet, relying exclusively on the acquisition of Boeing-727 aircraft. Starting with seventeen aircraft in 1970, the airline's fleet grew to forty-four by 1980, and all of these were 727s. In 1981, the first three DC-10s were added. This expansion program was funded largely by debt. In 1982, when rising interest rates and falling oil prices led to the Mexican debt crisis, Mexicana—reflecting its country's fortunes—had a debt crisis of its own. The company was unable to meet its debt obligations, and turned to the government for help. The government elected to acquire a 51 percent shareholding (terms were not disclosed), thereby making Mexicana a parastatal company.

Aeromexico was started as a private sector company in 1934; its first route was Mexico City–Acapulco.[2] Over the next several decades, it grew steadily, largely by acquiring smaller airlines in financial difficulty. Although this may have seemed like a cheap way to expand, it had a serious unanticipated cost: the airline ended with a hodgepodge of aircraft, which were therefore expensive to maintain. In 1940, Pan American acquired 40 percent of Aeromexico shares but did not take control of the company. In 1957, Pan Am sold their holding to a group of Mexican investors.

In July 1959, in response to a strike by the pilots' union and a perceived need to keep the airline operating, the government acquired all the shares of the company. For the next three decades, until its privatization in 1988, Aeromexico was a consistent money loser, turning a profit in only three years (1979–81). For the period 1982–87, the company received subsidies each year from the government equal to about 15 percent of its revenues. And although the subsidies were officially listed as capital subsidies (contributions of capital or absorption of debt), there was in fact a close correspondence between the size of the subsidy and the net loss of the company for that year. In a period of fiscal austerity, with Mexico facing pressure from its creditors to reduce its deficit, the continual drain of resources to Aeromexico was clearly undesirable.

Mexico has a medium-sized market for air transport services. In 1987, the last full year before the divestiture of Mexico's airlines began, a total of 13.5 million passengers were carried on 189,000 scheduled departures. By comparison, Malaysian airlines carried 7.4 million passengers on 101,000 departures; British airlines carried 33.7 million passengers on 523,000 departures, and U.S. airlines carried 439.6 million passengers on 6.3 million departures. Mexico has a larger market than Chile, Malaysia, and Argentina, a somewhat smaller one than Brazil, and less than half the size of the United Kingdom. Mexico City's Benito Juarez airport (which has about six times the activity as its nearest Mexican competitor, Acapulco) is most comparable in terms of traffic to the New Orleans airport.

In terms of its importance in Mexico's overall transportation system, air transport surpassed rail in terms of number of passengers in 1989 and is continuing its upward trend. Air freight remains relatively unimportant as a mode for transporting goods, but the passenger market, while medium-sized by international standards, has been growing fairly steadily.

The Domestic Market

A little more than 50 percent of Mexico's air traffic is domestic. This market has traditionally been dominated by Aeromexico and Mexicana, with a varying number of smaller airlines, ranging from five or six in the mid-1980s to fourteen in 1991, and a larger number of regional air companies providing unscheduled service. The smaller airlines had declined in importance, but since 1987 there appears to have been a resurgence in this category. Nevertheless, in 1991, the two trunk carriers dominated the market, carrying over 80 percent of the passengers and, in fact, accounting for 90 percent of passenger-kilometers (since their typical stage length was longer).

Until 1991, the domestic market was tightly regulated and entry both of new airlines and of new routes or flight schedules by existing airlines was strictly controlled. Further, fare increases also required prior approval of the Secretariat of Communications and Transport (SCT). Domestic fares were held at low, uneconomical levels, and increases generally lagged behind inflation. A sample of 1989 fares matched with fares for similar distances in the United States demonstrate how much lower Mexican fares were (table 8-1). Since both trunk airlines were state owned, there was little pressure to raise fares any faster. Competition was essentially nonexistent. A clear manifestation of this occurred during Aeromexico's bankruptcy in 1988, when Mexicana did not change its flight offerings at all to take advantage of Aeromexico's troubles. Deregulation of the airline market took place in July 1991, well after the divestiture of the two major airlines. Deregulation and its impact are considered later.

The International Market

The international market, while smaller in volume than the domestic market, is growing more rapidly. The number of passengers on international flights to and from Mexico grew by about 50 percent between 1980 and 1990, compared to just over 7 percent for domestic traffic. From 1981 to 1987, both Mexican airlines were steadily raising their share of the market, to a peak of 55.4 percent in 1987. In 1988, particularly with Aeromexico's bankruptcy, the Mexican share fell dramatically, and it had not yet recovered in 1994. According to data of the SCT, the Mexican

Table 8-1. Air Fares, United States and Mexico, Comparative Data, 1989

Route	Distance (miles)	Fare (US$)	Fare per Mile (US$)
Boston to Newark	206	178	.864
Mexico City to Acapulco	191	52	.273
New York to Cleveland	417	296	.710
Guadalajara to Monterrey	410	75	.182
Seattle to Los Angeles	1,133	472	.417
Mexicali to Guadalajara	1,113	142	.128

Source: Ruprah (1992).

share in 1990 was around 46 percent; the 1991 Mexican share is estimated at only 40 percent (Pizzimenti 1992).

In terms of geography, the bulk of Mexico's market is to and from the United States, which accounted for almost 90 percent of passengers. Several major airlines competed in this market, including three big American airlines: American, Delta, and United.[3] Because of the bilateral nature of international air traffic arrangements, the Mexican carriers had substantially the same number of flights as the foreign airlines and so had close to a 50 percent market share. Aeromexico, which flew to only six U.S. cities, had a relatively small share compared to Mexicana. The only other significant Aeromexico international destinations were Paris and Madrid, but it was far behind Air France and Iberia and had only about 10 percent of the passenger traffic between Mexico and Europe. Mexicana did not fly to Europe.

Because of the large size of the Mexico-U.S. market, compared to the small size of the Mexico-Europe market, international business was more important to Mexicana than to Aeromexico. This, combined with the fact that the domestic business was relatively unprofitable (because of fare regulation) while international business was relatively profitable, explains why Aeromexico had traditionally been a money loser while Mexicana had some profitable years.

The Transformation of the Airline Industry

The Divestiture of Mexicana

Because of Mexicana's mildly profitable history, it was seen as a much more viable candidate for divestiture compared to Aeromexico. The government decided in October 1986 to divest it, early for such a relatively large company.[4] Banamex was appointed as the agent bank. The first attempt to sell the company ended in July 1987; two bids were received, but they were deemed inadequate. A second attempt to sell the company followed. The government declared it wanted 225 pesos per share plus a minimum equity investment of US$75 million. Letters of intent were received from a number of potential buyers, including Gerardo de Prevoisin, who later that year bought control of Aeromexico,[5] Grupo Lanzagorta, which owned Avemex, a small private air carrier, Grupo Protexa, owner and operator of another small airline, and Roberto Hernandez of Acciones y Valores, who some years later bought control of Banamex.

Despite all the interest, Mexicana remained unsold. Each potential bidder was willing to pay the price of 225 pesos per share, plus to guarantee investment, but each had a list of requirements that they wanted satisfied, and it was these requirements that were the stumbling block. There were two important conditions that reappeared again and again:

—Mexicana was severely overstaffed, and the workforce had to be cut before the privatization sale. One bidder specifically mentioned the need to cut 3,000 workers from the payroll, at an estimated severance cost of 100 billion pesos (about US$45 million).

—Mexicana was too heavily indebted, and the government had to restructure or take over the debt before the sale.[6]

Negotiations over these and other preconditions for sale led nowhere, and eventually, in October 1988, the government declared the sale attempt a failure and closed the proceedings.

In May 1989, the government switched agent banks, appointing Banco Internacional, and a new scheme to privatize Mexicana was announced. The government would not sell its share but, rather, searched for an equity infusion into the company. It was willing to dilute its shareholding and to permit the new controlling group to be up to 49 percent foreign owned. Letters of interest were sought in June; by August, seven formal offers were received. The winning bid was filed by Grupo Falcon, a consortium of Mexican and foreign investors. The Mexican investors owned 51 percent, of which 33 percent was held by the brothers Pablo and Israel Brener, through their holding company, Grupo Xabre. Of the foreign investors, Chase Manhattan Bank held 35.7 percent of Falcon, Drexel Burnham Lambert owned 7.1 percent, and Sir James Goldsmith 6.1 percent. The consortium was put together primarily by the Breners, the sons of Lithuanian immigrants, who made a fortune in the 1980s by buying assets when everybody else in Mexico was trying to get their money out of the country. Their investments had included the Camino Real Hotel chain and the Las Hadas resort in Manzanillo, tourism properties that they regarded as synergistic with Mexicana. The foreign investors were largely passive; business associates of Pablo Brener, they had faith in his ability to make profitable investments.

The Falcon bid was a US$140 million equity infusion in exchange for 20 percent of the company's stock, implying a value for Mexicana of US$700 million. In addition, they were required by the terms of the agreement to buy an additional 5 percent of the shares in the open market. The ownership structure of the firm therefore evolved as follows (in percentages):

	Predivestiture	Postdivestiture
Government	50.83	40.60
Domestic shareholders	49.17	34.40
Domestic buying group	0.00	12.75
Foreign buyers	0.00	12.25

The government placed another 25 percent of the shares in a trust, over which Falcon had voting control until September 1992, thereby assuring the group control over the company for a period of three years. Falcon had the option to buy this block of shares at any time during this three-year period at a price implying the same valuation as the original bid plus interest at LIBOR (London interbank overnight rate) plus 2 percent. Finally, Falcon promised an ambitious US$3 billion, ten-year investment program, of which US$1.1 billion would be spent in Mexico, creating an estimated 21,500 new jobs.

The winning bid was announced on August 22, 1989, and the transfer of Mexicana took place in September. The basic strategy of the new airline was to prepare for and to capitalize on the expected boom in tourist traffic, which was also related to the Brenners' interests in resort properties. Thus the focus of attention was the pleasure traveler.[7] Also to this end, in August 1990, Mexicana placed an order for twenty-two Airbus-320 aircraft, with options to buy fourteen more. Delivery was to be spread over a period of seven years, 1991–97, and the total price (undiscounted) was US$1.6 billion. Because the program of aircraft retirement was considerably slower than this, this order constituted a commitment to expand the airline rapidly. Mexicana also leased four more Boeing-727 aircraft, raising the size of its fleet from forty-four in 1990 to fifty-two in 1991. As we will see, the rapid capacity expansion turned out to be a bad mistake.

The Divestiture of Aeromexico

Aeromexico had not been considered much of a prospect for divestiture because of its long history of losses and very poor reputation. Nevertheless, an opportunity presented itself in 1988, and the government seized it. In a contract dispute over wages and working conditions, the airline's ground workers went out on strike on April 14.[8] A few days later, on April 18, Aeromexico went into bankruptcy. Under Mexican law, workers are entitled to job security, but if a company goes into bankruptcy, its workers can be discharged. This is what happened to Aeromexico's workers. They were paid compensation according to the legal requirement (three months' pay plus another twelve days' pay for each year of service) but, otherwise, were let go.

Aeromexico—or rather, the company that owned it, Aeronaves de Mexico, S.A.—was placed in the hands of a trustee for administration during its bankruptcy. The trustee was a government bank, BANOBRAS (Banco Nacional de Obras y Servicios Públicos); it took control of Aeromexico on April 28 and moved rapidly to liquidate all of the company's contracts, except for its aircraft rental agreements, and to restart operations on a skeleton basis.

The airline recommenced operations in early May. Initially, only five aircraft were used (four owned and one rented DC-10s) to fly ten routes. The routes selected were the key routes between Mexico City and other destinations not served by any other airline. Sharp cuts were made in personnel: the ground crew for each flight at each station was 13 (instead of the previous 60) and the flight crew was held at 4 (instead of the previous 8). Seat occupancy rate in these early weeks was a little higher than 50 percent. As the situation stabilized, the flight schedule was slowly expanded, so that by mid-June eleven aircraft were serving twenty-one destinations. At this point, the airline was operating with 118 employees per aircraft, compared to 292 employees per aircraft in 1987.

Buoyed by the success in temporarily operating Aeromexico at a much reduced staffing level, the government announced its decision to privatize the airline. However, Aeronaves was in bankruptcy, and to resurrect it would be to also restore the labor union's contracts. The legal way out of this quandary was to create a new company—dubbed Aerovías de México, S.A. de C.V.—and to privatize it.[9] Accordingly, Aerovías was created on September 7 with a capital stock of 100 million pesos (approximately US$44,000), of which 35 percent was contributed by the pilots' union, ASPA, and the rest (temporarily) by BANOBRAS.

The new company quickly reached contractual agreements with its workers. Partly because they had been given a large equity share in the company, the pilots agreed to a 10 percent reduction in salaries, longer working hours, and other changes allowing the airline greater flexibility and efficiency. Similar efficiency-enhancing agreements were signed with ASSA, the flight attendants' union, and a new union for ground crew (National Union of Workers of Airlines and Related Companies, dubbed Independencia). The old ground workers' union no longer represented any workers.

Aerovías took formal control of Aeromexico on October 10. Ownership of the assets of Aeronaves, however, stayed in the hands of the bankruptcy trustee pending their sale. These assets were offered for sale to the private sector by the trustee. Legally speaking, therefore, the privatization of Aeromexico was not a divestiture (sale of an ongoing company) but rather a liquidation, involving sale of assets. The offer to sell these assets was made on September 26, when potential buyers were offered two options: (1) to buy all the fixed assets of Aeronaves, including all flight equipment and rental contracts, for a minimum price of 770 billion pesos (US$337 million); or (2) to buy all the assets except the owned aircraft and engines for a minimum price of 370 billion pesos (US$162 million). The sale of Aeromexico was, therefore, very different from the usual divestiture method in Mexico. Apart from the fact that this was a sale of assets, an unusual feature of this divestiture was the preannouncement of the minimum price, which was set as the higher of two measures of value: (1) the liquidation value of the assets, and (2) the present discounted value of future cash flows.[10] Of these, the so-called liquidation value turned out to be higher, and this was used to set the minimum bids.

The offer to sell Aeromexico's assets was announced on September 11, 1987. Interested bidders had until September 19 to express interest; nine such expressions of interest were received. On September 26, the minimum prices were announced. To continue further, potential buyers were required to deposit 500 million pesos (just over US$200,000), which would not be refunded if no bid was made. Only three buyers chose to continue; of these, only two actually made bids. One bid was by a large investment brokerage firm, Operadora de Bolsa, S.A. (OBSA), which offered to buy all the assets for US$245.5 million, 28 percent less than the minimum set by the government. They further required favorable tax treatment for lease expenses, permission to sell up to 49 percent of the company to foreigners, and renegotiation of various aspects including routes, tariffs and financial structure. The second—and winning— bid was from a consortium of investors under the corporate name of Dictum, S.A. de C.V. This was a joint venture of Bancomer, a government-owned (but since divested) commercial bank, and Icaro Aerotransportes, a holding company formed to hold shares of Aerovías. Icaro in turn was owned directly and indirectly by a number of different Mexican investors, of whom Gerardo de Prevoisin Legorreta—who controls Mexico's largest reinsurance company—eventually emerged in a dominant position.[11] Dictum's offer was of the minimum required (US$337 million) for all the assets, subject to their valuation and approval. They reserved the right to review all the assets and to reject those they deemed unnecessary. Further, the offer was for 75 percent of Aerovías stock (leaving 25% for the pilots' union, ASPA). Of the 75 percent, Bancomer was to own 20 percent and Icaro 55 percent.

Table 8-2. Aeromexico and Mexicana, Employment and Labor Productivity, 1981–1992

	Number of Employees		Revenue-Passenger-Kilometers per Employee	
Year	Aeromexico	Mexicana	Aeromexico	Mexicana
1981	9,448	10,212	705	781
1982	10,417	11,031	594	643
1983	10,463	11,910	704	708
1984	10,791	12,158	746	746
1985	11,010	12,980	754	724
1986	11,214	13,373	693	682
1987	11,505	13,906	681	700
1988	7,015	13,540	585	795
1989	4,218	12,783	1,295	824
1990	5,104	11,974	1,329	956
1991	6,004	11,289	1,256	952
1992	7,100	9,801	1,191	1,065

Source: Secretariat of Communications and Transport, company reports, and author's calculations.

The Dictum offer was accepted as the winning bid. Upon subsequent evaluation, Dictum did reject some of the assets, and the price was accordingly adjusted down by about 114 billion pesos.[12] The net price therefore was 655.2 billion pesos (approximately US$285 million).[13] However, I estimate that the government will actually receive no revenue from the sale of Aeromexico, as all sale proceeds will be used up in satisfying the liabilities of the bankrupt Aeronaves. Indeed, the creditors are not receiving full compensation and are, therefore, bearing some of the cost of divestiture.

The new owners of Aeromexico adopted an entirely different strategy than the owners of Mexicana. Rather than buying more aircraft, they sold almost the entire fleet, leasing much of it back, a move that gives the airline slightly greater flexibility. More important, and consistent with the fact that Aeromexico was fundamentally a domestic airline, a strategic decision was made to focus on the domestic business traveler. This strategy paid the airline handsome dividends, as we shall see. Finally, because the airline was now operated by a new company (Aerovías), the management was free to hire only as many workers as they needed. They took advantage of this to drastically reduce the size of the company's workforce (see table 8-2).

The Regulatory Environment and Deregulation

As Aeromexico and Mexicana were divested, no immediate changes were made in the regulatory environment. Thus the airlines were divested into a highly regulated environment, in which prior approval was required for practically all major decisions concerning route structures and fares, prices were held at extremely low levels, and price adjustments for inflation involved a considerable lag. Nevertheless, because the government was so vigorously pursuing deregulation in many other parts of the economy, it was clear that the deregulation of airlines would also come. What was not clear was the particular form deregulation would take. Thus the newly divested airlines were in a state of limbo, wondering and waiting for deregulation to arrive.

Deregulation was announced in July 1991, with the by-laws being published in September. The reform was far-reaching. Entry of new airlines is now free; airlines may add new routes and new flights on existing routes freely; and fares are arrived at almost freely. On routes served by more than one airline, or on regional routes where intermodal competition is strong, fares are totally free of regulation. On trunk routes served by only one airline, fares will continue to be regulated; however, carriers must now simply notify the secretary of transport of their intention to raise prices, and the secretary must decide whether to object—otherwise, the fare increases go through. For all practical purposes, the entire market is deregulated.

The Aftermath of Divestiture and Deregulation

Since divestiture and deregulation, the Mexican airline market has been in a state of some upheaval, not unlike the experience in the United States after airline deregulation. The most significant immediate event has been the rapid expansion of capacity. As mentioned earlier, Mexicana made a commitment to expand shortly after divestiture, by placing an order for twenty-two new Airbus-320 aircraft. After the Persian Gulf War in early 1990, however, the growth in international air travel came to an abrupt halt. The combination of slower demand growth and additions to the fleet created excess capacity. In addition, deregulation in the second half of 1991 resulted in some significant new entries. Not only did the incumbents, Aeromexico and Mexicana, increase their offerings, but several new airlines started to emerge, notably TAESA, a charter company that aggressively expanded into scheduled service. As a result, available-seat-kilometers (ASKs) in the domestic market grew by 25.6 percent in 1992, the first full year after deregulation, while actual traffic in terms of revenue-passenger-kilometers (RPKs) was growing only 11.4 percent. As a consequence, load factors (percentage of ASKs filled) were falling dramatically. Aeromexico's load factor fell from 62.1 percent in 1991 to 55.9 percent in 1992, while Mexicana's fell from 62.6 percent to 54.9 percent. Load factors below 60 percent are usually uneconomical, and indeed both airlines were operating in the red.

Despite the problem of excess capacity, prices (as measured by real yields, i.e., inflation-adjusted revenue per passenger-kilometer) tended

Table 8-3. Airfares from Mexico City, 1991 and 1992

Destination	Number of Passengers, 1990	Full Economy One-Way Fare (old pesos)		Ratio, Dec. 1991/ June 1991	Advertised Fares, One Way, January 1992
		June 1991	December 1991		
Guadalajara	995,265	160,370	239,360	1:49	167,550[1]
Monterrey	813,031	232,850	341,230	1:47	198,000[2]
Acapulco	751,242	143,620	214,370	1:49	
Tijuana	476,271	485,910	712,090	1:47	300,000[3]
Cancun	466,007	399,490	585,440	1:47	
Tampico	—	125,600	180,820	1:44	130,620[1]
Vera Cruz	—	143,020	205,910	1:44	150,000[1]
Minatitlan	—	173,130	242,590	1:40	190,000[3]

Source: Mexicana Airline; SCT price office; newspaper advertisements.

[1] Promotional fares advertised by Aeromexico.

[2] Promotional fares advertised by Mexicana.

[3] Promotional fares advertised by Saro, a new entrant.

— = not available.

to increase after deregulation. One of the first consequences of deregulation was a substantial increase in full economy fares. Table 8-3 shows these fares before and after deregulation for eight airline markets. In December 1991, prices were about 45 percent higher in nominal terms, or about 30 percent higher in real terms, compared to the June, preregulation prices. At the same time, there appears to have been intense competition in certain markets: Aeromexico may have touched off a price war in January 1992 by entering two markets hitherto served only by Mexicana, namely Mexico City–Vera Cruz and Mexico City–Tampico. Mexicana responded by aggressively expanding its Mexico City–Monterrey service, an Aeromexico stronghold. Also, new entrants began some aggressive marketing efforts of their own. The last column in the table shows some aggressively marketed one-way promotional fares. Thus it is clear that price discrimination became an important factor in Mexico's airline market, just as it did in the United States after deregulation. Full fares, paid largely by business travelers, were higher than before, while leisure travelers paid lower prices if they could plan ahead or meet other restrictions.

The bottom line on prices is really the yield—the revenue received per passenger-kilometer. Yields showed some increase, although much more moderate than might have been suggested by the changes in full fares. Table 8-4 shows the domestic market yields of Aeromexico and Mexicana. The first year after deregulation shows a small increase in yield, despite the large expansion in capacity. Given the low level of fares under regulation, this is not surprising. Early evidence from 1993 indicates a more pronounced increase in yields, particularly for Mexicana.

Table 8-4. Aeromexico and Mexicana, Domestic Yield, 1981–1992 (old pesos per RPK)

Year	Nominal Yield		Real Yield (1992 prices)	
	Aeromexico	Mexicana	Aeromexico	Mexicana
1981	1.9	1.8	317	300
1982	3.2	2.3	336	241
1983	5.5	6.0	286	312
1984	8.9	9.6	280	302
1985	12.3	14.6	245	291
1986	26.5	30.3	284	324
1987	71.9	87.0	332	402
1988	114.6	170.6	247	368
1989	176.3	185.0	317	332
1990	244.2	246.0	346	349
1991	296.0	285.0	342	329
1992	388.0	344.0	388	344

Source: Company reports and author's calculations.

This is related to developments in the market structure, which I consider next.

Prior to divestiture, as was mentioned earlier, there was no effective competition in Mexico's airline market, even though there were two major, or trunk, airlines operating in the domestic market. This changed after divestiture. Aeromexico, as the first company to be divested and with a strategy of focusing on the business traveler, began by transforming its image from a grossly inefficient airline ("Aeromaybe") to a modern, first-class one. By late 1991, when Aeromexico made a public offering of its stock, it could boast that it had the world's highest on-time performance rating (97%) and much-improved service in all other dimensions.

Competition between the airlines really took off after deregulation, however. Aeromexico entered markets it had hitherto not served (Vera Cruz and Tampico), thereby competing very aggressively with Mexicana. The intensity of competition was heightened by the entry of new airlines, particularly TAESA. By early 1993, the share of "other" airlines (i.e., other than Mexicana and Aeromexico) in the domestic market was over 25 percent, up from less than 8 percent in 1989 (Pizzimenti 1992). Thus the pressure on the trunk carriers was great. Aeromexico, thanks to its improved image, was able to hold its own, retaining a market share of around 44 percent, but Mexicana started to have serious troubles, suffering a drastic decline in market share from around 45 percent to just over 30 percent. In 1992, Mexicana's domestic revenue per passenger-kilometer actually fell 9 percent, while Aeromexico's was growing 9 percent (table 8-5). At the same time, Mexicana's yields (revenue per passenger-kilometer), which had been well above Aeromexico's prior to and up to divestiture and equal to Aeromexico's in 1990, fell to less than 90

Table 8-5. Aeromexico and Mexicana, Millions of Revenue-Passenger-Kilometers, 1981–1992

	Domestic		International	
Year	Aeromexico	Mexicana	Aeromexico	Mexicana
1981	3,877	3,161	2,782	4,819
1982	3,473	3,791	2,717	3,302
1983	4,619	4,093	2,744	4,339
1984	4,668	4,032	3,380	5,034
1985	5,449	4,390	2,849	5,004
1986	5,289	3,842	2,478	5,277
1987	4,630	3,296	3,202	6,440
1988	3,205	3,706	896	7,064
1989	4,253	4,005	1,209	6,532
1990	4,694	4,291	2,091	7,156
1991	4,780	4,715	2,737	6,028
1992	5,209	4,304	3,249	6,130

Source: Company reports and author's calculations.

percent of Aeromexico's by 1992 (table 8-4). Thus Mexicana was selling less, and what it was selling was fetching a lower price.

To add to Mexicana's troubles, its international business was doing poorly also. As can be seen from table 8-5, its international RPK's were 14 percent lower in 1992 than in 1990; this translated into revenues being lower by 18 percent in real terms. For Mexicana, where the international business was its bread and butter, these were serious numbers. The primary factor behind this trend is probably the intensified competition from the big U.S. airlines following the liberalization of the U.S.-Mexico market in 1991.

All these factors were showing up on Mexicana's bottom line—its profits. After having been profitable in 1988 and 1989, Mexicana made heavy losses in its first three years as a private company (see table 8-6). In sharp contrast, Aeromexico, which had been a heavy money loser prior to divestiture, turned a small profit in each of its first three years as a private company but suffered a loss in 1992, the first full year after deregulation (Mexicana's loss had more than doubled in real terms in 1992). Thus it appears that deregulation may have imposed some severe financial costs on the airlines. Information on the new entrants, particularly TAESA, is unavailable, because they are all privately held.

The most significant consequence of these events was the takeover of Mexicana by Aeromexico in March 1993, via a takeover of 80 percent of Grupo Falcon. Recall that, under the terms of Mexicana's divestiture, Grupo Falcon had acquired 25 percent of the equity and had an option to buy another 25 percent from the government any time before September 1992 at the same inflation-adjusted price. During 1992, however, the stock price of Mexicana was far below the strike price of Falcon's

Table 8-6. Aeromexico and Mexicana, Revenues and Profits, 1981–1992 (millions of old pesos)

Year	Nominal Revenue		Real Revenue (1992 prices)		Nominal Profits		Real Profits (1992 prices)	
	Aeromexico	Mexicana	Aeromexico	Mexicana	Aeromexico	Mexicana	Aeromexico	Mexicana
1981	12	15	2,000	2,500	0.2	1.5	33	250
1982	19	22	1,993	2,308	–3.6	–2.7	–378	–280
1983	48	61	2,494	3,170	–1.6	0.8	–83	42
1984	75	96	2,356	3,016	–5.1	4.0	–160	126
1985	120	162	2,390	3,227	–20.2	–6.9	–402	–137
1986	246	334	2,632	3,573	–38.9	–40.1	–416	–429
1987	640	867	2,954	4,002	–97.0	–81.6	–448	–337
1988	492	1,703	1,060	3,669	–228.2	48.4	–492	104
1989	981	1,881	1,761	3,377	10.3	20.1	18	36
1990	1,624	2,525	2,302	3,578	13.2	–255.0	19	–361
1991	2,095	2,746	2,420	3,172	3.2	–232.0	4	–268
1992	3,073	3,089	3,073	3,089	–132.4	–702.0	–132	–702

Source: Company reports and author's calculations.

option, so Falcon began to buy the stock in the open market. Aeromexico, at the same time, also began to buy Mexicana stock. By September, Aeromexico had acquired about 11 percent of the equity, and Falcon owned 43.7 percent. The March 1993 agreement gave Aeromexico 80 percent of the shares of Falcon, thereby giving it control over 55 percent of Mexicana's equity. The two airlines were expected to operate as separate airlines, for various legal reasons. The most important of these, no doubt, was to satisfy the formal requirement under the airline deregulation that there must be two airlines on any route to ensure pricing freedom. This would then allow the merged entity to charge monopoly prices on certain routes. Early evidence from 1993 indicated that there were significant upward price revisions—Mexicana's domestic yield appears to have risen 30 percent in real terms in the first half of 1993 over the average for 1992.

The Effects of Divestiture and Deregulation

We have already seen that Mexicana incurred serious losses in all three years after divestiture. It is therefore tempting to conclude that Mexicana's poor performance was due to divestiture. Aeromexico, on the other hand, had three profitable years and can be seen as a divestiture success story. In my earlier analyses of these two cases (Tandon 1994), this was how I characterized them: Mexicana was a "failure" of divestiture, Aeromexico was a "success." I also speculated that the market could probably not support both firms and that Mexicana would be the one to collapse. In light of more recent data and of having seen events unfold, I reassess that earlier analysis and draw implications for future policy.

In the earlier analysis, I gave great weight to the fact that Aeromexico appeared to be a much more efficient airline than Mexicana. Early bidders for Mexicana complained of its overstaffing and wanted to severely prune the labor force prior to divestiture. However, this did not happen. Aeromexico, also severely overstaffed, underwent a thorough labor restructuring: its entire labor force was fired when the company (Aeronaves) was declared bankrupt; when the new company (Aerovías) was created, management was free to hire only the workers they needed. In table 8-2, we see the dramatic cut in Aeromexico's workforce at the time of divestiture. This was reflected in an approximate doubling of labor productivity as measured by RPK per employee. Further, by 1989 Aeromexico's labor productivity was over 50 percent higher than that of Mexicana.

However, this gap has not persisted. Mexicana has done a creditable job in improving its productivity. By 1992, Aeromexico's labor productivity advantage was down to 12 percent, as Mexicana achieved substantial workforce reduction and Aeromexico seemed to be drifting backward. This tendency is also visible in calculations of total factor productivity (TFP), which take into account all factors of production. As can be seen from figures 8-1 and 8-2, Aeromexico experienced a dramatic increase in TFP immediately after divestiture but drifted slightly downward subsequently. Mexicana, on the other hand, experienced substantial TFP gains in 1987 and 1988, prior to divestiture. Actually, the 1988 figures should be seen as an aberration, as they stemmed from very high load factors during Aeromexico's bankruptcy year. If we take 1987 as a base, Mexicana appears to have done well by holding TFP constant since divestiture.

It appears therefore that productivity alone cannot explain the rise of Aeromexico and the fall of Mexicana. Both airlines raised productivity substantially above the average for 1981–86. In fact, Mexicana raised TFP about 25 percent, while Aeromexico seems to have a TFP only about 15–20 percent higher.[14] At the same time, Mexicana has had to "pay" for the efficiency improvements; in 1992 alone, the company paid over 100 billion (old) pesos in severance. Aeromexico, on the other hand, got its workforce reductions "free," since the workers were compensated by Aeronaves. Indirectly, it was the creditors of the old Aeronaves who bore the cost of the severance; on average, they received only about 70 percent of their claims on the company.

Two strategic decisions by Mexicana had specific effects. One decision was the massive investment program to which Mexicana committed itself shortly after privatization. Not only was this expensive—being reflected in sharply rising interest expenses—but also it created the excess capacity that put a downward pressure on yield. Second, Mexicana was unable to match Aeromexico's aggressive campaign to

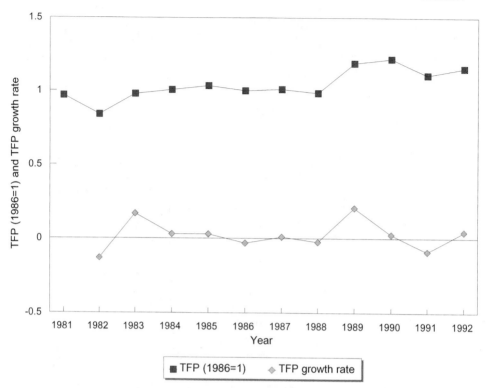

Figure 8-1. Aeromexico, Total Factor Productivity (TFP) and TFP Growth Rate.

improve service.[15] Combined with its implicit emphasis on the leisure traveler, this forced Mexicana to discount prices more than Aeromexico, which is reflected in the lower yields noted in table 8-4.

Mexicana faced particularly severe problems in its international operations, which had previously been its primary source of profit. In all likelihood, the key factor here was the liberalization of the U.S.-Mexico market in 1991, which permitted airlines from either country to add new routes and flights more freely. Competition from the major U.S. carriers therefore intensified, resulting in reduced traffic for Mexicana.

Finally, mention must be made of autonomous conditions in the airline market. The 1990s have not been good years for the airline industry in general. The U.S. market, for example, continues to be plagued by losses and even bankruptcy. The Mexican market seems to have followed some of the trends experienced in the United States since deregulation: greater price discrimination, periods of intense competition, periods of losses, and periods of consolidation. It is possible that Mexico has entered a period of consolidation now that Aeromexico has acquired Mexicana.

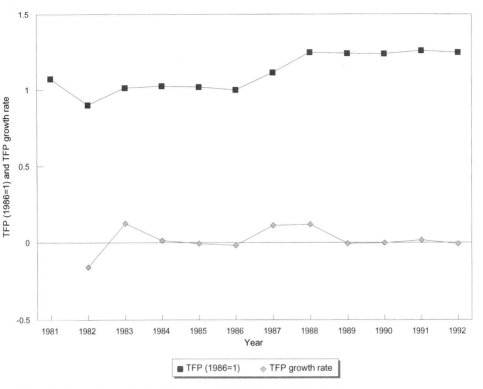

Figure 8-2. Mexicana, Total Factor Productivity (TFP) and TFP Growth Rate.

Whether this is desirable, however, is another question. Although it may spell some financial stability for the airlines, it is likely to be costly to consumers, as we already see from rising prices. In calling attention to the potential for monopolization implied in the merger, one observer criticizes the Mexican government for delaying the creation of an antitrust environment that might have prevented such a merger (Hanson 1993). But it is unclear whether free competition is sustainable in such a market. Further, it is unclear whether the Aeromexico-Mexicana "cartel" will be able to maintain itself in the presence of free entry.

Conclusions

The Mexican airline market is still in such a state of flux that it is impossible to reach any firm conclusion as to the impact of divestiture and deregulation. Five key points, however, can be distilled at this time:

1. The Mexican government has divested itself of two, potentially heavy, loss-making companies, thereby making a significant dent in the public deficit.

2. In particular, the divestiture of Aeromexico via bankruptcy provides an example of how to sell a significant money loser and effect a major (labor) restructuring at the same time.

3. Sometimes, owners of a privatized firm (such as Mexicana) may cause a net welfare loss to society, but this is a small price to pay. The market will quickly correct the problem (as it did by Mexicana's takeover).

The following points are speculative:

4. In order to allow the market to quickly correct problems, market forces must be allowed to work. In the Mexicana case, an impediment to the operation of the market was created when the government gave voting control to Falcon for three years following divestiture.

5. It is an open question whether the government could have done any better in the way divestiture and deregulation proceeded. On the one hand, deregulation seems to have created problems for the firms before they had a chance to establish themselves on a sound footing.[16] On the other hand, the creation of free competition is what privatization is all about. Whether free entry is sustainable in a market as small as Mexico's is still to be seen.

NOTES

This chapter draws heavily on my earlier work on the divestiture of Mexico's airlines, "Aeromexico" and "Mexicana de Aviacion," in Tandon 1994. It has been updated to include data through 1992. Further updating has become difficult because of the takeover, in 1993, of Mexicana by Aeromexico and the subsequent confounding of the data.

1. Much of this background is based on the Mexicana sale prospectus.

2. Much of the discussion on the history of Aeromexico and its divestiture is based on Genel Garcia 1988, Sales Gutierrez and Gomez Gordillo 1989, and Carrera Cortes 1990. It is interesting to note that the first two papers are virtually identical. Because the Genel Garcia paper had an earlier date, credit is generally given to that paper in what follows.

3. United Air Lines is a small but rapidly growing presence in this market. Its 1990 share was 2.7 percent, up from 1.5 percent in 1989 and 1.2 percent in 1988.

4. The discussion on the divestiture of Mexicana is based on conversations with various individuals at Mexicana and at the Mexican privatization office, on official documents of the sale process, on Echegaray 1990, and Centro de Análisis e Investigación Económica 1991.

5. This was in March 1988, before Aeromexico went into bankruptcy.

6. Interestingly, one bidder suggested allowing Mexicana to default on its loans and go into bankruptcy as a way of forcing a debt restructuring. Only two months later, the government did just that with Aeromexico, although the primary motive there was a labor restructuring.

7. In a way, this was a logical choice for Mexicana, because its U.S. operations accounted for approximately half their revenue but almost all their profits.

8. The wage demand was reportedly for a 30 percent increase, which may not appear excessive in light of the 159 percent inflation Mexico experienced in 1987. However, according to our estimates, average wages had already risen by a factor of two-and-a-half in 1987.

9. Technically, Aerovías was never a public sector company.

10. The methods used to calculate these were rather unsophisticated and probably were serious underestimates (for a brief discussion, see Tandon 1994). One key component of the liquidation value, however, was determined fairly accurately: the value of the owned aircraft was obtained as 398 billion pesos (US$174 million) on the basis of actual offers by potential buyers.

11. In September 1990, following a dispute over the strategic direction of Aeromexico, de Prevoisin and companies controlled by him or his associates bought all the shares of Icaro owned by the other investors. These amounted to 62.7 percent of Icaro's shares.

12. Dictum rejected about half the parts and inventories and two DC-10-15 aircraft.

13. In fact, it appears that the owners of Aerovías achieved a further price reduction in negotiations over the valuation of the parts and inventories. The 1991 income statement reports an extraordinary gain of 62 billion pesos for "amortization of surplus on business acquired," which I believe to be a settlement of some outstanding issues on the purchase price. It is possible that the final price paid was lower than the OBSA offer, although I was unable to obtain definite information on this.

14. Mexicana's improving trend started in 1987, two years before divestiture.

15. Some observers feel that this was, in turn, a consequence of Mexicana's inability to deal effectively with the unreformed labor unions and, hence, related to the lack of a labor restructuring, discussed earlier.

16. This comment particularly applies to Mexicana's international operations.

REFERENCES

Banco Internacional. 1989. "Contrato de Compra Venta Formal: Corporacion Mexicana de Aviacion." Mexico City.

Carrera Cortes, Emilio. 1990. "Aeronaves de Mexico, S.A." Case Study C379-PD-DIV. Instituto Nacional de Administracion Publica, Mexico City.

Centro de Análisis e Investigación Económica, A.C. 1991. "El Proceso de Privatizacion en Mexico: Un Estudio de Casos." Mexico City.

Echegaray, Gabriela. 1990. "Caso Final: Compañía Mexicana de Aviacion." ITAM, Mexico City.

Galal, Ahmed, Leroy P. Jones, Pankaj Tandon, and Ingo Vogelsang, eds. 1994. *Welfare Consequences of Selling Public Enterprises: An Empirical Analysis.* New York: Oxford Univ. Press.

Genel Garcia, Julio Alfredo. 1988. "Aeromexico: Metamorfosis Creativa." BANOBRAS, Mexico City.

Hanson, Gordon. 1993. "Privatization and Antitrust in Latin America." Univ. of Texas—Austin, Dept. of Economics.

Pizzimenti, David J. 1992. "Research Report on Aerovías de México, S.A. de C.V." Nomura Research Institute America, New York.

Ruprah, Inder. 1992. "Privatization: Case Study Compañía Mexicana de Aviacion." CIDE, Mexico City.

Sales Gutierrez, Carlos, and Ismael Gomez Gordillo. 1989. "Aeromexico." Case Study C395-AD-INAP. Instituto Nacional de Administracion Publica, Mexico City.

Tandon, Pankaj. 1994. "Aeromexico" and "Mexicana de Aviacion." In Galal et al., eds., *Welfare Consequences of Selling Public Enterprises.*

9. One Piece of a Larger Puzzle

THE PRIVATIZATION OF VIASA

Janet Kelly

In the 1980s, as takeovers and leveraged buyouts led to the restructuring of private firms, privatization became a popular method for restructuring state-owned enterprises. Since a hostile takeover of state enterprises is generally not possible, privatization can occur only when the public loses its patience with the state enterprise's results, when governments see privatization as less costly than incurring the voters' wrath, and when committed reformers dedicate themselves to overcoming the forces of resistance—not of course without political aims of their own.

Recent history shows that privatization does not come easily. The public only rarely organizes itself as an interest group in favor of selling off state-owned enterprises, and dedicated reformers are also extremely rare.[1] Given public apathy, privatization is not much of a platform for emergent politicians and is certainly a hard way to go about getting good press, given the number of enemies that may come out of the woodwork. Even when finally achieved, privatization does not always meet the objectives of the privatizers. State enterprises may suffer many ills, but so do private firms, which are only different in that managerial mistakes can lead to bankruptcy.

The story of the privatization of VIASA demonstrates the serious difficulties of the privatization process in Venezuela and illustrates that political leadership is a necessary component even for small successes. Privatization does not occur just because it makes sense. If that were the case, the public enterprise sector in Venezuela would be much smaller than it is and VIASA would have been privatized long before 1991. The regulatory context must also be taken into account. Privatizations are such intensely political events that even factors apparently unrelated to

241

the case at hand may play a dominant role. What is more, the measure of a successful privatization is not necessarily the better performance of the resultant firm: privatization can be an indirect route to liquidation, as well, or simply a first stage in a longer process of reversing negative patterns of behavior.

In this chapter, I recount the story of VIASA up to and beyond the sale of 60 percent of its shares to a consortium led by the Spanish airline Iberia, in September 1991. The case of VIASA illustrates the importance of individuals in reform processes and the way privatization is less an end in itself than a piece of a wider drama of political and economic change. An attempt to privatize the domestic state-owned airline Línea Aeropostal Venezolana (LAV) two years later illustrates how sensitive the privatization process can be to changes in the political fortunes of leaders. Neither the privatization of VIASA nor that of LAV provides good reading for those seeking success stories; rather, they serve to deepen our understanding of the complexity of decisionmaking processes that lead to profound, if slow, economic changes. Should VIASA's buyer, Iberia, eventually be privatized by Spain, it will be even clearer that privatization is not a discrete event but a progression of interconnected processes that develop over time in an ever more complex global system undergoing structural and regulatory change.

The First Time as Tragedy: VIASA's History

The date of VIASA's creation in 1960 coincided with the first privatization of the company, for at its start, this state-owned enterprise was placed under private administration.

The First Privatization: 1960

Before 1960, there were two Venezuelan airlines: Línea Aeropostal Venezolana (LAV), a state-owned enterprise, and Aerovías Venezolanas (Avensa), a private company controlled by the Boulton family, in which Pan American Airlines had a 30 percent share. Both companies had national routes and a limited number of international routes, although by 1960 they were both technologically behind the times, since they did not yet fly jets. Avensa, however, was a profitable and healthy company— although less international than LAV—and was in the process of buying its first jet; LAV was in serious financial difficulties, mostly in its international division. The new democratic government under Rómulo Betancourt assigned the source of LAV's problems not to the underlying market but rather to the abuses of the ten years of military dictatorship between 1948 and 1958.

After more than a year of negotiating in 1959–60, the government decided to create a joint venture with Avensa to be called Venezolana Internacional de Aviación, or VIASA, whose business it would be to consolidate the international operations of both LAV and Avensa: 55 percent of VIASA's shares would remain in government hands and 45 percent would be held by Avensa. By mutual accord, management control would go to Avensa. In this sense, VIASA began life as a joint venture in which government shareholder dominance was balanced by private sector administration in a classic attempt to improve public management through private sector intervention.

It is well to note a few enduring aspects of VIASA's creation. Throughout the negotiation, the issue of national control was foremost. Andrés Boulton had proposed a joint venture to the minister of communications in August 1959, but the government came to the conclusion that it was better to reorganize the international division of LAV and grant a long-term management contract for its administration to a foreign consortium composed of Swissair and the Scandinavian airline, SAS. The government favored the Swissair/SAS solution because it was simpler, required no change in the structure of LAV, and ensured experienced management in international markets, which Avensa scarcely had—although, according to Andrés Boulton (Gil Yepes 1981) Swissair/SAS did not have jet engines, while Avensa had already made its first purchase of a jet-powered plane.

A significant dose of statism is evident in the declarations of the minister of communications, when he said in 1960:

> I would like to express emphatically that this experiment in contracting out the management [of VIASA to Swissair/SAS] does not mean and cannot mean in any way that the administrator might participate as a shareholder in exploiting the Venezuelan state's international routes currently served by LAV, with so many difficulties. They may not acquire shares either in LAV or in a new company that might be formed to exploit the international routes. These routes will continue to be served by a 100 percent Venezuelan company owned entirely by the state. The administrator will participate only in future profits in a proportion not yet determined. The contract will be for a maximum of five years and the company will be obliged to train Venezuelan personnel. . . .
>
> The proposal presented by Swissair/SAS is the most attractive that the government has received, although the terms of the contract have not yet begun to be discussed. (Boulton 1973, 20)

In effect, and apparently without worrying too much about the details of the contract, the government preferred the control implicit in remaining as sole owner; under the Avensa proposal (later reversed to favor the state), the government would retain only 45 percent of the shares and would cede management control.

Avensa mounted an effective campaign to get the government to compromise, using its considerable influence in the businessmen's top organization, Fedecámaras, and in an important body dedicated to ensuring national (rather than foreign-dominated) development, Pro-Venezuela. Both fully supported the preference for the Boulton group on the grounds of its national character and the ancillary operations that would be carried out by Venezuelans in Venezuela. As a shareholder, Avensa would share not only in profits but also in possible losses (Swissair/SAS took no such risk). Avensa agreed to eliminate Pan Am from among its shareholders as part of the deal, and insisted on the commercial, profit-oriented character of the company. By November, the government had given in and negotiated the creation of VIASA with Avensa, rather than with Swissair/SAS, and the new company was born.

VIASA under the Boultons: Success and Failure

For fifteen years, VIASA enjoyed a period of relative success: growth, profits and, for many years, a reputation for good service. From a corrupt and loss-making division of a state airline, it had been transformed into a functioning company (see figure 9-1). From 1961 until 1967, the company enjoyed increasing success, increasing personnel, planes, routes, and profits. Avensa provided services both to VIASA and to its own operations, capitalizing on economies of scale.[2] Its president, Oscar Machado Zuloaga (who served until 1976) was a respected businessman who not only occupied a place of honor in the private sector as a member of the family group that today still holds a large share of the Caracas electric company (Electricidad de Caracas) and of one of the major private companies in the steel and steel products industry, but also had served briefly as minister of communications after the downfall of Marcos Pérez Jiménez in 1958. His credentials were impeccable.

Machado, in an interview some years after his retirement from VIASA, mentioned that the only serious problem that VIASA had at its start was a disagreement with the National Pilots' Union (Asociación Nacional de Pilotos, or ANP). This conflict became VIASA's central problem until (and beyond) its privatization in 1991. The union, which then represented the pilots in LAV and Avensa, wanted to ensure its role in the choice of VIASA's pilots and their contractual conditions. Certainly, the pilot's job in VIASA would be coveted, since international pilots tend to enjoy higher pay than local pilots, and they would gain training and experience in the new jet technology. Machado said: "Unfortunately, due to a variety of circumstances, the relationship with the union could not be developed in a normal way, because the aspirations of the ANP were outside the realm of the acceptable in terms of pay and working

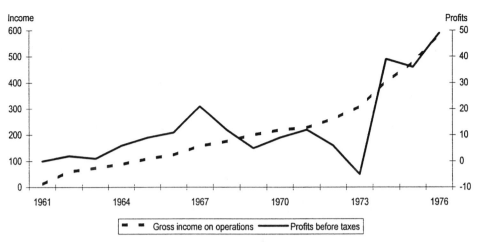

Figure 9-1. VIASA: Income and Profits under Private Management, 1961–1976 (millions of bolivars).

conditions. As a result, and after a regrettable press campaign, we had to come to a separate agreement with the pilots who would come to form the team in VIASA" (Gil Yepes 1981, 10). In November 1962, the VIASA Pilots' Union was created, and those who joined were forced out of the ANP.

In the meantime, the company also signed a labor contract with ground workers and with cabin personnel affiliated with the Association of Cabin Attendants (Asociación de Aeromozas y Mayordomos de Aviación Venezolana, ADAMA). The union of cabin personnel, like the pilots union, was not associated with any union federation (unusual in a country where company unions are the exception), nor was it allied to political parties.[3] The company unions ensured labor peace until 1968, when the Christian Democratic union federation began to make inroads. In 1968, indeed, union organizers sympathetic to the Christian Democatic party, COPEI, began to work hard to upset the company control of the unions. And little by little they had their way, aided in part by the victory of COPEI's candidate, Rafael Caldera, in the presidential elections of the year. In particular, a member of the cabin personnel, Franco Vecchiettini, worked to form the Association of Cabin Personnel of VIASA in 1968 and to affiliate it with the Christian Democrats.

It is not necessary to detail the ups and downs of Vecchiettini over the following years, except to say that what had been peaceful labor relations soon became tumultuous. Where in 1969–70, VIASA was rated second in service by the International Air Transport Association (IATA), it soon became involved in a series of strikes and conflicts that would sour labor-management relations. The government seemed to have supported the unions against the management, despite its own presumed interest in VIASA. Said Vecchiettini: "I recognize that I had the support of the Christian Democrats and of Caldera's government. Caldera's government allowed more union freedom. And COPEI was very weak in the union movement and at the time of the COPEI government [1969–74] it was looking for ways to strengthen itself" (ibid., 13).

During this period, the company unions affiliated themselves to labor federations, and new unions proliferated for all types of personnel. In one strike, the union took over the company's downtown offices; Vecchiettini admitted that the unions had the support of Caldera's minister of labor, who released the protesters arrested by the police. Vecchiettini received a decoration (honors) from the president in 1972. By 1973, there were six unions in VIASA (for 1,430 employees) organizing the pilots, cabin personnel, aeronautical technicians, ground workers, and general workers, with some groups being represented by competing unions. The unions had conflicts not only with the company but also with each other. In such a situation, it is not surprising that the private partner in VIASA was denounced for multiple sins, which besides the claims of various violations of labor law and collective contracts included a structural conflict of interest due to its control over services sold to VIASA and its continuing link to Pan Am. VIASA suffered a slight loss of US$1.8 million in 1972–73, for by that year, its internal problems had begun to affect its ability to make money.

The oil boom that began in 1972–73 fundamentally changed VIASA's prospects and tended to mask its managerial flaws. In the first place, Venezuelan demand for foreign travel increased during the 1970s as a result of increased incomes, the availability of foreign exchange, and the progressive undervaluation of the bolivar. Between 1973 and 1979, VIASA's number of passengers doubled, as did the number of employees. Indeed, during this period, Venezuelans gained the reputation of being the newest of the new rich visiting Miami and New York. Growth was such that passengers settled for any kind of service during peak traffic periods as long as a seat could be had. The tendency toward lower earnings was reversed with the growth in business. Curiously, VIASA also enjoyed an initial advantage over foreign airlines such as Pan Am (its competitor for the lucrative U.S. routes) because airfares generally were rising due to the oil price hike, while the government sold jet fuel to VIASA at a price below the international price given to Pan Am.

VIASA was riding the boom even as an excessive euphoria took possession in Venezuela. Oil was going up, income was going up, and the government was the great beneficiary. President Carlos Andrés Pérez announced his vision of the "Great Venezuela" that was about to take off. The same logic that informed the nationalization of oil, gas, and iron ore mining was applied to VIASA. Only the government represented the true welfare of the population as a whole; private industry tended to favor the few. Some industries had to be managed by foreigners because the country had been weak in technology and management, but now that period had ended: the state would take its rightful place as owner and administrator of the common assets of the country. While Avensa was hardly foreign, the fact that a private company was managing a public one, coupled with the tendency of the fractious labor unions to accuse Avensa of profiting from the arrangement, contributed to a certain distrust by the government with respect to the traditional arrangement for VIASA's management.

A serious sign of distrust manifested itself in 1974 when Avensa proposed a distribution of profits and the government insisted that the distribution be made in the form of shares. Then, in 1975, Leopoldo Sucre Figarella, a powerful politician with a penchant for large state-run projects, proposed to the board of directors that the state buy a portion of Avensa's shares in order to increase its control to 75 percent of the total and that it name the chief executive officer. According to Andrés Boulton (ibid., 20), "the government argued that by that time the company had matured and that now they could administer it along with its majority control. So, it was decided that Avensa would sell 20 percent to the Corporación Venezolana de Fomento," a state holding company.

In effect, the era of the Boultons ended in VIASA, despite the fact that they would hold onto their remaining 25 percent until 1980. But now the company fully assumed its public character. It was subjected to the rules of the game for public enterprises—budget controls, state comptrollers, politically named directors and executives, etcetera.

VIASA as State-Owned Enterprise: 1975–1989

To the casual observer, VIASA indeed became a troubled company under state control and management. The boom of the mid-1970s tended to permit laxness in management within a seller's market. Growth in number of passengers led to excessive spending on administrative services, unproductive offices abroad, and unsustainable concessions to personnel. Expansion was financed by debt, while managers thought that growth would never stop.[4] Small profits at the start of the 1970s turned into large losses after 1979, when the oil boom began to deflate. Serious losses were registered in 1980 and continued until the worst year of all, 1983, when a general financial crisis shook Venezuela. In that year, a foreign exchange crisis led to a brief closure of the market for foreign currencies, followed by a rigid system of exchange controls, which sharply curtailed foreign travel by Venezuelans. The number of passengers fell by some 38 percent. A casual observer would note, however, a gradual turnaround after 1983, despite my own prediction (Kelly and Villalba 1984) that there were reasons to think that VIASA, as a state-owned enterprise, would face difficulties in bringing about the changes needed in order to survive. The company turned a profit by 1985, and profits continued through 1989.

For many, the improvement could be attributed to a return to sound private-style management. In 1984, a well-known private sector executive, Luis Ignacio Mendoza, was named president of VIASA and was given authority to straighten out both the management and the finances of the firm. At that time, the company was almost put into liquidation. Some newspaper headlines from the period, depicting VIASA as sick, corrupt, overextended, and deeply in debt, convey the flavor of the situation:

"Report by Swissair: VIASA in Grave Financial Crisis,"
El Universal, Nov. 18, 1981

The report cites the lack of a planning system, politically motivated decisions and mid-level management in a confused and vacillating state. There has been personnel growth beyond control, service on board is disastrous as a result of the mass production of stewardesses with defective training.

"Manual of Corruption: How VIASA Was Destroyed in Five Years,"
El Mundo, Jan. 1, 1984

"Elias López: VIASA's Situation Is Poor, but It Has Been Worse,"
El Nacional, Jan. 17, 1984

"The Cabinet Analyzed Yesterday 'The Inherited Disaster': VIASA's Debt: 1.4 Billion Bolivars,"
El Diario de Caracas, Feb. 29, 1984

The situation of the airline is critical and the [new] government is making every effort not to shut it down. It will be necessary to close offices abroad. VIASA has 74 offices across the world but it only flies to 12 countries.

The naming of Mendoza put a quick halt to VIASA's decline. He immediately set about putting the house in order and communicated both confidence and a sense of crisis to the personnel, which encouraged their collaboration to save the company: the unions, seeing that the alternative was liquidation, rallied around Mendoza, creating a level of solidarity that had not been seen in VIASA since the 1960s. The pilots went so far as to say they would accept pay cuts on their salary supplements. On March 29, 1984, the Union of Ground Personnel published a declaration blaming all on the former administration in much the same way ("Paid Advertising by the Land Workers' Association" 1984):

> In a recent meeting between the unions and the president of VIASA, we were shown figures that illustrate clearly the disequilibrium and the financial disaster that characterizes the company at this time. It might be asked whether the former management was trying to destroy the company in order to justify its liquidation along with the firing of hundreds of workers as well as permitting certain interested parties to take over VIASA's routes, buy up its assets and thus displace the State from its leadership role in air transport through its direction of Venezuela's flagship airline.

A period of intense activity to restore profitability followed. Plans were announced that personnel would be reduced by some 700–800 persons, including pilots (despite their offer to sacrifice salaries in favor of conserving jobs), and new schemes were invented to stimulate travel and to eliminate unnecessary offices, planes, and routes. VIASA employed 36 pilots per plane, versus an average of 15 to 18 pilots for other airlines at the time.[5] To some extent, these plans were successful: some foreign offices were closed, personnel was reduced by 595 persons[6] in 1984–85 (although only 18 pilots lost their jobs, despite initial plans to fire 105), some old planes were sold, some contracts were rescinded, and generally, the crisis atmosphere was reduced. One local news magazine put VIASA's president on its cover and ran the story: "In VIASA, a Miracle Has Begun to Fly" (*Bohemia,* March 4–10, 1985). By the end of 1985, VIASA was announcing that it was in the black again.

Indeed, from 1985 to 1989, VIASA enjoyed profits. All was not, of course a rose garden. Relations with the pilots returned to their more normal prickly state. In 1986, a short strike led to the firing of eight pilots; they were all returned to their posts in early 1987 as a result of their appeal to the administrative courts. In 1988, another conflict with cabin personnel over per diem compensation led to long negotiations. But when Mendoza resigned his post in early 1989, soon after the inauguration of Pérez, he was proud of his results. He was interviewed on the most prestigious talk show and reflected on his experience ("I Left VIASA" 1989):

| *Marcel Granier* | The story of VIASA is a story of ups and downs. . . . |
| *(MG), Interviewer:* | What is the true situation of VIASA and what has happened in these last five years? |

Luis Ignacio Mendoza (LIM), ex-president of VIASA:	Well, the biggest problem the company had at the beginning was to really put the airline to work as a competitive company and an efficient one. . . . There was practically no way to meet the payroll, and now we can hand over the company with accumulated profits over the last three years that are over 700 million bolivars. . . .
MG:	Is there any special difficulty in managing a public enterprise, either with the bureaucracy or with political connections?
LIM:	In my first days at VIASA, I began to receive any number of communications of all types, from the government or people linked to it, and from the opposition too, in which everybody was recommending someone for a job . . . but I think we showed ourselves to be serious, and we demonstrated that VIASA was in very poor shape. . . .
MG:	Do you see any similarity between the situation of VIASA in 1984 and that of the country now in 1989, which finds itself in so many difficulties?
LIM:	Without any doubt, there are great similarities. . . . I think that the success of VIASA is due to the fact that a concrete plan was presented that people could understand and that the people who work for VIASA started working with great affection for the company in order to bring about the plan.

Such was the apparent situation of VIASA on the eve of the initiative to privatize it. Based on "the official story," VIASA had passed through several years as a troubled state-owned company whose management improved in the period prior to privatization. That it would enter the agenda for privatization decided on by the new, liberalizing (and bankrupt) government in 1989 might seem to have been a wise step for a government looking for "easy" privatizations to start out its program to reduce the state sector. Follow the advice of the British: produce some successful first privatizations in order to legitimize the process. Airlines were being privatized in many countries, so VIASA seemed a good bet. LAV, still mainly a domestic airline with a history of poor service, underinvestment in comunications, and a not very vibrant market, was not even considered as an alternative at the time. The defect in the plan to sell VIASA was that the state had come to believe its own stories. For, although real measures had been taken by Mendoza to improve VIASA's management, by 1989 the underlying situation of the company was still poor and the country's macroeconomic situation was worse still. Politi-

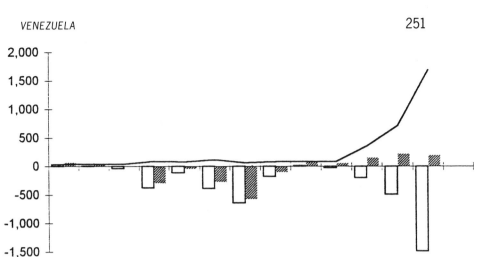

Figure 9-2. VIASA's Subsidies, 1977–1989 (millions of bolivars).

cians had done what they always do for public managers when given the chance: improve the balance sheet with hidden (and not so hidden) subsidies. VIASA's apparent financial health depended mostly on the huge subsidy on "exports" as well as on the equally huge subsidies implicit in the exchange control system operating between 1983 and 1989. As soon as the subsidies were removed in the liberalization period from 1989 on, VIASA's true situation became apparent (figure 9-2).

Getting On the Privatization Agenda

One hypothesis of how VIASA came to occupy an early spot on the privatization list is that the government that came into power in 1989 faced a grim macroeconomic situation and was also trying to recuperate from a popular uprising just one month after its inauguration, in which hundreds of persons were killed. It was looking therefore for candidates for privatization that would have certain characteristics: low political resistance, high cash flow effect, and good saleability. VIASA appeared to have these qualities, perhaps better than any other state-owned enterprise at the time. Soon, an all-out effort was made to bring it to the block, and after two years or so of eliminating various sources of opposition, 60 percent of the government's shares in the company were sold on September 9, 1991.

Despite the simplicity and persuasiveness of the above hypothesis, it is worthwhile examining the steps before privatization in order to understand the longterm effects and to capture some of the elements that would cloud the postprivatization picture. Privatization came about in 1991 after an entire decade of debate and economic change, which, little by little, overcame resistance to the sale. These forces opposed private sector participation in many industries, and especially in the airline industry.

Changes in the Environment

Two environmental changes undoubtedly contributed to making VIASA's privatization feasible. The first was the change in the international environment that led to widespread privatization in the 1980s. The second was the changing structure of regulatory arrangements in the international airline industry. The third was the change in Venezuela's economic environment that led slowly but surely to the virtual bankruptcy of the country in 1989.

The Example of Other Countries While the United States has long acted as a promoter of private enterprise throughout the world, it acted alone during much of the postwar period. Britain's Labourite governments consistently turned back the privatizing efforts of the Conservatives until Margaret Thatcher's accession to power in 1979. As Aharoni (1988, 27) puts it, "Capitalism for [the Labour Party] meant a dance around the golden calf—oppression of workers and a wrong distribution of wealth and power." France remained intransigently statist until Mitterand's Socialists were forced to recognize economic realities; Italy and Spain—both models for Venezuela for cultural and historic reasons—stuck to their large government holdings in industry and seemed, willy-nilly, to be doing quite well. In Latin America, state activity in the economy was practically regional doctrine, enshrined in the ideas of the United Nations Economic Commission on Latin America, known as CEPAL. In the 1970s, only dictatorial governments that had been condemned for human rights violations, such as the government of Augusto Pinochet in Chile, had ventured into privatization, marking the concept with a certain stamp of inhumanity and reducing the willingness of other Latin Americans to take the Chilean example as a model.

By the late eighties, attitudes toward privatization had radically changed worldwide, and this profound change inevitably affected Venezuelans' way of seeing reality. Countries, like individuals, can suffer a sort of collective cognitive dissonance when their worldview is at odds with the rest of the world's vision. Of course, psychologists tell us that the normal reaction to cognitive dissonance is to refuse to acknowledge disparities in terms of interpretation of reality, but little by little very strong signals will force a new evaluation of the "facts." Chile had the strongest economy in Latin America. Spain and Mexico, whose leaders were models for Venezuelan presidents (particularly for Acción Democrática) climbed onto the liberalization bandwagon as well. European countries began to go the way of Britain, and even the relatively privatized United States began to look for state activities to turn over to the private sector. The Soviet Union turned to perestroika and, eventually following Eastern Europe, rejected its own communist system. The Asian tigers were submitted to relentless study, and while the state undoubtedly played a huge role in their emergence, state-owned enterprises were nowhere to be found among the champions.

In short, the world had changed. State capitalism as a model had failed, and nowhere could its advocates find appreciative audiences. Even those who continued to support it now couched their arguments in new terms: "privatization is not a panacea," they would say—as if anyone had ever said it was.

The British privatization experience had a powerful effect on the process elsewhere, and not least in Venezuela. The British experience legitimized privatization, of course, but it also suggested lessons for privatizers: sell the idea that it will benefit both workers and middle classes; permit profits to the investors; sell big public service companies; keep the process open and transparent; and above all, avoid failures that might derail the process. The British, in fact, visited Venezuela frequently after its government began to seriously organize for privatization in 1989. Sir Allen Walters, adviser to Margaret Thatcher, gave a series of talks to relevant members of the policy community in which he analyzed the positive lessons to be shared. Madsen Pirie of the Adam Smith Institute in London expounded on the twenty-two varieties of privatization, to calm the fears of those who thought of it as just one thing: turning over business to a rapacious private sector.[7] The British government, seeing a market not only for consulting but also for investing, supported a privatization seminar in Caracas in April 1991, and its Department of Trade and Industry embarked on the so-called Project Venezuela, through which special attention was to be given to relations with Venezuela.

Deregulation Another background influence on events in Venezuela might be traced to the deregulation of the airline industry in the United States, which began with the Airline Deregulation Act of 1978. The act began a long process, still under way, of opening both national and international markets to greater competitive pressures. The influence of such a change in approach is, of course, impossible to measure, especially with regard to Venezuela. Nevertheless, at the same time that the privatization of VIASA was under way, the Ministry of Transport and Communications was announcing its new policy of deregulation. Certainly, the turn toward market-oriented solutions, present in air transport policy in general, underlay the new willingness to decrease the role of the state in the industry.

Privatization made sense in the context of liberalization. In its annual report for 1991 (Venezuela 1992, III), the Transport Ministry said, "The Ministry of Transport and Communications, through its general Office for Air Transport, has reoriented its new Air Transport Policy towards its liberalization, for the purpose of eliminating all unnecessary restrictions that affect the sector and in order to generate a competitive environment that will benefit the consumer."

In fact, deregulation had already started some years before in Venezuela, when the previous government began to revise its long-standing policy of permitting only single designations of the foreign airlines operating on routes that VIASA flew. This meant, initially, that Pan Am's duopoly on the lucrative routes between Caracas and Miami and New York would now be open to other competitors, both Venezuelan and American. The deregulation trend continued under the Pérez government, in particular with the signing of two major agreements just before VIASA's privatization in 1991: the decision of the Andean Pact to open up routes among its members and an agreement with Colombia that would completely open up all routes between the two countries.[8]

One aspect of deregulation to be considered was the effect of open competition on potential buyers. As the ministry showed itself ever more disposed to approve routes for multiple airlines, the value of VIASA's routes would drop. For instance, in the good old days of protectionism in the 1970s, the Caracas–New York route was exclusively the territory of VIASA and Pan Am. By 1993, VIASA had to compete with American, United, and Avensa. To improve the attractiveness of VIASA to potential buyers, the Venezuelan government promised to include in the agreement of sale the guarantee that VIASA would be the designated airline in agreements for route assignments with other countries for twelve years, while it would also be guaranteed continued rights for seven years as the exclusive airline on those routes where it had that privilege at the time of privatization (this applied to routes to Europe in particular). The tendency toward the breakdown of the old system of cartelization of international air transport markets, where routes between countries were invariably granted to only one airline from each country, contributed to the tendency to privatize. State-owned airlines were having an ever more difficult time competing profitably. Additionally, those airlines that stood to gain from deregulation could be expected to lobby in favor of deregulation (see Marcus 1991). Once a government privatizes, of course, it clearly loses interest in protecting the companies.

International Organizations While examples of successful privatizations were important, no less influential in Venezuela was the role of the international organizations, in particular the International Monetary Fund (IMF) and the World Bank. Until it faced its deep financial crisis in

1989, the Venezuelan government had been able to avoid agreements with the IMF and World Bank that involved policy quid pro quos. But the seriousness of the 1989 crisis left the government without any alternative, even if it had wanted to resist. The creditors were knocking at the door, public finances were in a shambles, and no acceptable model of opting out of the system existed. Peru had tried that under Alán García, and no one advised following suit.

The riots of late February 1989 served to put the international community on notice that Venezuela was in trouble and needed help, quickly. The World Bank reacted rapidly, and by June had in place a structural adjustment loan that required mainly macroeconomic changes in policy. By May 1990, Venezuela had signed the public enterprise reform loan, with cofinancing by the Inter-American Development Bank. The loan was to underwrite, among other things,

—the preparation and implementation of the restructuring of at least eleven public enterprises,

—the privatization of $150 million in assets,

—adjustments in prices for certain state-produced goods,

—and a phase-out of government transfers to commercial state-owned enterprises.

An internal World Bank document notes: "Virtually all enterprise restructuring will involve some degree of privatization, together with regulatory reform."

At the time of the loan, VIASA was not included in the list of companies to be privatized, although in an initial list published by the Venezuelan Investment Fund in March 1990, VIASA was under study as a possible candidate for privatization by the Advisory Committee on Privatization created by the president. The case of its sister company, LAV, was more complex, since it could not be privatized under the privatization law without first being transformed into a joint stock company through a law that would change its status as an autonomous institute.[9]

It is not easy to measure the role of the international organizations, however. There is ample evidence that Venezuela had come to the conclusion that privatization was necessary without help from the IMF or the World Bank (Kelly 1987). Under the Lusinchi government (1984–89), an initial privatization plan was undertaken and a privatization law approved. That plan limited itself to selling off small unimportant companies, of which there were more than 200.[10] What is clear, however, is that the loans from international agencies tied government policy to specific goals, gave a special urgency to the process, and extended privatization to large and politically prominent firms. Additionally, these organizations helped the government set priorities in its overall liberalization strategy, laying down the rules of timing and sequencing with its detailed schedules for policy transformation.

Changes in Ideology and People

How does a country change its collective mind? In the midseventies, Venezuela expressed a worldview that put it clearly on the side of government interventionism and state capitalism. In 1975, the oil and iron ore industries were nationalized and their foreign owners sent home. VIASA itself was swept into the nationalization frenzy. The Fifth National Plan stated categorically:

> Today the Venezuelan state can be described as a democratic government with a marked interventionist bent. . . . This tendency, which is becoming ever clearer, imposes on the state the obligation to intervene in the economic life of the country . . . the role of the state is no longer that of mere protector of private interests, but has now been transformed into that of the great agent of the community. The old concept of the liberal state has given way to the idea of the legitimate social state, such that the state's action in economic affairs is no longer a possibility but a true duty.[11]

In a paper written in the late seventies (Kelly 1982, 112), I noted that "Venezuelan governments have not only rejected the pure liberal claim that the free market produces the optimal outcome, they have also rejected the neo-liberal claim that pessimistically charges governments with inevitable incompetence. In fact, there is a remarkable degree of optimism in Venezuela with respect to what the state can do when it puts its mind to it."

The Ideological Revolution By 1978, some signs of change were evident. The huge expansion of government activity and debt-financed projects under the first Pérez government made the fiscally conservative camp nervous; hints of expansion in corrupt activities also raised doubts. The opposition campaign of presidential candidate Luis Herrera in 1978 called for a different approach, although without abandoning the state by any means. Herrera's "state as promoter" was to be less directly active, although in time, his government failed to change the drift of state capitalism. Facing a severe financial and balance of payments crisis in 1982–83, Herrera erected the final monument to state intervention—a detailed exchange control program called Recadi, which distributed scarce resources to favored sectors, especially public enterprises.

The government of Jaime Lusinchi (1984–89) is known principally for its mistakes in economic management and its penchant for unethical practices, so that little credit has been given to it for the important steps it took to liberalize at the microeconomic level. Lusinchi maintained the unsustainable and corrupt system of exchange control, subsidization, protectionism, and financial repression, taking it to extremes. Yet, during his government, there was a ferment of activity both outside the mainstream and on its fringes, a ferment that set the stage for the 1989 liberalization. Also, for the first time, the government constructed a formal plan for privatization and tried timidly to carry out Lusinchi's announced policy, that only "basic industries and services" remain under state control.[12] Lusinchi liquidated the large state holding company, the Venezuelan Development Corporation (CVF), that owned VIASA's shares. But since at that time VIASA was still considered "basic" or "strategic" by most opinion makers, its shares were not slated for sale but were turned over to the Ministry of Transport and Communications.

It was also Lusinchi who installed a powerful private businessman as president of VIASA, and in his government, the first steps were taken to introduce competition in the airline industry by giving routes to additional foreign and local companies, thus breaking the managed duopolies that had existed previously.[13] In December 1987, the Congress approved the first privatization law that established the rules of the game (still not referred to as "privatization" but rather the "transfer" of state property "not including 'basic' industries."[14] VIASA was still sacred state property, but progress was made in secularizing at least some state holdings.

At the level of ideas, even more important things were going on in the eighties. On taking power in early 1984, the Lusinchi government had created an independent reform commission called COPRE (Comisión Presidencial para la Reforma del Estado), whose mission it was to examine areas in which the state might be modernized. Named to the commission were some enterprising and committed private sector representatives who quickly set to work to free up the economy. One subcommittee sorted out the problem of how to reverse a standing policy under which the so-called economic rights enshrined in the Constitution of 1961 might be restored. (They had been suspended almost since their approval.) It was felt that restoring economic rights—while perhaps not so significant in terms of real policy change—would have a tremendous symbolic effect as a signal that the free market would heretofore be the norm, while intervention would constitute the exception.[15]

Another significant document was being prepared in the Lusinchi government: the Seventh National Plan (1984–88). The plan itself was not given much attention at the time; it is interesting more for what it says about the team that put it together in 1984 in the planning agency, Cordiplan, since it included important actors in the next government. The document argued that the prevailing model of the country was weak and vulnerable and favored inefficient production and use of resources. As was typical of the era, it did not address itself directly to privatization as such, much less mention concrete companies like VIASA. The plan reflected a compromise between Planning Minister Luis Raúl Matos (a left-leaning politician with tendencies toward syndicalism) and the person in charge of writing the plan, Ana Julia Jatar, who was linked to the liberalizing groups from the private sector that were organizing other activities, as we shall see below.

Equally (or more) important in the eighties were the voices from outside the government in favor of changing the government's role in the economy. A network of private sector representatives developed, with the explicit objective of influencing public and political opinion. Business organizations like Fedecámaras and the Caracas Chamber of Commerce held meetings and published documents supporting freer markets. Fedecámaras had sponsored a study of state-owned enterprises in 1983–84 that proposed a systematic review, company by public company, with the purpose of determining which companies might be privatized. VIASA was examined in detail in the pilot studies, and it was recommended that it be privatized as soon as market conditions permitted; in particular, it was argued, the company had been assigned "strategic value" due to faulty reasoning (Kelly and Villalba 1984).

At the same time, a group was forming composed of independent businessmen, whose purpose it was to lobby for a new liberal economic strategy. Called Grupo Roraima, it published in December 1983, on the eve of the new Lusinchi government, a document entitled "Action Plan: Proposition to the Country—Roraima Project." This document challenged the economic strategy of the previous years, in particular, government intervention in all phases of the economy. By today's standards, the Roraima project was mild; when it spoke of the state-owned enterprises, it never used the word *privatization* but suggested only that the public enterprises had failed to achieve their objectives. But despite the moderate tone of the document, it generated criticism for its radical promarket stance. It was said that it lacked the political underpinnings necessary to make it viable as a program.

In answer to the criticisms, the group published a second document, called "More and better democracy" (Granier and Gil Yepes 1987), that recommended a parallel opening in the political system that would, implicitly, break down the power of such traditional groups as political parties, labor unions, and political structures. Interestingly, even by 1987, many of the boldest voices were still highly reserved and unwilling to take on their enemies directly. The second Roraima report said of public enterprises, only two years before the policy revolution of 1989, that there were "strategic" companies that would remain under state control and "residual" companies that should be liquidated or sold (still without using the word *privatization*):

Certain development institutions and public services have been considered as strategic enterprises. Thus, it should be noted that the state includes among these strategic firms: the regional development corporations such as the CVG, financial institutions such as the BIV or the FIV, and public services such as Inos [water], CANTV [telephones], CADAFE [electricity], Ipostel [mail], VIASA, etc.

The public nature of these companies has for now been considered beyond discussion, and thus solutions for them will be based on improving management and control mechanisms, and in some cases there could be private participation in ownership or concessions.

It is evident that the authors of such documents were walking on eggs. Yet from about that year on, barriers to a frank discussion of privatization came down. In 1988, both major candidates espoused privatization and called it by its name. In the June annual meeting of Fedecámaras, Pérez, the leading candidate for president, announced that he would implement "total change in economic policy whose essence would include exchange rate freedom, privatization and the internationalization of the economy" ("The Candidates" 1988). The COPEI candidate, Eduardo Fernández, announced similar plans. Both insisted that privatization would democratize ownership and worker participation, perhaps following Thatcher's strategy of turning privatization into a popular policy. The most important change came with the victory of Pérez and his announcement that he would include among his ministers well-known advocates of privatization, many of whom had been involved in the ideological debates of the previous five years. The ideological revolution had begun.

People Behind the Ideology The story of ideological change has, as they say in Venezuela, first and last names. Those who challenged the old populist model also seemed to have an action plan for implementing the changes they espoused. It would be difficult to reconstruct the network that developed in the eighties, but it is possible to provide examples to show how a group of individuals linked mostly by common ideas and education took form as a political generation. The privatization of VIASA—and later, of the telephone company—gives us the essential clues to understanding the processes.

The chief actors in the privatization of VIASA included, most importantly, its president at the time of its privatization, Eduardo Quintero. Quintero, a quiet person, had risen to the position of chief executive officer of Polar, one of the largest and most successful private companies in Venezuela. In the eighties, he became interested in the strategic problems confronting the country and was impressed with the systems- and scenario-based thinking that had developed out of the planning group at Shell in the seventies. His first active step was to sponsor a research project at IESA in 1982, under the direction of Ramón Piñango and Moisés Naím (then dean of the business school), to explore the dynamics that were driving public policy.[16] His next step was to form, together with an impressive group of young, internationally oriented business leaders, Grupo Roraima. Quintero was project director for the Proposition to the Country. Naím established the link between his private sector connections and academic friendships, such as Carlos Blanco, who was a close adviser to newly elected President Lusinchi.

When the Lusinchi government accepted the idea of establishing COPRE, Blanco became its executive secretary, while both Naím and Quintero were selected as commissioners. Quintero threw himself into public affairs activities in COPRE and, together with a talented young economist in the COPRE staff, Gerver Torres, worked hard on the issue of the restoration of constitutional economic rights. In the Pérez government, Quintero was named to be president of the Venezuelan Investment Fund (FIV), the chief holding company for the most important state enterprises. He immediately set out on a quixotic campaign in favor of privatizing even the most sacred of industries and planned to liquidate the FIV in favor of a privatization agency to be called PRIBE (Empresa Privatizadora de los Bienes del Estado). The head of PRIBE was to be none other than Gerver Torres.

Quintero's enthusiasm gained him some powerful enemies, in particular, Leopoldo Sucre Figarella, president of the industrial state holding company Corporación Venezolana de Guayana (CVG) and the same gentleman who had suggested the full nationalization of VIASA some fifteen years earlier. Sucre won the battle: the president agreed to protect the CVG from Quintero's privatizing drive.[17] In the meantime, it was soon obvious that there was no political support for supplanting the FIV, although there was nothing to impede privatization either. Torres, a less controversial figure and one with more talent for getting the politicians to come around to his point of view, saw through the political jungle perhaps more clearly than Quintero. In mid-1990, Torres took over the presidency of the FIV, and Quintero was named president of VIASA, with the sole mission of carrying out a successful and model privatization in collaboration with Torres at the FIV. Quintero moved over to VIASA, together with Ellis Juan, who had worked with him at Polar, had collaborated on the Roraima project, and had served with him as vice president of the FIV.

Of course, these actors were not operating in a vacuum; the liberalizing network was much more extensive in the Pérez government. Moisés Naím played an important role in the cabinet as development minister, while his colleague from IESA, Miguel Rodríguez, was planning minister. Rodríguez, who attended to macroeconomic policy, charged

Roberto Smith with the job of writing up the new national plan, published in January 1990 and entitled "El Gran Viraje" (The Great Turn-around). Smith, after gaining fame with the plan, was named minister of transport and communications and would play a critical role in working with Quintero and Torres in the privatization of VIASA in 1991. Smith was a natural member of the young turks. A brilliant mathematics student at the Simon Bolivar University, he took an early interest in politics in a leftish student group called Study and Struggle. He formed a friendship there with Fernando Martínez, who had come to Cordiplan with him and whom Smith later backed as president of the telephone company during its privatization. Both had been master's degree students in political science and both earned their doctorates in public policy in the United States (Smith at the Kennedy School at Harvard, Martínez at Cornell). Smith had worked at Cordiplan with Ricardo Hausmann, who had in turn worked on Lusinchi's national plan, later joined Ana Julia Jatar as IESA professor, was successor to Rodríguez as minister of Cordiplan.[18] Another supporting actor in the cabinet was Gustavo Roosen. He had been head of one of Polar's divisions while Quintero was CEO, was a member of the Roraima Group, and although he was minister of education, participated in the cabinet committee on economic policy.[19]

The members of this group, with connections going back to the early eighties, were self-aware, were committed to bringing about privatization and liberalization, and were able to work together. The key ministers were Smith, Torres, Rodríguez, Naím, and Roosen; Quintero was strategically placed in the presidency of VIASA. Despite their universal lack of political experience and the distrust they tended to generate among traditional party leaders, they enjoyed the full support of the president and were ready to undertake the symbolic and important privatization of VIASA.[20]

Being Sold to the Highest (and Only) Bidder

The privatization of VIASA took about a year, once the green light was given to the company. To some extent, the decision was confused with efforts to change the whole privatization system. In the first year of the Pérez government, there was a presumption that VIASA would be re-formed in some way. The sanguine economic position of the company as reflected in the final financial results turned over by Luis Ignacio Mendoza was quickly shown to be somewhat artificial under the new rules of the game. Exchange rate liberalization had brutal effects on the balance sheet, as dollar-denominated debt soared in local values. The end of the dual exchange system created similar problems in the income statement, since preferential dollars were no longer available. Devaluation wreaked havoc on the purchasing power of Venezuelans, who stopped traveling abroad. Real GDP shrank by some 10 percent in 1989. The simultaneous phasing out of the system of export bonuses constituted the final blow. It turned out that in no year would VIASA have had profits if this subsidy had not existed and that the real cost of maintaining the company was much higher than had been suspected.

Eduardo Quintero at the FIV lost precious time in 1989 fighting for the creation of the privatization agency and the liquidation of the FIV. It was thought at the time that the legal requirements in place—the Law for the Transfer of State Assets—would present serious difficulties to the privatizers because of some clauses requiring the approval of a special privatization commission as well as somewhat troublesome procedures for valuation. It was also thought that its clauses with respect to worker participation were excessively problematic: the law could be interpreted to mean that any offer made by workers' representatives had to be favored over offers by other bidders, regardless of the price offered. While such a possibility might seem ridiculous, it nevertheless raised doubts (and constituted an insurmountable barrier in case of a hotel privatization). In the end, it was discovered that the law was not so inflexible. It also had to be realized that, in a democratic political system, it was not going to be possible to privatize without first achieving a minimum of political consensus, even if that meant boring and uncomfortable hearings by the congressional privatization commission. It was necessary to ensure that the process had the appearance of openness and participation; if not, it all might backfire.

When Torres took over at the FIV, he gave his attention to smoothing over political problems, while the more controversial Quintero took over the less public but nevertheless crucial job of president of VIASA. The cabinet approved the general plan for privatization presented by the FIV in August 1990. VIASA was included, along with LAV, in the list of companies to be privatized in the first phase.[21]

There was indeed a moment of consensus in October 1990, when the Special Commission on Privatization of the Congress celebrated a joint seminar with the FIV on privatization (Venezuela 1991). In that meeting, Eduardo Quintero presented his vision of the reasons for privatizing VIASA and how it would be carried out. He cited the changes in the world economy, the deregulation of airlines, the high cost of needed investments, and the necessity of a global strategy for international airlines competition. He emphasized the opportunity to permit worker participation in the shares of the company. Calming the opposition, he said that the state could maintain a minority interest as well and insisted that the process would be professional and absolutely transparent in its execution. Companies were being invited to bid as consultants in different aspects of the program, and discussions were under way with regard to the plan for worker participation and the percentages that would be assigned to the various shareholders.

About this time, the privatization process was unlinked from the discussion of whether to approve a new privatization law in Congress. One of the principal doubters in Congress with respect to privatization was Luis Raúl Matos, representative of the Chamber of Deputies in the Privatization Commission. He declared to the press in December 1990 that he believed that privatization could advance without serious problems within the existing legal framework ("Matos Azócar" 1990).

By January 1991 the advisers had been contracted. First Boston was the leader, with a number of local companies as specialists, including several auditors, the legal firm D'Empaire, Reyna, Bermúdez and Associates and financial consultants Kesai and Associates among others. Some doubts were raised about whether the choice of consultants had been open, but this did not result in any political backlash ("Surgen dudas de Transparencia 1991"). In February, the economic subcommittee of the cabinet recommended that external debt of US$58 million be absorbed by the government, thus clarifying the intention of the government to absorb the company's outstanding debt. It took four more months to decide on the conditions for companies permitted to bid:

—The bidder should be a consortium, with Venezuelan firms and at least one well-known international airline included.

—The international airline should have a minimum passenger-kilometer of 10 billion.

—It should have minimum income from operations of US$1 billion in the last three years and a minimum capital of US$250 million.

—Venezuelan partners should have minimum capital of 330 million bolivars.

The net effect on national control by Venezuelans would be that at least 51 percent of the shares would remain under the control of nationals, given the shares of the government (20%, later to be sold in the stock exchange), the workers (20%), and local members of the consortium (11%). The FIV published the following in full-page ads in newspapers: "Given its character as a strategic company, VIASA will continue to operate as a clearly national airline, with 51 percent of its shares in the hands of Venezuelan private capital. The privatization of VIASA responds to the great interests of a more efficient Venezuela, a more productive and competitive company and a state that takes up less space and in which citizens participate more actively." ("VIASA's Privatization Is Taking Off" 1991). From all appearances, things were going ahead well, although during the last months before the sale, several problems emerged, some of which would affect the company's postprivatization environment.

First, the international market had soured considerably. When the sale was decided on in mid-1990, its promoters were relatively sanguine; who would have guessed then that the end of the year would bring the Persian Gulf War and the unprecedented air traffic and airline losses that accompanied it? Many companies were losing their shirts and were not scouting for additional capacity. Second, the financial situation of VIASA stimulated little interest, and its dire economic straits would mean additional bureaucratic barriers, which would take time to hurdle. The supposed profits left by Luis Ignacio Mendoza had quickly turned into huge losses when the new government lifted exchange controls and protection in the beginning of 1989. The years of profit could be attributed to the export bonus that VIASA received, particularly between 1987 and 1989 (figure 9-2). Without such support, losses were 2.7 billion bolivars in 1990 and 2.4 billion bolivars in 1991, the year of privatization. The end of exchange controls tended to reduce income, since the system in place from 1983 to 1988 had favored both importers and exporters (at the cost of international reserves and debt).

When it was put on the privatization list in August 1990, VIASA was counted among the companies that would be sold in the second phase, since certain policies had to be implemented before the sale could take place—particularly getting out of debt, since according to a 1986 promise the Republic would assume a large amount of its debt. Indeed, as new losses began to pile up, it also became necessary to reinject capital in order to avoid a technical bankruptcy.

The firm of Keisai and Associates undertook a financial analysis of VIASA as a first step in setting the minimum bid amount. Keisai reported that, as of June 1990, the company had negative capital of some 438 million bolivars even after a capital injection by the government of some 1.5 billion bolivars.[22] By December 1990, the FIV had prepared a plan to formalize the debt assumption operation, but this in turn had to be approved by the Finance Committees of both houses of Congress. The Treasury Ministry approved the plan on December 12, and it was formally handed over to the Congress on April 25, 1991.[23] By the time of the opening of bids on August 9, the audited financial statement for 1990 was available, stating that the shareholders (i.e., the Venezuelan government) had to inject more capital to the tune of 4.8 billion bolivars (about US$70 million) within the terms of the bankruptcy law.

These altered circumstances—the decline in the international market and the deterioration in VIASA's financial situation—probably contributed to the fact that at the moment when possible buyers had to declare their interest, only two consortia appeared: (1) a group led by

Iberia, together with the Venezuelan Banco Provincial,[24] and (2) a group led by KLM, together with Northwest Airlines, another Venezuelan bank, Banco Mercantil, and two small private investors, Luis Ignacio Mendoza (former president of VIASA) and Peter Bottome.

A third problem that came up in the last month before privatization was a spurt of opposition that caused a flurry of resistance. The idea of worker participation had been a key element in selling the idea of privatization. Not only in the case of VIASA, but in practically all the other privatizations carried out by the Venezuelan government, shares were reserved for the workers and care was given to labor relations. At the same time, the government tried to ensure that worker participation was not equated with union participation and that shares were not given away. In the VIASA offer, the FIV suggested that the shares be paid for in lieu of benefits under the union contracts, plus a 5 percent discount from basic salary as well as the cession of part of the usual end of year bonus.

The pilots, ever intransigent in their relation with the company, decided to put off contract negotiations with VIASA until after privatization, putting possible buyers on notice that there might be a showdown in their future. They did not oppose privatization, but they were surely wary that the sale of the company might mean cutbacks in the number of pilots, which they had managed to avoid since the first efforts to fire excess personnel in the seventies. The lack of definition of contractual terms with the pilots meant in turn that the plan for labor participation, as well, would have to await the postprivatization period.

On Sunday, July 26, only two and a half weeks away from privatization, the most important newspaper, *El Nacional,* published four articles under the heading "The AD Party Comments" (1991). All of the articles criticized different aspects of VIASA's upcoming privatization. The headline of the principal article, the leader in the economics section, read as follows: "Is the Company Being Given Away? The Real Financial Situation of VIASA is not Reflected in its Balance Sheet." The article suggested a number of vague improprieties, based on "confidential information," such as that the chief of accounting at VIASA was not a certified public accountant, for which reason he was easily used by management (under various presidents) when they wanted to distort the figures; that VIASA's planes alone had cost US$210 million, while the company was to be sold for a minimum of US$135 million; and that in the proposed agreement of sale, there would be a contingency clause to the effect that liabilities not reflected on the balance sheet would be the responsibility of the seller. Mysteriously, the article also took issue with the fact that the government would receive only 60 percent of VIASA's value, fearing that the net value of the sale might be negative. VIASA had (allegedly) been a profitable company until Eduardo Quintero took over; now it was losing over 2 billion bolivars a year: "All of which reflects the fact that there appears to be a campaign to project a negative image of our flagship airline in order to sell it off at a bargain basement price, which is just about the same as giving it away."

The title of the second article revealed what was no secret: "The Plan for Worker Participation Fell Through." Here, the terms of the labor participation offer were presented and criticized as excessively hard on the workers, who, with the low salaries received by the majority, could not be expected to be able to sacrifice 5 percent of monthly income to pay for their shares.

The third article, entitled "Airline Manager Is Also in the Pay of KLM," took a position clearly more favorable to Iberia than to KLM, citing supposed evidence of undue KLM influence in VIASA's affairs. The KLM consortium was doubly suspect because it included Luis Ignacio Mendoza and Peter Bottome. (That Mendoza was interested in the company was not interpreted, oddly enough, as a vote of confidence by the man who perhaps knew it best.) Furthermore, the article claimed that Iberia was being questioned unjustly as a bankrupt company, when its losses could be attributed to the short-term consequences of the Persian Gulf War. The article finished thus: "Therefore, perhaps it would be well to listen to the voice of the congressman who recently suggested that this is not the best moment for selling VIASA. At times of crisis, those who have resources take advantage of the situation to buy up assets at low prices. And that is what may happen with VIASA if they insist on going ahead with the sale on the planned date."

The fourth article, "Privatization May Be Delayed," reflects best of all where the opposition was based. It reported the opinion of Luis Raúl Matos, president of the special privatization commission of the Chamber of Deputies, member of the government party, AD (soon to be thrown out of it, to be sure, after years of dominating its left wing), and dedicated enemy of the president and his liberalization program. Matos returned to the argument that the then-valid privatization law permitted the workers special privileges in privatization operations: all they had to do was form a buyers' group representing the workers, and the bidding process would be stopped. The existing company formed to buy shares for the workers, Provía, had gone beyond its mandate, since it had agreed to the terms offered by the company to sell shares to individual workers that would be paid for with their accumulated labor rights.[25] Matos claimed that only the unions could negotiate such terms. Other voices criticized elements of the sale in the discussion in Congress; a report was to be made within two weeks.

To prepare the joint report of the Privatization and the Administration and Services Committees, those in charge of the privatization were to be questioned. By the end of the week, doubts were openly expressed as well by Luis Emilio Rondón, deputy leader of the AD in the Chamber of Deputies and member of the executive committee of the party ("Privatization Cannot Be Held Up" 1991). He even opened the possibility that the privatization could be stopped and, instead, VIASA could be merged with the domestic airline, LAV, which would be an ironic return to VIASA's origins pre-1960 as the international division of LAV. Gerver Torres, seeing the political environment in sudden deterioration, responded with his own declarations, attributing the opposition to the interests of various actors: those who would like to buy, those who might be prejudiced by the sale, those related to the companies involved in various ways who were benefiting from their relations, and those who were enjoying benefits from the company. He said "there are all sorts of interests that come into play in a privatization. For just this reason, it is important to rely on the technical arguments" (ibid.).

Torres, Quintero, and Smith all appeared before the committee and made their arguments in favor of continuing with the bid date as planned. By Monday, July 29, Matos revealed that the committees would not stop the process, although they still had reservations. It was clear that the risk was the government's and that the Congress would not be responsible for anything going wrong. Torres promised that the sale terms would be modified to include a more precise account of the nature of worker participation and to ensure that the value paid would be sourced from abroad. He insisted that the sale price reflected real value and was based on a various methodologies: liquidation value, cash flow under optimum future conditions, goodwill, value of routes, etcetera. As a result of the accords, the opposition COPEI also announced that it would support the sale. Finally, the opposition was neutralized, and with the day set for opening the bids only days away, the plan could proceed.

On August 9, a somewhat embarrassing result came about: although both consortia appeared at the central bank for the formality of handing over their offers, in the end the KLM group decided not to bid, due to their judgment that the company had a net worth below the minimum sale price set by the FIV of US\$135 million (equivalent to US\$81 million for 60%).[26] The Iberia–Banco Provincial group offered US\$145 million for its share, well above the limit, and won as if by default. However, Torres declared that the final price was less important than the fact that the government was at last free of a company that had lost money for many years. And the president of Iberia hastened to ensure the workers that their jobs were not in danger but that, if they thought they could take advantage of the firm, they should pack their bags. He admitted that 1992 would not be a good year but declared that, by 1993, VIASA would achieve success ("VIASA's Final Price" 1991).

The Second Time as Farce? Postprivatization VIASA

Given the financial situation of VIASA, its long-term hostilities with the unions and lack of definition of the terms of labor participation, the decline in real income in Venezuela, and the continued presence of the government as shareholder, it should not be surprising that the postprivatization era was less than smooth. Some would even question whether it could be called privatization, since the shareholder division was not much different from that of VIASA at the time of its creation in 1960. On the other hand, the fact that Iberia was the chief buyer may have seemed less like a buyout by a foreign firm, since the new arriving managers spoke Spanish. In its analysis of the sale, *Veneconomía Mensual* ("VIASA's Privatization" 1991) hailed the privatization as "Good news for everyone." It was good news for Iberia, because VIASA would permit it to become the leading airline in Latin America, joining its own extensive network not only with the Venezuelan airline but also with Aerolíneas Argentinas and LADECO of Chile. It was good news for the government, because it would no longer have to cover VIASA's losses and because the privatization process would be fortified by the success of the sale. It was also good news for VIASA employees, whose jobs had been saved at least for the time being. It was admitted that Iberia was also a state-owned enterprise with a mediocre record, but (hope springs eternal) its reorganization in late 1990 promised better results.

Decreasing Losses?

Indeed, the first period of life for VIASA under the control of Iberia was a hard one. By December 1991, the company had accumulated losses of 4.1 billion bolivars (about US$70 million, for which the government was mainly still responsible). The end of the year was even more difficult as a result of a strike by pilots, starting November 19 and lasting until December 18 and ruining ticket sales in the peak period of travel. Iberia gave in to the pressure and settled for pay increases for the pilots. From the pilots' viewpoint, it was a first show of force on their part, and VIASA's future, they thought, might be in their hands. Of course, this was a twoway street: their jobs were in Iberia's hands. According to *Veneconomía Semanal*'s version of events ("VIASA's New President" 1992), an account retracted the following week, the settlement of the pilot dispute cost Javier Russinés his job for his having agreed to indexing pilots' salaries and to paying part of them in U.S. dollars.

By September 1992, a flurry of negative news afflicted Iberia. In particular, a study came to the Privatization Commission of the Chamber of Deputies citing the poor financial results of the privatization operation due to the large hidden liabilities that the government would have to meet. Ordozgoiti, executive vice president of VIASA, denied that VIASA was bankrupt and began publicizing Iberia's investments in VIASA, the reduction in financial losses, and the expansion of routes, number of planes, and personnel.[27] Iberia was starting to organize its more efficient system for sharing services among its subsidiaries in different countries. Ordozgoiti also stressed the generous terms on which the workers could buy shares: apart from the long-term payment period, it would also be possible to receive up to a 50 percent discount in return for reductions in contractual benefits.

Real losses exceeded the projections announced by VIASA's management for 1992 and 1993. Needless to say, the losses and the corresponding requirement that shareholders (including the government) underwrite these losses dismayed Venezuelans, who had been told that one of the chief benefits of privatization was that they would no longer have to cover its losses.[28] Political leader Leonardo Ferrer put it this way in his Sunday column in *El Universal* (Ferrer 1992):

> A year and a half after opening the bids, the renationalized company is undergoing financial problems due to uncovered liabilities of 2.3 billion bolivars. Operation costs have increased by 40 percent [not so bad, given inflation of over 30 percent], and IATA decided to suspend VIASA from the payments system because it is behind on its debts. These and other deficiencies lead me to conclude that VIASA under the Venezuelan government was just about as badly managed as it now is under the Spanish government. . . .
> I will be soliciting an investigation in the Congress with respect to [the proposal that the FIV join Iberia in reinjecting capital to cover the losses].

The story of VIASA continued as if it had never changed hands: the Congress still called for investigations and questioning of executives. Ordozgoiti defended himself before the same Luis Raúl Matos in the same Privatization Committee of the Chamber of Deputies; the president of the FIV, now Julián Villalba, had to come up with the arguments and the funds to put back into VIASA the money it had lost up until 1992. The FIV viewed additional investment with little enthusiasm, but its search for someone who would buy its shares was fruitless and the government did not want to face the political resistance that would inevitably come from the "strategic" school of politicians and military.

Yet, as other political issues captured attention, the privatization of VIASA slipped into the background. It seemed that if Iberia could put the company into the black, the questioning would stop.

Labor Relations: Hope Replaces Despair

In April 1992, the unions began one of their traditional press campaigns against management, claiming that it was creating an "artificial crisis" presumably aimed at setting the scene for reducing labor benefits. The *Diario de Caracas,* a proprivatization newspaper, said in its editorial ("What's Artificial in VIASA?" 1992):

> [The workers' complaints] are really about trying to criticize the process of privatization, when there has not yet been sufficient time for the new companies to start changing things and to begin to produce the positive results we are all waiting for.
>
> . . . In both cases [VIASA and CANTV] it is clearly a campaign mounted by groups whose politics are in favor of a statist approach to the economy and who hope that neither privatization is successful, in order to demonstrate the flaws of privatization in general.

The labor situation was further confused by the fact that it was very difficult to resolve the question of how, when, and at what price the employees would invest in the company. Indeed, given the financial situation of VIASA, it is not surprising that some workers had doubts about investing. Labor representative William Bracho put it this way ("VIASA Personnel" 1993): "If there is no guarantee by the airline and by the government that VIASA will recuperate and begin to make money again, the workers will not agree to buying shares in a bankrupt company."

At the same time, while it was agreed that the workers would pay the same price per share as did Iberia (US$14), it was still not clear what Iberia had paid, since under the hidden liabilities clause of the sale agreement the state had to pay for all liabilities that were not reflected in the end-of-1990 balance sheet. Provía, the company organized to represent the workers, suggested that a reference price be set to start the purchase system, with adjustments made later. In any case, the workers were to be given five years to pay, without interest.

It was not until April 1994—almost three years after privatization—that the plan for worker purchase of 20 percent of the company's shares was implemented. The sale was guaranteed at the 1991 exchange rate of 59 bolivars per U.S. dollar, despite the fact that the bolivar was already at almost 120 per U.S. dollar by that date and would be soon slide beyond 200, thus turning the deal into a giveaway. At the time of the agreement, Iberia began to announce that, while losses in 1994 would still be on the order of US$7 million (optimistic again?), the stabilization of, and improvement in, the company made it possible to predict profits for 1995. Some signs indicated that share ownership was beginning to effect a change of attitude on the part of the personnel.

Regulatory Framework

In another respect, VIASA's evolution did not appear to have changed from its government-dominated past. Unlike the telecommunications and electric sectors, the airlines did not have an independent commission to decide regulatory issues in the postprivatization era. This left VIASA at the whim of the ministry with respect to its routes. In one bizarre episode in August 1993, the ministry, now less neoliberal than in the Pérez period, announced its intention to study the possibility of rationalizing route assignments due to oversupply of passenger space. Immediately, the presidents of Avensa and LAV (not yet privatized) were known to be suggesting that they be assigned some of VIASA's best routes—in the interests of the country, of course. VIASA's directors were appalled. Such government actions show that, in regulated markets, it is still the government that determines who may play (contestability) and who makes profits (sustainability, in the terms of Gerchunoff et al. 1992). In another incident under the new government that came into power in 1994, there were attempts to place radical opponents of privatization on the boards of VIASA and the telephone company. Yet when the president discovered that the candidates were unsuitable, he ordered their names withdrawn. At best, the regulatory framework continued to be somewhat unpredictable. In any case, VIASA would enjoy its guarantee of exclusivity on most routes at least until 1998, according to the agreement of sale.

Parallel Cases: The Attempt to Privatize LAV

This recounting of the privatization of VIASA aims to show that important decisions about the economic order in a society depend on complex combinations of events and people in such a way that economic rationality determines outcomes only in the longest of terms and, even then, is not assured. The extraordinary team that was assembled to carry out the liberalization of the economy and that achieved its best moments in 1991 with the privatization of VIASA and the telephone company was soon disbanded as a result of the political assault on President Carlos Andrés Pérez that began with the coup attempts of February and November 1992 and ended with his impeachment in 1993. Under interim president Velásquez, there was little enthusiasm for privatization, although FIV president Julián Villalba made some valiant one-man attempts to continue the program. This was virtually impossible without presidential support and was even slightly illegitimate given the calls by major presidental candidates for an approach different from the prevailing neoliberal orthodoxy.

The attempt to privatize LAV, which ended as of this writing in May 1994 with the failure to get a single bid from potential buyers, provides an interesting parallel to the story of VIASA. LAV, it will be remembered, is a mostly domestic airline, operating in a virtual duopoly with the private airline Avensa, owned by the Boulton family (the same company that ran VIASA in the 1960s). The Venezuelan domestic market was long characterized by low technological investment, mediocre but extensive service, and a negotiated division of routes, although the opening up of Venezuela's domestic market was increasingly a fact after 1991, with the object of introducing competitive factors. Indeed, the Antimonoply Superintendency submitted an opinion to the effect that Avensa could not bid for LAV because it would substantially lessen competition in the domestic market, creating a dominant firm in a situation in which problems of access to airport space would create high barriers to entry (Venezuela 1993).

LAV's privatization was of lower priority than VIASA's and depended on a law to be approved in Congress to convert it into a saleable company. A private sector executive, Andrés Duarte, was named president to guide the sale, but he soon found that the political situation of 1993 did not favor action. The company began to lose money in large amounts, and only because of threats that the company would be shut down did the Congress include the necessary legislation in an emergency law at the end of 1993 that would finally permit privatization.

While the logic of the situation demanded a quick sale, the politics led in another direction. Recently elected Rafael Caldera appointed a rather reluctant privatizer to head up the FIV in early 1994, Abdón Vivas, who said he favored privatizing LAV but insisted that he would not sell off state assets at unfairly low prices. He put off the sale date a number of times and finally came up with a minimum price of US$62 million, which observers agreed was unduly high. Duarte resigned in disgust, although he later agreed to stay on until the bidding date. On May 17, as predicted, no bidders presented themselves, and the sale had to be put off again. Vivas was fired days later and replaced by Carlos Bernárdez, an original member of the Roraima Group, which had lobbied for liberalization back in 1983. In the end, LAV was liquidated when its workers refused to negotiate terms for a new privatization effort in 1994.

Conclusions

Economic rationality probably explains the trend toward privatization of the last fifteen years. Yet such a broad theory is not useful for understanding why certain countries privatize while others do not nor why in one country the advance of privatization is so irregular. Why did Argentina differ so from Brazil, and why did Venezuela adopt such a zigzag course? This chapter suggests that a closer reading of key variables leads to an explanation. It would be comforting to have found that policy decisions on privatization were based on social cost-benefit analysis and on calculations of the net present value of the firm under private and public ownership, but over the medium term, political factors were predominant. VIASA was privatized in 1991 in a political climate totally different from that which would characterize the country when the privatization of LAV was attempted just two years later. Additionally, privatization does not end government intervention in industries where regulation continues to be important.

Another lesson of the postprivatization period of VIASA is that privatization did not get the state out of the market. Especially in this case, where the government retained an important share (in reality, 40 percent, counting the unsold workers' shares), the dynamics of the company seemed unchanged by privatization. Indeed, it could be argued that the big problem with VIASA's privatization was that it did not truly privatize the company—the state still had a big stake. Others might argue that partial privatization was the only possible way to change management because of nationalistic sensibilities and the vulnerable image of the government. Such a partial privatization would (it was hoped) make total privatization easier to swallow at some future date.

VIASA has been privatized twice in the story we have told, and it is likely that it will be privatized a third and fourth time. Should political resistance subside, the government will sell off its remaining 20 percent of shares in the company in the stock market. And should we widen our lens beyond the case at hand to include Iberia itself, we will find an enlarged version of VIASA: a state-owned enterprise struggling to survive (its reported losses in 1993 were US$498 million) in a world market that permits gains only to the truly efficient. Iberia's strategy of building a network of subsidiaries in Latin America, of which VIASA is one, and of seeking alliances with the likes of Lufthansa and United Air Lines, will work only if Iberia reaches efficiency levels that are in fact difficult to achieve in state-owned enterprises. Progressive deregulation makes the old strategy of protected destinations less and less viable, while privatization makes governments less and less willing to subsidize and protect their costly flagships. Just as political changes permitted VIASA's privatization through a window of opportunity in 1991, it is not difficult to envisage that, in Spain, a government to the right of Felipe Gonzalez's socialists or perhaps even the socialists themselves, faced with dwindling fiscal prospects, would turn to privatization as the Venezuelan government did before it. The story of privatization and deregulation is ongoing.

NOTES

1. These enterprises have vast resources for covering up their flaws, while the public at large normally dedicates its limited attention span to things politi-

cal rather than to monitoring accounting statements and the like. In fact, the public often perceives itself vaguely as a beneficiary of the state-owned company even when it recognizes that perhaps it might be better run.

2. The relation between VIASA and Avensa generated suspicion from the time of VIASA's creation onward, particularly among those with natural distrust of the more powerful economic interests in Venezuela. Critics always accused Avensa of squeezing profits from its service to VIASA at the expense of the state. Defenders of Avensa claimed that costs would be much higher were VIASA to go it alone.

3. The dominant union federation since the restoration of democratic rule in 1958 has been the Venezuelan Workers' Confederation (Confederación de Trabajadores Venezolanos, CTV, allied since its inception with the political party Acción Democrática, AD). Competing with the CTV was a much weaker Christian Democratic union federation.

4. VIASA's conduct in this period mirrors exactly the economic conduct of practically all agents in Venezuela during the oil boom. Similar patterns can be observed in other state-owned enterprises, although it is notable that the private domestic airline owned by the Boultons did not fall into such excesses.

5. IATA figures for pilots per plane were United, fourteen; British, eighteen; American, seventeen; TWA, seventeen; Iberia, fourteen; Lufthansa, twenty-one; VIASA thirty-six. See *Número*, Aug. 26, 1984.

6. This represented a reduction of 21 percent in total personnel. Passenger loads fell by some 45 percent in 1983 and 1984, during the worst of the financial crisis.

7. Pirie's work was made accessible in Spanish (Pirie 1985) and distributed in Venezuela by Cedice, an organization devoted to the promotion of free markets.

8. The Andean Pact agreement was published as Decision 297 of the Commission of the Cartagena Agreement, *Gaceta Oficial* 4284 Extraordinario, June 28, 1991. The agreement with Colombia was published in *Gaceta Oficial* 34749, July 4, 1991.

9. Congress never got around to passing the law. When, after the downfall of President Pérez, it was decided to grant extraordinary powers to the interim president, Velásquez, in mid-1993, LAV was finally converted from autonomous institute to joint stock company. The Venezuelan Investment Fund immediately started to prepare its privatization, scheduled initially for November 1993—although this was later repeatedly postponed.

10. Venezuela had accumulated a large number of firms owned by the government. While about one-fourth could be said to be important, the total number of independent entities (including foundations, nonprofit institutes, and companies with state participation) was more than 400 by the late eighties. Of these, the Advisory Committee counted 177 majority-owned firms in 1992.

11. Decree 1454, *Gaceta Oficial* 1860 Extraordinario, Mar. 11, 1976.

12. Lusinchi's campaign program was published as "Un pacto para la democracia social" in 1983.

13. By *duopoly*, I refer to routes in which VIASA and one foreign carrier would

operate, with a cartel-like division of the schedule. The most important were the routes to New York and Miami, whose lucrative markets VIASA and Pan Am had divided for many years.

14. See "Ley Orgánica que Regula la Enajenación de Bienes del Sector Público No Afectos a las Industrias Básicas," *Gaceta Oficial* 3951 Extraordinario, Jan. 7, 1988.

15. See especially COPRE 1988 and Kelly 1986. In 1986, I argued that, while COPRE might not succeed due to the opposition of traditional forces, it nevertheless was injecting daring ideas into the system and was playing an important role in advancing change.

16. This project resulted in the publication in 1984 of the influential book *El Caso Venezuela: Una Ilusión de Armonía.*

17. Sucre won that battle but not the war. Sucre was removed from his post at the CVG in the following government, and in May 1994, another Roraima member was named to the privatizing job at the FIV.

18. Smith brought interesting talents to his job as planner. He had worked as a consultant in McKinsey & Company in Washington after completing his doctorate. There he absorbed the McKinsey style of succinct and graphically persuasive presentations that develop a powerful logic around a few key strategic points. The Eighth National Plan abandoned the traditional heavy bureaucratic text of former plans and was full of McKinsey-style charts, with arrows, pictures, and strong conclusions. It was possible to trace his influence by looking for government documents with this look, at least up until the time that Keisai and Associates began to consult for the FIV and VIASA, since one of Keisai's partners was also an ex-McKinsey consultant.

19. In another twist of fate, Roosen would emerge as an important actor in the government of Rafael Caldera, who came to power in early 1994 after a campaign that stressed interventionism and resistence to "neoliberalism." Roosen would resuscitate the liberalizing tendencies supposedly rejected by the president.

20. For reflections on the liberalization program by one of the members of the group, published after the derailing of the Pérez government's initiatives, see Naím (1993).

21. As noted above, LAV would have to pass through the difficult first phase of congressional approval, since its legal status as an autonomous institute required a special law previous to a privatization of the business.

22. The Keisai estimation (internal VIASA document, 1991) was based on unaudited accounts. In the Alice in Wonderland of exchange controls, it was never quite clear how to value foreign liabilities denominated in other currencies. Since in the eighties, VIASA's debt was guaranteed at 7.5 bolivars per US$. By 1990, the exchange rate was at 47.

23. Letters from minister of the treasury to the presidents of the Permanent Commission on Finance of the Senate and the Chamber of Deputies. The finance minister was never a friend of the liberalization program of the government, despite his being brother-in-law to the minister of transport, Roberto Smith.

24. The fact that its CEO was of Spanish origin may have led the Banco Provincial, the largest bank in Venezuela, to embark on a joint venture with Iberia.

25. Under Venezuelan labor law, companies acquire significant liabilities toward their workers based on salaries and seniority; these are paid on separation of the worker from the company for any cause.

26. According to *Veneconomía Mensual* ("VIASA's Privatization" 1991), KLM had revealed its intentions to its associates on August 5, but its secret was well kept. It is not known whether the FIV knew ahead of time that only one bid would be made. Certainly it is a fact that, had KLM announced its withdrawal early, the doubting congressmen might well have raised a ruckus in order to stop the operation, since the remaining buyer would have no motive to bid above the minimum price. Given its bid, we can assume that Iberia did not have information about KLM's retirement.

27. In a press conference reported in *El Diario de Caracas* ("Airline Executives" 1992) and taken from a wire service, Ordozgoiti predicted that, while losses in 1991 had reached US$98 million, these would be reduced to only US$27 million in 1992. The realized losses in 1992 were in fact US$53 million, still quite considerable, especially for a company like Iberia that was also losing money on its investment in Argentina. Despite new rosy forecasts, VIASA's losses reached US$45 million in 1993 ("Debt and Exchange Rate Differential" 1994).

28. Under Venezuelan law, if losses in a company are more than two-thirds of capital and reserves, shareholders must pay in the value of the losses or declare bankruptcy. Government-owned companies have been known to survive for years without conforming to this provision, however.

REFERENCES

Aharoni, Yair. 1988. "The United Kingdom: Transforming Attitudes." In *The Promise of Privatization: A Challenge for American Foreign Policy,* ed. Raymond Vernon. New York: Council on Foreign Relations.

Boulton, Andrés. 1973. *Origenes y Formacion de VIASA.* Caracas: Andrés Boulton.

COPRE (Comisión Presidencial para la Reforma del Estado). 1988. *La Reforma del Estado: Proyecto de Reforma Integral del Estado.* Vol. 1. Caracas.

Ferrer, Leonardo. 1992. "VIASA: Lamentable Reestatización." *El Universal,* Dec. 6.

Gerchunoff, Pedro, et al. 1992. "Las Privatizaciones en la Argentina." Working Paper 21. Inter-American Development Bank, Washington, D.C.

Gil Yepes, José Antonio. 1981. "Caso VIASA I." Case study prepared for the annual meeting of the Grupo Santa Lucia, IESA, Caracas.

Granier, M., and José Antonio Gil Yepes. 1987. *Más y Mejor Democracia.* Caracas: Grupo Roraima.

Kelly, Janet. 1982. "Venezuelan Foreign Economic Policy and the United States." In *Economic Issues and Political Conflict: U.S.–Latin American Relations,* ed. J. Domínguez. London: Butterworths.

————. 1986. "Reform without Pain: The Commission on State Reform in the Lusinchi Administration." Paper prepared for the annual meeting of the Latin American Studies Association, Boston, October.

————. 1987. "Privatization in Venezuela." In *The Promise of Privatization*, ed. Raymond Vernon. New York: Council on Foreign Relations.

Kelly, Janet, and Julián Villalba. 1984. "Venezolana Internacional de Aviación, S.A.: VIASA." In *Información y Criterios para la Orientación de Decisiones Acerca de las Empresas Pública Venezolanas*. Caracas: IESA for Fedecámaras.

Marcus, Alfred. 1991. "Airline Deregulation, Business Strategy, and Regulatory Theory." In *Public Policy and Economic Institutions*, ed. M. J. Dubnick and A. R. Gitelson. Greenwich, Conn.: JAI.

Naím, Moisés. 1993. *Paper Tigers and Minotaurs: The Politics of Venezuela's Economic Reforms*. Washington, D.C.: Carnegie Endowment.

Pirie, Madsen. 1985. "Teoría y Práctica de la Privatización." *Revista del Instituto de Estudios Económicos: La Privatización de la Empresa Pública* (Madrid) 1:1–12.

"Surgen dudas de Transparencia en Privatización de VIASA." 1991. *El Diario de Caracas*, Jan 13.

Venezuela. Various years. *Gaceta Oficial*.

————. 1991. *La Privatización: Un Diálogo Necesario*. Caracas: Fondo de Inversiones y Congreso de la República.

————. 1992. *Memoria y Cuenta*. Vol. 1. Caracas: Ministry of Transport and Communications.

————. 1993. *Informe Especial sobre la Eventual Participación de las Líneas Aéreas Venezolanas en el Proceso de Privatización de Aeropostal*. Caracas: Ministerio de Fomento.

III. ROADS

10. The Mexican Toll Roads Program

··

William M. Emmons III

In early 1989 Mexican President Carlos Salinas de Gortari launched a major economic development plan, which included a novel approach to highway infrastructure development. Under Mexico's traditional strategy for highway development, the public sector took responsibility for the financing, operation, and maintenance of roads, while private sector firms typically carried out road construction. Yet, through the terms of the new program, the Mexican government would award concessions of up to twenty years to private companies to finance, construct, operate, and maintain an upgraded and expanded network of toll roads along Mexico's key economic corridors. Although the initiative has been referred to loosely as a road privatization program by some observers, all highways constructed under the concession mechanism revert by law to public sector ownership at the end of the concession term.

The Salinas administration initially proposed the development of 4,000 kilometers of concession toll roads over five years at a total cost of approximately 11.5 trillion 1989 pesos (US$5 billion). (Figure 10-1 presents a map of the toll road master plan.) In late 1991 the Mexican government accelerated its original timetable, increasing its target to 5,330 kilometers of highway concessions by the end of Salinas's term in office (Stanfield 1991, 9). As of July 1994 a total of 3,476 kilometers of concession toll roads were in operation, while another 1,884 kilometers were under construction (table 10-1).

This chapter presents an overview and preliminary assessment of the Mexican toll road concession program through mid-1994. The first section explores motivations underlying the introduction of the concession approach to highway development in Mexico. The next section provides a description of both the traditional approach to highway development in Mexico and the alternative toll road concession mechanism,

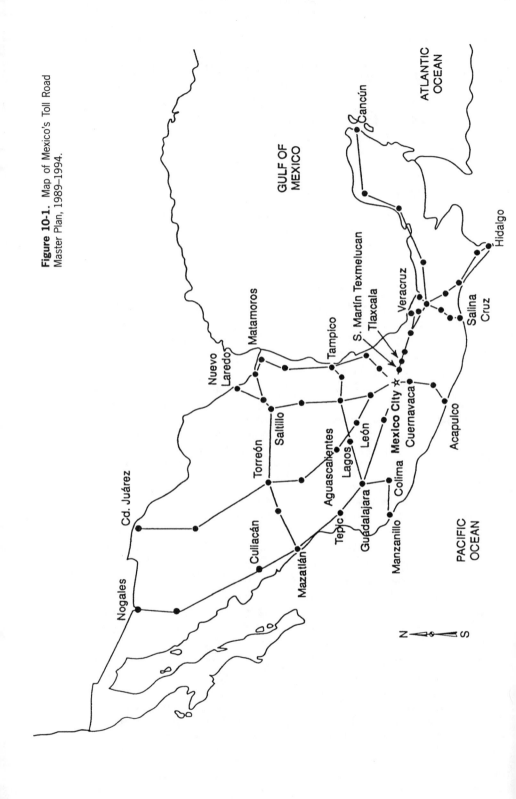

Figure 10-1. Map of Mexico's Toll Road Master Plan, 1989–1994.

Table 10-1. Status of Mexico's National Highway Program, July 14, 1994

Highway Type	Highways in Operation Kilometers	Highways in Operation Percentage	Highways under Construction Kilometers	Highways under Construction Percentage	Total, 1989–1994[1] Kilometers	Total, 1989–1994[1] Percentage
Concessioned toll roads						
Owned by private entities	2,380	49	1,104	52	3,484	50
Owned by state governments	859	18	665	31	1,524	22
Owned by BANOBRAS	237	5	0	0	237	3
Total	3,476	71	1,769	83	5,245	75
Federal toll roads (CAPUFE)	102	2	14	1	116	2
State toll roads	371	8	0	0	371	5
Free federal roads	809	17	0	0	809	12
Free state roads	112	2	0	0	112	2
SCT-managed roads	0	0	342	16	342	5
Total	4,870		2,125		6,995	

Source: Secretariat of Communications and Transport.

[1]Almost 90% accounted for by roads of four or more lanes.

while the third section offers a comparative analysis of the two approaches from a theoretical perspective. Section four examines outcomes associated with the concession program in practice and provides case studies of Empresas ICA and Grupo Tribasa, major private sector participants in the program. The final sections offer a provisional evaluation of Mexico's highway concession program and suggest lessons for other countries based on the Mexican experience.

Motivations for Mexico's Toll Road Concession Program

Mexico began constructing its high-performance road system in the 1950s under the auspices of the Secretariat of Communications and Transport (the Secretaría de Comunicaciones y Transporte, or SCT), financing these projects through public sector borrowings and taxation. By the late 1980s, Mexico had approximately 13,000 kilometers of roads handling daily traffic volumes of 5,000 vehicles, including 4,000 kilometers of four-lane highway. Although the majority of these highways were free roads, approximately 1,000 kilometers consisted of toll roads operated by the federal toll road authority, Caminos y Puentes Federales de Ingresos y Servicios Conexos (CAPUFE), an agency of the SCT.

Most of Mexico's highway infrastructure was completed prior to the 1980s. New road development reached a virtual standstill after 1982 owing to the fiscal constraints imposed by Mexico's severe economic crisis. During this period, President Miguel de la Madrid ended CAPUFE's financial autonomy, allowing the government to divert toll revenues to nonhighway uses. By the end of his term, it appeared that the limited scope and poor physical condition of Mexico's highway infrastructure might serve as an impediment to renewed economic growth as the nation strived to emerge from years of austerity. Nevertheless, the magnitude in 1988 of Mexico's public external debt obligations (US$83.7 billion) and federal budget deficit (12% of GDP) severely restricted the ability of the Mexican government to finance a major highway infrastructure program through public borrowings. Within this context, a toll road concession program that would place primary financing responsibility for highway infrastructure development on private construction companies and financial institutions appeared quite attractive to resource-constrained public sector policymakers.

Although Mexico's principal motivation for adopting a toll road concession approach to highway development could be attributed to government financial constraints, the program—at least in theory—could also generate gains in efficiency with respect to highway construction and maintenance as a result of the incentives created by the ownership structure, bidding process, and other features of the concession mechanism. In the next sections we examine the concession mechanism in more detail, focusing in particular on the differences in the incentive structure of the new versus the traditional approaches to highway infrastructure development in Mexico.

Alternative Approaches to Highway Development

To provide a context within which to analyze the impact of the shift in the Mexican government's approach to highway infrastructure development, we begin by describing the key features of the traditional contracting strategy and the more complex concession process introduced by Mexico in early 1989.

Traditional Contracting Mechanism

Under Mexico's traditional approach to highway development, the SCT planned the expansion of the nation's route structure in cooperation with the Secretaría de Hacienda y Crédito Público (Secretariat of Finance and Public Credit), which worked to arrange financing through a combination of infrastructure bonds and general tax revenues.[1] The SCT in turn contracted with private sector construction companies to build individual highways in accordance with detailed technical specifications determined in advance by the SCT. Contracts were typically awarded through a competitive bidding process; the SCT selected the lowest unit cost bidder among those companies judged technically qualified to execute a specific project. (Unit costs included a markup for overhead costs and profit.)

During the construction period the winning bidder was reimbursed for work completed on the basis of unit labor and materials costs specified in the contract and applied to the reported volume of inputs

employed. Contracts typically contained escalation clauses that protected firms from unit cost increases resulting from inflation. Although
all requests for reimbursement were subject to review by the contracting
agency, in practice, the government challenged company invoices only
rarely. However, payments were sometimes delayed due to temporary
budget constraints. In some cases, budgetary shortfalls were so significant that work in progress was suspended, leaving the construction firm
exposed to the costs of idle capacity.

Once completed, highways were maintained by the SCT. In the case
of toll roads, CAPUFE was responsible for toll collection and highway
maintenance. Toll rates were determined by the SCT, with input from the
Secretariat of Finance.

Toll Road Concession Mechanism

The toll road concession mechanism introduced by the Salinas administration was considerably more complex than the traditional contracting
approach to highway development. In essence, potential concessionaires
bid for the right to collect toll revenues on a particular route in exchange for constructing and operating the highway over a specific period of time. Under this system, the winning bid was based on shortest
length of concession proposed, as opposed to cost- or price (toll)-related
criteria.[2] To ensure that road users had access to a road regardless of
users' financial circumstances, the government required that at least
one "free road" be available along the route served by any toll road
concession. In most cases, the free road was simply an existing (precon-
cession) highway along the route.

Broadly speaking, the toll road concession mechanism encompassed
six phases: concession specification, preparation of bids, concessionaire
selection, construction, operation and maintenance, and reversion.

Concession Specification   The SCT was responsible for preparing detailed technical specifications for each highway covered by the government's master toll road plan and for securing rights of way along each
route. (Most concessions were granted by the federal government, but
state governments also had the authority to award concessions.) In addition, the SCT, along with the Secretariat of Finance, set the maximum
toll rates that the concessionaire would be allowed to charge, prepared
estimates of traffic usage for each route, and determined what conditions, if any, would be placed on the financial structure of the concession. Since toll road concessions were limited by law to a maximum of
twenty years, the SCT had to take care to set the parameters of the
concession in such a way that the term of the winning bid would not
exceed this duration.[3]

The SCT tried to carefully define the technical specification of the route, which included such information as highway path, locations of interchanges, bridges, and toll booths, number of lanes, and minimum standards for construction materials, so that potential concessionaires could estimate construction, operating, and maintenance costs with sufficient accuracy to prepare a bid. If the SCT changed specifications during the construction phase, the concessionaire could petition for an extension in concession length in order to recoup costs incurred in complying with such changes.[4]

The stipulation of maximum toll rates and the estimation of traffic levels were critical components of the specification process, since the combination of the two determined the level of revenues implicitly guaranteed by the government to the concessionaire. If usage volume fell below the level forecast by the SCT, the concessionaire could petition for an extension in the term of the concession; conversely, if traffic estimates proved too conservative, the government could reduce the length of the concession. Concessionaires were also protected in large part from the effects of inflation. In particular, the SCT was authorized to permit compensatory toll rate increases after a 5 percent increase in the consumer price index had taken place. Alternatively, the SCT could choose to grant an extension in the concession term as a means of offsetting the impact of inflation on the concessionaire's rate of return.

The concessionaire was typically expected to provide a minimum of 25 percent of the total capital requirements from its own resources, while the remaining capital could take the form of bank loans or other debt instruments. In some cases, the SCT permitted public sector entities—including CAPUFE, state and local governments, and even PEMEX (Mexico's state owned petroleum company)—to contribute equity capital to a particular concession.[5] In general, such public participation was allowed only when the concession's revenues were projected to be so low, or the required investment believed to be so great, as to discourage full private sector financing of the venture.

Preparation of Bids Bids were prepared by concessionaires affiliated with individual Mexican construction companies or joint venture consortia of two or more firms. (However, any Mexican public or private entity could act as a concessionaire.) In most cases, parent construction companies established a wholly owned concession division or subsidiary to manage its participation in a number of concessionaires. Each concessionaire was incorporated separately in order to isolate the costs and revenues associated with a given toll road concession.

Before a would-be concessionaire could submit a bid, it had to secure a commitment from a financial institution to contribute debt capital to the concession. Bidders typically explored arrangements with several different banks with the goal of obtaining the best possible terms with respect to loan size, interest rate, and maturity. Banks sought to match the terms of their lending commitments to the riskiness of the particular project, and thus they carefully reviewed the proposed construction timetable, estimated costs, and concession length of the bidder in conjunction with the concession specifications in deciding whether or not to support a bid. In some cases, a bank would make a commitment to more than one bidder for a particular concession, although not necessarily on the same terms.

Concessionaire Selection Each bidder was required to submit extensive documentation providing cost estimates, financing plans, and professional qualifications. The SCT and the Secretariat of Finance reviewed each proposal and awarded the concession to the bidder offering the shortest concession period—inclusive of construction time—provided that the proposal as a whole was judged to be feasible on both a technical and a financial basis.[6] Upon determination of the winning bid, the SCT, the Secretariat of Finance, the concessionaire, and its financial partner finalized the concession title, which established the length of the concession, capital structure, maximum toll levels, the implicit rate of return to the concessionaire, and responsibilities of the parties during the construction and operating period. The following is a summary of the terms of a representative concession title:

—Concessionaire:	Autopistas Mexicanas Concesionadas (Amecon), 100 percent owned by Empresas ICA.
—Development:	Two-lane toll road between Guadalajara and Tepic, denominated Plan de Barrancas.
—Financial entity:	Banco Internacional.
—Grant:	Right of way provided by the SCT, which will not award concessions for competing roads though the life of the highway.
—Term:	Eight and a half years from signing date (August 23, 1989), maturing February 23, 1998.
—Capital:	Resources for construction financed with no less than 25 percent equity and no more than 75 percent debt.

—Toll rates and traffic:	Maximum toll rates based on estimated average daily traffic of 7,500 units, of which initially 75 percent (5,625) would use the road as follows: cars (60%), 10,000 pesos per unit; passenger trucks (10%), 18,000 pesos per unit; other trucks (30%), 21,000 pesos per unit. Annual traffic growth projected at 4 percent. Tolls can be increased only with inflation rates greater than 5 percent. Concessionaire may appeal for extension of concession term if traffic falls below projections.
—Duties:	0.5 percent of annual toll revenues.
—Extension:	Road can be extended by an additional sixty kilometers on terms agreed to by the participating parties.
—Estimated construction time:	One year and six months, starting in November 1989.

Construction At the beginning of the construction period, the concessionaire's bank (or bank syndicate) typically established a *fideicomiso* trust (fiduciary trust, or escrow) to manage all cash flows related to the concession (figure 10-2). The initial flow of funds consisted of bank loans, and in some cases public sector equity, placed in the fiduciary trust. As the concessionaire incurred expenses in the form of services performed by its construction affiliate or other contractor, it submitted invoices to the trust for reimbursement (typically on unit-price basis). Cash payments to the concessionaire, however, were discounted by a percentage equal to its (equity) capital stake in the project. Therefore, the concessionaire's capital share in the concession accumulated over time in the form of "sweat equity." From the perspective of a construction company acting simultaneously as a concessionaire, the firm's construction division received full payment for construction services provided, while its concession division was required to make an investment in the concessionaire equal to the sweat equity share and subject to amortization over the life of the concession.

If all of the original capital available to the concession was depleted before the end of the construction period, several responses were possible. On the one hand, the participating bank could simply increase its capital contribution, thus enlarging its claim on toll revenues once the highway was operational. Although the concessionaire would continue to receive (discounted) reimbursement for expenses, its equity stake in the venture would become less valuable. Alternatively, the SCT might

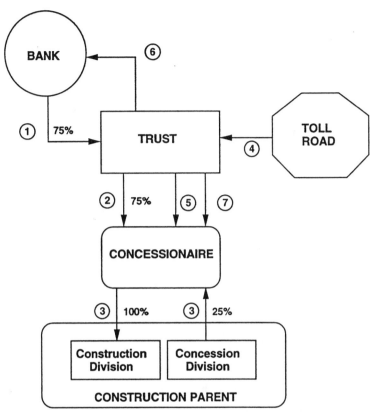

Figure 10-2. Financial Flows Associated with the Mexican Toll Road Concession.
Key: 1 = loans to concession; 2 = reimbursement based on construction invoices; 3 = payment for construction services; "sweat equity" investment in concessionaire; 4 = toll revenues; 5 = road maintenance and operation costs; 6 = debt service; 7 = dividends.
Note: Percentages relate to anticipated level of total investment in concession (debt plus equity). This example assumes that debt capital accounts for 75% of concession investment, while "sweat equity" by the concessionaire accounts for the remaining 25%.

encourage some public sector entity to make an equity contribution to the venture. If no additional capital contributions could be obtained from these sources, the concessionaire would be forced to finance the remaining construction on its own or withdraw from the project.[7]

Operation and Maintenance During the life of the concession, the concessionaire was responsible for the operation of toll facilities and the maintenance of the highway in accordance with government standards. The concessionaire could subcontract these activities to third parties, including CAPUFE; however, it retained full responsibility for their performance. At the same time, the concessionaire was given the right to develop and operate roadside services (rest stops, food, lodging) for up to two years beyond the term of the concession.

During the operating period, all toll revenues flowed through the fiduciary trust, which used the income to pay operating expenses and service the concession's debt. Residual revenues were paid to the concessionaire as dividends. Depending on the maturity profile of the concession's debt, the concessionaire might receive dividends across the entire operating period or, alternatively, be required to wait until the entire debt had been liquidated before receiving residual revenues.

Reversion The expiration of the concession period led automatically to the reversion of the toll road to Mexican government ownership. However, during the term of the concession, the government reserved the right to seize or expropriate—with fair compensation to the concessionaire—all assets related to the concession in the event of major disruption in communications, war, or economic or public order. In addition, if the concessionaire failed to perform its obligations—for example, in the areas of road operation and maintenance—or to comply with restrictions under applicable law, the government could terminate the concession without compensation before the scheduled expiration of the concession term. In such cases, the concessionaire would be ineligible for additional participation in the concession program for five years.

Concession Mechanism versus Traditional Contract Bidding: A Theoretical Analysis

As discussed above, the primary motivation for the adoption of the toll road concession program was the government's desire to attract a significant amount of private capital into the development of highway infrastructure in support of broader economic growth. In particular, the program was designed to spur the construction of 4,000 kilometers of high-performance toll roads over the period 1989–94. Yet, how appropriate was the incentive structure underlying the concession program for achieving these objectives? Furthermore, what impact was the shift from contract bidding to concessions likely to have on other outcomes, such as efficiency in highway construction and operation, road quality, prices charged for highway usage, profitability of construction companies, allocative efficiency in the use of Mexico's scarce resources, and overall costs of program administration? These questions are explored in more detail below.

The Mexican government hoped that by shifting from contract bidding to toll road concessions it would significantly increase the level of private investment—and thus total investment—in Mexico's highway infrastructure. Under the traditional approach to highway development, private investors were unable to invest directly in a specific road project but could fund highways only indirectly, through loans to Mexican government entities, whose debt repayment record in the 1980s was irregular and unpredictable. In contrast, highway concession financiers would theoretically recoup their investment through toll revenues generated by traffic on a specific route over the life of the concession. Furthermore, the riskiness of investor returns under the concession mechanism appeared to be minimized through government policies designed to offset the effects of specification changes, inflation, and unanticipated traffic shortfalls. Since these guarantees involved increases in toll rates and concession extensions, investor returns did not appear to depend on the fiscal condition of the Mexican government, as was the case under the traditional approach to infrastructure financing. Finally, construction companies (which served simply as contractors under the traditional approach) were in effect required to provide capital for concession projects through sweat equity contributions, thus creating an additional pool of funds available for infrastructure development.

Therefore, a priori, it seemed reasonable to expect that a shift to toll road concessions would result in higher levels of private sector investment in highway construction. However, if the SCT in practice failed to compensate concessionaires adequately for deviations in route specifications, price levels, and traffic volumes, private investors might come to shun the program. Furthermore, the requirement that construction companies take equity stakes in toll road projects through their investments in concessionaires raised the possibility that, over time, construction firms might become increasingly capital constrained and thus reluctant—or simply unable—to participate in toll road concessions.

The Salinas administration's goal of completing 4,000 kilometers of new toll roads within six years suggested that speed of construction was an important performance measure with respect to highway infrastructure development. Within the concession framework it appeared that the winning bidder indeed had powerful incentives to complete construction as rapidly as possible since the duration of the concession incorporated the construction period; thus, every additional day of construction represented a forgone day of toll revenues. In contrast, contractors under the traditional system faced no comparable incentives to complete construction work in a timely fashion. Also, budgetary shortfalls experienced by the SCT could lead to suspension of work in progress, thus delaying completion of individual routes indefinitely.

In terms of the cost of construction, the concession mechanism appeared to offer certain advantages over the traditional approach. In theory, the Demsetz-style auction underlying the concession bidding process would lead to the minimization of total construction costs by producing a winning bidder whose proposed concession length would generate just enough toll revenues to cover the cost of the most efficient bundle of resources required, including capital (Demsetz 1968). In contrast, the traditional contract bidding approach, while minimizing unit costs, did not appear to offer strong incentives for minimizing total costs, given the difficulty associated with monitoring input volumes. Furthermore, to the extent that the concession mechanism helped to eliminate construction delays, which sometimes resulted in connection with lags in government financing, one would also expect the overall costs of concession construction to be below levels incurred under the traditional approach.

Nevertheless, the concession approach did entail a possible source of cost disadvantage. Specifically, the cost of capital enjoyed by government borrowers was typically lower than that available to private borrowers, especially on an after-tax basis. Yet, the extent of the (pretax) capital cost differential would be determined by the market's assessment of the relative riskiness of the future cash flows from which returns on investment would be paid. The riskiness of these investments would in turn be highly influenced by the degree to which the Mexican government protected concessionaires from the effects of specification changes, inflation, and traffic shortfalls. Therefore, it was difficult to predict a priori whether the total costs of construction would be higher or lower under the concession mechanism than those incurred in the context of the traditional approach.

As for the operating and maintenance costs related to toll roads, the concession approach seemed to provide superior incentives for efficiency. Traditionally, CAPUFE was charged with toll road operation and maintenance, leaving these functions subject to the X-inefficiencies typically associated with public ownership (Leibenstein 1966). Yet, under the concession approach, the winning bidder was responsible for toll road operation and maintenance in addition to construction. Therefore, in theory, costs would be minimized across all three activities. However, with respect to capital costs associated with operation and maintenance, private concessionaires would presumably be at a cost disadvantage relative to public sector entities, as discussed above.

Based on these analyses of costs, it would seem that, at least in theory, the concession mechanism would limit the profitability of construction companies to normal returns. In contrast, the unit-cost bidding process underlying the traditional approach to road development might more easily enable private construction companies to earn excess returns. However, certain factors could conceivably allow construction companies to also earn excess returns under the concession mechanism.

For example, if the intensity of competition in the concession bidding process was mitigated by collusion among the bidders or by the limited number of qualified bidders willing and able to compete, the lowest bid submitted might still incorporate monopoly rents.[8] On the other hand, construction companies might actually earn below-normal profits on their concession business if the government failed to compensate concessionaires adequately for unanticipated changes in specifications, prices, and traffic volumes.

With respect to quality of construction, operation, and maintenance, it was not clear, a priori, that a shift to toll road concessions would have a significant impact on outcomes. Under both the traditional and the concession approach, the SCT was responsible for monitoring the quality of construction materials and the workmanship of private builders. In the case of toll road operations and maintenance, the SCT was responsible for monitoring the performance of CAPUFE under the traditional development process and the performance of the winning bidder under the concession mechanism. Since it was unclear whether CAPUFE or a private concessionaire would have a greater proclivity to slack behavior, quality differences between the two regimes were difficult to predict. However, given that a reduction in maintenance expenditures by concessionaires translated directly into higher dividends, there appeared to be significant incentives for the winning bidder to underinvest in toll highway maintenance. Nevertheless, this incentive was tempered by the SCT's authority to terminate any concession found to be in noncompliance with government maintenance standards.

The price charged for toll road usage was likely to be higher under the concession approach than under the traditional approach. Since highways constructed under contract bidding were publicly owned, the government could choose to recover the costs associated with any particular road through tax revenues or tolls. And even if costs were to be covered exclusively through tolls, the government would be able to set toll levels based on the expected life of the highway. In contrast, toll levels for concession highways had to be set high enough so that investors could recover all costs by the end of the concession term, a period presumably shorter than the life of the highway. Therefore, it appeared that the concession mechanism would lead to relatively higher toll rates unless (1) cost savings achieved through concession bidding more than offset the shorter investment recovery period, or (2) the tariffs charged on CAPUFE-operated toll roads were set at a premium in order to subsidize other government activities in addition to providing a return on highway investment.

The likely impact on allocative efficiency of a shift from the traditional to the concession approach seemed generally positive. The output of "highway services" had been suboptimally constrained under the traditional development approach, at least during the 1980s, as a result of the government's limited borrowing capacity combined with the absence of any mechanism through which direct private investment in highway projects could take place. However, the concession approach allowed for the willingness of road users to pay for additional highways to be translated into higher levels of toll road construction. Also, since concessionaires were granted the right to develop roadside services along toll highways, at least some of the positive externalities associated with road development would be internalized into the bidding process. If the government wished to provide additional encouragement to toll road development in areas where it believed that externalities extended significantly beyond roadside service profits, it could subsidize concessions along these routes through the infusion of public sector equity in the projects.

The concession mechanism, however, did raise an important concern with respect to allocative efficiency. Since toll levels were set so as to allow the concessionaire to recover total costs over a period of under twenty years, the price charged for road usage would presumably exceed the marginal cost of road usage by a substantial amount. Thus, the more elastic the demand for highway usage, the greater would be the loss in allocative efficiency resulting from toll road underutilization. Nevertheless, this average cost-pricing approach could still be regarded as a second-best strategy, since a first-best strategy—such as the use of general tax revenues or lump-sum charges to recover fixed costs of highway development—appeared to be impractical in the Mexican context at the time the concession mechanism was introduced. Therefore, it seemed that the shift to highway concessions, while theoretically providing a more socially optimal level of highway infrastructure development, would not at the same time lead to optimal utilization of this infrastructure.

Finally, the net impact of the shift to the toll road concession mechanism on government administrative costs was unclear. In particular, the adoption of a more private sector approach to highway development could not be equated with a reduction in the level of government regulatory activity. The SCT not only continued to be responsible for setting technical specifications under the new approach but was also required to develop traffic projections based on alternative toll scenarios. Although the fiduciary trust oversaw the disbursement of investment funds during the construction period and the distribution of toll receipts during the operating phase, the SCT was still charged with monitoring and enforcing highway quality standards over the course of the concession. In addition, the SCT was responsible for reviewing and responding to requests for concession extensions and toll rate increases during the concession period. If such requests led to the repeated renegotiation of concession terms, the concession mechanism in practice would appear less like a Demsetz-style (one-time) auction and more like franchise bidding processes identified by Williamson (1976), in which the transactions costs associated with ongoing recontracting lead to outcomes (in terms of administrative costs) little different from those found under traditional regulation. Thus, ironically, a shift to privately financed and operated toll road concessions would not necessarily imply a reduction in administrative costs relative to those incurred under the contract bidding system.

In theory, Mexico's shift from a reliance on its traditional contract bidding approach for highway infrastructure development to the use of a complex toll road concession mechanism could lead to increased highway investment, more rapid completion of new roads, improved technical efficiency in highway construction, operation, and maintenance, and net gains in allocative efficiency, without sacrificing road quality or increasing administrative costs. However, depending on the government's implementation of the program, some if not all of the putative benefits of a shift toward concessions could be illusory in practice. The following section provides evidence on the performance of the toll road concession program through mid-1994 and thus allows us to compare theoretical predictions with actual outcomes.

Trends in the Mexican Toll Road Concession Program

In late 1987 the de la Madrid administration initiated an experimental toll road program, which served as a forerunner to the highway concession approach adopted two years later. Under the terms of the experiment, two toll roads totaling 215 kilometers were developed under the auspices of BANOBRAS and two state governments, which collectively provided the majority of the financing for the projects. However, several private companies involved in the construction of the roads were asked to make investments in the highways in exchange for dividends paid from future toll revenues generated over a twenty-year period. Based on this experience, the Mexican government developed the more complex concession mechanism introduced by President Salinas in 1989.

The evolution of Mexico's highway concession approach from 1989 through mid-1994 is reviewed below in terms of both general performance and government policy responses. A more detailed analysis of outcomes follows in the form of short case studies of two major private sector participants in the concession program: the construction-engineering firms Empresas ICA Sociedad Controladora, S.A. de C.V. (ICA), and Grupo Tribasa, S.A. de C.V. (Tribasa).

General Trends

With respect to a number of indicators, the Mexican toll roads program got off to a promising start early in the Salinas administration. Mexican construction firms and financial institutions demonstrated strong interest in the program, and winning bids during the early rounds of concessions averaged approximately ten years, only half of the allowed maximum concession term. During 1990 and 1991, roughly 500 kilometers per year of high-quality concessioned toll roads were placed in operation, rivaling output levels during the peak years of the French and Spanish private toll road programs (Gómez-Ibáñez and Meyer 1993, 155). Over time, Mexican capital markets developed increasingly sophisticated financial instruments to support concessioned toll roads, including both medium-long-term infrastructure bonds secured by banks and by certificates of participation (debt securities secured solely by the toll revenues of a specific concession).[9] Foreign investors also displayed growing interest in the toll roads program through their purchases of international offerings of certificates of participation as well as debt and equity securities issued by major Mexican construction companies.

In spite of these favorable trends, the concession program experienced a number of serious difficulties in the early years, particularly in the areas of construction cost and traffic volume. Cost overruns, in one case (the Cuernavaca-Acapulco highway) exceeding 100 percent of the original projected budget, were attributed to a variety of factors. Concessionaires cited changes in the original (government-stipulated) technical specifications as the chief source of higher costs and, typically, construction delays as well. For example, unanticipated difficulties involving terrain along certain routes sometimes compelled the concessionaire to make costly adjustments to the construction plan. In other cases, specifications were altered as a result of pressure from environmentalists or local property owners. However, another possible source of cost overruns was the cost padding of concession-related construction services. Although concessionaires maintained that their construction expenses were fair and reasonable, it was virtually impossible to determine the degree of reasonableness, particularly for projects beset with significant changes in technical specifications.

Following the construction phase, many concessionaires were faced with another serious problem: actual traffic volumes significantly below levels forecast by the SCT. In effect, the SCT overestimated the demand for concession toll roads at the high price levels it had set to attract investors to the program: about 500 pesos per kilometer (US$0.28 per mile) on average (Stanfield 1991, 11).[10] Apparently, historic data on demand for Mexico's publicly owned toll roads were of little help in guiding the estimation of demand elasticities for the concession highways, given that the rates charged on CAPUFE's highways were only a fraction of the levels envisioned for the new toll roads.[11] Traffic forecasting was further complicated by the need to estimate the impact of the availability of parallel free roads on demand for concession highways.

Reacting to both cost overruns and traffic shortfalls, virtually all concessionaires approached the SCT during the early 1990s to obtain relief. The concessionaires appeared to be in a fairly strong negotiating position, for two reasons. On the one hand, concession agreements explicitly included provisions that protected firms against changes in technical specifications and specific traffic volumes. In addition, if the government refused to grant concessionaires satisfactory compensation, construction companies and financial institutions might simply avoid participation in future concession offerings, thus placing in question the long-run viability of the toll road program and perhaps other related government initiatives.

The Government Response

The Mexican government responded to concessionaires' concerns in several ways. With respect to existing concessions, the government compensated concessionaires for cost increases and demand shortfalls by sanctioning public sector capital infusions, tariff increases, concession extensions, and more complex schemes on a case-by-case basis. Regarding future concessions, the government worked to refine its capabilities in the areas of technical specification and traffic forecasting while, at the same time, shifting more of the risk for cost overruns and traffic shortfalls onto the concessionaires.

Renegotiations The problem of cost overruns was most dramatic in the case of the Cuernavaca-Acapulco concession, a high-profile project awarded in 1989 to a joint venture concessionaire owned by Mexico's three largest construction companies. The technical specifications of this highway were based primarily on an extrapolation of the analysis completed on the initial third of the highway, which traversed the least complex terrain of the route. After it became clear that the actual scope of the project was substantially greater than estimated, the SCT secured additional financial commitments for the project in the form of (non-dividend earning) equity contributions from CAPUFE, PEMEX, and the state government of Guerrero. In general, an increased willingness of the Mexican government to subsidize toll road construction during the early years of the concession program is borne out by data showing a rise in participation of government capital in concessions from 10 percent of total investment in 1990 to 23 percent in 1992 (Gómez-Ibáñez and Meyer 1993, 157–58).[12]

Although it was not obligated to do so, the SCT in some circumstances permitted concessionaires to raise toll rates to compensate for insufficient traffic volumes. For example, the concessionaire for the Constituyentes–La Marquesa highway was allowed to raise tariffs 60 percent (from approximately 455 pesos per kilometer to 727 pesos per kilometer) after actual traffic levels were found to be 25 percent below projections. Although demand fell by 17 percent after the price increase, total revenues increased sufficiently to compensate for the original shortfall (*Mexico City–Toluca Toll Road* 1992, A-9, A-11, A-39).

In principle, the Mexican government preferred to deal with unfavorable specification changes and traffic shortfalls through concession extensions, since this mechanism entailed neither additional public sector outlays nor toll increases to the general public. However, the SCT's ability to lengthen concessions was initially limited by Mexico's twenty-year restriction on the concession term. In June 1992 the government extended the maximum allowable highway concession length to thirty years, and the trickle of concession renegotiations became a flood. By 1994 virtually all of the concessions granted during the early years of the program had been extended or were in advanced stages of renegotiation. In a number of cases, original concession terms were doubled or tripled.

At times, the SCT's negotiated settlement with a concessionaire was more complex. For example, in one instance (the Guadalajara-Tepic concession), the government coupled a concession extension with the grant of an additional concession over a preexisting government-owned toll road as compensation for difficulties encountered in the construction and operation of the original concession. In another cases (the Mexico City–Toluca Highway), the SCT granted a concession extension in conjunction with a privately initiated concession refinancing that included a lump-sum payment to the government to be used for public sector equity investments in other highway projects.

Policy Changes Government officials and private sector participants in the toll road program acknowledged that, in spite of difficulties associated with many of the early concessions, by 1992 the concession mechanism had begun to function more effectively for new highways. The SCT's accuracy with respect to design specifications and traffic projections improved dramatically and, at the same time, construction contractors and financial investors became increasingly sophisticated as participants in the program. At this time, the Mexican government began to implement several policy changes designed to leverage off the growing predictability of the concession mechanism.

The lengthening of the maximum concession term from twenty to thirty years in June 1992 was not only useful with respect to renegotiation but also made the concession mechanism more attractive for new toll roads, particularly in areas where traffic density or income levels might be insufficient to support a shorter-term concession. The government announced that same year that it was willing to promote larger public sector equity shares in new concessions but with an important change from previous policy: government contributions would henceforth be eligible to receive dividends on the same terms as other concession equity holdings. This change allowed the government to increase the attractiveness of certain marginal concessions and yet participate as a co-owner, as opposed to merely a subsidizer, of these highways.

The improved planning and forecasting abilities of both the public and private sector with respect to toll roads led the SCT by 1993 to omit guarantees with respect to cost overruns and traffic levels in some concession specifications, in effect shifting supply and demand risk to the concessionaires and their financial partners. For example, the SCT awarded a fixed-price contract (subject to adjustment for inflation) for the construction of a portion of the Mexico City–Guadalajara concession; concession for the La Venta–Colegio Militar highway explicitly denied the winning bidder the right to petition for a concession extension in the case of traffic shortfalls (Grupo Tribasa 1993, 8, 18). In the case of the latter concession, however, if traffic levels *exceeded* projected levels, the SCT retained the right to reduce the length of the concession.

One more significant change in policy occurred in January 1994 as a new federal law took effect that required competitive bidding in the award of all future concessions. In essence, the new policy prohibited the SCT from granting uncontested concessions for toll routes as part of negotiated agreements with existing concessionaires or other entities. Although this reform reduced the SCT's flexibility in the renegotiation of concessions, it reduced the chances that new concession awards would be subject to favoritism and made more transparent the terms of negotiated settlements that the SCT did reach in conjunction with the toll road concession program.

Program Outcomes

The relatively accommodating posture of the Mexican government with respect to toll road concessionaires during the early 1990s presumably helped keep the ambitious master highway plan on schedule. By mid-1994, more than 5,200 kilometers of toll road concessions had been granted, almost 3,500 kilometers of which were in operation. Thus it appeared that Mexico would attain Salinas's initial goal of developing 4,000 kilometers of concession highways by the end of 1994. In addition, the government was able to draw on its track record with respect to road concessions to attract investments for concessions in other infrastructural areas, including ports and harbors.

In terms of costs, the performance of the program was somewhat more difficult to evaluate. Total expenditures through mid-1994 were estimated at 33.0 billion new pesos, a figure that would appear to exceed by 200 percent the program costs of 11.5 trillion pesos estimated at the outset of the initiative.[13] Yet, this comparison is deceptive given the greater number of highway kilometers under construction in 1994 than originally anticipated and, more significantly, the considerable price inflation experienced over the period.[14] Therefore, although the costs of the Mexican highway concession program exceeded original projections, it is not clear how uncharacteristic these deviations were for heavy construction projects of this nature.

What impact did the Mexican highway concession program have on the concessionaires themselves from 1989 to 1994? An examination of the experiences of the construction firms Empresas ICA and Grupo Tribasa provides not only a private sector perspective on the program but also insights into the actual government mechanisms. The following sections present brief case studies of ICA's and Tribasa's participation in the toll road concession program through early 1994.

Empresas ICA Sociedad Controladora, S.A. de C.V.

Mexico's largest construction firm was founded in 1947 as Ingenieros Civiles Asociados, S.A. de C.V. (ICA) and participated subsequently in a wide variety of projects for private sector and public sector clients, including highway construction. During the 1980s, ICA responded to the bleak state of Mexico's construction industry by diversifying increasingly into other businesses. Late in the administration of President de la Madrid, ICA was invited to participate in an experimental concession program to build and operate a toll road from Guadalajara to Colima. Although ICA's share in the project was relatively small, its participation provided an excellent opportunity for the firm to learn about the concession program from its inception.[15]

ICA bid aggressively for concessions in 1989 and won participation in three toll roads: the Cuernavaca-Acapulco, the Guadalajara-Tepic, and the Tampico-bypass highways (table 10-2). However, the SCT significantly revised the technical specifications for each of these highways during the construction period. When these roads opened in 1991, traffic levels were significantly lower than originally projected. Shortly thereafter, ICA began negotiating with the SCT for changes in the

Table 10-2. Empresas ICA Sociedad Controladora, Highway Concession Investments, 1989–1994

Concession Route	ICA ownership share (%)	Length (km.)	Year Awarded	Original Concession	Year Renegotiated	Renegotiated Concession	ICA Investment on 12/31/93 (1993 NP mill.)
Cuernavaca to Acapulco	33	262	1989	14 yrs., 8 mos.	1993[1]	30 yrs.[1]	492
Guadalajara to Tepic	100	194	1989	8 yrs., 5 mos.	1992	20 yrs.	1,211
Tampico bypass	81	15	1989	12 yrs.	[2]	n.a.	124
San Martín to Tlaxcala to El Molinito	20	26	1990	10 yrs., 3 mos.	1994	25 yrs., 5 mos.	5[3]
León to Lagos to Aguascalientes	40	116	1990	18 yrs., 5 mos.	[2]	n.a.	92
Mazatlán to Culiacán	40	291	1990	17 yrs., 5 mos.	1994	30 yrs.	169
Torreón to Saltillo	40	230	1992	7 yrs., 5 mos.	1994	25 yrs.	9
Mexico City to Guadalajara	34	340	1992	18 yrs., 3 mos.	n.a.	n.a.	74
Guadalajara to Zapotlanejo	100	26	1992	20 yrs.	n.a.	n.a.	4[4]
Total		1,500					2,176

Source: Empresas ICA Sociedad Controladora 1992a, 1992b, 1993.

Note: Includes developments through mid-June 1994.

[1] Agreement in principle reached with the Mexican government in late 1993 would extend concession to 30 years.

[2] ICA in discussions with Mexican government in 1994 with aim of concession renegotiation.

[3] Estimate.

[4] Included within Guadalajara-Tepic investment.

n.a. = not applicable.

concession agreements to compensate for cost increases and revenue shortfalls.

From 1990 to 1992 concessionaires owned in part or in full by ICA won bids on five additional toll roads. On average, the tariff levels specified by the SCT for these routes were considerably lower and the winning concession term was of longer duration than those associated with 1989 concessions awarded to ICA.[16] Although ICA experienced some problems with respect to technical specifications and traffic volume associated with concessions awarded after 1989, these difficulties were not as serious as those encountered with earlier concessions. In the case of the Mexico City–Guadalajara highway, it appeared by early 1994 that the project's total cost would be substantially below the initial estimate on which the concession was based. These results would seem to provide support for the contention that the government had indeed moved rapidly down the "learning curve" with respect to concession design.

A major challenge faced by ICA and other construction companies participating in the highway concession program was generating sufficient capital to support the equity stakes they were required to take in the toll roads. By the end of 1991, investments in concessions represented almost one-third of ICA's total assets, and the firm's equity base appeared inadequate to support any additional toll road investments. To help relieve this constraint, ICA launched an initial public equity offering in April 1992, raising US$450 million on international capital markets (or approximately 25% of ICA's equity base after the public offering). ICA also pursued several opportunities for reducing its equity investments in completed toll roads. In May 1992 the firm arranged to sell its equity interest in the Guadalajara-Colima concession at book value to a trust established by BANOBRAS and financed through bonds secured by the concession's toll revenues and guaranteed by BANOBRAS. Later that year ICA was able to sell a portion of its equity stakes in the Mazatlán-Culiacán concession and the León-Lagos-Aguascalientes concession to other firms involved in the construction of those projects. Through these efforts, ICA was able to lower its investments in toll road concessions by approximately 35 percent by the end of 1992.

ICA's efforts to renegotiate the terms of its concessions began to bear fruit in late 1992, when a complex arrangement was reached with the government with respect to the Plan de Barrancas (Guadalajara-Tepic) highway. Whereas the original concession entailed the construction and operation of a 22-kilometer toll road over a period of eight years and five months, the amended agreement granted ICA a twenty-year concession for an extension of the original highway to cover the entire 194-kilometer route from Guadalajara to Tepic. As part of the settlement, ICA was also granted a twenty-year concession to upgrade the existing 26-kilometer Guadalajara-Zapotlanejo (government-owned) toll road from two lanes to four, as well as operate and maintain the road, in exchange for the toll receipts collected on the route. However, ICA agreed to pay the Mexican government a total of 249 million new pesos out of residual toll revenues earned on the Guadalajara-Zapotlanejo route over the life of the concession.

ICA renegotiated the terms of three other toll roads with the government through mid-1994, resulting in each case in a substantial lengthening of the concession period: on average, the terms were more than doubled (table 10-2).[17] In addition, the firm obtained a waiver from the government with regard to the 249 million new pesos it initially agreed to pay in conjunction with the Guadalajara-Zapotlanejo concession. As of June 1994, ICA was still in negotiations with the SCT to revise the terms of the Tampico-bypass and the León-Lagos-Aguascalientes concessions. At the same time, ICA—along with its joint venture partners—were actively exploring options for refinancing the Cuernavaca-Acapulco concession, which was able to meet only half of its debt service obligations after payment of operating and maintenance expenses.

In light of the difficulties encountered along the way in conjunction with the highway concession program, how profitable has the toll road concession business been for ICA? The data presented in table 10-3 suggest that ICA's returns on its concession construction activities have been quite high since the inception of the program. Specifically, gross margins on concession construction exceeded 33 percent during every year from 1990 to 1993, almost twice the percentage earned by ICA on its other construction activities. Also, over time concession construction accounted for an ever larger share of ICA's total construction revenues and gross profits.

How has ICA been able to earn such impressive returns on its concession construction contracts, in spite of the competitive bidding process that underlies the program? There are several possible explanations. First, competition for concessions may not have been very fierce, particularly during the first few years of the program. On the one hand, most construction firms were capital-constrained after a decade of austerity and in many cases may not have had the requisite equipment and technical skills to undertake sophisticated highway projects. In fact three firms—ICA, GMD, and Tribasa—accounted for over half of all concession investment in 1989–91, and in some cases, these firms worked together as concessionaire partners. On the other hand, the volume of concession business projected at the beginning of the program was enormous: 11.5 trillion pesos over five years (65% of the 1990 revenue of Mexico's entire construction industry). Therefore, the few competing firms probably felt that, at least in the short term, they could each

Table 10-3. Empresas ICA Sociedad Controladora, Financial Indicators, 1990–1993 (thousands of constant new pesos, as of December 31, 1993)

Financial Indicator	1993	1992	1991	1990
Revenues				
Concession construction	2,043	1,540	708	415
Other construction	3,129	3,694	3,506	2,376
Concessions	298	92	71	5
Gross profits				
Concession construction	747	515	275	140
Other construction	595	708	753	374
Gross margin (%)				
Concession construction	36.6	33.4	38.9	33.4
Other construction	19.0	19.2	21.5	15.7
Operating Earnings				
All construction	954	808	734	263
Concessions	–43	–24	10	–2
Assets (year end)				
All construction	6,239	5,096	2,789	2,291
Concessions	2,303	1,819	2,838	780
Operating return on average assets (%)				
All construction	16.8	20.5	28.9	13.4
Concessions	–2.1	–1.0	0.5	–0.5

Source: Calculated from Empresas ICA Sociedad Controladora (1992b, 1993).

Note: "Other construction" includes industrial, urban, housing, transportation (subway), and major nonconcessioned infrastructure construction. "Concessions" includes all investments in concessionaires, whether involving majority or minority ownership. In the case of minority investments, net earnings are used in lieu of operating earnings.

secure a comfortable share of the concession business without resorting to bids with razor-thin margins.

A second possible explanation relates to changes in specifications and the delays associated with many of the early projects. Although concessionaires insisted that all cost increases experienced on these projects could be attributed to government actions, it is possible that the firms padded their costs to some extent under the guise of "public sector mismanagement." Since the government compensated for these cost overruns by contributing public sector equity to some of the projects, participating firms may have been able to raise their margins.

A third interpretation is that the high margins may be an incomplete and possibly deceptive measure of the long-run profitability of the toll road business. Although firms generate substantial profits during the construction stage of the concession, they are able to accomplish this only by investing significant sums of capital in the concessionaire in the form of equity capital. Depending on debt repayment terms and toll revenues, this equity may or may not generate substantial profits over the life of the concession. In the case of ICA, the firm's concessionaires collectively incurred losses in 1990, 1992, and 1993 as a result of toll revenues that were inadequate relative to operating and maintenance costs, amortization, and debt service (table 10-3). Although ICA reduced its absolute and relative exposure to concession investments after 1991, concession assets still accounted for over 2,300 new pesos at year-end 1993—an amount greater than the sum of gross profits in ICA's concession construction since the program began. Concession renegotiations should help improve the profitability of ICA's concession investments by extending the years of toll revenue flowing to the firm and by reducing annual amortization charges. However, the expected returns on these investments are still considerably below those earned on construction activities and remain subject to future uncertainty with respect to toll revenues and government policy.[18]

In summary, Empresas ICA appears to have profited handsomely in the short term from construction contracts associated with concession toll roads but in return has thus far incurred ongoing losses related to its required sweat equity investments in the concessionaires. Although the firm has been relatively successful in renegotiating concession terms with the government, it is unclear whether ICA's long-run returns associated with the toll road business (both construction and concession activities) will prove to be higher or lower than the returns on its traditional (nonconcession) construction business. Below, we compare ICA's experience with that of Tribasa, one of its principal partners and competitors in the program.

Grupo Tribasa, S.A. de C.V.

Although Mexico's second largest construction firm in 1993, Tribasa was founded in 1969 as Triturados Basálticos y Derivados, S.A. de C.V., a firm devoted to the production of construction aggregates and asphalt concrete. In 1974 the firm expanded its activities to include construction of roads, drainage facilities, and other public works projects. Between 1989 and 1993, Tribasa experienced compound annual (real) growth in revenues and assets of approximately 100 percent as a result of its active participation in toll road concession projects. The rapid expansion of the firm was facilitated by partnerships and an eventual 1993 merger with Cimentaciones y Edificaciones, S.A. de C.A., a firm specializing in bridge construction, and Gimsa Industrial, S.A. de C.V., a company experienced in industrial construction.

Table 10-4 profiles Tribasa's role in highway concessions through mid-1994, including participation in ten federal-sponsored and two state-sponsored toll roads.[19] As was the case for ICA, Tribasa faced con-

Table 10-4. Grupo Tribasa, Highway Concession Investments, 1989–1994

Concession Route	Tribasa Ownership Share (%)	Length (km.)	Year Awarded	Original Concession	Year Renegotiated/ Securitized	Renegotiated Concession (months)	Gain from Securitization (1993 NP, mill.)	Tribasa Investment on 12/31/93 (1993 NP, mill.)
Cuernavaca to Acapulco	30	263	1989	14 yrs., 8 mos.	1993/n.a.	30[1]	n.a.	1,007
Constituyentes to La Marquesa	100	22	1989	2 yrs., 4 mos.	1991/92	13	203	0
Mazatlán to Culiacán	40	294	1990	17 yrs., 5 mos.	1994/n.a.	30	n.a.	250
Armería to Manzanillo	100	37	1990[2]	9 yrs., 3 mos.	1992/93	14[2]	56	0
Ecatepec to Pirámides	100	22	1991[2]	3 yrs., 11 mos.	1992/93	21[2]	3[3]	170
Chamapa to La Venta	100	14	1991[2]	16 yrs., 0 mos.[2]	n.a./1993	n.a.	32	103
Chamapa to Lecheria	100	27	1991[2]	18 yrs., 4 mos.	n.a./n.a.	n.a.	n.a.	1,060
Torreón to Saltillo	40	246	1992	7 yrs., 5 mos.	1994/n.a.	25	n.a.	9
Mexico City to Guadalajara	25	340	1992	18 yrs., 3 mos.	n.a./n.a.	n.a.	n.a.	54
Peñón to Texcoco	100	16	1993[2]	20 yrs., 0 mos.	n.a./n.a.	n.a.	n.a.	126
La Venta to Colegio Militar	100	26	1993	20 yrs., 0 mos.	n.a./n.a.	n.a.	n.a.	0
Reynosa to Matamoros	100	79	1994	22 yrs., 0 mos.	n.a./n.a.	n.a.	n.a.	0
Total		1,386					291	2,779

Source: Grupo Tribasa (1993); *Mexico City-Toluca Toll Road* (1992); Stanfield (1991, app.)

Note: Includes developments through mid-June 1994.

[1] Agreement in principle reached with the Mexican government in late 1993 would extend concession to 30 years.

[2] Estimate based on highway opening date and other relevant data.

[3] Gain included under the Armería-Manzanillo concession.

n.a. = not applicable.

siderable specification changes and traffic shortfalls with respect to concessions received in the early years of the program. However, rather than simply work to renegotiate concession terms with the government, Tribasa also explored opportunities for refinancing its initial concessions so as to liquidate all or part of its investment stake in each venture. This innovative "securitization" strategy enabled Tribasa, by 1993, to reduce its investment in four highway concessions, while realizing an aggregate gain of 291 million new pesos.

The first of Tribasa's securitizations was completed in June 1992 with respect to the Constituyentes–La Marquesa toll highway running from Mexico City to Toluca. Tribasa's initial concession for this route, the Reforma–La Venta toll road, had been awarded in July 1989 for a twenty-eight-month term and covered only eleven kilometers. Specification changes in response to protests from environmentalists contributed to construction cost overruns, and when the highway began operations in October 1990 traffic levels fell 25 percent below government estimates. In February 1991 the government allowed the concessionaire to raise toll rates by 60 percent, and by December 1991 the SCT agreed to extend the concession an additional ten years in exchange for Tribasa (1) extending the highway to encompass an additional eleven kilometers, and (2) making a payment of 320 billion pesos (approximately US$103 million) to the SCT for use as public investment in other toll road concessions.

The SCT agreed that its supplemental payment could be funded through a refinancing mechanism, proposed by Tribasa, that involved the issue of debt securities backed solely by the concession's anticipated toll revenues. With the help of a financial syndicate led by Lehman Brothers International, Tribasa was able to successfully market the so-called toll revenue indexed participation securities (TRIPS) to international and domestic investors, raising a total of US$312.7 million. After applying the net proceeds to retire the concession's existing debt and to fund the payment to the SCT, Tribasa realized a gain of approximately 190 billion pesos on its remaining book equity of about 40 billion pesos in the concession.[20] Tribasa agreed to reinvest the entire (after-tax) gain in new highway concessions.[21]

Encouraged by investor interest in toll road receipts, Tribasa pursued additional securitizations during 1993. In October the company completed a securitized financing in the Mexican capital markets based on toll revenues from the Chamapa–La Venta highway, enabling the firm to reduce its investment in the concession by approximately 170 million new pesos while realizing a gain of 32 million new pesos on the transaction. However, since the term of the securities was shorter than the remaining life of the concession, Tribasa retained a book investment of 103 million new pesos in the concession. In November, the company securitized the toll revenues from two additional concessions, the Ecatepec-Pirámides and the Armería-Manzanillo highways, in a single international placement.[22] Through this transaction, Tribasa reduced its concession investments by 280 million new pesos, realized a gain of 56 million new pesos, and retained an investment of 170 million new pesos in the Ecatepec-Pirámides toll road (Grupo Tribasa 1993, F-18). In addition to its toll receipt securitizations, Tribasa made two offerings of common equity to the international capital markets. These issues included an initial public offering in late 1993 and a second issue in early 1994, which together raised approximately US$200 million for reducing Tribasa's short-term debt and for increasing its investment in toll roads and other projects. During this same period, Tribasa was awarded two additional concessions. As an amendment to its Constituyentes–La Marquesa concession, Tribasa received a twenty-five-year concession to build and operate the La Venta–Colegio Militar toll road. However, this concession was not subject to extension if traffic volumes fell below projections. This nonextension provision was also included in the Reynosa-Matamoros highway concession awarded to Tribasa in early 1994.

How profitable has the toll road concession business been to Tribasa as compared to ICA? Data in table 10-5 suggest that Tribasa's gross margins on concession construction have been as attractive as ICA's. However, disaggregated data from the company's financial statements indicate that Tribasa's construction margins on its wholly owned concessions have been considerably higher than the margins attained from concessions in which it holds a minority stake. As was true for ICA, Tribasa's operating return on concession assets was negative in 1992 and 1993, contrasting sharply with returns on the construction business. These negative results appear even more worrisome in the case of Tribasa, since by 1993, more than 50 percent of its total assets were accounted for by concession investments, as opposed to about 20 percent for ICA. Although Tribasa has realized several impressive one-time gains from its securitization initiatives, its cumulative reduction in concession investments made possible by these offerings (approximately 490 million new pesos) is dwarfed by the level of investments in highway concessions held by the firm as of December 1993 (2,779 million new pesos). Thus, overall, it is as hard to evaluate for Tribasa as it is for ICA what the combined long-term return on concession construction, plus sweat equity investment, will be for the firm.

Preliminary Assessment

Given the experience of the Mexican highway concession program from 1989 to mid-1994, what can we say about the effects of Mexico's shift

Table 10-5. Grupo Tribasa, Financial Indicators, 1991–1993 (thousands of constant new pesos, as of December 31, 1993)

Financial Indicator	1993	1992	1991
Revenues			
All construction	2,128	1,779	1,301
Majority-owned concessionaires	689	345	199
Other concessionaires	1,253	1,403	1,002
Concessions	160	165	162
Gross profits			
All construction	807	570	451
Majority-owned concessionaires	376	132	84
Other concessionaires	347	425	327
Gross margin (%)			
All construction	37.9	32.0	34.6
Majority-owned concessionaires	54.5	38.3	42.3
Other concessionaires	27.7	30.3	32.7
Operating earnings			
All construction	727	465	358
Concessions	−35	−20	36
Assets (year end)			
All construction	3,109	2,085	1,448
Concessions	2,298	1,992	898
Operating return on average assets (%)			
All construction	28.0	26.3	n.a.
Concessions	−1.0	−1.0	n.a.

Source: Calculated from Grupo Tribasa (1993).

Note: "Other concessionaires" include concessionaires in which Tribasa holds a minority equity share as a joint venture or associated partner. "Concessions" includes all investment in concessionaires, whether involving majority or minority ownership. In the case of minority investments, net earnings are used in lieu of operating earnings.

n.a. = not available.

from its traditional approach for highway development to the toll road concession mechanism? With respect to the level of private investment, the program appears to have been relatively successful in attracting new sources of private capital for highway infrastructure development. The sizable returns earned on concession-related construction business, combined with the flexibility that the government has shown with respect to concession renegotiation, have helped to attract not only investment but also new financial instruments tailored to the long-term characteristics of concession projects. Private domestic investors have supported the program, and foreign investors have helped finance toll road concessions as well, both through equity investments in Mexican construction companies and through purchases of bonds backed by toll revenues generated by specific highways.

Public sector entities have contributed over 20 percent of total investment in toll road concessions, both where the government believed the positive externalities associated with a route's development to be high and in certain cases in which changes in initial specifications led to major construction cost overruns.[23] However, the government has been less willing over time to regard its concession equity stakes as grants, preferring instead to treat them as investments, with all the corresponding rights and obligations of ownership.

In terms of the speed of construction, the program appears to have been very successful, since as of mid-1994 more than 5,200 kilometers of concession toll roads were either in operation or under construction. Although construction delays were experienced on a number of toll road projects early in the program, these lags were largely attributable to changes in technical specifications made by the SCT after the concession had been awarded. Construction delays have become much less frequent over time, however, as both the SCT and the concessionaires have accumulated experience with the program.

The effects of the concession mechanism on construction, operating, and maintenance costs are difficult to assess. Although it seems reasonable to assume that technical efficiency has improved as a result of the cost-minimizing incentives inherent in the concession bidding process and from the reduction in construction delays achieved under the new approach, there are no hard data to support the conjecture that a shift to toll road concessions has reduced the costs of highway infrastructure development. In addition, the higher cost of capital faced by private investors relative to the government would tend to offset, at least to some extent, the putative cost advantages associated with the concession mechanism. Finally, the substantial changes in technical specifications that affected many of the early concessions during the construction period presumably led to increases in construction costs that could have been avoided if the SCT had correctly specified the relevant parameters during the bidding phase.

The toll road concession program appears to have had a highly favorable impact on the profitability of construction companies, at least in the short run. Although the high margins earned on concession construction may be attributable to a lack of effective competition at the bidding stage or cost padding during construction, they may alternatively serve to offset the low and uncertain profitability of equity investments that construction firms must make to gain access to the toll road concession business in the first place. In other words, the fact that construction companies have made substantial profits "up front" on concession construction does not ensure that their total return on concession-related investments will be above normal, as defined by the ex ante riskiness of these stakes.

During the first few years of the toll roads program, the government adopted a number of policies designed to offset risks associated with concession investment in order to assure program participants that their long-term returns would be protected. However, as concession specification and construction has become more precise and as traffic projections have become more accurate, the government has begun to offer fewer safeguards to investors in its terms for new concessions. Although these policy modifications should shift a larger share of concession risk from the government to concessionaires, the greater predictability of program parameters in general should lower overall risk and, therefore, preserve the attractiveness of the toll roads to investors.

To the extent that construction companies are able to employ a toll revenue securitization strategy to "cash out" concession equity investments at or above book value soon after construction has been completed, concerns regarding long-term profitability may be rendered moot. To date, Tribasa has pioneered this approach by selling participation in highway concessions to investors willing to accept the lower "utilitylike" returns commensurate with the lower risk of completed toll roads. Ultimately, if construction companies come to view their sweat equity concession stakes as relatively easy to divest early in the concession term, one would also expect these firms to accept lower margins on concession construction on future projects.

Although the quality of Mexico's concession toll roads has proved quite extraordinary relative to alternative free roads and older government-owned toll roads, the quality differential can be attributed not to the concession mechanism per se but instead to the specifications set by the SCT with respect to concession highway construction, operation, and maintenance. Given that few concession highways have been in operation for more than several years, it is too early to assess the SCT's effectiveness at monitoring the condition of concession roads over an extended period of time.

The prices charged for concession highway usage have been quite high relative to tariffs on government-owned toll roads in Mexico and have even exceeded the typical rates charged in most industrial countries. Although these high prices have attracted substantial investment in the Mexican toll road program, they have also served as a significant deterrent to concession highway usage. In spite of the fact that the government has actively promoted the time savings, greater safety, and improved riding comfort provided by concession highways relative to the alternative free roads, many drivers of passenger as well as commercial vehicles have yet to find that the value of these benefits exceeds their price. As a result, the SCT has tended to set lower toll rates over time for new highways. Of course, the ability of the SCT to lower toll rates has been facilitated by an increasing willingness of investors to provide capital for long-term concessions, combined with the change in Mexican law that, since mid-1992, has permitted the granting of concession terms of up to thirty years.

The implications of the toll road concession program for allocative efficiency have been mixed to date. The movement of substantial scarce resources into highway infrastructure has probably been justified from a social welfare perspective, given the magnitude of benefits provided by these highways relative to the costs of development.[24] However, the high toll levels charged on most of these roads have caused much of the potential benefits of the infrastructure to remain unrealized.[25] Nevertheless, efforts on the part of the scT to extend concession terms and to lower tariffs are presumably helping to increase social welfare by increasing highway utilization.

Finally, the shift from the traditional approach for highway infrastructure development to the use of toll road concessions cannot be said to have reduced government administrative costs. Both the scT and the Ministry of Finance have expended innumerable person-hours in support of the concession program, in the design of new concessions, and in the monitoring and renegotiation of existing concessions. Yet, although Mexico's toll road concession mechanism has thus far demonstrated greater similarities to an ongoing (Williamsonian) franchise mechanism than to a one-time (Demsetz-style) auction, the growing predictability of program parameters and the increasing rigidity of concession terms may over time lead to a substantial reduction in the program's administrative burden.

Conclusions

The Mexican toll road concession program demonstrates that a nation can develop a high-quality highway infrastructure in a relatively short period of time by relying primarily on private sector investors to finance, construct, and operate it. Perhaps most surprisingly, the experience suggests that this feat is possible even in a developing country emerging from a prolonged period of economic stagnation and hyperinflation. At the same time, Mexico's record suggests that the start-up costs of such an ambitious program may be considerable and that the price of toll road services, especially for lower-income drivers, may be prohibitive.

In general, the Mexican experience provides certain lessons for other nations hoping to embark on toll road concession programs. First, unless capital markets are well developed in the country, the government may have to offer a combination of high tolls and short concession terms in order to attract private investment, at least during the initial period of concession bidding. Unfortunately, this combination is costly from a social welfare perspective, since it tends to place the price for road usage far above its marginal cost. Second, to attract any investment at all, the government may have to assume many, if not most, of the risks associated with road development in the initial program phase by offering explicit and implicit guarantees to offset the impact of unanticipated changes in highway design, traffic levels, inflation, and other parameters.

An additional lesson is that the regulatory body responsible for managing the concession program must be well trained not only in the technical aspects of highway construction but also in statistical and economic analysis. Even Mexico's Secretariat of Communications and Transport—an agency filled with highly educated technocrats—struggled during the first years of the concession program to master the intricacies of the bid specification process. Furthermore, the regulatory body must continue to play an active oversight role not only during the bidding phase but also over the course of the entire concession term.

A particularly encouraging aspect of the Mexican case is its demonstration of the virtuous cycle, which may result over time as private and public sector entities become more experienced in and secure with the concession process. In particular, if the regulatory body can establish a reputation for fairness and consistency, private investors will be more likely to supply capital to future concessions, perhaps for longer terms and at lower rates. Similarly, as concessionaires establish solid profitability levels from concession construction, more firms will be attracted to the program, thus leading to greater competition at the bidding stage.

On balance, Mexico's toll road experience suggests that the benefits derived from the rapid implementation of a concession-based infrastructure initiative may well exceed the costs associated with a swift expansion of the program. In 1989, Mexico was emerging from a period of austerity, and the Salinas administration was determined to return the country to a condition of stable economic growth. By putting the toll road concession plan quickly into place, the government signalled its commitment to building a sustainable foundation for growth and to providing an environment in which the private sector could invest in and share the benefits of economic expansion. Although the speed with which the SCT added toll road concessions in 1989 and 1990 may have exacerbated the types of difficulties associated with start-up programs, it allowed the agency to move quickly along the "learning curve" and to establish the credibility of the government as an innovator and as a reliable partner for the private sector with respect to existing and future development initiatives.

NOTES

1. Infrastructure bonds were typically issued by two state-owned financial institutions: Mexico's national development bank, Nacional Financiera (NAFIN), and the national bank for public works, Banco Nacional de Obras y Servicios Públicos (BANOBRAS). Since 1960 the World Bank had also provided debt capital for road construction and maintenance.

2. This competition based on concession length distinguished Mexico's road privatization mechanism from those employed by other countries, e.g., France and Spain, which awarded concessions on the basis of cost criteria such as the level of equity invested, government subsidies requested, and toll rates proposed.

3. This constraint was relaxed in June 1992, when legislation was adopted extending the maximum length of toll road concessions to thirty years.

4. Most concessions entailed the construction of a completely new highway. However, in some instances, concessions were granted for the substantial upgrading of an existing road. Even in cases where the SCT changed specifications, concessionaires were officially required to absorb 15 percent of the cost overrun.

5. Initially, public sector "equity" was in effect a pure subsidy, since government equity holders were not entitled to receive dividends. However, by early 1992, the terms of new and renegotiated concessions typically conferred full ownership rights on public sector equity holders. See discussion below.

6. If multiple bids with identical concession periods were received, the government made its selection based on (in priority order): (1) shortest construction period, (2) total cost, (3) reliability of the proposed financing, and (4) experience and qualifications of the bidder.

7. Other financing sources might include internally generated funds, debt or equity contributions from the concessionaire's parent company, or external borrowings denominated in pesos or dollars.

8. One factor that could limit the number of qualified bidders was the condition that the concessionaire provide sweat equity in addition to construction services.

9. These developments were favorably influenced by the Salinas administration's policies to bring down inflation, renegotiate the country's foreign debt, and return the banking industry to the private sector.

10. The toll level specified in the concession documents for ICA's Tampico Bypass highway was 1,000 pesos per kilometer.

11. For example, rates for public toll roads in the Mexico City area were approximately 50 constant 1990 pesos per kilometer during the 1980s (*Mexico City–Toluca Toll Road* 1992).

12. Private concessionaire equity averaged 28–29 percent of total investment over the entire period.

13. The new peso replaced the old Mexican peso in January 1993. One new peso carried the value of 1,000 old pesos.

14. Inflation, as measured by Mexico's consumer price index (the INPC), was 30 percent in 1990, 19 percent in 1991, 10 percent in 1992, and 8 percent in 1993 (Banco de México 1993).

15. Seventy percent of the project investment was provided by public sector

entities, and the remaining capital took the form of sweat equity contributed by the construction firms Grupo Mexicano de Desarrollo (GMD), Gutsa, and ICA.

16. The average toll rate specified for ICA's 1990 concession highways was 227 pesos per kilometer, as compared with an average rate of 831 pesos per kilometer for its 1989 concessions. These figures were calculated from data provided in Stanfield (1991, appendix).

17. The extension of the Torreón-Saltillo concession from 7.5 years to 25 years was granted after protests by local residents led to fundamental changes in the highway design. Specifically, instead of upgrading an existing two-lane free road to a four-lane toll road, the amended concession required the concessionaire to construct a new two-lane toll highway that would run parallel to the preexisting free highway.

18. ICA's expected rate of return on individual concession investments at the time the concessions were awarded ranged from 6.0 to 12.1 percent (Empresas ICA 1993, F-16).

19. Tribasa participated as a joint venture partner with ICA in concessions for the Cuernavaca-Acapulco, Mazatlán-Culiacán, Torreón-Saltillo, and Mexico City–Guadalajara highways.

20. The book value of the investment at the time of the offering was estimated from data included in *Mexico City–Toluca Toll Road* (1992, 8, B-6).

21. Tribasa continued to be responsible for operating and maintaining the Constituyentes–La Marquesa highway after the securitization. However, the fees charged for these activities would be deducted from toll revenues before the (net) receipts were made available to the new security holders.

22. Prior to the securitization, the SCT had agreed to extend the concession terms for both of these highways to compensate for inadequate toll revenues, particularly on the Armería-Manzanillo highway.

23. State governments have been increasingly active in the toll roads program over time. However, their share of participation in total kilometers does not necessarily reflect their share in terms of peso investment.

24. Actually, not all of the resources flowing into the road concession program should be regarded as scarce from Mexico's perspective. In particular, it is quite possible that much of the foreign capital invested in concession highways, as well as capital repatriated from abroad by Mexican nationals, would, in the absence of the toll road program, have remained outside of Mexico. Furthermore, to the extent that the demonstration effect of toll road concessions has attracted foreign capital to other areas of the Mexican economy, the program may provide positive spillovers in terms of resource generation.

25. These unrealized benefits may frustrate segments of Mexico's population that feel bypassed by the type of economic growth programs, fuelled largely by private sector investors, implemented under the Salinas administration.

REFERENCES

Banco de México. 1993. *Indicadores Económicos.*

Demsetz, Harold. 1968. "Why Regulate Utilities?" *Journal of Law and Economics* 11 (Apr.): 55–66.

Empresas ICA Sociedad Controladora, S.A. de C.V. 1992a. *Prospectus.* Apr. 8. Mexico City.

————. 1992b. *Form 20-F.* Mexico City.

————. 1993. *Form 20-F.* Mexico City.

Gómez-Ibáñez, José, and John R. Meyer. 1993. *Going Private: The International Experience with Transport Privatization.* Washington, D.C.: Brookings.

Grupo Tribasa, S.A. de C.V. 1993. *Form 20-F.* Mexico City.

Leibenstein, Harvey. 1966. "Allocative Efficiency versus X-Efficiency." *American Economic Review* 56 (June): 392–415.

Mexico City–Toluca Toll Road: Toll Revenue Indexed Participation Securities Prospectus. 1992. May 29. Mexico City.

Stanfield, Mitchel. 1991. *Modernizing Highway Infrastructure through Toll Concessions in Mexico.* Washington, D.C.: U.S. Dept. of Transportation.

Williamson, Oliver E. 1976. "Franchise Bidding for Natural Monopolies—In General and with Respect to CATV." *Bell Journal of Economics* 7 (spring): 73–104.

11. Regulating Private Toll Roads

José A. Gómez-Ibañez

The private provision of toll expressways, bridges, and tunnels is becoming increasingly common in Latin America and elsewhere in the developing world. Many developing countries are experiencing rapid increases in truck and automobile ownership and in traffic and are under growing pressure to improve their highway systems by building modern, limited access expressway systems and other facilities. Expressways are expensive to construct, however, and these governments typically face many competing claims for the tax receipts they collect and limits on the amount of new debt their international creditors will allow them to issue. In such cases it is often attractive to grant a concession to a private company to build and operate the needed new expressways, bridges, or tunnels as toll facilities.

Private provision raises special problems, however, particularly with regard to the control of potential monopoly power. A private toll road company might be tempted to exploit any monopoly power it enjoys by raising toll rates well above costs or by constraining capacity or service. These problems occur with other industries as well, of course, but are often not as serious. In cases such as trucking or airlines, the prospects for competition are stronger because capital requirements are modest or capital assets can be shifted easily from one market to the next, as competitive opportunities arise. In cases such as electricity generation or long-distance telecommunications, the facilities required are expensive and immobile but often can provide effective competition with one another at a distance.

Most private toll roads do face competition from parallel public untolled roads. These untolled alternatives are typically not built to expressway standards, however, and are usually slower and often more circuitous. Moreover, a toll road must have either advantages or market

317

power over the free alternatives if it is to be successful, since otherwise all motorists would use the free road. Rarely are traffic volumes sufficient along any one corridor to justify the construction of two parallel expressways, so effective competition from other tolled facilities is usually not available either.

Private Toll Road Programs

The experience with private toll roads actually predates modern motor vehicles.[1] An extensive private toll road network developed in the United States in the late eighteenth and early nineteenth centuries, for example, only to disappear under competition from canals and railroads. Several southern European countries pioneered modern private toll roads after World War II, particularly Spain and France. Spain relied on private concessions when it began building its modern intercity expressway network in the 1960s; by the early 1980s, Spain had opened nearly 2,000 kilometers of private toll expressways. By that time, it had decided that additions to the network would be built as untolled and publicly owned facilities. France created public toll road companies in the late 1950s, when it began to build its intercity expressway system. In the 1970s, however, France granted four large private toll road concessions, partly in the hope that the private concessionaires would stimulate better performance among the public toll road companies. Three of the four French private concessions went bankrupt soon thereafter, thanks in part to the energy crises of the 1970s, but one private company with over 700 kilometers of expressways remains in operation.

Interest in the private provision of roads revived in Europe and elsewhere during the late 1980s, usually because the public sector was facing growing financial constraints. Several industrial countries began granting private concessions, although these concessions have not amounted to a very important share of their systems—in part because they had already completed fairly extensive expressway networks. Britain granted two concessions for private bridges in the 1980s, for example, and France offered several new, small, private concessions as well. In the United States, nearly a dozen states passed legislation authorizing private toll roads, although only two concessions, both for roads less than twenty miles long, were under construction by 1994.

Private road concessions have been much more important in the developing world, particularly among those countries that are just beginning to build an extensive expressway network.[2] In Asia, for example, Indonesia, Malaysia, and Thailand all switched from relying on public toll road companies to private toll road companies to build and operate the new segments of their emerging expressway systems. China granted several major expressway concessions, and concessions were being studied by several of the former Soviet bloc countries in Eastern Europe.

In Latin America, Mexico, Chile, Argentina, and Puerto Rico have been most involved with private road provision. Between 1989 and 1994, Mexico built the largest private toll expressway network in the world with over 3,000 kilometers open or under construction (see chapter 10). Argentina granted a number of concessions, including concessions to maintain and upgrade existing roads as well as build new ones. By 1994, Chile had awarded one new tunnel as a concession and was in the process of soliciting or evaluating bids for many other road links, including a project to widen the Pan American highway in central Chile. Puerto Rico granted a concession for a new bridge over the San José Lagoon near San Juan, which opened for traffic in 1994.

All of these countries have had to decide whether and how to regulate the potential market power of toll road concessionaires. Each country has adopted a slightly different scheme, none of which has proven wholly satisfactory.

Basic Regulatory Objectives and Options

Any regulatory scheme must strike an appropriate balance between user and investor interests. If regulation is too lax, concessionaires could raise toll rates well above their operating and investment costs, so that users are charged more than is necessary and the toll road is underutilized. If regulation is too stringent, however, private investment will not be forthcoming. The hallmark of successful regulation is to strike a balance between protecting the public from excessive tolls or reduced quality and allowing the investors the opportunity to earn a reasonable rate of return on their investment (recognizing and adjusting for the risks they are assuming).

All else being equal, the regulatory scheme should also be clear from the outset. Uncertainties about future regulation will add to the project risks for investors. At the very least, they will insist on a higher rate of return to compensate for the added risk; this, in turn, is likely to be reflected in higher tolls for users. If the regulatory risks are too high, many will be unwilling to invest at all. Foreign investors are likely to be particularly sensitive to regulatory uncertainties, since they are less familiar with the local political situation. Domestic pension funds, insurance companies, and others whose investment risks are strictly controlled by other government agencies are likely to be precluded as well. Indeed, if the regulatory scheme is perceived to be too subject to political interference, only investors who are politically well connected or allied with politicians will be willing to invest.

Within this basic framework, however, there is a wide range of regulatory possibilities. At the risk of some simplification, three main options are available:

1. Relying on *competition* from parallel free roads.

2. Establishing a *regulatory commission* that, within the confines of its statutory authority, controls toll rates and the quality of service provided.

3. Designing a *concession contract* that specifies future toll increases and other matters, that can be enforced by normal commercial law and courts rather than a specialized regulatory commission, and that is put out for competitive bidding to ensure that the public receives the best terms.

Regulatory economists have long debated the merits of these options, although usually in the context of electricity, telecommunications, and other industries that have more experience with private ownership and public regulation.[3] Between the commission and the contract approaches, the commission approach has generally been employed for power distribution, telecommunications, and other infrastructure systems that involve complex networks that must be continually upgraded or expanded and that face rapid technological change, significant demand uncertainties, or other complications not easily written into long-term contracts. The contract approach is generally employed only with projects, such as power-generating stations, that are discrete, one-time investments and that face relatively fewer technological uncertainties or other complications.

In the case of private toll roads, no country has been willing to rely entirely on competition from free roads to control a potential monopoly power; all of the Latin American countries (and most others) have opted so far for contract regulation, although often with interesting variants. While the decision to not rely entirely on free-road competition appears sensible, the choice of contract over commission regulation may be premature.

Competition from Free Roads

There is almost always some form of free alternative to a private toll road and, in theory, it might be possible to design the concession and the free alternative so that the concessionaire enjoys just enough market power to recover a fair return on investment but not enough to abuse the public.

In practice, however, governments have not been confident that they can achieve such an appropriate balance. Although the concession laws in most countries require that a free alternative be available to motorists, this seems to be more symbolic than practical. The concession laws do not specify how good the free alternative must be and require, instead, some government regulation of tolls or rates of return to supplement the free-road competition. Experience suggests that governments are justifiably skeptical that they can design and maintain the right level of free-road competition. Cases where there is too little free-road competition are not usually obvious, since other regulatory schemes help prevent the road concessionaire from abusing its market power.

Cases of too much free-road competition, on the other hand, have developed in several countries; the most notable examples in Latin America are in Mexico, where several concessions apparently lost much of their potential traffic to parallel free roads. The Mexican government set very high allowable toll rates because it wanted the concession periods to be relatively short, even on lightly traveled segments. But the high toll rates encouraged significant diversion to the free alternatives, particularly in Mexico's northern deserts, where low population, low traffic densities, and level terrain allow relatively high speeds on the competing free roads.

Too much competition from free roads not only threatens the financial viability of the concessions but also can cause a serious misallocation of traffic and resources. Congestion and traffic delays may be excessively high on the free road, while the new expressway is underutilized. Indeed, if there is so much potential competition from existing free roads, as apparently has been the case in some sections of Mexico, then it probably would have been wiser to postpone the construction of the new toll expressway until traffic volumes had increased to the point where there was more need for the added capacity.

Regulatory Commissions

Under the commission approach, a special regulatory body determines whether the toll rates or other conditions of service are appropriate. The commission is usually guided by a statute that sets out the factors it is to consider, and its decisions are usually subject to judicial review. Nevertheless, the statute is usually written so that the commission must exercise some independent judgment or discretion in interpreting its mandate. Indeed, the need for limited discretion to cope with unforeseen complications is the fundamental reason commission regulation is often advocated over contract regulation.

There are many variants of commission regulation, but the two most important are (1) rate of return regulation as traditionally practiced by public utility commissions in the United States and (2) the price cap regulation introduced by the British in the 1980s.[4] In the United States, private electric, gas, telephone, and other utilities petition a special regulatory body, usually a state utility commission, when they desire an increase in tariffs. The request triggers a rate of return investigation, in which the utility commission calculates the return being earned or proposed by the utility and compares it to returns earned by private companies in competitive industries facing similar risks. If the utility's actual or proposed rate of return is higher than that in comparable industries, the tariff increase is denied or reduced. The basic idea is that the returns earned in other comparable but competitive industries are determined by competitive forces; that is, they are just high enough to attract the capital needed for new investments but not so high as to generate excess profits. Aside from the requirement that the company be allowed a fair rate of return, the commission often has wide latitude in the requirements it may impose on the regulated company. But the requirement for a fair rate of return, arrived at through published analyses and open hearings, provides a basic protection for both the customer and the investor.

The major drawback to the rate of return system is the need for frequent return investigations by the regulatory commission. Picking the appropriate rate of return is difficult and often controversial. The central issue is deciding which private industries face risks comparable to those of the regulated industry, so that their rates of return can be used as a benchmark. If the regulators overestimate or underestimate the needed rate of return, the regulated company will have incentives to overinvest or underinvest. The burden of these investigations on the regulated company and the government is therefore substantial, especially in inflationary periods, when tariffs may need frequent adjustment.

The price cap approach differs primarily in requiring less frequent commission investigations of the profits of the regulated firm. Between investigations, a company's allowable annual price increases are capped at the annual rate of increase of the retail price index *(RPI)* an estimate of the expected annual rate of productivity improvement *(X)* in the industry. The formula is revised periodically—every five years in the case of British industries—based on a new investigation by the government commission responsible for the industry. The commission considers whether the rate of productivity improvement has been faster or slower than anticipated in the previous period or than that expected in the next period. In practice, the commission relies heavily on an assessment of the profitability or returns of the firm to decide whether *X* was set too high or too low in the previous period. If the rate of return is greater than the returns earned in private companies in competitive industries facing similar risks, *X* is increased for the following five-year period. If it has been less than that earned by other comparable industries, *X* is reduced. The British have used this system for various public utilities privatized during the 1980s, including electricity, telecommunications, water supply, and airports.

Proponents of price caps argue that the regulated firm has a stronger incentive to control costs because the rate of return is not capped during the five-year period between investigations. If the company can reduce its operating costs during this period, it can keep the profits from dropping. Price caps are also thought to build more rate stability when a new regulatory regime is inaugurated for a newly privatized industry, thus helping those making new investments in the industry to make plans. Skeptics of price caps respond that the long period between investigations creates some risks and that the investigations require as much or more information and analysis as those for rate of return regulation.

The commission approach has not been used to regulate private toll roads in Latin America or elsewhere in the developing world, even though it has been popular for regulating newly privatized electricity and telecommunications companies in these same countries. Apparently, commission regulation is thought to subject investors to more political risk and regulatory uncertainty than contract regulation, and thus contract regulation is preferred where it is practical. Although contracts must be enforced by courts, which, fairly or not, are often seen as subject to political manipulation in developing countries, a new regulatory commission, without long-established procedures or the constraints of a body of case law and precedent, is often viewed as even more vulnerable to political interference.

Private toll roads are seen as inherently less complex concessions than other utilities and, thus, more susceptible to contract regulation. Many highway concessions are commonly thought of as simple, one-time investments, particularly tunnels, bridges, and expressways. The initial investment is the only major investment contemplated during the life of the concession (other than routine maintenance). A second tunnel or bridge or additional traffic lanes are generally not expected to be needed until after the end of the initial concession period (that is, after the original project has reverted to the government). These major rounds of new investment might then be awarded as a new concession.

Commission regulation, by contrast, was designed for industries such as telecommunications and electric utilities, where continuing investments and improvements are the norm and, thus, where constant monitoring of the issues that potential investors face and the returns they require is necessary to ensure continuing modernization or expansion. Telecommunications is also subject to great technical uncertainties, for which regulatory flexibility may be needed. Thus, for example, both the government and private investors in Mexico, Chile, and Argentina have accepted the need for commission-style regulations for their newly privatized telephone and electricity companies but not for their new private road concessions.

Competitive Concession Contracting

Contracting was first proposed as an alternative to commission-style regulation in 1968 by U.S. economist Harold Demsetz. The simplicity of the Demsetz proposal (Demsetz 1968) attracted immediate attention. A one-time contract for the life of the concession would, in theory, remove political uncertainties for the investor by clearly fixing, at the outset, the rules that would govern tolls or rates of return and other key economic issues. The potential for monopoly abuse would be eliminated if the contract were awarded competitively. Most of the toll road concession programs in Latin America follow the Demsetz model in principle, although in practice the contracts and procedures are sometimes fairly complex. In a few cases, most notably Puerto Rico, competition is based on the preliminary proposals of potential concessionaires, and the franchising authority then negotiates the key details of the contract with the winner. The prospect of subsequent negotiations may encourage bidders to be unrealistic, although the authority can always threaten to open negotiations with the runner-up if the winner is too resistant to authority demands.

In Mexico and Chile, there are, at least in theory, no subsequent negotiations. In Mexico, the draft concession contract issued with the solicitation specifies highway alignment, construction and maintenance standards, and the maximum toll that the concessionaire can charge. This maximum toll is indexed to future changes in the Mexican consumer price index.[5] The franchising authority, the Secretariat of Communications and Transport, also guarantees a minimum traffic volume, with the compensation for low traffic being an extension of the duration of the concession. The franchising authority will also grant extensions to compensate for construction cost overruns that the concessionaire can demonstrate are the result of design changes ordered by the authority or errors or omissions in the preliminary engineering studies the authority supplies the bidding package. The concession is awarded to the bidder who proposes the shortest concession period, which in no case can exceed twenty years.

Chile's solicitations also specify the alignment, construction standards, and maximum allowable toll, indexed to consumer prices.[6] In its first concession, for a tunnel to provide an alternative to the El Melon pass on the Pan American Highway, the Chilean government also offered to guarantee 1 percent annual traffic growth, but it required, in return, that if traffic growth exceeded 6 percent per year the concessionaire had to pay the government 30 percent of the toll revenue attributable to the traffic growth in excess of 6 percent. Chile also awards its concessions on the basis of multiple criteria rather than simply the life of the concession; these criteria and their weights are spelled out clearly in the bidding documents and include, for example, toll rates, concession duration, and requests for subsidy from, or offers of payments to, the government.

So far, these schemes appear to have been acceptable to private investors. The solicitations have attracted a reasonable number of bidders, for example, although this has not always been the case. Puerto Rico's solicitation for its bridge concession attracted only two serious bidders, and the Mexican toll road program initially had only a few bidders per project. Over time, however, the number of bids per concession has increased, which provides some assurance of competition.

A variety of problems have developed, however, which suggest the limitations of the contract approach to regulation, even for apparently simple projects such as toll roads.

The Award Criteria

One difficulty is establishing criteria for awarding contracts that are specific enough to clearly identify the winning bid and yet rich enough to capture the legitimate concerns of the franchising authorities. The Mexican contract illustrates some of the perils of an excessively simple criterion. Mexico awarded concessions on a single criterion—concession duration—because the officials in charge of the program hoped to convince potential bidders that the selection process was transparent and fair. While it probably did increase the perception of fairness, it also encouraged bidders to charge the maximum toll rate allowed in order to reduce the concession duration. The maximum tolls were set fairly high in many of the early solicitations, moreover, which resulted in some very short concessions (in some cases, five years or less).

Mexico's choice of concession duration as the award criterion can be faulted on at least three grounds. First, it did not protect highway users from monopoly abuse but, rather, transferred the monopoly rents from the concessionaires to the government in the form of an earlier date for the transfer of the new road.[7] Second, the high tolls caused congestion on the parallel free roads and the underutilization of the new toll roads. Finally, the short concessions might undermine the concessionaires' incentives to build durable roads, although the franchising agency claims that it avoided such problems by specifying construction standards and supervising construction.

Mexico might have done better by using toll rate rather than concession duration as the criterion for selecting the bids, although it also would have had to set a maximum concession term to avoid bids for indefinite concession. Alternatively, Mexico might still have used the concession term as the sole criterion but reduced the toll maximums to more reasonable levels. In either case, picking, in advance, the socially optimal constraint on term length or toll rate would be difficult, especially because traffic levels are often uncertain.

The Chilean concession law allows multiple criteria, but in the name of transparency, the government accounting agency requires that all criteria be quantifiable and that the relative weights for each criterion be specified in advance. This led to a variety of criteria being used in the El Melon concession solicitation, for example, but with some seemingly arbitrary formulas and weights.

This is not to say that sensible and transparent criteria cannot be developed but, rather, that the task is not an easy one. The task becomes more complex, moreover, when one recognizes that concessions face a variety of cost and revenue risks, which the franchising authority and the concessionaire need to anticipate and apportion.

Coping with Commercial Uncertainties

Before a toll road is opened, neither the concessionaire nor the franchising agency can be sure how much it will cost to build and operate or how many vehicles will use it. The franchising agency may face problems if the road is either more or less successful than expected. If the road generates far more traffic than the bidder expected, for example, then the toll level allowed in the winning bid may be much higher than is socially desirable or efficient.[8] Conversely, if the road attracts far less traffic than expected, the franchising agency may be faced with the choice of renegotiating the concession terms or of declaring the concessionaire in default and then coping with the delays, disruptions, and litigation that are likely to follow.

Some of these problems are already apparent in the Mexican concession program, perhaps because the Mexican program is the oldest and most ambitious in Latin America. According to one observer, cost overruns amounted to 62 percent of the original estimates for the roads completed by late 1992, and most of these roads had traffic at least 20 percent lower than the minimum guaranteed (Oks 1993). The design of the concession program is probably partly to blame: concessionaires may have been lax in controlling costs, knowing they might be able to negotiate concession extensions; traffic shortfalls were caused by the high tolls that bidders were encouraged to charge by the government's award criteria. Nevertheless, some cost overruns and traffic shortfalls might have been expected even under an alternative concession bidding scheme, especially since Mexican highway planners had little experience with comparatively high tolls and did not know how traffic would respond.

The result in Mexico has been extensive negotiations between the franchising agency and the concessionaires over the extent to which the cost overruns were due to errors in the preliminary engineering documents and how long concession extensions should be to compensate for cost overruns and traffic shortfalls. In effect, the franchising agency began to act more like a regulatory commission rather than a contract monitor, although without the benefit of an explicit rate of return or price cap framework to guide it.

Chile and Puerto Rico have tried to alleviate this problem by including in the concession contract explicit rates or contingencies for various uncertainties. Chile's El Melon tunnel concession, for example, includes a minimum traffic growth guarantee and a formula for revenue sharing if traffic growth exceeds certain levels. Even more interesting is the scheme negotiated for Puerto Rico's San José Lagoon bridge. This contract also offers minimum traffic guarantees, but it differs in that it regulates the rate of return the concessionaire receives on its investment, rather than the toll rate. The concessionaire has broad flexibility to set the toll, but if it earns more than 18 percent on its investment the government gets 60 percent of the earnings in excess of 18 percent; if the concessionaire earns more than 22 percent, then the government gets 85 percent of the earnings in excess of 22 percent.

The attraction of the El Melon and San José Lagoon contracts is, of course, that the government shares in the profits if the road is more successful than anticipated. The San José Lagoon contract is particularly interesting because it protects against other sources of uncertainty than traffic volume. Nevertheless, both schemes probably can be faulted in that the more efficient response to unexpectedly high traffic volumes is probably to reduce allowable toll rates rather than to have the government share in the surplus.[9] In effect, the El Melon and San José Lagoon schemes simply ensure that the government as well as the concessionaire profit from excessive toll rates. Moreover, the specific traffic or rates of return at which government profit sharing is initiated may be somewhat arbitrary. In neither case were these traffic or return levels the subject of competitive bidding, for example, so it is unclear whether they appropriate all the potential monopoly rents for the government.[10]

It would, of course, be possible to draft a concession contract that varied the allowable toll rate with actual traffic level. Getting the appropriate formula might be difficult, however, and traffic is just one of the uncertainties that the concessionaire and the franchising authority face.

Discrete versus Continuing Investment

A related and even more difficult problem with the competitive contracting approach is that it is more suitable for a single discrete investment than for a continuing investment. Many road investments are of the former type, particularly bridges and tunnels. Neither the El Melon tunnel or the San José Lagoon bridge can be easily expanded; when they reach their capacity, a new tunnel will have to be bored or a new span added. Because bridges and tunnels are "lumpy" investments, moreover, highway planners tend to design them with enough spare capacity to accommodate many years of growth. Thus it is likely that the concessions for the El Melon tunnel and the San José Lagoon bridge will expire before a second tunnel or span will need to be provided. That makes the design of the concession contract simpler, because one does not have to cope with the problems of adding a massive new investment late in the life of the concession. These problems arise because granting a concession for a second tunnel or bridge would greatly affect the profitability of the first tunnel or bridge.

For many other types of highway projects, such as an expressway, capacity is far less lumpy than for bridges and tunnels. Expressway capacity can be added gradually, in small increments: a third traffic lane can be added in each direction, for example, or a hill can be regraded or an alignment straightened. If traffic is growing at a reasonably healthy rate, new investments are likely to be advisable every ten years or so, less than the lifetime of many toll road concessions.

The Spanish and French, who have had by far the longest experience with modern private toll roads, have experienced this problem on a number of their concessions (Gómez-Ibañez and Meyer 1993). Their usual remedy is to negotiate an extension of the existing concession in return for the construction of the third lane or other needed investment. These negotiations fall far short of the competitive contracting model, however, in that the government is often faced with the unattractive choice of finding some pretext for breaking the existing concession contract, going without the needed investment, or meeting the terms of the concessionaire.

Chile faces such a situation in the design of its concession programs for the upgrading of the Pan American Highway. The Chilean Ministry of Public Works has been slowly improving the highway, especially around Santiago and between Santiago and the turnoff for Concepcion, where traffic volumes are heaviest. On some segments, the highway has separate two-lane carriageways for each direction of traffic, for example, but full access control and bypasses around towns are needed to improve safety and capacity. Other segments still have only a single carriageway, with one lane in each direction, and will soon need second carriageways and, ultimately, full access control. The ideal concession program would continue this gradual upgrading process, as traffic warranted, rather than move immediately to a level of investment that would be sufficient for the traffic volumes expected in fifteen or twenty years.

Concession contracts could in theory include provisions for the investment needed before the end of the concession. One attractive possibility, for example, is to allow the concessionaire and the government to negotiate the terms of new investments as the need arises, with the proviso that if they fail to reach an agreement the government could buy the concessionaire out for a fee established in the contract. Specifying the appropriate buyout price is more difficult than one might expect, however (see Williamson 1976). And there is, in general, a limit to our ability to anticipate problems and design effective contingencies in contracts. Since roads, bridges, and tunnels are very durable investments, unexpected problems are likely to arise in the lifetime of the concession.

Private Concession Proposals

A final difficulty is how to allow private entrepreneurs to propose concession projects to the government. Several states in the United States have run competitions in which concessions are proposed by the private sector rather than by the government.[11] Those competitions have generated many innovative ideas, ranging from novel road alignments and designs to new ideas about how to price and manage road capacity. Judging the bids in such competitions is more complicated, however, since there is so much more variety among the proposals.

It is especially difficult to devise a fair procedure if the government merely wishes to be open to innovative private proposals rather than to run a competition in which they are solicited. Chile's concession law, for example, specifies that a private company can propose a new idea for a concession. If upon review the government determines that the idea is original and meritorious, then the concession will be put out to bid, with the original proposer enjoying a 10 percent rating advantage when the bids are ranked. This advantage in any subsequent bidding has not proven sufficient, however, to induce private companies to make the investment needed to develop a proposal to the point where the government might be able to judge its merits. Some proponents of private toll roads have proposed that the government reimburse the originator of a novel concession scheme for the costs of developing the idea, but this raises difficult questions as to how such reimbursement should be calculated, especially given that investments in new ideas are risky since many are likely to prove infeasible or be rejected.

Regulating private toll roads is a fascinating and complex problem, but we are only beginning to learn about and experiment with the concept. None of the obvious alternatives is wholly satisfactory: designing an alternative free road that offers just the right degree of competition is both difficult and can involve a wasteful duplication of investment, the commission approach has the discretion to accommodate change but subjects the concessionaire to the vagaries of politics, while the one-time contract may be unrealistic for long-lived investments in a rapidly changing world.

If the contract approach does prove unrealistic, then toll road franchising agencies will assume, over time, more and more the role of regulatory commissions. Unanticipated problems and needs will gradually render most concession contracts obsolete, and breaking the contracts and rebidding the concessions will prove impractical for a variety of economic and political reasons. The impasses will, in effect, be negotiated, with the franchising agency trying to ensure that the public is protected while the concessionaire earns a reasonable return or, at least, is not bankrupted. This commission-like role may be more difficult and controversial than need be, however, because it was not anticipated and because franchising agencies have little experience or guidance in the task.

NOTES

1. For a more complete description of the experience of Europe, the United States, and several developing countries with private toll roads, see Goméz-Ibañez and Meyer 1993.

2. For a list of the many projects in operation, construction, or planning, see "1994 International Major Projects Survey."

3. For the classic articles in the debate between contract and commission regulation, see Demsetz 1968, and Williamson 1976. One of the few applications to highways, which advocates, not very convincingly, the contract approach, is Fielding and Klein 1993.

4. The relative merits of rate of return and price cap regulation have been the subject of intense debate among regulatory economists. For an overview, see Liston 1993, and Acton and Vogelsang 1989.

5. For descriptions of the Mexican system, see chapter 10, Gómez-Ibañez and Meyer 1993, and Oks 1993.

6. For a description of the Chilean system, see Ortega 1993.

7. The ultimate beneficiary of the monopoly rents might be future motorists (if the government decided to abolish or greatly reduce tolls once the road reverted to public ownership) or taxpayers (if the government continued to impose high tolls and use toll revenues for other purposes).

8. The private toll road company is assumed to be constrained by public policy to set its prices so that it is financially self-sufficient. It is also assumed that these prices are higher than would be socially optimal, since, because of economies of scale or temporary excess capacity, the marginal cost of highway provision is below average cost. If traffic is higher than expected, however, then the gap between the price bid and actual marginal cost may be even larger, and thus the social inefficiency of the tolls will be greater.

9. As noted earlier, tolls set to recover the toll road concessionaires' costs are likely to be higher than marginal cost.

10. In the El Melon tunnel, the franchising agency specified the traffic levels at which profit sharing would begin, while the San José Lagoon sharing scheme was negotiated after the winning concessionaire had been selected.

11. These states are California, Arizona, and Washington. For a description of the California experience, see Gómez-Ibañez and Meyer 1993.

REFERENCES

Acton, Jan Paul, and Ingo Vogelsang. 1989. "Symposium on Price Cap Regulation." *RAND Journal of Economics* 20 (3): 369–72.

Demsetz, Harold. 1968. "Why Regulate Utilities?" *Journal of Law and Economics* 11 (Apr.): 55–66.

Fielding, Gordon J., and Daniel B. Klein. 1993. "How to Franchise Highways." *Journal of Transport Economics and Policy* 27 (May): 113–30.

Gómez-Ibañez, José, and John R. Meyer. 1993. *Going Private: The International Experience with Transport Privatization.* Washington, D.C.: Brookings.

Liston, Catherine. 1993. "Price Cap versus Rate of Return Regulation." *Journal of Regulatory Economics* 5:25–48.

"1994 International Major Projects Survey: Public-Private Partnerships in Infrastructure Development." *Public Works Financing* 28 (Oct.).

Oks, Daniel. 1993. "Mexico: Private Sector Participation in Infrastructure Development." World Bank, Washington, D.C.

Ortega, Alejandro Magni. 1993. "Chilean Infrastructure Concessions." *International Supplement to Public Works Financing* (July–Aug.): 1–12.

Williamson, Oliver E. 1976. "Franchise Bidding for Natural Monopolies—In General and with Respect to CATV." *Bell Journal of Economics* 7 (spring): 73–104.

IV.   OTHER PERSPECTIVES

12. Multinational Enterprises and Telecommunications Privatization

Mabelle G. Sonnenschein and Patricia A. Yokopenic

The 1980s saw an increase in the privatization of state-owned enterprises (Kikeri et al. 1992; Ramamurti 1991). Between 1981 and 1991, privatization in the telecommunications sector alone raised more than US$104 billion (Golob 1992). The two main drivers for privatization in developing countries have been the need to fulfill demand for modern telecommunications services at reasonable cost and to raise funds to amortize the country's debt. In the 1990s the pace of such privatization increased, particularly in the telecommunications sector.

Common carrier privatizations continue to unfold, particularly in Latin America and Europe, and many more countries are expected to sell their state-owned telephone companies in the near future. Among the countries that began to privatize their telecommunications industries through strategic sales and equity offerings in 1994 were Belgium, the Czech Republic, Germany, Greece, India, and Nicaragua. We look for the following to similarly privatize in the future (EIU 1992, 1993; Morgan Stanley 1993; Pyramid 1993; Nash 1993):

1995–96	*Longer term*
Bolivia	Bangladesh
Colombia	Brazil
France	Bulgaria
Honduras	Ecuador
Indonesia	Guinea
Ireland	Israel
Italy	Kenya
Kuwait	Madagascar
Morocco	Panama

1995–96	*Longer term*
Nigeria	Paraguay
Pakistan	Poland
Portugal	Puerto Rico
Sweden	Romania
Taiwan	Saudi Arabia
Thailand	Uruguay
Turkey	
Zimbabwe	

Recent sales have even generated bidding wars among investors and escalated the price paid per line in countries like Hungary and Peru.

Not only the pace but the nature of recent telecommunication privatizations has changed. Many recent privatizations have attracted foreign investors, especially other telecommunications carriers, which have the knowledge and the capital necessary to revitalize the ailing infrastructures of developing nations. Network improvements are typically difficult and expensive, since they involve expanding, digitizing, and integrating the infrastructure. To spread and reduce risks, therefore, carriers have joined forces with one another and with other investors to form bidding consortia rather than go solo.

Various methods have been used to transfer state-owned enterprises to private investors (Nankani 1988; Ramamurti and Vernon 1991; Vuylsteke 1988). The first large-scale transfers of telecommunications operations from public to private status took place in the industrialized world, in the United Kingdom (1984) and Japan (1985). Both of these privatizations were part of a larger, ideological movement toward deregulation (Kok 1992). Both involved the sale of stock to the public, but neither involved strategic investors as partners.

In the developing world, the history of telecommunications privatization begins in Chile in 1988 (Ambrose et al. 1990; Kikeri et al., 1992). The Chilean privatization and subsequent others in the developing world have nearly all involved foreign strategic investors, especially U.S. and European network operators, financial institutions, and equipment vendors. In the strategic partnership model, privatization is not an ideological end in itself but a means of financing and creating a modern communications infrastructure (Kok 1992). And while the public flotation of shares to individual investors and the private sale of shares to strategic partners both raise money for the government, a strategic partnership can bring technological and managerial expertise to the enterprise. Thus apart from raising capital, the developing country benefits from the strategic partnership with other large telecommunications carriers, although this approach may entail relinquishing some degree of control in operating the privatized company.

Whichever privatization model is adopted by a government, the final impact of the privatization will be affected by the balance achieved between a country's need to create the desired infrastructure and the investors' need to recover their cost of capital. Properly managed, these needs are complementary rather than conflicting, and the right balance between them provides the opportunity to achieve a beneficial situation for the country, the investor, and the consumers. Two critical elements of this balance are (1) the establishment of objectives and priorities related to the privatization, and (2) the creation of an "institutional infrastructure," meaning the restructuring of the sector and the enterprise and the creation of supporting institutions and policies that provide the basis for the future development of the telecommunications sector.

The sale of government-owned enterprises involves numerous local stakeholders, including government planners, politicians, managers, and others, all of whom view the objectives of privatization somewhat differently (Aharoni 1991; Kok 1992). Another set of stakeholders are international financing agencies such as the World Bank and the International Monetary Fund, which encourage privatization and lend funds for debt restructuring and economic development.

The strategic partnership introduces yet another player in the process of telecommunications privatization—the strategic investor. In addition to supplying capital, the strategic investor brings an external view of the experience, the resources, and the conditions required to fulfill the privatization objectives. The strategic investor usually becomes involved in the process after many related activities have already occurred, such as sector and enterprise restructuring. But before the die is cast, the private investor can influence the privatization process. Private investors may send company representatives in advance of the privatization process. During the early meetings, the potential investor may discuss the company and its qualifications, share the company's experience in past divestitures, and offer assistance in developing a privatization plan that would present an attractive investment opportunity. In addition, the investor may also present the private company's perspective of the business and economics of providing telecommunications services. The purpose of such a presentation is to share the investor's expectations that the concession documents, usually written by international legal firms, will both reflect the country's interests and allow the healthy operation of national and international investors. In any case, if privatization ensues, the investor will exert considerable influence during the negotiations surrounding the concession documents.

In some instances, privatization efforts fail at very early stages of development because the legislature or the public do not support them. In Panama, cabinet ministers could not agree on a privatization proposal, and none was initially passed in Congress. In Uruguay, certain factions in Congress opposed the privatization law that proposed the sale of several state enterprises, including the telephone company (ANTEL). Consequently, the law was subjected to a public referendum and was resoundingly rejected by nearly three-quarters (72%) of the electorate (EIU 1992; Luxner 1993d; Pyramid 1993). The degree of popular opposition had not been anticipated in Congress and, perhaps, indicated a general approval of the management of public companies in Uruguay, where such companies had improved their performance in recent years and had not attracted charges of corruption (EIU 1993). It is possible that the initial results of privatization in Argentina, where the government sold the national carrier ENTel in 1990, also shaped public opinion in Uruguay. In Argentina the government approved a large telephone rate increase, which generated a significant uproar (see chapter 4); meanwhile, network improvements were slower than expected during the first year of privatization.

Despite the political setback in Uruguay, ANTEL embarked on an ambitious development plan, raising its investment budget from less than US$50 million in 1991 to US$120 million in 1993 and made significant progress in the provision of basic and other telecommunications services (Pyramid 1993). In addition, ANTEL recently financed the expansion and modernization of its pay phone system through a build-operate-maintain-and-transfer arrangement, enabling the company to make the required network improvements despite a lack of public support for privatization.

More recently, the Greek privatization experience demonstrated how a country's political situation can discourage potential bidders and derail the sale of state-owned enterprises to strategic investors. Labor opposition to telecommunications privatization in Greece essentially forced the economic ministry to change the enabling legislation, making it more palatable to OTE employees and the public but less attractive to investors (Hope 1993). A new Greek government ultimately changed the method of privatization from the sale to foreign strategic investors, which involved relinquishing management control, to the sale of shares on the Athens stock exchange.

Privatization of a state-owned telecommunications company is normally an extremely lengthy and complicated process, which can fail completely or be delayed interminably by political forces. This chapter offers some insight into the strategic investor's view of the privatization process. Specifically, it discusses the strategic investor's motivations, investment criteria, expectations of sector restructuring prior to sale, expectations of the bidding, negotiation, and due diligence processes, the role of strategic partnerships, the risks as seen by the investor, and the conditions for a successful privatization. The issues are addressed in the context of the sale of government-owned telecommunications entities.

Stakeholders and Their Objectives

Ultimately, the success of the privatization will be measured against the objectives of the various stakeholders, including the government and its various ministries, the firm's employees, and the public at large. Many authors delineate and discuss the various objectives that characterize the process of privatization (Aharoni 1991; Kok 1992; Kikeri et al. 1992), but since a failure to outline and embrace clear and unified privatization objectives can discourage potential investors and derail the process in its early stages, it is worth reviewing, briefly, some typical government objectives of privatization.

Different government entities usually have different and perhaps conflicting objectives. Economic planners seek development through the modernization and expansion of the telecommunications sector, which in turn facilitates the expansion of the manufacturing and service sectors. This undoubtedly means large investments to expand and upgrade the existing network. Financial planners, under the influence of the international financing agencies, seek to reduce or eliminate debt and to raise capital. This means maximizing the sales price of the enterprise. Transport and communications planners often seek to deploy state-of-the-art technology, replacing obsolete networks and introducing new, expensive technologies, which may require skills and expertise not available in the country. In many cases, new owners may need to train local labor or bring foreign expertise to implement new systems and technologies.

Politicians may want low prices for their constituents, while economists seek efficiency in the market. Economists and some politicians see competition as a means to achieve their efficiency and pricing objectives, but both groups must recognize that the large cross-subsidies between local and long-distance services, which suppress usage, must be eliminated before the entire telecommunications sector is fully opened to competition—so that the investors in the newly privatized company will not begin to expand and modernize while prices are still being rebalanced. Finally, another objective of the government may be to obtain an experienced operator. To accomplish this, many countries (e.g., Chile, New Zealand, Argentina, Mexico, Peru, and Venezuela) have required that potential buyers be prequalified before they can bid for the national telecommunications firm.

Clearly some of these objectives—high sales price, network expansion and modernization, low prices and competition—are at odds with each other. The privatization process works best if the government integrates the conflicting objectives. If investors do not feel confident that the government's objectives are unified, they might decide to forgo the investment opportunity. Good leadership within the government can contribute greatly to the development of clear and unified objectives. International advisers can also play a key role in helping governments achieve this goal.

Investor's Interest and Incentives

In 1989 and 1990, the world's common carriers of telecommunications committed US$11 billion to international investments (Serrano et al. 1991). Why are large telecommunications companies turning to the developing world to make such large-scale investments? Among the primary incentives are (1) the saturated domestic markets of most large telecommunications carriers, (2) the profitable growth opportunities in the world's developing regions, (3) the success of recent strategic alliances and joint ventures in the telecommunications sector, and (4) the globalization of markets and customers. Especially attractive to U.S. carriers is the opportunity to be a full-service provider, which has not been possible in the United States.

Growth in telecommunications revenues is expected to decrease in industrialized regions. This is the result of several factors, including slow population growth in the industrialized nations and increased competition in the telecommunications sector. Moreover, the domestic markets of most advanced telecommunications carriers are largely saturated. In the United States, for example, at least 94 percent of all households already have telephone service (FCC 1991–92). And government regulations in some countries may restrict carrier entry into new services or geographical markets. For example, local U.S. carriers are limited in scope and geographic region of operation. Although these restrictions may be easing somewhat, they are currently stringent compared to those in many developing countries, where the strategic telecommunications investor can operate as a full-service provider. In Venezuela, for example, CANTV provides local service, national and international long-distance service, value added service, and cellular service. As a matter of fact, the United States might be the only country where carriers are restricted to providing either local or long-distance service.

In contrast to the situation in North America and Europe, where penetration rates (main lines per 100 population) average 50.9 and 36.8, respectively, penetration rates average only 5.3 in Central and South America, 2.3 in Africa, 2.7 in the South Pacific, and 8.1 in the Middle East and Southeast Asia (AT&T 1993). Limited capital has meant years of insufficient investment in telecommunications in these regions (Nulty

1989; Saunders et al. 1994; Wellenius 1989). This insufficient investment has resulted in obsolete networks and considerable unmet demand, which is evident from the long waiting lists and waiting periods (ten years is not uncommon) traditionally characteristic of state-run telecommunications (Ambrose et al. 1990). In addition, many of the government-owned firms have suffered from years of poor management and suboptimal use of financial resources. The use of prices and public sector jobs as political tools and the use of government-managed assets to generate cash for other sectors have also restricted the development of telecommunications.

Developing countries increasingly recognize that economic growth is tied to trade in the service sector, which depends on, and spends heavily on, telecommunications. Service sector trade is now estimated at US$600 billion a year, or about one-fifth of total world trade (Jussawalla 1992). Even in developing countries, the service sector often accounts for nearly half of total GDP (ibid.). Telecommunications render banking, insurance, financial, travel, and other services tradable. The importance of information flow to the world's business, especially in financial and other service sectors, is forcing developing nations to upgrade and modernize their telecommunications networks.

Although developing countries recognize the limitations of their telecommunications networks and seek to expand and modernize them, they typically lack the required capital and expertise. And so the world is witnessing a historic trend among developing nations to privatize their large, state-owned telephone companies through the sale of private shares to strategic investors, which will require huge, cumulative capital investments. In addition, privatized companies have a need for later-stage financing to upgrade their networks or to invest in value added or higher band widths. The compelling need for basic service and the desire for advanced services has created a window of opportunity for the large, experienced operator to bring the capital and the expertise required to meet the national telecommunications objectives of developing nations.

The past performance of foreign telecommunications stocks signals high growth opportunities for the owners of newly privatized telecommunications companies. And while domestic telecommunications remain one of the most attractive investments (U.S. telecommunications stocks with large market capitalizations have substantially outperformed other industry stocks; Thompson 1992), telecommunications companies in developing countries have become even more attractive. In fact, the composite price of six of these telecommunications stocks has outperformed the Standard & Poor's index throughout the 1980s and into the 1990s (ibid.).

The stock performance of recently privatized firms also indicates the success of the strategic partnership model. The stock value of shares issued by Telefónica de Argentina, Telecom Argentina, Compañía de Teléfonos de Chile (CTC), Telecom New Zealand, and Teléfonos de México increased between 1991 and 1994, during which time they have been traded on the New York Stock Exchange (figure 12-1). These same stocks significantly outperformed the Standard & Poor's 500 and the Dow Jones Industrial Average in 1993 (figure 12-2).

In addition to the pent-up demand in developing countries, current economic and political developments such as free-trade agreements, a surge in offshore business, and the movement toward free-market economies are creating new and increased demands for telecommunications in the developing regions of the world. At the same time, the number of multinational firms operating in global markets is on the rise. The United Nations estimates that roughly 35,000 multinationals are now in operation, compared to 7,000 in 1970 ("Survey of Multinationals" 1993).

Large corporations increasingly operate in global markets to remain competitive. The relative decline in telecommunications costs and the proliferation of new electronic services has enabled manufacturers, retailers, and others to increase their usage of telecommunications in doing business (Cronin et al. 1992a; Cronin et al. 1992b; Nulty 1989). In the manufacturing and retailing of women's apparel, for instance, companies are able to purchase labor and materials around the world and to electronically integrate their dispersed worldwide sources and production with inventory and orders (Nulty 1989). Such global operations supported by integrated global information systems help ensure the minimum cost of production. In financial markets, integrated global systems are practically indispensable (Warf 1989). Financial transactions are increasingly carried out over electronic media. For example, transactions on the Society for Worldwide Interbank Financial Telecommunications (SWIFT) grew from 20,000 per day in 1977 to 700,000 in 1985 (Nulty 1989). Other service sectors, such as travel and tourism, likewise have come to depend heavily on global telecommunications. In light of the globalization of their customers, telecommunications carriers want to retain corporate account control by offering integrated global communications solutions and "one-stop shopping." Facility ownership abroad helps reduce the cost of providing these types of solutions.

The incentives discussed here have come together in the 1990s to create mutually beneficial opportunities for the developing nations and for private, strategic investors with the knowledge and the capital to construct and manage modern telecommunications systems.

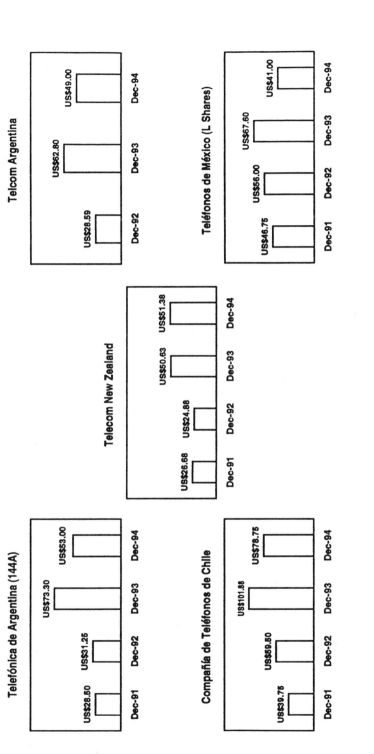

Figure 12-1. Stock Performance of Five Recently Privatized Telecommunications Firms.
Source: Compiled from Lehman Brothers (1995).

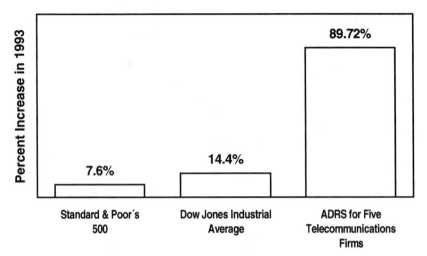

Figure 12-2. Privatized Foreign Telecommunications Stock Performance and Stock Market Averages (1993).
Source: Compiled from Lehman Brothers (1995).
Note: Simple average of change in value of American depository receipts (ADRS) for the following firms: Telefónica de Argentina, Telecom Argentina, Compañía de Teléfonos de Chile, Telecom New Zealand, and Teléfonos de México.

The Evaluation of Privatization Opportunities

The evaluation of the privatization opportunity entails a lengthy and thorough review of the country's conditions, the degree of sector and enterprise restructuring completed prior to the offer of privatization, the projected capital required to expand and modernize the company, the expected financial performance under new ownership and management, and the strategic value of the investment. In general, however, what the private investor seeks is an economically attractive opportunity in a stable environment.

The telecommunications sector—its institutions and regulatory framework—and the individual enterprise structure provide the environment in which the newly privatized company will operate. Its dealings with other state-owned enterprises and the regulatory rules under which it operates will greatly influence the newly privatized company's financial performance. A thorough evaluation of these factors is required to ensure the company's sustainable financial performance.

Other critical aspects of the evaluation process include projecting the capital required to expand and modernize the networks, identifying sources of funding, and evaluating the facility integration and traffic agreements among subsidiaries of the parent company (the right combination of facilities and traffic might enhance the valuation of a foreign telecommunications opportunity). Finally, the risks presented must be analyzed, usually using both domestic and foreign sources.

Management Control

The opportunity to exercise management control or substantial influence in the operation of the privatized company, although not required, is regarded as highly desirable by the strategic investor, given the expansion and modernization commitments that are usually required by the government at the time of sale. Management control will support the telecommunications carrier's ability to leverage its expertise in pursuing greater efficiency and productivity from the privatized company.

In Mexico, for example, Southwestern Bell and France Telecom— partners in the investment consortium that bought a stake in TELMEX— have not gained the right to name the telephone company president, who according to Mexican law has to be a Mexican national. Nevertheless, these strategic investors exert considerable influence by virtue of their experience and their right to appoint some members to the TEL-MEX board of directors. In this case, since January 9, 1991, the TELMEX board of directors has consisted of nine directors named by the Mexican investor group, four named by Southwestern Bell Holdings Corporation, three named by France Cables et Radio, and two more directors named by the holders of class L shares and by the federal government (Telé-fonos de México 1990). This new board of directors ratified the appointment of Juan Antonio Pérez Simon as president of TELMEX (ibid.).

In Venezuela, the GTE-led consortium obtained management control of the company, with the right to name the president of CANTV. This arrangement facilitates the tracking of compliance with network and service objectives, which is necessary to meet concession mandates and to make informed decisions about future expansion and modernization.

Country Conditions

In evaluating a country's stability, the strategic investor will consider the nature of its political institutions, its legal system and tax structure, its fundamental economic and social conditions, the nature of the local and regional marketplace, and the various risks associated with doing business in the country.

Stability in the country's political institutions is critical to the large, private, strategic investor. Instability can mean a high risk, and returns must be commensurate with the risks. The investor will consult and consider the country's risk ratings, which provide some measure of the political, financial, and economic risks associated with doing business in a country. While successful privatizations have occurred in countries with various degrees of political risk, political instability decreases the attractiveness of an investment. As a matter of fact, it may totally deter the large, corporate investor, who generally will not consider investment when a country is classified as unstable.

Of critical importance to the investor is the country's constitution and general legal framework, especially its treatment of property rights. Does the constitution guarantee the right to own property and prohibit the taking of private property for public use without the payment of just compensation? Does legislation exist to authorize the sale of the state-owned enterprise? The investor will also review the country's foreign investment laws. Do they allow for the repatriation of profits? Do they permit the potential buyer to obtain some degree of legal control of the company? While such control may not be an a priori requirement for the investor, it may help ensure the viability of a long-range investment.

Nature of the Market

Lack of a free market and a legal system supporting it will be an obstacle to privatization through the sale of private shares. The economy may be in transition to a free market. If so, when did the transition begin? And is it supported by the government, the institutions, and the people? Any economic stabilization programs will also be studied prior to and during the due diligence process. Specifically, what are the objectives, and the results to date, of the economic reform program? In addition, the strategic investor will evaluate local demographic and economic trends to determine if they ensure sufficient future demand to support the mandated service objectives and the healthy growth of the business.

Sector Restructuring

Economists and investors seem to agree that in most developing nations it will be necessary to reform the telecommunications sector prior to its privatization (Ambrose et al. 1990; Vuylsteke 1988; Wellenius 1989). The required reforms generally encompass changes in the telecommunications and foreign investment laws and the establishment of a regulatory body and policies. Where private investment capital is sought, however, it is generally agreed that regulatory and operating functions must be separate and distinct (O'Neill 1993). From the private investor's point of view, a successful privatization can occur only if the necessary restructuring of the telecommunications sector has been completed before privatization begins. Furthermore, the nature of the legal and regulatory framework will, to a great extent, determine the future value of the company being privatized.

The need to create an institutional infrastructure is typical of most developing countries. For one thing, there has been no need for a regulatory structure in most of these countries, since the public utilities are usually government-owned monopolies and price changes are allowed by law and approved by the government. Furthermore, budgetary cross-subsidies usually exist among the various utilities in these countries. Under this arrangement, the profit from one company covers the losses from another; if the utilities all lose money, then their deficits are covered by national budgets. Although public utilities may have large, outstanding balances due from other government institutions, these typically remain on the books for long periods of time, sometimes being written off entirely. In some cases, services are bartered between government institutions, creating financial distortions. When companies are privatized, it is necessary to create the proper budgetary infrastructure to ensure that the private company will be paid for services rendered. Finally, some mechanism or procedure must be created to resolve the conflicts that inevitably arise, especially as competition is introduced among private carriers of telecommunications.

One possibility is to proceed through the legal system at the national level, as Telefónica de España has done in Chile, in its attempt to enter the long-distance and international market.[1] Another is to turn to international agencies, such as the Geneva-based International Telecommunications Union (ITU), which is currently mediating the access charge dispute between the Dominican Republic's telephone company (CODETEL) and All America Cable and Radio, a competitor in the long-distance market (Campbell 1993). A third possibility, as we have observed for Peru, is arbitration, which allows a company to resolve conflicts without going through the local courts.

Efforts at institutional restructuring have met with varying degrees of success in those countries with newly privatized telecommunications networks. Argentina, Chile, New Zealand, and Venezuela have succeeded in separating regulatory and operating functions, a condition necessary for successful sector restructuring, particularly when private capital is sought. While the regulatory scheme has apparently worked in Chile, which restructured the sector well before divestiture (Galal et al. 1994), some false starts have been observed in Argentina. Many countries have also instituted some form of price regulation. But given the relatively recent history of telecommunications privatizations, it is perhaps premature to evaluate efforts at institutional reform in developing countries.

Enterprise Restructuring

Some governments have recognized a need to make their telecommunications company as attractive as possible. New Zealand, for example, hired an experienced executive, Peter Troughton, from England, to operate the New Zealand telephone company for two years prior to the sale. He recruited a new management team and achieved drastic changes in the company so that it could successfully be sold (Jones 1992).

Actually, few government-owned enterprises are ready to be sold to the private sector without some examination and reform of their finances and operations (Vuylsteke 1988; Takano 1992). The common steps required prior to sale have been listed and discussed in other publications (Vuylsteke 1988). Of particular concern to potential investors, however, are the financial accounting system, the pension plan and employee benefits, and the quality and the attitude of the labor force.

The rate-rebalancing process and the related requirement of capturing billing details are the most difficult and expensive tasks for the new owners. Old equipment is not usually capable of traffic measurement, so the new owners will be required to install modern equipment and systems that permit the tracking and cost accounting of local and long-distance calls. Identifying international traffic is usually an easier task, because many firms have installed modern international gateways to keep pace with international carriers.

Corporate and cost-accounting systems will facilitate the privatization process and help the investor valuate and value the company (Takano 1992). Ideally, the privatizing company and the potential investor understand the details of the historic revenues and costs by service category (e.g., local, long-distance, and international). The availability of cost-accounting data by service category will shape the investor's assumptions about subsequent rate rebalancing and potential revenues under the new management.

Contrary to what some authors report (Vuylsteke 1988), the profitability of the company being sold is not necessarily one of the determinants of how easy or difficult the sale will be. When dramatic changes are required in the company, the past financial performance will be largely irrelevant. What is important for assessing value, besides the physical condition of the company, are the terms and conditions of its future operation and the requirements for expansion, modernization, and introduction of new services. These become a matter of negotiation during the bidding process.

The Regulatory Framework

The investor's evaluation of the company's future performance depends almost entirely on the rules of the game, that is, the regulatory conditions under which the company will operate. These include the method for determining future rate increases, the rules for incorporating inflation and productivity effects on rates, and the regulatory scheme imposed upon the company. The regulatory scheme under which the new owners will operate is, in fact, shaped in part by the companies that are bidding. Before these companies present their qualifications to bid, and during the bidding process, company representatives usually meet with the government to discuss and negotiate the regulatory rules. Companies that find the rules unacceptable do not bid. Rejection of the regulatory scheme is one of the primary reasons that companies drop out of the bidding process.

Given a lack of cost-accounting data bases and the time and expense required to develop them, private investors regard those regulatory schemes that require filing cost data by line of business as particularly burdensome. Preferable is price cap regulation, which allows the government to control the amount of revenues the operators realize while they rebalance rates. In general the new owners will find less burdensome those regulatory schemes that tie price regulation to market forces than those that require proof of cost.

In Argentina the regulatory structure developed at the time of privatization did not succeed. The structure collapsed due to lack of government commitment. The original decision to create a regulatory body was a political one and did not grow out of sector policy: the president perceived that a regulatory structure had to be created, and a skeleton structure was hurriedly developed (in only four days) as a matter of expedience (personal conversation with Judith O'Neill, Sept. 7, 1993). The members of the regulatory directorate labored their first five months with no salary; one year after its creation the directorate was disbanded, with the functions reverting back to the secretariat. Fortunately, the government of Argentina has since focused on the need to regulate its telecommunications sector and is now committed to overseeing it.

In Mexico, even though the regulatory function was not taken out of the secretariat, the government did have a clear commitment to regulate and oversee the sector, and this commitment was spelled out in the written concession. Perhaps some of the regulatory success observed in Mexico after privatization can be attributed to the fact that the regulators were not part of TELMEX before privatization.

Capital Requirements

The strategic investor must project the capital required to fulfil the unmet and future demand for telecommunications services and to meet the government's network and service mandates. Besides satisfying the demand for basic telephone lines, the recently privatized company must provide new services to meet the needs of the country's business customers. Therefore the capital required during the expansion and modernization phase is typically huge. The buyers, who have already invested a substantial amount to purchase the company, will usually require that funds for further investments be internally generated or borrowed from capital markets, in which case the company must have the appropriate leverage to borrow. The CANTV expansion, for example, was financed by internally generated funds and leveraged borrowing; no fresh money was generated by private investment the first and second years of operation.

Strategic Value

A global telecommunications investor will also evaluate factors that contribute to the strategic value of a company. Such factors include "hubbing" and "transiting" opportunities that stem from the geographical location of the country relative to the purchasing company's other subsidiaries. The strategic location of its facilities allows a company to use them and its overall cost position optimally by concentrating and transiting traffic over its own networks rather than paying outside carriers to do so. The right opportunity could enhance the ability of an operator such as GTE (which has operations in the Dominican Republic, Canada, Venezuela, Hawaii, and Micronesia) to carry much international traffic exclusively over its own facilities.

Other synergies can be gained in marketing and sales. Market analysis and segmentation techniques, usage forecasting driven by cultural and ethnic usage patterns, and other market planning and analysis "technology" can be transferred from the parent company to the subsidiary, and among subsidiaries, these factors can reduce the cost of product planning, design, development, and deployment.

Risks

The strategic investor faces many risks when becoming an owner or operator of a developing country's telecommunications system. Private consultants and research organizations offer country-risk rankings showing the relative political, economic, financial, and composite risks associated with doing business around the globe. Such rankings may be reviewed by the telecommunications investor when formulating overall strategy and when evaluating a particular telecommunications investment. The initial evaluation of risk, however, is usually based on the investor's perception of a country's stability and is then adjusted depending on further information about the political and economic risks.

A high degree of country risk may limit the investor's ability to raise capital. The cost of capital in the United States is usually the floor for the discount rate, which increases as risk increases. Some of the risks factored into the value and represented by the discount rate assigned to the valuation project include the political situation, various economic factors (GDP growth, inflation, and exchange rate fluctuation), the degree of competition in the market, the pace of change to a market economy, and the management of relations with government, regulatory agencies, labor unions, and partners. The strategic investor also faces other risks in the operation of foreign telecommunications networks: the possibility of the nationalization of the enterprise, as occurred in Chile (Galal et al. 1994), Argentina (see chapter 4), Jamaica (see chapter 2), Venezuela (Francés 1993), and Mexico (see chapter 3).

Personal risks to management employees in the newly privatized foreign company must not be overlooked or understated, either. In Venezuela, for example, the government issued arrest orders for some top executives of GTE and AT&T in connection with a natural gas line explosion that killed commuters in Caracas. The telephone company executives were initially held responsible because CANTV had contracted the engineering firm that cut through the gas pipeline that exploded. (Some observers, however, attributed the arrest orders to preelection politics.) The executives were eventually cleared of any responsibility (Luxner 1993c). In Argentina, Enedor (power company) executives were incarcerated for cutting power to shantytown residents who did not pay their bills (Nash 1993). These cases illustrate the perils of privatization when a country's judicial process is easily influenced by political pressure.

The Bidding Process

From the investor's point of view, the bidding process has to fulfill certain requirements to ensure the representatives of the potential investing consortium that the process is a fair one. The primary requirement of the bidding process is that it be transparent, meaning that the process be open and competitive (Jones 1992; Kikeri et al. 1992). Lack of transparency could lead to the perception that the process is unfair and could discourage the best firms from bidding. Furthermore, the perception of unfairness can result in a subsequent political backlash and create public relations problems for the new owner. The bidding process should provide for enough time for comprehensive due diligence visits, should outline clear criteria for evaluating the bids, and should provide disclosure of the final purchase price and the buyer. In addition, the review process must be consistent and well defined and have realistic deadlines. If at all possible, there should be a single point of contact between potential investors and government agencies. One authorized voice representing the government helps eliminate confusion and facilitates the meeting of deadlines.

Setting an unrealistic minimum bid can result in failure to privatize, as happened in Puerto Rico (Kikeri et al. 1992; Thompson 1992). Based on unrealistic advice, the Puerto Rican enabling law set a minimum price of US$2 billion plus assumption of US$1 billion of debt, prohibited any increase in tariffs, and prohibited termination of any employees as a result of the sale. With only about 900,000 lines, the terms and prices proved unrealistic, and the government was unable to attract a bid. Subsequently, the enabling law expired without the sale of the company (Kikeri et al. 1992). In addition, there were negotiations between the Puerto Rican regulatory body, GTE, and Telefónica de España for TLD (Telefónica Larga Distancia), Puerto Rico's second-largest long-distance company. These negotiations also failed because the legislature set unrealistic price expectations. Subsequently, the government changed its expectations and reached a private deal with Spain's Telefónica to buy 80 percent of TLD for US$142 million. Incidentally, the sale was opposed by the major long-distance carriers in the United States, where the FCC had to approve it, given Puerto Rico's status as a U.S. commonwealth. In the end, the FCC did approve the sale, with conditions that would comply with the U.S. Communications Act of 1934, which prohibits foreign ownership of more than 25 percent of a U.S. radio licensee (Luxner 1993a, 1993b; Burkhart 1993).

Negotiations

Various documents negotiated during the privatization process spell out the terms and conditions of future operations. These documents usually include a charter, a license or concession agreement, and the regulatory rules. The concession contract method has been applied for over a century in France, but its typical provisions vary among countries (Vuylsteke 1988). In Venezuela, for example, the concession is essentially a franchise that sets forth the scope of the permitted business during the period of exclusivity. In the telecommunications sector, it typically contains requirements for network development, quality improvement, and regulation of prices. The method has also been used extensively in the power and water sectors.

The concession establishes the right of the company to be in specific businesses, such as voice, data, video, and value added services. The concession also spells out the terms and conditions under which the company will operate in the future, the terms and conditions for interconnection requirements, and the company's obligations with respect to the network and to customer service. The extent to which the business will be subject to competition, the period of exclusivity, and the methods for determining future rates and rate increases are part of the regulatory rules.

The concession obviously is of critical importance in valuing the future streams of earnings. In past privatizations, succeeding drafts of the concession have been available to all potential bidders for their input and comment. The bidders must discuss the concession while they conduct a due diligence review of the company. Any changes made in the concession during the bidding process usually substantially affect the investors' view of the company's prospects and, therefore, its valuation. Most of the discussion and negotiation surrounding the concession agreement in previous privatizations have focused on the issues of eliminating cross-subsidies, introducing competition, and rebalancing rates. While service mandates also generate discussion, the issues of competition and rate rebalancing usually generate the most disagreement between the investors and the government; typically, these issues continue to be debated following privatization, as in Venezuela.

Competition and Exclusivity

Lack of competition is said by some to be an impediment to privatization. Various World Bank studies generally endorse the idea of reducing monopoly and introducing competition into the telecommunications sector as part of the privatization process, especially as a means of ensuring increased efficiency and productivity (Kikeri et al. 1992; Vuylsteke 1988; Wellenius 1989). One study called protection from competition an "exorbitant advantage" (Vuylsteke 1988). Other authors endorse competition as a way to protect the public interest following privatization (Goodman and Loveman 1991). From the strategic investor's point of view, however, some protection from open competition will facilitate the privatization of telecommunications in developing countries. Investors may argue against competition in the profitable sections of the telecommunications sector until basic expansion and service quality improvements are completed and rates are rebalanced. When local exchange rates are heavily subsidized by national and international long-distance tolls, as is true in many telecommunications markets, it is unrealistic to expect a commercial company to provide universal service and invest in new facilities. Some observers recognize a need to delay competition in the newly privatized markets of developing countries and most understand that doing so will also increase the franchise value of the existing service provider (Kok 1992; Takano 1992; Thompson 1992).

For competition to be beneficial, it is necessary to allow for the development and upgrading of the basic network infrastructure and the availability of service at reasonable prices. Government priorities during the first stages of privatization, when telephone penetration is very low, are the expansion of the network and the provision of basic services to all who can afford them, along with the modernization of the telecommunications infrastructure. It is one thing for a country with a developed telecommunications infrastructure to introduce competition. When telephone service is widely available, competition can result in efficiencies, innovation, greater customer choice, and lower prices to the consumer. For these reasons, New Zealand, which had a well-developed telecommunications network, decided to allow full competition when it reorganized the telecommunications sector beginning in 1986 (Lojkine 1992). It is quite a different matter, however, to allow competition when the telecommunications infrastructure is not developed and when the issue is the availability of telephone service at any cost. In those countries where local service is drastically underpriced at the expense of national and international long-distance tolls, the objectives of improving service and expanding the network are incompatible with the introduction of competition.

A country's advisers may shape the government's initial position with respect to competition. In Venezuela, for instance, the government's advisers proposed a concession agreement and regulations that had the effect of opening the profitable sections of the telecommunications sector to competition while requiring the company, CANTV, to develop and expand the national telecommunications infrastructure and improve service. These objectives ignored the fact that CANTV's rate structure contained heavily subsidized local exchange rates, and the proposal did not present an effective method for eliminating these subsidies. It was unrealistic to expect a business to invest in new facilities and sell service below cost. In Venezuela, the flat rate component of local service charges was about US$0.75 a month, and local service was heavily subsidized by national and international long-distance service. Allowing competition in the overpriced national and international markets would result in CANTV quickly losing large customers in these markets and losing the revenue streams necessary for the required development of the basic telecommunications infrastructure. The various bidders explained these issues to the government group in charge of privatization. Subsequently, the government changed advisers and made significant changes to the proposed concession and regulations (Sonnenschein 1993). Had there not been a change in these rules, some major investors would not have bid for CANTV.

Rate Rebalancing

The ultimate goal of rate rebalancing is to align prices with costs to prepare the newly privatized company to operate in a competitive environment. Albeit difficult to estimate joint costs in the telecommunications industry, industrialized countries (mainly the United States) have considerable experience in either cost accounting or statistical methods to determine service cost. The proxy for the cost of providing local service is the cost of the "local loop," meaning the wire from the closest central office to the customer premises. The local monthly rebalanced rate should reflect this cost. In the case of Venezuela, the rebalancing went from US$0.75 to US$7.00, following an equation established by the government. The total price change is expected to be achieved during the nine-year period of exclusivity. A crucial point in this negotiation, from the point of view of the investor, is therefore the local rate and the flexibility to make the price changes. The price control mechanism must (1) promote competition by allowing price restructuring, (2) allow flexibility to establish prices that ensure the financial viability of the company, and (3) provide economic incentives to increase operational productivity, which will benefit the company and the consumers.

Price ceiling regulation offers the flexibility to achieve these objectives. Generally, the price ceiling system addresses the composition of service baskets, the controlling factor (to adjust for inflation), and the rule of maximum price adjustment. Essentially, price ceiling control allows the change in the composition of revenues among the various service elements, allowing the rationalization of prices in alignment with costs. Under this scheme, the growth of gross revenues will depend on the growth of the subscriber base, productivity increases, and the price elasticity of demand. Allowing the company operators to benefit by productivity increases, which will be shared with consumers, will provide economic incentives and financial viability, which is necessary to prepare for open competition. The terms of the concession will guide the value assigned to the company by the prospective investor. Ideally, tariff rebalancing will begin early. The interests of buyers and sellers will be served if the principles behind tariff modifications are transparent and follow internationally recognized procedures.

Service Objectives

The concession will usually mandate specific objectives for expansion and service improvements. Service objectives usually include expansion and quality of service objectives, such as number of lines to install per year and percentage improvement of call completion rate, repair response time, etcetera. The costs associated with service mandates have considerable impact on the valuation of the company. For instance, during its first four years as a private company, TELMEX of Mexico is required to expand the number of lines in service by an average minimum annual rate of 12 percent. The CANTV of Venezuela is required to grow from approximately 1.6 million lines in 1991 to more than 4.4 million lines by the year 2000. At the same time, the companies must meet increasingly higher quality standards, so that by the end of the decade quality will equal or exceed that currently provided by U.S. telecommunications companies.

The first issue of concern to the investor in evaluating such objectives is whether they are realistic. The investor, being market driven, would normally aim to exceed the mandate for customer demand and quality service. Therefore, although the objectives may be aggressive (as is true in Mexico and Venezuela), the investor will evaluate whether they are also realistic, given the marketplace. The second issue that concerns the telecommunications investor is its ability to develop the required infrastructure in the newly privatized environment. Meeting these mandated objectives will depend on the stability of the concession. Assuming the concession is balanced, proposals to change it in order to achieve other political reforms could upset the balance. The agreements in the concession must not be changed for political expedience; any changes must be agreed upon by the company and the government. Stability in the concession is critical to the investor, because the value placed on the company is derived from the rules established during negotiations. Such stability can be enhanced if the negotiators indeed represent the country and have the authority to negotiate without being overruled. Creating a professional regulatory agency separated from the political process will also enhance the stability of the concession.

Due Diligence

Due diligence means that the investor evaluates the changes required in the privatizing company and the cost of making these changes. During due diligence, potential bidders collect, review, and evaluate information about the company being privatized and the country conditions. The process is lengthy, taking several months to complete. Ideally, due diligence entails a review of company records and the information memorandum provided to all qualified bidders. In addition, bidders interview company managers and customers. Site visits to the company, permitting a review of the physical facilities, a review of the actual records, and interviews with company managers, facilitate the due diligence process.

Due diligence encompasses the review and analysis of the fundamental aspects of the business, which include a review of (1) records of lines and subscribers, (2) operation records and service indicators, (3) financial records (treasury, accounting, and auditing), (4) systems, (5) billing and customer service operations and access to commercial and business offices, (6) supply and inventory systems and access to warehouses, (7) operation systems and access to operation facilities, and (8) the human resources situation (employees' records, salary and benefit structure, pension plan, and organizational structure).

To ensure that the process is fair (that all bidders have access to the same information), due diligence and access to information is monitored by the government. Documents in the data room should be accessible for reviewing and copying. During this period, the government needs to make available to potential investors (1) the records of the company, (2) the management personnel, and (3) the facilities (e.g., office buildings, commercial offices, switching centers, earth stations, and communications towers).

Governments may engage an investment banking firm to monitor the due diligence process, as occurred in New Zealand, Mexico, and Venezuela. Argentina controlled the due diligence process by creating a special office of privatization to oversee its fairness to all bidders. In all of these countries, bidders had access to company officials and personnel, buildings, records, etcetera. (In Greece, union opposition and opposition by officials to the privatization of the OTE was such that bidders had limited or no access to company records and buildings.)

Valuing the Company

Large telecommunications corporations currently have many opportunities to invest at home and abroad; investment in a foreign company is only one of various opportunities they consider. When evaluating opportunities, corporations utilize the portfolio management approach to select those investments presenting the highest potential for return. They also establish investment criteria, which may include synergy with the core business and returns on investment commensurate with the risks of operating in a foreign environment.

The approach usually taken to determine the value of an investment opportunity is based on projections of the future business and not on the historic financial performance of the company. The investor begins by assessing the stream of revenues expected from the lines of business allowed by the concession and by calculating the capital required to develop the necessary telecommunications infrastructure. The nature of the business means that acquisitions are usually viewed as very long-term commitments. Investments in telecommunications infrastructure are recovered quite slowly. Large, new investments are needed each year to develop and expand the network and to improve quality. Funds for this new investment usually come from internally generated cash and from the ability of the privatized company to raise new capital in the financial markets. Thus, the financial viability of the business depends upon striking a balance among modernization and expansion requirements, competition, and rate regulation.

The evaluation process may vary among companies, but most investors will evaluate a project from two complementary points of view: (1) a stand-alone valuation and (2) a valuation from the point of view of the investor. The stand-alone valuation represents the perspective of a local investor (or any other investor); it is usually called the local value and is based on the company's free-cash flows, its weighted average cost of capital, and the terminal value, represented by earnings before interests, taxes, depreciation, and amortization (EBITDA multiple) and by the growth of free-cash flow.

The valuation from the point of view of the investor is ultimately the way the strategic investor looks at the value of the company to be acquired. This approach is usually termed *value to the parent company* and is based on cash flows of dividends net of U.S. taxes, the cost of capital (represented by the cost of equity adjusted for country risk), and the terminal value (represented by EBITDA multiple and net dividend growth). In some circumstances, investors may forgo an attractive investment because the effect on their operations and stock performance are not deemed worth the risk or not agreed upon by their board of directors.

Strategic Partnerships

Although large, modern telecommunications carriers are usually able to bid alone, they may decide to form a bidding consortium, primarily to spread the financial requirements and the risk of the investment. Another reason corporations seek partnerships is to form joint ventures and strategic alliances that will allow them to be global players in the telecommunications market. Each consortium partner probably has a specific objective: U.S. local operating companies (such as GTE and the Bell companies) look for expansion into profitable, growing markets; European, full-service providers and global long-distance carriers may seek strategic alliances as protection against competition; all international traffic carriers seek to consolidate transiting and hubbing agreements and to facilitate the optional use and sharing of hubs; and equipment vendors undoubtedly view consortium membership as an opportunity to sell equipment to the local market, especially during the early postprivatization years, when large network expansion occurs. Usually, consortia form from the list of qualified bidders. The successful formation of a consortium among a number of firms depends on the relations and interests of the various parties. Therefore, consensus in major decision-making should be an overriding goal of the consortium.

Having the right partners can enhance the chances of success before and after the bid. The stability of the consortium will also be enhanced if the members complement each other and each brings a specific expertise to the management of the new company. In the privatization of TELMEX, for example, the winning consortium consists of a holding company, Grupo Carso and two advanced operators, Southwestern Bell and France Cables et Radio, a subsidiary of France Telecom. The holding company, Grupo Carso, brings expertise in managing business in highly competitive markets, more specifically, lending expertise in general administration and government-labor relations (Teléfonos de México 1990; Luxner 1992). Southwestern Bell assists TELMEX with network maintenance, customer service, billing, Yellow Pages, and office procedures, while France Telecom lends expertise in network planning, long-distance, and credit card phones (Luxner 1992). The long-term commitment of these partners in the management of TELMEX is ensured through restrictions on transfers of holdings and requirements on bloc voting.

In Venezuela, GTE formed a consortium that included Telefónica de España, AT&T, and two local partners—Banco Mercantil and Electricidad de Caracas. Telefónica's experience in managing both sophisticated data networks and elementary networks in rural communities was very valuable, especially during the period of intense network development following privatization in a country like Venezuela. AT&T, being one of the largest international carriers, lent its experience in the development of the international traffic sector of Venezuela. The local partners brought knowledge of the local financial and labor markets. Banco Mercantil, one of the largest banks in Venezuela, brought knowledge of local cash flow management, local capital and consumer markets, and advertising. Electricidad de Caracas, the private power company, brought its experience in outside plant construction, local subcontractors, subcontract arrangements, and the local labor market. These areas of knowledge were all invaluable to GTE in meeting the expansion requirements of CANTV during the first year of operation. While local ownership and control may not be a privatization requirement, an international consortium with substantial local participation may be very desirable. Local ownership may also take the form of stock flotation in the domestic market and employee stock ownership. Broad-based local ownership can be a stabilizing force, and employee stock ownership can help transform the state-owned company to an efficient, responsive, private company.

The large telecommunications carrier brings not only capital but management and technical expertise to privatization. In the United States, for example, the large local carriers (GTE and regional Bell holding companies) together manage about 128 million customer lines, or an average of about 16 million lines each (FCC 1991–92). Furthermore, their expertise in managing these large networks is evident in the extremely high local completion rate found in the United States, where the percentage of local calls that fail is only 0.5 for the holding companies (OECD 1993). In France and Spain, where France Telecom and Telefónica de España provide all local and long-distance services on a monopoly basis, the local call failure rates are only 0.7 and 2.0, respectively. Low failure rates indicate that the networks are well managed and are large enough to handle the traffic.

Besides their network management skills, the major telecommunications carriers, particularly in the United States and, to some extent, in Great Britain, also bring market management, forecasting, and restructuring skills. Due to the trend in the United States to make telecommunications more competitive, the carriers have had to develop marketing skills to sell new services and retain customers. And through their continued efforts to lower costs, local exchange carriers have developed organization restructuring skills, which allow them to eliminate duplication of effort and reduce the labor force. These same skills will enhance the U.S. carriers' ability to manage the transition from a public to a private telephone company.

Although the state telephone company could obtain capital from one source and hire expertise from another, the ability to raise capital and manage key technical functions has made high-caliber network operators the favored private equity investors in such privatizations. There is some indication that privatized telephone companies in developing countries may grow more rapidly and operate more efficiently when managed by another network operator-investor than when managed by private investors without telecommunications experience. In Chile, for example, under Telefónica de España, the CTC has outperformed its record under Alan Bond, the Australian investor with no background in telecommunications who bought the CTC in January 1988. (Standard & Poor's 1986–91; CTC 1992). The firm can expect faster deployment if the assessment of technical requirements and capital budgets are under the same management umbrella. It can also expect more accountability if the same organization is responsible for the budget and its management.

Attracting Buyers

Telephone company privatizations have attracted many potential bidders, including many of the large, well-known telecommunications firms around the world. However, relatively few of these firms continue through the entire privatization process and actually bid. If one sees the privatization of state-owned telephone companies and the liberalization of telecommunications in other countries to be a positive development, it is relevant to inquire why many firms with an obvious interest—and that even prequalify as bidders—nevertheless fail to complete the process.

The conditions that promote a bid can be broadly grouped as those involving the country itself, the process being followed, and the company to be privatized. Since no two privatizations are the same, the conditions (listed below) may or may not be encountered in a particular telephone company divestiture:

Country

—Popular support provides opportunity to privatize.

—Political and economic stability lowers risk-adjusted cost of capital.

—A free market and private ownership of property support large, long payback investment.

—A liberal foreign investment law and currency translation facilitate company management and repatriation of dividends.

—Economic growth and telecommunications demand provide attractive opportunity.

Process

—Wide government support facilitates unified objectives.

—Strong leadership, good advice, and enabling legislation create realistic expectations and present attractive investment opportunity.

—A fair process attracts the best firms.

—Available, accessible information facilitates company valuation.

—Well-thought-out regulatory rules ensure benefits for the country and enable the sustained viability of the business.

—A well-defined and well-communicated review process eliminates confusion and ensures that bidders can meet deadlines.

Company

—An acceptable network and plant condition ensure fundable investment to expand and upgrade.

—A reasonable debt/equity ratio ensures the ability to raise capital to expand and modernize.

—Reasonable cross-subsidized rates ensure a price/cost alignment before competition commences.

—Reasonable bureaucracy, staffing, and financing of pension plans and flexible personnel policies ensure the ability to improve efficiency.

—Work ethics ensure the acceptance of the parent company's ethical standards.

Advice to Investors

Each privatization presents unique challenges, but some general insights may be gleaned from previous divestitures. Some of these points have already been discussed, but others deserve further comment:

—Conduct preliminary evaluation of the politics and economics of the country.

—Get involved early in the privatization process, to participate in the development of the privatization plans and the conditions of the concession.

—Engage local legal representation.

—Devote personnel to study the history, culture, customs, and language of the country before conducting the evaluation.

—Select local partners that can contribute to the management of the company.

—Be aware of the possibility of personnel risks.

—Be prepared to manage in a different cultural environment.

—Ensure the early preparation of transition plans. Ensure ready and able personnel available to manage the ownership changeover in the subsidiary as well as in the parent company.

Summary

With a successful telephone company privatization, everyone wins: the government, the customers, the employees, the investors, and the country. The government not only obtains a large amount of money, it also acquires an experienced operator with the knowledge, expertise, and obligation to expand the network, provide service to the entire country, and improve quality. In Venezuela, for example, where CANTV invested some US$500 million in 1992, major improvements have been recorded (Bottome 1993). In one year, the total number of lines increased by more than 300,000, or 10.59 percent, the number of pay phones rose by 42 percent, and call completion rates improved in all categories: local rates rose from 47.9 percent to 53.4 percent, national rates from 30.5 percent to 39.1 percent, and international rates from 19 percent to almost 33 percent. Improvements in repairs were also evident after the first year of privatization: fewer breakdowns were recorded, and the percentage breakdown repaired within forty-eight hours rose from 58.1 percent to 77.7 percent.

The mere availability of service is the primary, initial benefit to customers, who also reap more benefits as the quality of that service improves. In Venezuela, over 200,000 subscribers were connected to the network during the first year of private operation (ibid.). The various service improvements were reflected in customers' opinions. In one year, the proportion of satisfied pay phone users increased from 27 to 55.7 percent, satisfied residential customers increased from 46.8 to 52.8 percent, and satisfied business customers increased from 36.1 to 51.3 percent (ibid.).

Employees benefit from privatization by their association with a growing, dynamic company and, in many cases, by receiving salary increases and the funding of their retirement plan accounts, as in Venezuela. In addition, they may be given the option to purchase shares in the company on very favorable terms, as in Argentina and Venezuela.

Investors benefit from a successful privatization by seeing their investment achieve positive change in the company's operations. Such change is reflected in the telephone company's stock value and its revenues, as in Venezuela, where CANTV's revenues rose 70 percent after one year of private operation and for the first time climbed to more than US$1 billion ("GTE Consortium Reports" 1993, 9).

Finally, and perhaps most importantly, are the benefits of successful telephone privatization to the country and its economy. The initial investments following privatization will, of course, immediately benefit local contractors and suppliers. The long-term effects of such investments, however, are perhaps incalculable.

NOTE

1. The CTC, which is owned in part by Telefónica de España, began preparing to enter the long-distance market by investing about US$75 million in a fiber-optic network, along with an earth station and transponders. In response, ENTel Chile, the primary long-distance carrier, filed an antimonopoly suit in 1989 with Chile's Fair Trade Office, claiming that it was unfair for the CTC to enter the long-distance market before developing the less-profitable rural markets. Meanwhile, ENTel also applied for a concession to enter the local market in Santiago. The CTC in turn objected to ENTel's efforts, arguing that the latter should not be allowed to skim the profitable service areas while ignoring less attractive markets. Rulings and appeals continued into 1993, when a final decision on the million-carrier system was reached, allowing the CTC to enter the long-distance business with some initial restrictions and if it set up a separate company (now called CTC Mundo) to handle it (Orgill 1994; Morgan Stanley 1993).

REFERENCES

Aharoni, Yair. 1991. "On Measuring the Success of Privatization." In *Privatization and Control of State-Owned Enterprises*, ed. Ravi Ramamurti and Raymond Vernon. Washington, D.C.: World Bank.

Ambrose, William W., Paul R. Hennemeyer, and Jean-Paul Chapon. 1990.

Privatizing Telecommunications Systems: Business Opportunities in Developing Countries. Discussion Paper 10. Washington, D.C.: World Bank.

AT&T. 1993. *The World's Telephones.* Morris Plains, N.J.: AT&T International Marketing.

Bottome, R. 1993. "CANTV: The Giant Stirs." *VenEconomy Monthly* (Mar.): 12–15.

Burkhart, L. A. 1993. "FCC Approves Overseas Purchase of Puerto Rican Telco." *Public Utilities Fortnightly* 131 (Jan. 15): 40.

Campbell, Catherine. 1993. "Telephone War Afoot." *Business Latin America* 28 (May 17): 6.

Cronin, Francis J., Mark A. Gold, and Steven Lewitzky. 1992a. "Telecommunications Technology, Sectoral Prices, and International Competitiveness." *Telecommunications Policy* 16 (Sept.–Oct.): 553–64.

Cronin, Francis J., P. Herbert, and E. Colleran. 1992b. "Linking Telecommunications and Economic Competitiveness." *Telephony* 223: 38–42.

CTC (Compañía de Teléfonos de Chile). 1992. *Annual Report.* Santiago.

EIU (Economist Intelligence Unit). 1992, 1993. *Uruguay, Paraguay.* Country Report 4 (1992). Country Report 1 (1993). London.

Francés, Antonio. 1993. *¡Aló Venezuela! Apertura y Privatización de las Telecomunicaciones.* Caracas: Conetel Ediciones IESA.

Galal, Ahmed, Leroy P. Jones, Pankaj Tandon, and Ingo Vogelsang, eds. 1994. *Welfare Consequences of Selling Public Enterprises: An Empirical Analysis.* New York: Oxford Univ. Press.

Golob, J. 1992. "Will Telecommunications Remain a Golden Sector?" *Telecommunications Policy* 6 (Dec.): 738–43.

Gonzales-Lanuza, Luis M. G. 1992. "The Argentine Telephone Privatization." *Telecommunications Policy* 16 (Dec.): 759–63.

Goodman, John B., and Gary W. Loveman. 1991 "Does Privatization Serve the Public Interest?" *Harvard Business Review* 99 (Nov.–Dec.): 26–38.

"GTE Consortium Reports Billion Dollar Revenue in Venezuela." 1993. *Global Telecommunications Report.* Potomac, Md.: Phillips Business Information.

Hope, K. 1993. "Greek Telecommunications Workers Seek to Halt Sell-Off." *Financial Times,* Aug. 13.

Jones, Andrew. 1992. "Remarks Delivered to CONATEL." July 1. Caracas.

Jussawalla, Meheroo. 1992. "Is the Communications Link Still Missing?" *Telecommunications Policy* 16 (Aug.): 486–503.

Kikeri, Sunita, John Nellis, and Mary Shirley. 1992. *Privatization: The Lessons of Experience.* Washington, D.C.: World Bank.

Kok, Bessel. 1992. "Privatization in Telecommunications: Empty Slogan or Strategic Tool?" *Telecommunications Policy* 16 (Dec.): 699–704.

Lehman Brothers. 1995. *Global Telecommunications Team Comments.* New York.

Lojkine, S. M. 1992. "The New Zealand Experience." *Telecommunications Policy* 16 (Dec.): 768–76.

Luxner, Larry. 1992. "Mexico Reaches for New Telecom Heights." *Telephony* 222:22–28.

———. 1993a. "FCC OK's Telefónica's Puerto Rico Buy." *Telephony* 224:9–10.

────. 1993b. "Puerto Rico Privatization: Down to the Wire." *Telephony* 223:13–17.

────. 1993c. "Top GTE Executives Arrested Following Explosion at Venezuelan Telco." *Telephony* 225:9.

────. 1993d. "Uruguay Voters Kill Privatization." *Telephony* 224:3.

Morgan Stanley and Co., Inc. 1993. *Emerging Markets Investment Research.* New York.

Nankani, Helen. 1988. *Techniques of Privatization of State-Owned Enterprises: Selected Country Case Studies.* Vol. 2. Washington, D.C.: World Bank.

Nash, Nathaniel C. 1993. "Unrest Shows Argentina the Perils of Privatization." *New York Times,* June 15.

Nulty, Timothy E. 1989. "Emerging Issues in World Telecommunications." In *Restructuring and Managing the Telecommunications Sector,* ed. Bjorn Wellenius, Peter A. Stern, Timothy E. Nulty, and Richard D. Stern. Washington, D.C.: World Bank.

O'Neill, Judith D. 1993. "The Legal/Regulatory Dynamics of the Changing Telecommunications Environment." Paper prepared for the meeting of Caribbean/Latin American Action, Panama City, June 14–16.

Orgill, Margaret. 1994. "The More the Merrier." *Business Latin America.* May 30.

Pyramid Research. 1993. *Pyramid Research Latin America* 1 (Jan.): 10; (June): 2.

Ramamurti, Ravi. 1991. "The Search for Remedies." In Ramamurti and Vernon, eds., *Privatization and Control of State-Owned Enterprises.*

Ramamurti, Ravi, and Raymond Vernon, eds. 1991. *Privatization and Control of State-Owned Enterprises.* Washington, D.C.: World Bank.

Saunders, Robert J., Jeremy J. Warford, and Bjorn Wellenius. 1994. 2d ed. *Telecommunications and Economic Development.* Baltimore: Johns Hopkins Univ. Press.

Serrano, Ronald, P. William Bane, and W. Brooke Tunstall. 1991. "Reshaping the Global Telecommunications Industry." *Telephony* 221:38–42.

Sonnenschein, Mabelle. 1993. "Evaluation of Investment in a Foreign Operating Company: The Case of Venezuela." Paper prepared for World Bank seminar sponsored by A. D. Little, Washington, D.C., Mar. 10.

Standard & Poor's. 1986–91. *Standard Corporation Records.* New York.

"A Survey of Multinationals." 1993. *Economist,* Mar. 27.

Takano, Yoshiro. 1992. *Nippon Telegraph and Telephone Privatization Study: The Experience of Japan and Lessons for Developing Countries.* Discussion Paper 179. Washington, D.C.: World Bank.

Teléfonos de México, S. A. de C. V. 1990 *Annual Report.* Mexico City.

Thompson, Samme. 1992. "Telecommunications Privatizations and International Capital Markets." *Telecommunications Policy* 16 (Dec.): 732–37.

Vuylsteke, Charles. 1988. *Techniques of Privatization of State-Owned Enterprises: Methods and Implementation.* Vol. 1. Washington, D.C.: World Bank.

Warf, B. 1989. "Telecommunications and the Globalization of Financial Services." *Professional Geographer* 41 (3): 257–71.

Wellenius, Bjorn. 1989. "Beginnings of Sector Reform in the Developing World." In *Restructuring and Managing the Telecommunications Sector,* ed. Bjorn Wellenius, Peter A. Stern, Timothy E. Nulty, and Richard D. Stern. Washington, D.C.: World Bank.

13. Infrastructure Concession Design and Financing Issues

. . . .

José Luis Guasch

By the early 1990s, it was evident that gaps in infrastructure in Latin America and the Carribean were extremely wide, in terms of both the number of people with no access to service and the quality of service. For example, an estimated 18 percent of the population had no access to water supply, 42 percent did not have sanitation facilities or proper health care (witness the cholera outbreaks in the region in 1993), and 30 percent lacked electricity service, not to mention power shortages estimated at 10 percent of service capacity.[1]

To meet the need through the year 2000, annual investment needs were estimated at about US$12 billion for water supply and sanitation, US$24 billion for electricity, US$14 billion for transportation and upgrading highway networks to reasonable standards, and about US$10 billion for ports, pipeline, and telecommunications. Overall, in the 1990s, Latin American countries were estimated to require around US$60 billion per year, or about 5 percent of regional GDP, to finance their infrastructure needs. The average infrastructure investment in developing countries is 4 percent of GDP. In Argentina alone, according to one detailed study, the figure for the infrastructure investment needs was put at over US$4 billion annually for the 1993–2000 period, or about 2 percent of 1992 GDP (Melconian and Bour 1993). Also, the efficiency of the realized investments and operations was quite low. According to the World Bank (1994), power losses were close to or more than 20 percent; 45 percent of paved roads were in poor condition; unaccounted water, including leakages, was more than 50 percent of water produced; and it often took three or four tries to place a telephone call. In consequence, the annual maintenance requirements were also considerable. In the early 1990s, the total infrastructure capital stock was estimated at US$350 billion (power, US$170 billion; transportation, US$100 billion; water supply and sewerage, US$60 billion; and telecommunications, US$20 billion). Most of those investments required long-term capital, which was scarce or nonexistent in most Latin American capital markets, particularly in domestic markets and domestic currency.

To some extent, these significant investment needs were part of the legacy of the past. Through the 1970s and 1980s, the infrastructure sector experienced inadequate spending on new projects and maintenance, which led to the deterioration of a capital stock that was already very deficient, insufficient financing to expand the system, inefficient operations (due among other things to low labor productivity), poor performance by public enterprises in recovering costs from customers, and distorted pricing for social reasons. By 1993, the economic and social consequences of such shortcomings were abundantly clear to national policymakers. As those economies geared to take off, there was an urgency, from a social and economic point of view, for the improvement of infrastructure services, since otherwise bottlenecks and cost increases were likely to arise, which would stifle growth and cause social conditions to deteriorate, thereby impacting poverty levels. There was a realization that the situation was untenable, was slowing growth, and was unlikely to improve without radical changes in policy. At the same time, many Latin American countries were going through severe economic stabilization and structural adjustment programs that requires significant austerity measures and tight fiscal policies. As a result, expenditures on infrastructure development were slashed. By 1993, many of these countries were unable to provide for even the most urgent infrastructure needs.

This dire predicament and the inferior and disappointing historic performance of public enterprises in the provision of infrastructure services motivated many Latin American governments to question current and past approaches and to explore uncharted paths. Many governments began to seek alternatives to the public provision of infrastructure services that entailed greater private sector participation. The driving force behind the privatization of infrastructure and the awarding of concessions to private parties was the urgency of infrastructure improvements, the tight public sector budget, the growing belief that public enterprises operated in a highly inefficient manner, and the understanding that there was no strategic or economic argument for a direct government role in the provision of a number of infrastructure services.

Therefore, for reasons of both improving efficiency and alleviating the pressure on public funds, many Latin American countries have chosen a privatization-concession approach for infrastructure operations. Private financing is larger in Latin America than in other regions and larger in the telecommunications and power sector than other sectors. Literally no infrastructure subsector has been left untouched, and many countries have scheduled or are considering further infrastructure privatization in the upcoming years. Table 13-1 shows the progress of infrastructure privatization by sector in developing countries during 1988–92. Most of those privatizations took place in Latin America. Privatizations or concessions or management contracts took place or will soon take place in telecommunications, airlines, gas, water, sanitation, electricity, solid waste disposal, hospital operations, toll services, parking operations, railroads, ports, bus transports, subway, and roads.

In Latin America, the process started in Chile in the second half of the 1980s, and by the early 1990s a number of other Latin American countries had followed suit. The stage and progress of privatization varied from country to country, and the experience of the privatized firms is relatively short. Argentina, Mexico, and Chile took the lead in Latin America, in terms of the scope and speed (Boeker 1993). In Chile the pace was gradual; in Argentina and Mexico privatization began suddenly and proceeded briskly. By 1993, Peru, Venezuela, and Jamaica slowly began privatizing infrastructure operations, and still others were drawing up plans to follow suit, usually on a smaller scale and in a more selective manner. By 1994, countries that had engaged in infrastructure privatizations included the following: in telecommunications, Argentina, Barbados, Belize, Chile, Jamaica, Mexico, Peru, and Venezuela; in power generation, Argentina, Belize, Chile, and Mexico; in ports, Argentina, Colombia, Mexico, and Uruguay; in roads, Argentina and Mexico; in water supply, Argentina, Mexico, and Peru; and in airline transportation, Argentina, Brazil, Chile, Ecuador, Honduras, Mexico, Panama, Peru, and Uruguay. Often, privatization would have been faster had it not been for shortages in administrative capacity, the need to build political support through early successes, the lack of finance, and the absence of interested private parties.

The mechanisms, procedures, and terms used in the privatization of infrastructure sectors varied across countries and subsectors, ranging from full or partial sale to the awarding of concessions (build-own-transfer and build-own-operate-transfer), leases, and management contracts. Concessions and leases were becoming increasingly common, particularly for the water and sewage, road, and transport sectors and, to a lesser extent, the power sector (Guasch and Spiller 1995). Each mode elicited different incentive structures and risk burdens, whose assessment is a part of the privatization design process. For example, under a lease arrangement the commercial risk but not the financial risk of the large investments is borne by the operator, since the government provides the major investment. On the other hand, under a concession

Table 13-1. Infrastructure Privatizations in Developing Countries, 1988–1992

Infrastructure	1988 Value (US$m)	1988 Number of Countries	1989 Value (US$m)	1989 Number of Countries	1990 Value (US$m)	1990 Number of Countries	1991 Value (US$m)	1991 Number of Countries	1992 Value (US$m)	1992 Number of Countries	1988–1992 Value (US$m)	1988–1992 Number of Countries
Telecommunications	325	4	212	2	4,036	7	5,743	9	1,504	4	11,821	14
Power generation	106	1	2,100	1	20	2	248	2	1,689	3	4,164	9
Power distribution							98	1	1,037	2	1,135	2
Gas distribution									1,906	2	1,906	2
Railroads							110	1	217	1	327	1
Road infrastructure					250	1					250	1
Road transport							1	1	12	2	13	3
Ports									7	2	7	2
Shipping							135	1	1	1	136	2
Airlines	367	2	42	1	775	4	168	5	1,461	7	2,813	14
Water									175	2	175	2
Total	798	6	2,354	3	5,082	11	6,504	15	8,009	17	22,747	24

Source: Sader (1993).

arrangement, the concessionaire usually has to provide the investment and thus bears both commercial and financial risks. While the transfers were usually made through a competitive bid, on occasion, the less desirable bilateral negotiation process was utilized.

The privatization of infrastructure operations continues throughout Latin America, but bottlenecks are beginning to appear, especially difficulties in securing financing (long-term credit). The sectors encountering the most difficulty in securing financing, and thus drawing less interest from private sector parties, are roads, railroads, urban transport, and to some extent water and sewage. The transfer process in these sectors has often required some form of direct or indirect government participation, be it a subsidy, a guarantee, or infrastructure financing. Most of the effort by governments, private sector firms, and multilateral agencies are devoted to developing new sources of infrastructure financing. The paramount objective is not simply to secure private sector participation but to secure *efficient* private sector participation.

The Characteristics of the Infrastructure Sector

Privatizing infrastructure or transferring the rights to provide the services presents challenges often not present in other kinds of privatization:

1. A number of infrastructure activities display natural monopoly characteristics, network structure, or common carrier features and, consequently, require a level of regulatory oversight not present in other commercial activities.

2. Inexperience in regulatory matters, weak regulatory agencies, and lack of administrative capacity impose risks to all parties involved.

3. The investment requirements are considerable, since the revenue flows extend over a long period of time and the investment must be amortized over the long term. Asset requirements per dollar of annual revenue are as follows: water systems, $10–$12; toll roads, $7; telephone companies, $3; electric utilities, $3–$4; railroads, $2, and airlines $1 (Wade Miller 1987).

4. Infrastructure requires long-term financing and is typically highly leveraged in most developing countries, but long-term financing is often unavailable.

5. Because infrastructure activities often generate significant externalities, the direct cash flow revenues associated with optimal social pricing and tariffs are often not sufficient to amortize the required investment.

6. Most often infrastructure services involve nontradable goods or services.

7. The concession agreement for some infrastructure activities creates incentive problems not present in other privatizations.

8. The heterogeneity across infrastructure operations precludes a common privatization financing blueprint. Thus, a range of approaches to secure

financing is demanded, depending on sector, market, location, initial conditions, country, and stage of development.

9. Infrastructure activities are highly visible and consumer sensitive, bringing into play powerful sociopolitical forces, which increase the risks of infrastructure investments and lessen its attractiveness to private operators.

10. Foreign investors, a major expected source for infrastructure financing, face exchange rate risks and expropriation risks.

Lessons from Privatization

As Latin American countries began to privatize infrastructure operations, a number of practical problems became apparent, most clearly in securing financing for new private infrastructure and for refinancing construction loans (as in Mexico). Often the roots of the problems were more fundamental and derived from deficiencies in the framework established for the private sector to operate in the infrastructure sectors and from constraints in the financial sector. Among the framework deficiencies were the determination of concession terms, bidding processes, and regulatory framework; among the financial constraints were restrictions on certain forms of investment, the unavailability of certain forms of risk insurance and hedging instruments, the lack of long-term credit, and the incipiency of capital markets.

Overall, privatization and concession programs, while hurried, have been reasonably successful in terms of number of transactions, particularly if one considers the comprehensive scope of the programs. However, a more relevant criterion to measure the success of these programs should be increases in operating efficiency and in coverage and investment. While the preliminary results are encouraging, a number of problems have surfaced, some of which have been induced by following a piecemeal approach rather than a comprehensive approach, overemphasizing high sale values for fiscal reasons and granting lengthy exclusive rights (thus compromising long-term efficiency, in, for example, the telecommunications sector). Other problems include the failure of controlling agencies to ensure that social efficiency superseded their own interests (e.g., roads), the failure to address risk allocation issues (e.g., water), the failure to address pricing issues in subsectors with network structures (e.g., electricity, communications, and railways), the lack of experience in regulation and enforcement, and the tendency to follow a hurried approach that often did not allow adequate parallel development of effective regulatory mechanisms and often with rules that gave excessive discretion to regulators (e.g., electricity, water, and sanitation).[2] Thus, to improve the postprivatization operational efficiency of the sector, privatizing governments should take the following steps:

—Create a single, independent agency responsible for the privatization or concession program. This will limit potential conflict of interests and jurisdictional problems.

—Apply commercial principles. This will increase competition and involve users.

—Create either a commercial-corporate public sector, a private operation with public ownership (including leases and concessions), or a private operation and ownership.

—Assess the trade-offs between speed of transfer process and postprivatization efficiency.

—Develop a policy framework and an efficient structure for each subsector and identify the competitive and noncompetitive segments for each infrastructure operation.

—Design the optimal level of unbundling according to technological characteristics and extent of potential competition.

—Evaluate regulatory requirements before privatization; identify sources or stages exhibiting market imperfection needing intervention.

—In parallel with privatization, establish independent regulatory agencies and transparent enforcement criteria.

—Consider regulatory frameworks based on incentive regulation and self-regulation before reaching for external regulation.

—Secure credible and binding regulation through legislation, reimbursement funds, posted bonds, contingent contracts, and guarantees consistent with country endowments. This will induce more efficient postcontractual behavior and lower regulatory risks.

—Legislate competition policies to address noncompetitive practices in access pricing, nonprice barriers, and the provision of complementary services.

—Award the concession or privatization through competitive bids rather than negotiated agreements.

—Foster competition through bidding and through the design of the preprivatization market structure.

—Foster transparency and the control of opportunistic behavior both during the concession and during the postprivatization period.

—Transfer some benefits at the expiration of a concession to the previous operators as an incentive for good maintenance.

—Account for externalities, social as well as private, and incorporate them into the privatization and pricing structure.

—Decentralize decisions and procedures to the levels where the benefits and cost will be felt.

The payoff from improved efficiency, estimated at US$55 billion a year, will release resources to finance new investments. Likewise, the payoff from price reform in telecommunications, power, and water (estimated at US$123 billion a year) can reduce claims on public sector funds (World Bank 1994).

Current Options for Financing Infrastructure Investments

While the steps described above provide the framework for a sound infrastructure privatization program, its success depends on private sector interest in participation. One persistent issue, besides the anticipated rate of return on the investment, is how to finance the investment.

The domestic capital market, when effective at all, has shown a limited absorbing capacity, while demanding higher rates and offering shorter maturities than off-shore markets. In the early 1990s, domestic financing of infrastructure investments in the region was infeasible; Chile, and to some extent Mexico, were the only exceptions. Most countries have, at best, incipient capital markets. As of 1994, large domestic placements or maturities of over three years were not feasible in most of Latin America, with the exception of Chile. For example, in Argentina, during 1990–92, there were forty-six domestic debt issues by enterprises and ten by banks, for US$883 million and US$162 million, respectively. The median value of the placement was US$12 million, and only four issues exceeded US$50 million. The median maturity was three years, and with only three exceptions, all maturities were no greater than five years (even though one country, Argentina, has one of the most developed capital markets in Latin America). Equity finance appears also questionable as evidenced by the scant number of new listing and new issues. Therefore, given the investment amounts required for infrastructure projects in most countries, the domestic capital market, in the near term, is unlikely to be a significant source of financing.

The path of current and expected reforms in Latin American capital markets, if not derailed, will eventually produce an active and extended long-term credit market. The expectation is that, as capital markets develop and mature and as institutional investors emerge, the possibility of domestic financing will improve. However, this will be a slow and time-consuming process. In many countries, the optimism that privatized pension funds might solve long-term financing problems is excessive, especially in Chile. While the contribution of privatized pension funds to long-term financing has been notable, it did not happen overnight. By 1994, pension funds in Chile had operated in private hands for more than fifteen years. In 1994, in Argentina, Mexico, and Peru, privately managed pension funds were just beginning to operate. Elsewhere, they were nonexistent. While potentially important, their effect is unlikely to be felt for a number of years, particularly given the restrictions that prudent regulation imposes on the portfolios of pension funds.

As a result, private sector options for infrastructure financing are limited. They are (1) the placement offshore of medium- to long-term bond issues, (2) limited domestic placement of short-term notes: less than three years for the most advanced countries (Chile being the exception) and less than a year everywhere else, (3) short-term bridge loans from banks, (4) the securing of a foreign partner who can provide, directly or indirectly, equity or debt finance, (5) access to government cofinancing or guarantees, (6) retained earnings, particularly in cash-rich sectors, and (7) loans from the private sector lending arms of such multilateral institutions as the World Bank and the Inter-American Developing Bank. However, experience indicates that most of these options are open only to the "blue chip" companies in Latin America and to established foreign companies.

In most countries, almost all private infrastructure financing has been through direct equity participation, the placement of debt offshore, a few bank bridge loans, or occasional government guarantees.[3] Only a small number of companies have had access to offshore markets, which has greatly limited the number of participants in the bidding process. More generally, access to financing and costs of capital for infrastructure has varied across sectors and firms, and often such variations were highly correlated. Firms operating in the cash-rich subsectors, such as oil, gas, telecommunications, and power, appeared to have little problem finding long-term financing, and often 50 percent or more of the required financing could come through retained earnings. In addition, firms operating in tradables such as gas and oil had access to export credit, as was the case for Colombia Corpoven for its US$470 million Accrogas liquid natural gas complex project. In sectors where private companies were heavy users of the output, such as power, financing by user consortia has been an added alternative.[4] On the other hand, firms operating in cash-poor subsectors, like roads, water and sanitation, solid waste disposal, railroads, subway systems, and electricity, face financing difficulties and have to rely on costly bridge loans, rollover loans, and more complex financial engineering.

There is a further segmentation among the Latin American countries into those with and those without access to international financial markets. Most of the high-income countries, like Chile, Argentina, and Mexico, secured financing from international markets. On the other hand, low- and middle-income countries, which are the majority in Latin America, faced significant obstacles and lacked credibility in international financial markets. As a result, external financing for investment in these countries came largely from official sources and multilateral organizations. As of 1994, these countries had neither an advanced capital market nor the credibility and solvency that would allow them to place debt issues offshore, whether public or private.

A common financing pattern was the one- or two-year bridge loan obtained from a local bank for the construction period. Once revenues started flowing, medium-term negotiable obligations or offshore bonds were employed. The blue chip companies in Argentina, Mexico, and Chile secured attractive financing offshore, such as seven-to-ten-year Eurobond and, domestically, two-year commercial paper for operating capital and shorter term investments, both at very attractive interest rates, such as three percentage points over the seven-to-ten-year U.S. Treasury notes, or around 100–200 basis points above the government Eurobond rates.[5] However, the debt issues were against general obligations rather than revenue-based bonds or an infrastructure project.

Foreign participation, often through consortia, was a major reason for the success of infrastructure privatization and financing. International firms were major sources of infrastructure financing in Latin America, particularly in telecommunications, power, and water. The maturity and slow growth of these sectors in industrialized countries prompted firms in these countries to seek growth opportunities elsewhere. All of the privatized telephone companies in Latin America were bought by consortia of foreign firms and local companies. In the water sector, the French company Lyonnaise des Eaux Dumez led the consortia that won the concessions in Mexico, Argentina, and Peru.[6]

While equity finance, through both domestic and international markets, could be another attractive alternative, it has seldom been used. For example, in Argentina as of 1994 only four companies had used this alternative through international markets, often through the mechanism of American depository receipt. And of those four companies, only one, Pérez Companc, was involved in infrastructure operations. The most common instrument used by top infrastructure firms in Latin America to raise equity on the U.S. capital market was the American depository receipt. Its main advantage is that the firm need not be listed on a U.S. stock exchange (World Bank 1994).

Similarly, with a few exceptions, the experience with municipal banks has been disappointing. They have seldom shown a capacity for sustained investment and often have been undercapitalized, have been poor at recovering costs, and have accumulated arrears. Among the exceptions are provincial banks in Brazil and FINDETER, an autonomous agency under the finance minister in Colombia. FINDETER has obtained funds through urban formation bonds, profits on foreign exchange transactions, and credits from bilateral and multilateral sources. It operates as a discount agency, lending at the market prime rate to twenty-two private and state-owned commercial banks and nine financial corporations that make the loans, appraise the projects, and monitor performance. They finance up to 70 percent of a project's total cost. Water supply and sewerage have been priority areas of investment. During its two decades of operation, FINDETER has not experienced any major financial or loan recovery problems.

A variant of the development bank, particularly in the power sector, were the private sector energy funds. These were often capitalized by the government through loans from multilateral organizations and were used to finance power-generating projects that complied with certain efficiency criteria. In addition, the government tended to guarantee the payment obligation to the private developer under each power purchase agreement. The specifics of the Jamaica case, where one such fund was developed, are presented below (World Bank 1994, 104):

> In Jamaica a 1992–93 study financed by the World Bank concluded that the country's power market was too small to achieve full competition as in the UK and Chilean models. The study instead proposed that the Government restructure the monopoly utility, the Jamaica Public Service Company (JPSCO) into one generating entity and one integrated transmission and distribution (T & D) company, with the T & D unit responsible for purchasing power from Independent Power Producers (IPPs) to meet its demand requirements. A Private Sector Energy Fund was set up to provide part of the financial resources for private sector projects. The Fund was capitalized with two loans to the government of Jamaica from the World Bank and the Inter-American Development Bank of US$40.5 million each. In order to encourage private investment in the energy sector, there is a need for a clearly defined process for review, selection and approval of sub-projects. The Fund can finance generating projects that form a part of the least cost investment program for the energy sector and are competitive in price. The Fund provides long-term debt subordinated to commercial lenders, and the energy price would be specified and sufficient to cover the operating costs, debt service, and returns on equity for private investors. The Government of Jamaica guarantees the payment obligation to the private developer under each Power Purchase Agreement, in the process of assuming full market risk. The Fund financing of a sub-project is limited to 70% to become available in the fifth year if all construction criteria have been satisfactorily met, and with the developer responsible for the remaining amount. It is key to the Fund that procurement of goods does not require International Competitive Bidding because the bids are solely to supply electric energy at the lowest possible cost.

Another source of financing that figures to play an increasingly important role is private closed-end funds. A number of these funds were established in the 1990s to channel international capital to infrastructure projects in developing countries, such as the Scudder Latin American Trust for Independent Power (see table 13–2). Formed in 1993, it was expected to grow to at least US$300 million. Likewise, to tap into the savings of small investors, a number of mutual funds were successfully developed in the 1990s to invest in the listed securities of infrastructure firms in developing countries. The following is a list of selected mutual funds for small investors (and their size in millions of U.S. dollars):

Super Asia Infrastructure Fund	16
Nomura Asian Infrastructure Fund	40
Emerging Markets Infrastructure Fund	223
Emerging Markets Telecommunications Fund	125
Gabelli Global Telecommunications Fund	120
Gartmore Global Utilities Fund	20
GT Global Telecommunications Fund	2,100
Montgomery Global Communications Fund	70
Ridgewood Electric Power Trust	30

Multilateral organizations were also a significant source of infrastructure financing in Latin America. Over the 1971–93 period, the Inter-American Development Bank committed an annual average of US$1.8 billion for infrastructure projects. Its capital increase in 1993 will allow that lending to expand further. Moreover, 5 percent of its total lending will be to the private sector, without government guarantee. The International Finance Corporation, the private sector financing branch of the World Bank, also took an aggressive approach to private sector infrastructure investments. In 1993, its lending and investment in that sector worldwide grew to US$330 million, which was leveraged to finance up to US$3.5 billion of infrastructure projects. Its investments were primarily in power and telecommunications projects; much less was invested in toll roads and water projects. Worldwide, IFC's investment projects represented between 15 percent and 25 percent of all private investment in infrastructure, which was estimated between US$14 and US$20 billion a year. In addition, multilateral organizations continued lending for public infrastructure projects especially in low-income Latin American countries; it was the main source of financing for these countries, since their access to commercial international markets was limited.

Problems in Securing Financing

The success of major firms in the wealthier Latin American countries in securing financing does not preclude problems. Certain problems need to be addressed for the success of infrastructure privatization programs.

Limited Domestic Financial Markets Latin American financial intermediaries have been geared almost exclusively to short-term lending.

Table 13-2. Specialized Infrastructure Investment Funds

Fund	Core Investors	Region	Sector	Size
		Investment Targets		
		Region	Sector	Size
AIG (Asian Infrastructure Fund); Manager, AIG Asian Infrastructure Management Company, Ltd.	American International Group; Government of Singapore; Bechtel Enterprises	Asia-Pacific: 35–50% in China	Power, telecommunications, transportation	US$1,000–1,200m
Alliance ScanEast Fund L.P.; Manager, ScanEast Managing Partner, Ltd.	Alliance Life Assurance; American International Group; International Finance Corp.; EBRD	Eastern Europe, Baltics, CIS	Power, telecommunications, other industries	US$22–50m
Asea Brown Boveri Funding Partners; Manager, ABB Funding Partners, L.P.	Asea Brown Boveri Institutional Investors	North America	Power, transportation, related industries	US$500m
Asian Infrastructure Fund; Manager, Asia Infrastructure Fund Management Co., Ltd.	Peregrine Investment Holdings; Soros Fund Management; International Finance Corp.; Asian Development Bank; Frank Russell Co.	Asia (40% in China)	Power, telecommunications, transportation	US$750–1,000m
Central European Telec Investments, L.P.; Manager, Central European Telec Investments Managers, Ltd.	Creditansalt Bankverein; Pan European Financial Services; International Finance Corp.	Central and Eastern Europe (Poland and Hungary)	Telecommunications	US$42–100m
Global Power Investments Company, L.P.; Manager, Global Power Investments Company, Ltd.	GE Capital Corp.; Soros Fund Management; International Finance Corp.	Global emerging markets	Power	US$550–2,500m
Scudder Latin America Trust for Independent Power; Manager, Scudder, Stevens, & Clark, Inc.	International Finance Corp.; NRG Energy, Inc.; CMS Energy, Inc.; Corp. Andida de Fomento	Latin America and the Caribbean	Power	US$200–600m

Source: Fund memorandums. 1993–94.

They rarely offer the long-term funds so essential for many infrastructure project financing. Similarly, local capital markets are not developed enough to offer long-term funding. The current capital market environment in many countries has precluded a number of potential firms from participating in the process, thus limiting competition. The domestic capital market, when effective, has shown a limited absorbing capacity and demands higher rates and shorter maturities than offshore markets.

Large domestic placements or maturities above three years appear questionable as of the mid-1990s. Therefore, given the investment amounts required for infrastructure projects as of now and for the near term, the domestic capital market will not be an option for securing financing. The youth of the capital market and the novelty of the investment makes the selling of infrastructure projects to the general public and underwriters neither viable nor attractive. Equity finance appears questionable for the near future, as illustrated by the scarcity of new listings in the stock markets and by the very small number of primary offerings in Latin America.

Selective Country and Firm Access to Offshore Markets The international sources of financing grew in importance only for Chile, Argentina, Mexico, and, to a lesser extent, Colombia, and Brazil. And only the major blue chip companies appear to be able to secure financing. The consequences are limited competition and, thus, higher service prices and limited participation. While these problems are not apparent, since the transferring of infrastructure operations to the private sector has just begun, they will eventually surface as transfer programs keep evolving.

The Limited Capacity of Major Domestic Companies Firms with easy financing access are becoming overextended in infrastructure activities and are unlikely to absorb new operations. These major companies can take only so much debt exposure, so there is a limit to the amount of infrastructure operations in which they can get involved. As a result, for the second wave of infrastructure investment, the government might need to implement a much more proactive approach.

The Limited Use of Revenue-Based Bond Issues Most of the secured financing has been for general obligations and not the infrastructure projects themselves. Company bonds, rather than revenue bonds, have been the norm. For the long-term success of the program, revenue bonds ought to be the mainstream instrument, since revenues determine the financial viability of the project.

The Risks Associated with Foreign Currency Financing Most financing has been secured offshore or domestically in foreign currency. The reasons are twofold. First, lower interest rates and longer maturity can be secured abroad, and second, the domestic capital market is still reluctant to absorb long-term paper and its capacity to absorb large volume issues, at attractive prices for issuers, is still limited. Two types of risks emerge from this pattern of financing. First, existing long-term financing tends to be in U.S. dollars and not in domestic currency. However, most of the revenues from infrastructure operations tend to be in local currency. This mismatch brings an additional devaluation risk, which is countered with higher service prices. Second, large dollar indebtedness as a result of external borrowing is used to finance nontradables and infrastructure and is unlikely to generate direct exports revenue (foreign currency). Leaving aside devaluation risk, such indebtedness threatens macroeconomic stability, as imbalances in the current and trade account develop. Of course, instability can be countered by an increase in product competitiveness induced by improved infrastructure.

The Absence of Long-Term Institutional Investors or Government Regulatory Policies The domestic absorption of long-term issues essential for infrastructure financing is affected by a lack of institutional investors with long-term perspectives. In addition, a lack of clear government regulatory policies in some of the sectors increases operating and revenue risks, decreases interest in participation, and makes financing more difficult (Guasch and Spiller 1995).

Poorly Performing Infrastructure Banks Major players in infrastructure finance in the past, these banks have performed quite poorly and have been plagued by significant inefficiencies. They seldom have been financially viable and have often granted loans for unsound business prospects. As a result, they have fallen out of favor. There are ongoing efforts in some countries to restructure them into efficient second-tier institutions. The challenge is to turn them into effective, financially efficient, self-sustaining institutions.

The Future of Financing Infrastructure

As described, there is significant heterogeneity in the infrastructure sector in terms of internal resource generation, extent of regulatory constraints, and predictability of cash flows. This heterogeneity calls for a multiplicity of approaches to management, financing, and ownership.

As a country's capital market develops and institutional investors appear, other alternatives for infrastructure financing will arise. Banks will lend a higher proportion of their funds in long-term loans. Domestic bond issues will become more feasible, and their maturity periods will lengthen. Domestic equity financing will become viable and attractive. Domestic institutional investors, pension funds, insurance companies, and mutual funds will become increasingly important sources of domestic long-term financing. Sustained positive growth rates, liberalized financial markets, and developed capital markets will provide more favorable rates of returns on savings and thus will increase aggregate domestic savings, increasing the supply of investment funds. The securitization of the receivables of infrastructure companies could become a major source of financing.

Once project histories have been established, infrastructure intermediaries should be able to package their loans for the market or—which would be much more attractive to investors—to package securities from different projects and sell shares in those packages. Revenue-sharing bonds represent another alternative. Even consumer financing need not be out of reach.[7] Deposits and advance billings could become a complementary source of infrastructure financing, particularly for municipality-led projects. Bonds for a utility could be issued to a utility's customers, with fees being deducted from the bonds' returns. Clearly, the domestic financing of infrastructure would significantly increase efficiency since it would eliminate any devaluation risk. And, of course, offshore financing would still be an alternative, but with an increasing number of firms being able to access it. If macroeconomic stability is sustained and the environment is friendly to foreign investors, larger direct foreign investment participation will also result.

Government Policies that Facilitate Infrastructure Financing

For the above-mentioned financing possibilities to become a reality, the government needs to take a number of steps. The focus of government policies ought to be on how to reduce financial costs, how to reduce the risks of infrastructure investment, and how to improve the allocation of risks. The emphasis should be on the development of long-term credit markets, other sources of funds, risk sharing, hedging instruments, and capital markets in general. Most of these actions may not have an immediate impact on infrastructure finance; waiting for the effects would imply having to postpone the infrastructure privatization program.

Given the urgency of infrastructure development, an argument for jump-start policies can be made. These policies tend to be, by definition, interventionist and are likely to induce some distortions. That is the trade-off. Other arguments for intervention are more traditional: (1) many infrastructure activities generate externalities, (2) there is lumpiness in investment needs, (3) a critical mass is needed, so policies that favor initial participants are appropriate, (4) this is to some extent an infant industry and might need to be nurtured, (5) the lack of record of some financial instruments and mechanisms might argue for the positive effects of teaching by example, and (6) the government is better prepared to bear certain risks and facilitate the allocation of others.

Overall, a comprehensive program of government policies aimed at facilitating the financing of infrastructure should entail the following four types of policy: (1) broad policies directed at sustaining macroeconomic stability and promoting savings, (2) direct infrastructure policies directed at reducing the risks of infrastructure investment and operations (the lower the risk, the more attractive the investment, and the easier the securing of financing), (3) financial markets policies directed at reducing the price of credit and at lengthening the terms of credit in order to increase the pool of potential investors, particularly institutional, and to foster capital market development, and (4) jump-start policies directed at providing funds or guarantees for infrastructure operations. These policies would facilitate infrastructure financing through reducing the cost of capital, lengthening maturities, increasing the profitability of the infrastructure investments, or reducing risk, operational and otherwise, and risk premiums. The relevant policies within each category are as follows.

Broad Policies and Direct Infrastructure Policies

Broad policies would sustain fiscal balances and reduce debt so as not to crowd out credit markets. Stability enhances predictability and confidence, both of which are essential for long-term investments. The policies would also provide for incentives to increase savings rate—for example, the favorable tax treatment of participation in infrastructure trusts. The positive externalities of those investments can justify differential treatment.

Direct infrastructure policies include the policy recommendations described in the lessons from privatization section. Additional recommendations are as follows:

—Assume policy risks (it is highly inefficient and undesirable to pass on policy risks to operators and users).

—Minimize sectoral regulatory risk, enacting credible and binding regulation.

—Establish concession contracts with reference to unambiguous and measurable parameters.

—Establish clear and credible compensation in the event of breach of contract, such as posted bonds or insurance policies with penalty clauses.

—Implement schemes to share the risk among the government, the operators, and the investors.

—Build risk-sharing contingencies into financial contracts, since it is much less costly than renegotiating contracts when unspecified but predictable impacting events occur.

—Allow for a transfer of rights (to operate or to own) to third parties.

Financial Markets Policies

The broad objectives of these policies are to reduce the cost of credit and risk premiums, to develop alternative sources of credit, and to increase the supply of credit and the pool of potential suppliers.

—Develop the three components of capital markets: legislation, supervision, and enforcement.

—Remove barriers to entry (for domestic and foreign entrants) into the financial sector.

—Facilitate and encourage the development and use of regional rating companies.

—Facilitate the development of institutional investors, like insurance companies, mutual funds, and pension funds.

—Reduce restrictions on the use of funds by insurance companies, mutual funds, and pension funds. For example, if the securities or the infrastructure trust receive the highest rating from two ratings companies, allow for additional investment.

—Eliminate legal impediments to the issuance of financial instruments relevant to infrastructure finance, such as inflation-indexed infrastructure revenue bonds.

—Reduce the costs of issuing securities and any unwarranted waiting time. Streamline disclosure rules.

—Facilitate the securitization of infrastructure projects by issuing shares (or convertible bonds) of an infrastructure portfolio. Permit infrastructure companies to securitize their accounts receivable.

—Facilitate the development of infrastructure investment trusts with favorable tax policies and with guarantee services at market prices. Such favorable treatment can be justified by the positive externalities generated by infrastructure projects.

—Facilitate the development of secondary markets to provide liquidity for investors.

—For municipalities, consider granting credit for service to investors.

—To attract foreign equity investment, revise and liberalize foreign investment laws and procedures. To reduce foreign investors' unwarranted costs, risks, and waiting time and to facilitate the mobility of capital, provide a level playing field for domestic and foreign investors. Facilitate the listing of an American depository receipt and a global depository receipt. Facilitate targeted, professional marketing and explain the country, the sector, the regulatory regime, etc., to foreign utilities, mutual funds, and other potential partners. Enact tax treaties with major investor countries. Create and facilitate local depository agencies. Eliminate transaction taxes.

—To access foreign bond markets, establish free-market sovereign risk pricing by issuing appropriate external bonds. Provide guarantees and affiliation with the Multilateral Investment Guaranty Agency.

Jump-Start Policies

These policies are quasi-direct government interventions in financial markets designed to accelerate the provision of infrastructure financing. The objective is to provide or facilitate immediate long-term credit or liquidity. While a number of the jump-start options, or at least the best designed, foster financial viability, they might induce distortions.

Two of the salient jump-start initiatives are guarantee funds and infrastructure financing. A backup fund has been developed in Argentina with assistance and funding from the International Bank for Reconstruction and Development and the Inter-American Development Bank. Infrastructure financing facilities, a type of public-private infrastructure fund, are being considered in Mexico, Colombia, and Jamaica.

A compelling argument for these jump-start funds and facilities is that they can be thought of as seeds for further development of financial markets, especially when these mechanisms guarantee against certain risks, which the investors or the financial institutions are not prepared to bear. The potential distortions they may induce in financial markets and in the allocation of financial assets ought to be balanced against the long-term fostering of new financial instruments and their contribution to confidence building in financial markets.

A Backup or Guarantee Fund The objective of a backup fund is to facilitate the lending of long-term credit by financial institutions in environments where banks can secure funds for only the short or medium term. In the absence of long-term funds (to the banks), the banks are obviously reluctant to give long-term credit. (The premium they would require for bearing the risk induced by the mismatch of terms would price out demand.) A number of factors inducing uncertainty and discrepancies in the pricing of risk are responsible for the lack of a single, mutually accepted price and for the absence of a long-term credit or bond market. Most of these factors are structural, some are policy induced, and some are difficult to grasp since they involve perceptions. For efficiency reasons it is important to keep them in mind when looking for a solution or an intervention, since efficient solutions address the root of the problem. Governments ought to keep working on addressing these factors directly.

While a backup fund does not address these factors directly, it can provide a short-run, operationally useful transformation scheme and might help develop confidence in a long-term market. The challenge is how, with a minimum of distortion, to facilitate a sustainable long-term credit or bond market. The unwillingness of economic agents to hold long-term bonds is based on lack of liquidity and the price risk. An active secondary market can dispose of the lack of liquidity factor but not of the price risk factor, which requires the opportunity to redeem the bonds at face value. Indexed bonds can go a long way toward surmounting the price risk factor. There are two other ways to handle this factor, one through the sequential purchase of short-term bonds, the other through the purchase of a long-term bond with put options or insurance (to allow the redemption of the bond at face value) throughout the life of the bond. But both of these options presents the issuer bank with either the risk of being unable to place the subsequent bond at a profitable price or the risk that the bondholder will exercise the put option, inducing a mismatch of terms.

This is where the backup fund can make a contribution; it guarantees the bank the rolling over of short-term bonds. As a result, the bank can make long-term loan commitments even though the maturity of its liabilities is much shorter. For example, having made a nine-year loan and placed three-year bonds, in the event that at the end of the third year the bank cannot place a new three-year bond, the backup fund would be used to purchase the new issue. A variant is the issuing of long-term bonds with put options, marked with increasing interest rates, at each interval. The backup fund would guarantee the funds in the event that the bondholder exercises the put option. This variant appears to be more efficient, since it builds in incentives to hold the bond to maturity and saves on issuance costs and needs to be issued only once. The backup fund would address how to price forward the purchase of bonds. It can materially help create a market for the long-term bond. Strict eligibility criteria for accessing the backup fund and an insurance fee for its service or a market for the rights to use the backup fund would complete the design.

Finally, a caveat. A backup fund implies an implicit subsidy, since the price of the bond is bound to be lower than what it would be without a backup fund, and the backup fund would be transacting only at below-market rates (in cases of shortage of demand for the bonds or an exercising of the put options). The fees or the price for the rights to use the fund will partially correct this distortion.

Financing Facilities and Infrastructure Funds   Another jump-start option is to create a joint public-private-multilateral financing facility, an investment company, for private sector infrastructure projects. There are a number of variations within this theme, ranging from an essentially government institution (a last-resort option) to partnerships with multilateral organizations and the private sector.

Ideally, it would be a postconstruction option with investment grade rating achieved through direct and indirect capital contributions of first-class international risks combined with callable capital from the government. Management would be provided under a private-public partnership by a government institution and a well-reputed international bank or investment company, both exposed to first risk of loss and able to provide long-term political and commercial confidence. Significant private equity of 50–80 percent and private management ensure a commercial outlook, signal departures from traditional developmental financial institutions, reduce government costs, and facilitate future privatization. Multilateral participation would bring credibility to private investors. In addition, requiring government guarantees de facto would enhance government exposure. Forms of private-public infrastructure financing facility are being considered in Mexico, Colombia, and Jamaica.

The Role of Multilateral Organizations

Multilateral organizations would play a key role in infrastructure financing, particularly in low-income countries, which have much more limited options than middle-income or upper-middle-income developing countries. Multilateral agencies would continue providing technical assistance and structural adjustment loans to develop financial and capital markets and would continue to lend for those projects that remain in the public sector. The latter will be the case for most low-income Latin American countries. Direct lending for the infrastructure sector is likely to increase.

Both the Inter-American Development Bank and the World Bank will continue to have an important presence, directly or indirectly, in the financing of infrastructure. The International Finance Corporation of the World Bank has been expanding its investment and lending to the private infrastructure sectors in Latin America; its activities have an important multiplier effect through its syndication of loans to other lenders in its projects. It has supported projects in the power, telecommunications, transportation, and water and waste sectors in Argentina, Belize, Chile, Colombia, Costa Rica, El Salvador, Guatemala, Jamaica, Mexico, and Venezuela. To expand its lending without reaching its internal exposure limits, the IFC is planning to securitize and sell part of its portfolio. In addition, the World Bank is launching an infrastructure initiative for Latin America that will increase the scope of its presence in the sector.

Equally as important, multilateral organizations can promote and assist countries in implementing the kind of policies and regulatory environment that would facilitate private sector participation. Multilateral institutions can also help put in place the policies required to jump-start private investment in infrastructure through the provision of policy and political guarantees either for individual projects or as a line of credit for certain projects and risks. Through the use of specially structured loans or some form of guarantee, multilateral organizations could also support efforts to extend maturities, support that could be structured as a backup fund facility in a form similar to a contingent underwriting facility or through refinancing facilities.

NOTES

This chapter reflects solely the views of the author and should not be attributed to the World Bank, its board of directors, its management, or any of its member countries.

1. As of 1990, the social-economic cost of forgone (not available) electric power in developing countries has been estimated, on average at the margin, at US$1 per kilowatt hour of electricity. (Obviously the figure depends on initial conditions.)

2. Examples of hasty privatization are to be found in the other countries, notably Argentina (see chapters 4 and 7).

3. There is a macroeconomic risk to be considered. Large dollar indebtedness finances nontradables, and thus is unlikely to directly generate exports (foreign exchange). Leaving aside devaluation risk, it presents a potential macroeconomic imbalance risk through the current and trade account balances.

4. This is the case for the precedent-setting Colombia Mamonal, a US$71 million, 100-megawatt generating facility. It was undertaken by ProElectrica, a consortium of twenty-four industrial companies. All members were shareholders and customers of the new plant and established fourteen-year power contracts with the company. Chase Manhattan Bank underwrote US$57 million, and it also arranged US$1 million in working capital for the project. Along with developer K&M Engineering of Washington D.C., Scudder Stevens and Clark, and the Rockefeller Group, the World Bank invested US$14 million of equity.

5. In Argentina, for instance, a company called ROGGIO, working with a variety of partners in each case, won the concession for the Buenos Aires subway, for cellular telephone service in parts of the country, for toll roads, for garbage collection, for parking operations, and for hospital maintenance. Most of the financing was through two-year bridge loans from banks, expected to be followed by the floating of five-year notes. The only exception was the subway, where the government of Argentina financed the investment needs for the following few years. That concession was awarded to the firm with the smallest demanded subsidy. Other Argentine companies with this kind of financing are Techint (which won concessions in communications, energy distribution, gas and railroads) and the Pérez Companc group (which was involved in gas transport and distribution and electricity generation, transmission, and distribution).

6. The private Aguas de Argentina consortium won a thirty-year concession that would require a capital investment of at least US$3 billion. The consortium consisted of Lyonnaise des Eaux (28.1%), Aguas de Barcelona (14%), Generale des Eaux (8.9%), UK Anglia Water (5%), and three local partners. The group invested US$120 million in equity and secured a US$200 million credit facility from French and German banks. It also began a US$100 million commercial paper program. In Mexico, Lyonnaise had a 44 percent share in one of four consortia that were awarded ten-year contracts to clean up the city's water and sewage systems. Its partners were Anglia Water and two Mexican companies. Lyonnaise was also involved in improving water supply in Lima, Peru.

7. For example, in 1993, in the Corpoven gas project in Colombia, CS First Boston successfully securitized a U.S. Export-Import Bank guarantee into

a US$65 million medium-term note, the first time a guarantee had been so used.

REFERENCES

Boeker, Paul H., ed. 1993. *Latin America's Turnaround: Privatization, Foreign Investment, and Growth.* San Francisco: ICS Press.

Guasch, J. Luis, and Pablo Spiller. 1995. *Regulation and Private Sector Development in Latin America and the Caribbean.* Washington, D.C.: World Bank.

Melconian, Carlos, and Enrique A. Bour. 1993. "Financiamento de Infrastructura en al Argentina: Problemas y Perspectivas de la Postprivatizacion." Fundacion de Investigaciones Economicas Latinoamericanas (FIEL), Buenos Aires.

Sader, F. 1993. *Privatization and Foreign Investment in the Developing World, 1988–1992.* Washington, D.C.: World Bank.

Wade Miller Associates, Inc. 1987. *The Nation's Public Works: Report on Water Supply.* Washington, D.C.: National Council on Public Works.

World Bank. 1994. *World Development Report.* Washington, D.C.

Contributors

Ravi Ramamurti, associate professor of business administration, Northeastern University, was a visiting professor at Harvard Business School in 1986–88 and is a faculty member of Harvard's Public Enterprise Workshop. He is the author or editor of three books, including *State-Owned Enterprises in High Technology Industries: Studies in India and Brazil* and (with Raymond Vernon) *Privatization and Control of State-Owned Enterprises.* He is a consultant to several governments and international agencies.

William M. Emmons III, associate professor of business administration, Harvard Business School, has done extensive research on economic regulation issues in the United States and abroad. His publications include articles in the *Journal of Economic History* and *Business and Economic History* as well as fifteen case studies in the field of business and public policy.

Antonio Francés, professor and director of research, IESA, Venezuela, was an adviser to the Venezuelan government on the privatization of the national telephone company and is a member of Venezuela's national telecommunications regulatory agency, Conatel. He is the author of *¡Alo Venezuela!* and co-author of *Venezuela: The Challenge of Competitiveness.*

José A. Gómez-Ibañez, Derek C. Bok Professor of Public Policy and Urban Planning at Harvard University, holds a joint appointment at the John F. Kennedy School of Government and the Graduate School of Design. He has published numerous articles on transportation and land planning and is co-author of several books, including *Regulation for Revenue: The Political Economy of Land Use Exactions; Autos, Transit, and Cities; Cases in Microeconomics;* and *Going Private: The International Experience with Transport Privatization.* He has served as senior staff economist to the president's Council of Economic Advisers (1980–81), as chair of the mayor's Transportation Advisory Committee in Boston (1985–86), and as a consultant to several governments and international agencies.

Robert Grosse, chairman, World Business Department, American Graduate School of International Management (Thunderbird), has directed the Center for International Business Education and Research, University of Miami and has published extensively on Latin America. His titles include *Multinationals in Latin America; Private Sector Solutions to the Latin American Debt Problem; Foreign Exchange Black Markets in Latin America;* and *International Business.*

José Luis Guasch, principal economist and adviser in the Latin American Region of the World Bank, is professor of economics at the University of California—San Diego. He has been involved in advising and formulating policy for Latin American countries on privatization, infrastructure finance, capital market development, regulation, and technology issues, especially in Argentina, Brazil, Jamaica, Mexico, and Peru. He has published more than fifty articles in leading economic and finance journals.

Janet Kelly, dean of IESA, Venezuela's leading business school, was a research fellow at the Harvard Center for International Affairs from 1976 to 1979 and has served on the faculties of the University of Massachusetts at Boston and Simon Bolivar University in Venezuela. She is the author or editor of three books on public policy and has published several articles on state-owned enterprises and privatization, including chapters in *Public Enterprise in Less Developed Countries* and *The Promise of Privatization.*

Ricardo Parades-Molina, associate professor, Department of Economics, University of Chile, has written extensively on matters of regulation and antitrust rules. From 1990 to 1993 he was one of five members of Chile's antimonopoly commission and has been a consultant to several Latin countries on regulation and labor issues. He is a visiting faculty member of Harvard's Public Enterprise Workshop.

Ben Petrazzini, assistant professor of business administration systems, the Hong Kong University of Science and Technology, is the author of several studies on telecommunications privatization in developing countries. He previously taught at the National University of Buenos Aires and worked as a congressman's adviser in the Argentine National Congress.

Mabelle G. Sonnenschein, director, International Marketing, GTE Telephone Operations, previously taught at Boston University and worked as a senior consultant on the telecommunications industry with Arthur D. Little, Inc. Her current responsibilities include the evaluation of international investment opportunities in the telecommunications sector.

Pankaj Tandon, associate professor of Economics, Boston University, is the author of several articles and books on state-owned enterprises and privatization, including (with Leroy Jones and Ingo Vogelsang) *Selling Public Enterprises: A Cost-Benefit Methodology* and (with Ahmed

Galal et al.) *Welfare Consequences of Selling Public Enterprises: An Empirical Analysis.*

Alvin G. Wint, professor of business administration, University of West Indies, Jamaica, has published extensively on the regulation of foreign direct investment in developing countries, including two landmark reports on the subject (co-authored with Louis T. Wells Jr.), *Marketing a Country* and *Facilitating Foreign Investment.* He is a consultant on foreign direct investment matters to the World Bank Group, the United Nations, and several national governments.

Patricia A. Yokopenic is a staff member of International Marketing, GTE Telephone Operations. She worked previously in GTE's market research and human resource management departments. Prior to GTE, she worked for the state of California and on research teams at UCLA's School of Public Health and the Institute of Social Science Research.

Index

Library of Congress Cataloging-in-Publication Data

Privatizing monopolies : lessons from the telecommunications and transport sectors in Latin America / edited by Ravi Ramamurti.
   p. cm.
Includes index.
ISBN 0-8018-5135-1 (alk. paper)
   1. Privatization—Latin America. 2. Telephone companies—Latin America.
3. Airlines—Latin America. 4. Toll roads—Latin America. I. Ramamurti, Ravi.
HD4010.5.P765 1996
388'.049—dc20   95-18040

Heterick Memorial Library
Ohio Northern University

DUE	RETURNED		DUE	RETURNED
1. 2/29/00 MAR 7 2000		13.		
2.		14.		
3.		15.		
4.		16.		
5.		17.		
6.		18.		
7.		19.		
8.		20.		
9.		21.		
10.		22.		
11.		23.		
12.		24.		

WITHDRAWN FROM
OHIO NORTHERN
UNIVERSITY LIBRARY